The Autobiography of
Brother Marcel Van

Les Amis de Van

The Association of the **Friends of Van** (Les Amis de Van) is
recognised as a 'private association of the faithful'.

By its international vocation it participates in the communion between
the Churches and in the building of the universal Church.

Its main activities are:

The sponsorship of Vietnamese seminarists.
The publication of Van's story and his writings in several languages.
The preparation of the dossier for the beatification of Van.
The setting up of a Marcel Van house in Vietnam.

The cause for the beatification of Van as a Confessor of the Faith,
began on March 26 1997 in the diocese of Belley-Ars.

If you have any witness to give or if you have received a grace
through Van's intercession, if you have any information on his
life, you can write to:

Les Amis de Van
15, rue de l'Orangerie
78000 Versailles
France
Tel: 33 (0) 1 39 51 30 90
Fax: 33 (0) 1 39 51 30 89
e-mail cause@amis devan.org

The Autobiography of Brother Marcel Van

Translated into French and introduced by
Father Antonio Boucher CSsR

and thence translated into English by
Jack Keogan

with a foreword by
Mgr F.-X. Nguyễn Văn Thuận

GRACEWING

Originally published in French as
Autobiographie de Marcel Van Complete Works Volume 1
by Éditions Saint-Paul, BP652 – 78006 Versailles CX

This edition published in 2006

Gracewing
2 Southern Avenue
Leominster
Herefordshire HR6 0QF

ISBN 0 85244 597 0

Typesetting by
Action Publishing Technology Ltd, Gloucester, GL1 5SR

Printed in England

Contents

Foreword

There is a Vietnamese proverb which says, 'Heaven sends you that which you wish to avoid'. I must admit that I admire the work of those experts who examine the causes of saints; it is a work which demands one to be conscientious, meticulous even, and scientific: to analyse writings, look for witnesses, to verify and discriminate. I admire them in this, but I am afraid of this work and ... lo and behold! I am asked to be the postulator for the Cause of Marcel Van.

I was sceptical. I wished to decline the invitation because I was too busy, but it is delicate in view of the circumstances in which we live. It is necessary to search for the truth, to avoid divisions and try to create communion: to pray, to work, to hope, solely for God's glory and the service of souls.

I began to read the documents, to meet the people who work fervently for this Cause. Little by little, I entered more profoundly into the life of Marcel Van.

I adore the unfathomable intentions of God who allowed me to be sent to prison in North Vietnam, 1700 kilometres from my diocese, from December 1976 until November 1988, and then to spend three years in exile. I have had the opportunity to visit the places where Marcel was born and spent his religious life. I have met people who knew him; I have heard ordinary people tell about the poverty, the war, the ordeals they have had to put up with. All of this has helped me to understand better the writings of Marcel Van and the context in which the entire life of this little Redemptorist Brother has unfolded.

The first thing I have noticed is that Marcel is the same age as me; he was born on 15 March, and I on 17 April, 1928. Like me, he had poor health, and, more especially, he also had spent some time in prison. All of these aspects and many others bring him close to me and facilitate a better mutual understanding of our sufferings, our pains and our hope.

I went back, step by step, to the source. In 1925, at the time of Monsignor Eugène, Joseph Allys, the Apostolic Vicar of Huê, the ancient imperial city, there arrived Father Eugène Larouche, the founder of the Redemptorists in Vietnam. He and his confrères lived in one of the houses belonging to Mr Sắc, the brother-in-law of my grandfather, five minutes from the house where I was born. This is why I have always had a great liking for and attachment to the Redemptorist Fathers. When Marcel speaks of Father Dionne, of Father Paquette, of Father Louis Roy and of Father Joseph Bích, he seems to revive for me a story of only yesterday.

Rays shine in the firmament but threatening clouds remain which announce storms, tempests and thunder ...

A Cause for beatification demands scientific work, minute and inspired solely by faith. It is necessary to undertake it sincerely and impartially.

I ask myself why the process of beatification has begun in Canada, and why it then continues in Ars and not in Vietnam, in Marcel's diocese of origin of Bắc-Ninh in North Vietnam.

It is necessary to go back each time to the source. In 1954 after the division of Vietnam into two parts at the Seventeenth Parallel, Marcel's family left the North to settle in South Vietnam in the diocese of Xuan Loc. Twenty-five years ago, Monsignor Dominic Nguyễn Văn Lãng, one of my old friends whom I had known at the Urban University in Rome in 1956, became bishop of this diocese. Now Lãng when he was a seminarist knew the little Van and escorted him to the train to spend a probationary period with the parish priest of Quảng Uyên. When Lãng became a bishop he was interested in the cause of someone who came from the same diocese as himself, and a part of whose family lived in his current diocese. In view of the difficulties of the years 1975 to 1988 Monsignor had asked for the transfer of the cause to Quebec, and the bishop, Monsignor Charles Valois, agreed, considering that a certain number of the members of Van's family were exiled in his diocese of St Jerome, particularly his younger sister Tế who was with the Redemptorist Sisters of St Thérèse. Another very useful reason for this transfer is that the former Redemptorist superiors of Marcel Van, Vietnamese and Canadian, former missionaries in Vietnam, and, in particular Father Boucher, his spiritual director, were then in Canada, which facilitated enormously the collection of the necessary information.

Father Boucher was called to his Father's house after fulfilling his mission. Generally speaking the necessary information had been assembled in Canada. It was then that the association 'Friends of Van' judged it more practical to transfer the work to Europe, on the advice and with the agreement of Monsignor Charles Valois, and Monsignor Guy Bagnard has accepted this new transfer. The different steps have been submitted to Rome on each occasion and approved by the authorities of the Congregation for the Cause of Saints.

The transfer of Marcel Van's cause to Europe was necessary because it was good not to be too far from Rome where the canonical process takes place, and also where the mother house of the Redemptorists is located. The cause passed, therefore, to Ars since Monsignor Guy Bagnard has had the kindness and the courage to agree to the request of the association, 'Friends of Van'. Marcel was a great friend of France, he had a very special devotion to Saint Thérèse of the Child Jesus, and his spirituality has a special message for the seminarists of Ars.

The documents were, again, a problem. At the beginning I shared the opinion of a great number of people. I was sceptical: a weak boy, poor and without any secondary studies, what can he write? Then again, what should one think of his spirituality, of his intimacy with Jesus, Mary, Thérèse of Lisieux? Can one have confidence in him? I have met many people – priests, faithful, young people: Vietnamese, Canadian, French – who were charmed by the writings of Marcel Van. Personally, I took time to read them and my preconceived ideas disappeared progressively. It is not for nothing that Father Boucher asked him to put his experiences in writing, which proves that he acted after a long period of discernment. If anyone sets about reading the 326 letters Marcel has left after his death, addressed to numerous people, he might have said what a retired French general confided to me: 'I put these documents on computer, and I often had to interrupt my work to pray'. Here is another, more vivid testimony: I once saw a video cassette of an interview that Father Boucher, then retired in Canada, had given to some Vietnamese friends who had come to visit him. Father Boucher began to tell them the story of Marcel Van. Sometimes he burst out laughing; sometimes he shed tears of tenderness when speaking of the physical and moral trials of little Van. And then, days later, Father Boucher died, suddenly, of a heart attack.

And that is not all. We have at hand the 326 letters of Marcel Van, but of his life in Vietnam, of his imprisonment, has he left any record? Who knew him? Certainly, in view of the many special vicissitudes, it has not been easy, but, thanks to God, all of these witnesses have taken an oath on the Bible in retracing the diverse episodes of his life. They have told, for example, how he escaped from prison disguised as a woman for the sole purpose of bringing back to the prison the Blessed Eucharist. He was captured, brought back to prison and was severely punished as was to be expected for such an offence. These witnesses have also told of his death on 10 July 1959 at thirty-one years of age in the Camp for Re-education No. 2 at Yên Bình where he had been transferred in the month of August 1957. They have given details. It was at midday; all the prisoners were in the dining room. Marcel Van's friends had noticed that he was nearing his end. They rushed to the dining room to get Father Joseph Vinh, the Vicar General who hurried to assist Van in his final torments. Then Marcel joined his Lord. He died of exhaustion and illness after four years, two months and three days in prison. Forty years have passed. Many witnesses are still alive to tell the truth.

We have seen how the Lord has led Van and allowed the minutest details of his life to be collected under almost impossible conditions. I prefer you to discover for yourself, through the pages you are going to read, the mystery of grace, of the love of God acting in a very humble little soul, to make of it the instrument in the transmission of his message. By his life and his writings Marcel Van leaves us a message: the message of the Gospel and of Hope.

The writings of Marcel Van are important in more than one respect because they draw attention to the situation and needs of our world of today through the experiences of a young boy from North Vietnam who bears witness to his hope, following Thérèse of Lisieux. He has known how to change suffering into joy all his life, be it during his difficult childhood or during his life as a religious Redemptorist, offered until his death.

In our Church in Vietnam there are actually 6 million Catholics out of 75 million inhabitants, that is 8% of the population. Regarding the proportion of Catholics in Asia, we are, therefore, the second after the Philippines. As for perseverance in tribulation, our Church has already suffered more than three centuries of persecution. In 1988 the Holy Father, John Paul II, canonised in a single day and for the first time a group of 117 martyrs of Vietnam, including some bishops and French and Spanish missionaries. The Church in Vietnam and the Church in France are two sister churches. We have received the faith from missionaries but, more especially, since the seventeenth century, from priests of the Paris Foreign Missions. Other religious came after them, notably the Canadian Redemptorists of the province of St Anne of Beaupré. It is with them that Van discovered and brought to fruition his vocation. The Church of France and the Church of Vietnam are both 'eldest daughters' of the Church. One still recalls the cry of John Paul II at Bourget at the time of his visit to France in 1980: 'France, eldest daughter of the Church and educator of peoples, what have you made of your baptism?' For the Vietnamese Church it was Pope Pius XI in 1933 who consecrated the first Vietnamese bishop, Monsignor Nguyen Ba Tong and said to him: 'You are returning to your country, Vietnam, in the Far East. Continue the missionary apostolate since Vietnam has a great vocation and mission; it is the eldest daughter of the Church in the Far East.' Our two Churches are united not by political, diplomatic, cultural and economic ties but by the most important ones, those of the faith shared between our two countries. These ties are sealed by the blood of our martyrs, priests, religious and lay people. Marcel Van had always prayed and hoped that these links of faith would progress and develop more and more so as to fulfil the mission to go to Vietnam that Thérèse of the Infant Jesus had received when she was selected for the Carmel at Hanoi. It was her precarious health which prevented her from going there but her heart is in Vietnam. Marcel Van, her 'little brother' has received the mission to continue, with her, the evangelisation of Vietnam; to carry the gospel, not only to Christians to make them more perfect and sanctify them, but to all, above all to the non-Catholics and even the Communists.

The cause of Marcel Van is important because it offers us a vision for the future, not only for the next few years but also for the whole of the third millennium. The future looks not only to Vietnam but to the whole of the Pacific Basin.

In presenting to you the first volume of the Complete Works of the Writings of Marcel Van, I want to respond to the wish of the Holy Father in *Tertio Millenio Adveniente,* to collect the memories of witnesses of the faith in the twentieth century. As for his beatification, I respect-fully leave it to the decision of the Church.

The publication of the Writings of Van reminds us that in our time we are still living the Passion and the Resurrection of Christ. We see outside, and even inside the Church, so many challenges, temptations, trials, crises, persecutions, vices, dechristianisation and indifference. Fortunately, God never abandons the Church because in each epoch he continues to guide it, through the *Magisterium* certainly, and also through the great institutions, but often thanks to the witness of the humble. We can recall Saint Joan of Arc, Saint John Mary Vianney, Saint Bernadette and Thérèse of the Child Jesus. Vatican II tells us that they build the signs of the times. The saints are signs. The sign must be different; if not, it is no longer a sign. The sign demands courage and perseverance in order to be always present there where one has need of it. God has sent to us a little Vietnamese religious, come from the end of the earth, to bring the message to the entire world: a simple way, a humble way, an evangelical way, a way of service to the church in the community. And the saints mark their times. Thérèse is a sign for her time: Van marks his time.

Van's spirituality fascinates us. For my part there is one sentence engraved forever in my memory: 'And this is now the last word I am leaving to souls: I leave to them my love and with this love, so small that it is, I hope to satisfy the souls which wish to make themselves very small to come to Jesus. That is something I would wish to describe but, with my lack of ability, I have not got the words to do so.'

God wished to choose this little servant as he chose David, Joan of Arc, Thérèse, to confound the sensible and the strong, and to show his mercy to the world. Marcel Van is one of the hundreds of faces of young people which shine with the joy and love which comes from the heart; there, where God lives, to give back hope to today's world.

He has chosen him in his simplicity, his humility – I mean his humiliation ... his father's passion for gambling and alcohol, as well as the floods which reduced all of the family to poverty. Marcel Van became a 'slave' at the presbytery of Huu-Bang in 1938, at the age of ten years. In July 1944, after the Redemptorists had refused him entry because he was 'considered too weak and too small' he was admitted as an assistant gardener, thanks to a letter that his good mother had given him for Father Letourneau. He was still not in the community.

Marcel Van is a true son of Vietnam. He writes to Father Dreyer Dufer: 'Vietnam, my dear country, has known the horror of a war which has lasted for more than two years and nothing suggests it is going to end ...' And, in accordance with Vietnamese culture, filial piety is very important, consistent with the worship of the ancestors. He suffers because of his father's faults but continues to love him, to respect him and even to convert him: 'Mammy, I felt overwhelmed by your own sadness and that of the family on seeing that Papa, from day to day, became good for nothing and could hardly make everyone's burden heavier ... I am going to write a personal letter to Papa ... I am going to invite him to a personal retreat ...' In this letter he writes: 'I see that the situation gets worse from day to day, Papa. Are you aware of the husband's role as head of the family, what you should do to Mammy? ...' In fact, his father was moved by his supplications. Marcel wrote afterwards to Brother Andre ... 'Thanks to his conversion my family was able, once more, to be united as formerly.'

Marcel Van prays for Vietnam and for France: 'Give a true peace to France ... I do not know if it will be given to me to see Vietnam in peace during my time here on earth or simply after my death. It will be all the better in the latter case, since I have the great wish to be the victim of the love of God to beg him to grant peace to my dear country, Vietnam.'

Marcel Van was a true son of Vietnam, a pious child of his family, a sincere friend of France, but the culmination of his life is his message of love: 'My sole occupation is to love you ... Whatever my life may be, I can only love ...'

Monsignor Francis-Xavier Nguyễn Văn Thuận,
Former Coadjutor Archbishop of Saigon,
President of the Pontifical Commission of Justice and Peace.

A Brief History of Vietnam

Vietnam resembles in shape those yokes which the peasants used to carry on their shoulders: a pole balancing two baskets of rice, potatoes or fish. Vietnam stretches for 1650 kilometres from the 'door of China' to its southern extremity, but the narrow, central waist is hardly 50 kilometres wide, opening on to two plains of paddy fields, one on the delta of the Red River and the other on the Mekong in the south. They are surrounded by mountains and plateaux which cover three-quarters of the country. Van belonged to the rural community as did most of the Vietnamese people. Like many of his countrymen Van could become quite lyrical when describing its beauty.

Situated in the centre of south-east Asia on the eastern rim of the Indo-China peninsula, Vietnam is solidly attached to China in the north and hangs on to Laos and Cambodia in the west. Its predominantly secular history consists of confrontations with these two neighbours, tempered, however, by numerous political or religious influences as, for example, Buddhism or Confucianism. It is largely exposed in the east and the south to the maritime horizons of the Pacific and Indian oceans from whence came, in the seventeenth century, the Gospel with the Jesuits, including Alexander of Rhodes but, above all, in the nineteenth century, the many contacts with the Western world. 'Vietnamese-ness' and modernity intertwined, bore fruit and clashed in the different wars of this century, from which sprung up a new state of the socialist type, imitating the systems of the USSR and China. Marcel stands in this century of many upheavals, very much aware of his Vietnamese history and Catholic faith.

From the beginnings until the colonisation of 1883–1885

Like all national histories that of Vietnam is steeped in a legendary past. The Vietnamese people were forged, progressively, from Mongol immigrants from the north who mixed with the native people who were there since neolithic times. This new people developed in Tonkin and established themselves in the basin of the Red River. They controlled the water, built dykes and devoted themselves to an irrigated cultivation with brave, intelligent and unremitting labour which was imitated by their descendants century after century.

Chinese Domination

Tonkin emerged as a distinct entity about 208 BC, but China eliminated this first Vietnam in 111 BC. A Chinese model was imposed bringing with it the worship of ancestors, the pattern of village life and the family structures linked to it, writing and the mandarin[*] establishment. During ten centuries of domination and satellitisation (11 BC to AD 939) numerous uprisings took place of which the most famous was that of the Trúng sisters, AD 38–43. Independence was finally regained in the tenth century. The first national dynasty was established in AD 1010.

The Great National Dynasties (1010–1527)

They created a state with a solid political, administrative and military framework. They fought against China, Champa (whose current centre is Annam [in east-central Vietnam]), and the kingdom of Angkor. By these wars the dynasties of Lý (1012–1225), Trần (1225–1400) and Lê (1428–1527) gained their legitimacy. Each victory over Champa was followed by a Vietnamese territorial advance. Each victory over China furthered the 'Vietnamese-ness' of the whole country.

The Time of Fragmentation (1527–1802)

Feudal wars undermined the central state. The Trinh (lords of the north) and the Nguyễn (lords of the south) wished to re-create unity but each one worked to his own advantage. They sought help from abroad, the former from Holland and the latter from France. After 1771 three brothers from the village of Tây-Sơn mobilised a large number of peasants, and, supported by important merchants, had the

[*]   Mandarin. An educated official, representing the central power in the provinces, who was selected by competition.

same idea and massacred all of the pretenders. Only Nguyễn A'nh (the future Gia Long) escaped death. He re-established the unity of the country and was invested by the Emperor of China as King of Vietnam. He awarded himself the title of emperor. The *nam-tien* that is, the 'march towards the south', was also accomplished. It entailed the conquest of new territories of a population of land workers firmly organised in villages knitted together in real agricultural communities.

The Nguyễn Dynasty until the arrival of the French (1802 to 1883–1885)

Gia Long chose Huê as the capital of the new state, called Vietnam (the south of the Viets). He allied himself politically and culturally with China, revived the traditional religion of heaven and earth, but remained tolerant towards the Christians and, above all, towards the French who, with Monsignor Pigneau of Béhaine, had helped him to regain his throne. His successors Minh-Mạng and, above all, Tự Đức (1848–83), pressurised by the mandarins, the traditional scholars, closed ranks against foreigners and persecuted the Christians, 'destabilisers' of the old order. Social agitation and ethnic uprisings gained ground in this multi-nation state.

It was at this time that an expansion of the western world towards all of the world's horizons, including the United States, was gaining ground. It was the beginning of the colonial era. From 1862 to 1883 France became established in Vietnam. The year 1884 saw the end of Vietnamese independence. The court of Hue had no more than a nominal authority. In 1885 China accepted French tutelage of Vietnam.

The proclamation by Hôchí-Minh of the Democratic Republic of Vietnam (1885–1945)

The Indochina of colonisation (1885–1930)

Traditional Vietnam was followed by a new entity, Indochina, or, more exactly, the Indochinese Union. Cambodia and Laos were, from then onwards, associated with the 'three Ký', Tonkin, Annam and Cochin-China, of which the two former were protectorates[*] whilst the third was a colony.[†] In fact, authority was exercised by a governor-general residing in Hanoi. France projected Indo-China into an era of

---

[*]   Protectorate. A territory which partially kept its own administration under French control.
[†]   Colony. A territory totally under French administration.

modernisation at the same time that China was looking inwards and Japan, opened by the USA to western influences, chose to reform itself. It was the time of the Meiji.

The representatives of France were men of the Third Republic dedicated to the universality of the rights of man as proclaimed by the French Revolution and with a lay emphasis, spread essentially by teaching, to which more than any other colonial power France was attached. It was a work of ideological propaganda and of intellectual persuasion and, in the last analysis, incompatible with any suggestion of national independence.

The First World War, 1914–18, ruptured this story. The Indo-Chinese, 100,000 at the service of France in the beginning, saw the great western nations tearing themselves apart, heard the recommendations of President Wilson in favour of the claims of the colonies, and had followed the first developments of the Bolshevik Revolution. Nguyễn-Ái-Quốc, the future Hochi Minh, was present at the famous Congress of Tours (1920) when the French Communist Party broke away from the French Socialist Party, the French section of the International Workers.

Disputes in Indo-China (1930–1940)

The anti-colonial movement grew. The VNQDD*, the first national Vietnamese non-Communist party, was officially created in 1927. It fought for independence. It organised the mutiny of Yen Bay (Tonkin) in 1930. This was a failure and marked the end of the party. The Indo-Chinese Communist Party with Nguyễn-Ái-Quốc dates from the same year. Its objectives distinguished it completely from the preceding one. It belonged to that group of parties guided by the Comintern† of which they are the national forerunners.

Vietnam entered a new era. Her history was, from now onwards, linked to the history of the modern countries of the Far East. The old Chinese Empire had foundered. Sun Yat-sen Chiang Kai-shek‡

---

* VNQDD. Việt-Nam Quốc Dân Dảng. National Democratic Party of Vietnam, founded in 1927.
† Comintern. The Third International founded by Lenin in March 1919 to counter the Second Socialist International.
‡ Chiang Kai-shek was the main director of the Kuomintang at the death of Sun Yat-sen. He supported the war against Japan from 1937 till 1945 and against the Communists. In 1949 he withdrew to Taiwan (Formosa). There he was President and chief of the nationalist Chinese forces until his death.

and Kuomintang* had reintroduced China into the concert of great nations. Very serious political war broke out between the holders of opposing ideologies with the appearance of Mao Tse-tung and the foundation of the Chinese Communist Party, from 1921. Then a militarised Japan sprang up, which, in the name of the solidarity of the yellow peoples, got ready to control the Far East and to get rid of the western countries. In 1937 the Sino-Japanese war broke out. China was almost completely overrun. The Mikado's† troops at the end of the 1930s reached the Yunan Mountains near Chinese Indo-China.

Van's story unfolds between these attractive and often hostile worlds. In these difficult times a Christianity grew, served by the priests that Van met, as much in the parish of his birth as in the 'house of God' of Huu-Bang where this institution, created in the seventeenth century in the areas of evangelisation, as a sort of pre-junior seminary, prepared young candidates for the priesthood. However, the important ecclesiastical institutions, the seminaries and the universities, remained generally in foreign hands.

There were the Spanish like the Bishop of Bac Ninh, the heir of the missionaries who had come from Mexico and the Philippines in the seventeenth century, the French Dominicans at Lang Son and in the upland region of Tonkin, without counting a certain number of religious houses such as the Carmels of Hanoi and Saigon who knew Van well, or the Redemptorists (the Congregation of the Holy Redeemer) founded in 1732 by Saint Alphonsus Liguori, who were recently arrived in Hanoi from French-speaking Canada. The Catholic Church knows no frontiers, but in the struggles of the 30s this foreign religious presence was denounced and the total Vietnamisation of the church was regarded as necessary. Van served the Church during a particularly difficult time in its history.

The last years of Indo-China (1930–1945)

Europe flared up again in 1939. France, quickly overcome, signed the armistice with the Germany of Adolf Hitler on 25 June 1940. The German/Italian axis appeared to be succeeding. A partner, Japan, joined them at the time of the Tripartite Act of 25 September 1940.

---

* Kuomintang. the national party of the Chinese people founded by Sun Yat-sen on three principles: nationalism, democracy and socialism. Sun Yat-sen, Chinese statesman (1866–1925) was responsible for the revolution of 1911 which caused the old Chinese Empire to fall. He was the president of the Chinese Republic in 1921.
† Mikado. The title of the Japanese Emperor.

This was a kind of division of the world into zones of occupation and exploitation. Indo-China was swept along by the gigantic maelstrom of the Second World War. Japan, whilst recognising French sovereignty, placed troops in Tonkin from September 1940, controlled the naval bases and airfields of Southern Indo-China in 1941 and made Indo-China the base for a general offensive in south-east Asia, its 'sphere of co-prosperity'. Then, in December 1941 Japan attacked the United States. The war of the Pacific had begun. It was necessary to withdraw most of the forces of occupation from Indo-China.

Admiral Decoux, the Governor-General of Indo-China, successfully organised a strategy of survival, encouraged the expression of a certain kind of nationalism, revived the monarchist ideal and even went so far as to use the term Vietnam. At the same time the Communist Party emphasised the anti-imperialist line of its programme. At the end of 1939 it was well placed in southern China. In 1941 the Vietminh* was formed with as objective the independence of Vietnam. It was a kind of democratic front to regroup the progressive forces directed, surreptitiously, by Communists like Phạm-Văn-Đồng and Võ-Nguyên-Giáp who called for a general insurrection. France, Japan, Vietminh were the three entities whose future was closely linked to the unfolding of the world war.

The Japanese withdrew. They decided to 'defrenchify' the country. They launched a surprise attack on 9 March 1945. It was the end of the French in Indo-China. Nothing remained but an administrative, military and technical framework. The Vietnamese thought: 'Heaven has abandoned the French', and they rallied round an independent Vietnam under the auspices of Japan which chose, at the time of its defeat on 15 August 1945, to give its arms to the Vietminh, who gradually infiltrated the whole of the territory.

History was turned on its head. On 20 August the Vietminh took control in Hanoi, followed by Huế and Saigon. On 25 August the Emperor Bảo-Đại abdicated and gave to the Vietminh the seal of the state, thus giving it a historic legitimacy as the heir of the great Nguyễn dynasty. On 2 September 1945, the day of the official Japanese surrender, the future of Hồ-Chí-Minh, who had already formed a government of the Republic of Vietnam with a large majority of Communist ministers, announced 'the independence and unity of Vietnam'.

---

*   Vietminh. A contraction of Việt-Nam đoc lập đồng minh hội ... League for the independence of Vietnam, founded in May 1941.

From 1945 until reunification (1975–1976)

The end of the worldwide conflict did not bring peace. A powerful anti-colonial revolution lit up Asia, mixing wars of national independence with wars of Communist inspiration. Faced with the incertitude of the Fourth Republic intent on reconquering lost territories and offering them new statuses but unable to present a clear political objective, Hồ-Chí-Minh* called for a general war at the end of December 1946.

In addition the Cold War had begun in 1947. In this new, polarised world, 'Vietnam–Indo-China' became an important battlefield for Russia and the United States, both looking to extend their influence or to contain the enemy. China entered the Soviet orbit with Mao's victory in 1949. This greatly helped the Vietminh.

The United States, fearing a Communist victory in the Indo-Chinese peninsula, brought their assistance to the French who were thus called to be in the forefront of the 'free world' in the Far East. This was an inextricable engagement both militarily and ideologically. Van, with the Redemptorists at Hanoi and then at Dalat, looked on all these events in the heart of the beloved Jesus whilst suffering for the hurt of his country.

The first Indo-Chinese war ended for France with the defeat at Điện Biên Phú in May 1945, and in July, with the International Accords at Geneva, French troops evacuated the territory; Vietnam was divided into two zones at the Seventeenth Parallel: a North Vietnam in the hands of the Vietminh, and an independent South Vietnam with Ngô Đình Diệm, an anti-colonialist from the beginning, a Francophobe, a intransigent Catholic and a fierce anti-Communist. In reality he was supported by the United States which wished to make South Vietnam a bastion against the Communist flow towards southern Asia.

In addition the North Vietnamese population was free, during an short period of time, to remain where they were or to choose South Vietnam. (The latter was the choice of about a million Vietnamese Catholics.) As for Van, he chose North Vietnam, the land of his birth, to which he was deeply attached. He died there in 1959.

With the return of peace Hanoi had aligned the country on the Marxist–Leninist model already in place in the USSR and China, including the priority given to the development of heavy industry and the reform of society through the class war: the latter by means of auto-cratic meetings and popular tribunes with the death penalty, and labour camps for the more notorious opponents, where the category 'objectively hostile' included major proprietors and westernised minds

---

* Hồ-Chí-Minh: 'the luminous'.

faithful to a Catholic Church linked to Rome. The latter was considered as a foreign power.

Ngô Đình Diệm, the President of the Republic of South Vietnam in 1955, soon had to face opposition including that of an organisation of the Communist Vietminh type, the Việtcộng. Assassinations and coups followed under the auspices of the United States which undertook a direct war of intervention in 1964. This was the second Vietnamese War (1964–73) which finished with the Paris Accords in 1973. The Amerians, in their turn, evacuated the country but they still helped and advised the South Vietnamese army: they did not, however, stop a complete Communist victory in 1970 with the taking of Saigon. Reunification was achieved in 1976.

For ten years the Socialist Republic of Vietnam (RSVN), followed the radical socialist path of economic nationalisation. It was a failure. The 'Socialist new man' was not able to take root so, in 1986, there was a strategic turn-round to see new norms for a time of peace at the heart of a 'Pacific zone', soon to be the centre of the world. In 1995 the RSVN was admitted as the seventh member of the Association of Nations of South East Asia (ASEAN). This was a date as significant as that of 1976, the new date of its foundation. Franco-Vietnamese relations have since resumed: the Catholic Church is totally Vietnamese.

Vietnam, at the beginning of the third millennium, has all the attributes needed to become a great country in the Asia–Pacific zone.

Monique Mennerat (Geographer-Historian)

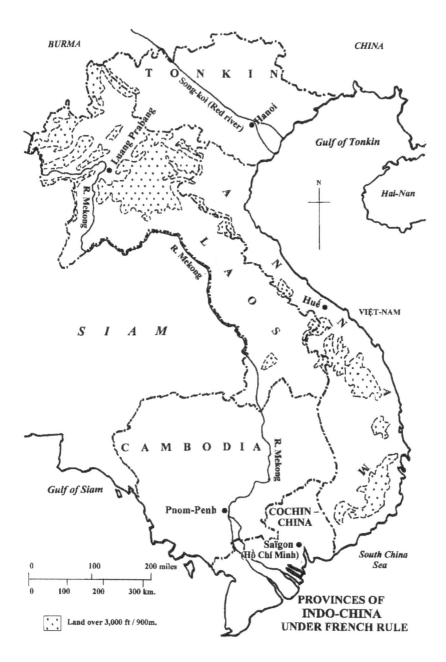

Provinces of Indo-China under French Rule

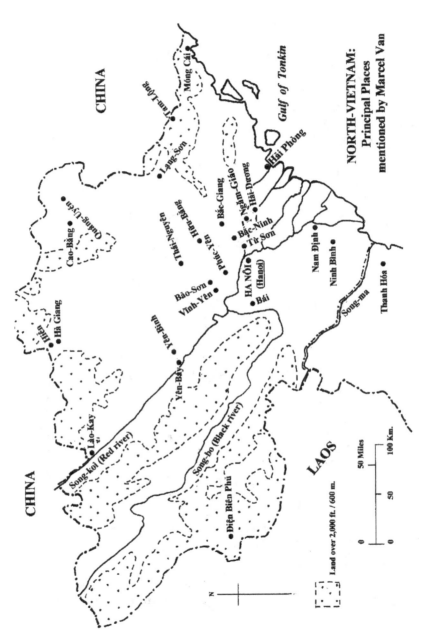

North-Vietman: Principal Places mentioned by Marcel Van

Preliminaries to the French edition

On 15 August 1945 I welcomed to the Redemptorist novitiate in Hanoi some young men who, after a time of voluntary postulancy, wished to become religious brothers in our community. One of them became noticed very quickly. He was only seventeen years of age but he was so small that he could have passed for fourteen. His civil name was Jaochim Nguyen tan Van, and he became in religion Brother Marcel. He came from a modest family in a village of the Bac Ninh province on the Red River. He left home at the age of seven to pursue his studies at different presbyteries and then at the junior seminary at Lang Son which was directed by French Dominicans. It was the boy's wish to become a religious with the Redemptorists at Hanoi. He got his wish. When his novitiate was over he lived for nine years in houses of our community from 1946 to 1955. He volunteered to be among the group of brave souls who remained in Hanoi after the division of Vietnam into two (1954), and he was arrested by the Communist police on 7 May 1955 and kept in detention under harsh conditions until his death which came on 10 July 1959. He was thirty-one.

Now Brother Marcel has left us a memorial of a short existence given totally to his Lord. This is the account that we present, a kind of spiritual autobiography which reveals a manner of behaviour which seems to us to come close to that of a Francis of Assisi or, better still, to that of Thérèse of Lisieux whom he called his older sister.

What gave rise to this account? From my first encounter with the boy I was struck by the account he gave me of the details of his childhood and adolescence, not so much because of the colourfulness of the events as of the existence of an unusual interior life. So I asked him to put it in writing for me. He applied himself to this work through obedience, above all during the twelve months of his novitiate, and continuing afterwards during the course of the five following years (1946–51). At the end I found myself with a copious Vietnamese text which covered almost nine hundred pages of exercise books.

I must admit that the French version of the text caused me much trouble because I had to translate it with the greatest fidelity. I had it looked at by confrères, by Brother Marcel's sister, today a Redemptorist nun, and by friends. They are numerous who have expressed the wish that the witness of this young religious, in whom the work of grace has performed wonders, be more widely known.

Father Antonio Boucher, CSsR

Additional Information

At the request of his Father Master, Van (Brother Marcel in religion), wrote his life story. This account covers 882 pages of scholar's exercise books (13cm × 19cm). It was a hard task for Van who dedicated to it all of his free time. Three attempts at writing it preceded this account. The first, composed during his novitiate during 1945–6 was 348 pages long. The second, written during the years 1947–51 was 875 pages long and the third, during the years 1951–52, consisted of 564 pages.

The fourth, definitive version, was translated from the Vietnamese by Father Boucher* on his return to Canada in 1964. It was a hard task which gave him plenty of problems. His work was studied by Professor Lê Hữu Mục† who concluded: 'The translation of Van's manuscript has been done by the hand of a master and with an astonishing fidelity.'

In the French edition there has been some retouching in changing some outmoded expressions, some heaviness of style and, in accordance with Father Boucher's wish in employing the familiar form 'tu' for the conversations of Van with his family and in his prayers.‡ We have done this to show Van's simplicity with Jesus and the saints whom he loved to invoke. Furthermore, we have added some explanatory notes; those which concern the family life have been rewritten from the notes which Tế, Van's little sister and now a Redemptorist, drew up at the request

---

* Father Antonio Boucher was Van's Master of Novices and afterwards his spiritual director until the end of his life.
† Professor Lê Hữu Mục, Doctor of Letters of the University of Saigon, head of the Vietnamology Department of the University of Saigon, author and literary critic of the Vietnamese language and the Promoter of a programme of Vietnamese studies in the scholastic networks of Canada.
‡ It is impossible to translate the numerous degrees of sentiment and respect between the generations, much more numerous in Vietnamese than in French, which is limited to two expressions. In English there is not even this distinction.

of Father Boucher; others are from the 'Friends of Van' (*Les Amis de Van*).

We have decided to reproduce the orthography of Vietnamese names with their precise accentuation. Only four words are given English orthography: Vietnam (Việt-Nam), Saigon (Sãi-Gon), Hanoi (Hà-Nôi), Van (Văn).

To make reference to the text as simple as possible it was decided, in the French translation, to maintain the numeration of the pages of the original copybooks. They appear in the text in brackets, for example (251).* The sub-titles are Van's. We have simply indicated the division of his life into three stages and have given titles to the first two, Van having given a title only to the third.

Translations into French of other of Van's writings are in preparation or have been completed. These include:

'The Dialogues' – A collection of conversations with Jesus, Mary and Thérèse of Lisieux. They are a wonderful witness of the way of child-like simplicity leading to heroism in little things.

'Correspondence' – A collection of almost three hundred letters from Van to those close to him. Through these letters the reader discovers Van's great solicitude both at the material and spiritual level, these two aspects being always linked in Brother Marcel's concern.

'Other Writings' – A collection containing the intimate notes of Van (retreat notes, personal reflections, poetry, scattered reflections), all collected here. Through these pages the depth of Van's soul will be revealed: his doubts, his hesitations, his anger and his total confidence in Jesus, to whom he commits himself to serve as best he can all his life.

The friends of Van (*Les Amis de Van*).

---

*   In the English edition these numbers appear in the margins.

The Autobiography of
Brother Marcel Van

For the love of the Child Jesus and of my Mother Mary
[†]
J.M.J.A.T.*

Reverend Father,

I have already tried three times to write the story of my soul but each effort has been a failure. I must, therefore, begin again. To tell the truth, it is not brilliant, and I think you must be tired of waiting.

That this is so is partly because of my lack of skill. Not only have I not got my sister Saint Thérèse's expertise in story-telling but I continue to be hesitant, not knowing how to express myself in a fluent manner. Above all, since it is a question of speaking of oneself, the bad as well as the good, of course, it boils down to singing one's own praises.

But after having weighed the pros and the cons and especially after having read this sentence which Thérèse applies to herself in *The Story of a Soul*: 'If a little flower could speak it would say, simply, what the good God has done for her'. She would frankly admit that she is a fragile crea- (2) ture, quick to fade but she would, also, be proud of her beauty, of the crispness of her colours, of her delicate scent and of all the other qualities that nature has adorned her with. I tell myself that my soul is also like one of God's flowers. It is God himself who has preordained all that I possess and all the events of my life. I can also therefore recount all the graces with which the good God has embellished my soul, so that together, my Father, we can sing a canticle of praise to the infinite mercy of God. But I have already told my story to you three times and, on each occasion, I have noted that there were big mistakes. It is because I have had to make several versions of my story that you may have some difficulty in understanding me.

Let us suppose that you have followed my development since my childhood as Pauline followed that of her sister (Thérèse), you would understand clearly, in spite of my clumsiness, in what my childhood consisted. But the Lord has decided otherwise and now He wishes that I make a personal effort so that the stages of my past life may become clearer and in this way, my Father, you will help me to become a more beautiful flower before the face of God.

In accordance with your wish I will once again take up my story. I will (3)

---

* J.M.J.A.T. Jesus, Mary, Joseph, Alphonsus, Thérèse. (Alphonsus Liguori is the founder of the Redemptorists.)

collect all the thoughts which are crowding my mind to present to you a detailed account of all that has happened to me from my childhood until now. Therefore, consider simply as drafts the two attempts I have already written.* I ask God to help and not let me stray from your wish.

My dear Father, I do not know if what I write will have any influence on those souls who will come after me. Nevertheless, my aim in writing this story is to fulfil, perfectly, the holy will of God. It never occurred to me until now that I would wish to serve as an intermediary between souls and divine grace. My only wish is to be a flower which does not know how to speak and which hides its beauty in God's heart. God, however, is not bound by this wish. He must, on the contrary, realise his own words: 'Nobody lights a lamp to put it under a bushel.' It is his wish, therefore, that I display my beauty and spread my scent in the daylight to fulfil perfectly my vocation as a flower.

God makes his will known

(4)   My Father, from the time of my first meeting with you as my spiritual director when I entered the novitiate, you questioned me, unexpectedly, on the graces which I had received since my childhood, and I felt that you had received the grace to understand deeply my child's soul. Being neither astonished nor embarrassed by your attitude, I spoke quite naturally. I say that I spoke naturally because I have never spoken to anybody, whoever it might be, of these graces, for the simple reason that, temperamentally, I was shy. On another occasion you asked me to commit to writing the graces that God has given me since childhood.

My Father, I fear nothing so much as to speak of these things. However, when I recognised that it was the will of God which you represented I immediately collected my rudimentary thoughts for you. Now, my Father, you see me as a rose which God has adorned with innumerable choice gifts. But to make of me a beautiful rose he had to weed and water me through many trials and tears.

(5)   ## What's to become of me?

Before beginning my story allow me to throw myself on my knees to ask Mary the most beautiful Mother really to help me in this work. Indeed,

---

*   The first compilation that Van made of his life was done on little loose sheets which he considered as a draft. The second and third accounts were made on pupils' exercise books, and these are the ones that Van mentions.

all the graces given to me by God have come through her maternal hands. Moreover, she is at the origin in my heart of all the good feelings and beautiful thoughts which have ascended from me to heaven. It is through obedience that, once again, I recall in writing these precious favours. The heart of Mary is indeed a book in which is clearly recorded the life of each of her children. Everything which happens, as it unfolds, is engraved in her heart. Thus, therefore, O Mary full of goodness, I seek your help. Direct my hand and do not allow me to write according to my personal thoughts but simply according to the facts as they are imprinted in your heart.* O my guardian angel and all the saints in heaven, I ask you to come to my help and obtain for me more patience and enlightenment so that I can fulfil perfectly God's will.

I turn most especially to you my sister, Saint Thérèse of the Child Jesus, the most beautiful of all the sisters that I have met in my life. It is thanks to you that I have known my vocation; it is with you that I have (6) loved Jesus. And if, today, I understand something of the heart of God, if faith and confidence have become my haven of peace, it is, again, thanks to your instruction. My life resembles yours completely: the same stem, the same scent, the same beauty. If there is any difference it comes from the grace of God which varies according to the times. Today, my sister, I ask you not to forget me. Help me again as you have done so often. Point out to me the songs of love and the intimate words that you used formerly to instruct me. Help me to recount once more the story of my soul, as formerly by obedience you had to do. My little soul has nothing worth telling. However, to respond fully to the demands of God's perfect love, I am obeying promptly. All I want is the will of Jesus.   *simplicity.*

That's what you have insisted many times that I do. I rely on your help.

Let us now begin.

A flower's detached petal. Thérèse of the Child Jesus, my (7) venerated sister

My Father, after having read the title of my story, you will have already

---

* I find in this very simple prayer the secret of Van's inspiration, which has enabled him to write hundreds of pages so quickly that I cannot yet understand how he has managed to do so, and at the same time do the work that Jesus asked him, 'to be his little secretary', to serve as an intermediary, to teach his Vietnamese compatriots how to love him and converse familiarly with him. This was done only in his free time, outside his working hours. [Father Antonio Boucher.]

formed some idea of the fragile and languishing life of this unfortunate petal. It has become detached, and if at this moment you see that it still retains a beautiful appearance, it is thanks to the vital strength that divine love has given it. Although it has often known bitterness and constraint, crushed as it has been by the wind's violence, it is still alive, however, and at this moment it can relate its own destiny as proof of the infinite love of God's heart.

In the shade of bamboo trees

Since my destiny is to be a detached petal I think that in my life there will be hardly any sweetness. Suffering is the image of my entire life. Yes, my Father, it is quite true that I knew suffering very early, and nearly all of my life has been a trial.

(8)   In speaking so I do not intend to relate straight away the painful moments of my life because, as you will have noticed, before becoming detached from the corolla the petal has also enjoyed a beautiful, fragrant springtime.

I will, therefore, divide my life before my entry into the congregation into three stages. These resemble those in the life of my sister Saint Thérèse. Furthermore, and speaking in all simplicity, I wish to take as my model that very same story of Saint Thérèse. Consequently, if in my story there are similar passages, it is necessary neither to laugh nor to accuse me of plagiarism because, really, they are the meeting places of our two souls. Each flower has its individual scent. Thérèse is the flower, and I being the petal of this flower, how can I not resemble her?

Part 1
Childhood (1928–1935)

The First Stage

The first period of my life includes the time from the day when I reached the age of reason until my seventh year, that is to say, until the time of my leaving home. I spent these seven years like a rose under the warm days of the springtime sun. Everything around me radiated joy, (9) everything reflected beauty, especially in my family, and I will never be able to describe the sweetness of my childhood nor the love of my parents. Moveover, since God has given me from an early age the use of reason, all these memories remain engraved in my heart. This is again a privilege that I share with little Thérèse, and the blessings that God gave me during this time of my life were also similar to those which my holy sister had received, although our family circumstances were different.

In the modest house of a country village my father plied the trade of tailor, and my mother, as well as being a housewife, worked in the paddy field so that we did not have to buy provisions elsewhere.

My older brother Joachim Liệt, my big sister Anne Lê and I, the third child, lived with our parents.

Here is my mother's pen picture of this third child: 'He is a very strange child. He loves fun and mischief, but he is also very sensitive and cries very easily.' Because of my unusual nature I was the object of a special love and attention on the part of my parents. My mother (10) would add: 'All those who came to the house took pleasure in teasing the little one. Sometimes that pained me because, when he was happy, everything was fine, but when he began to cry, goodness, only heaven could console him.'

My mother was perfectly correct in speaking in this manner, but she had also to admit that my love for her was no ordinary love like that of my brother and sister. I followed her all day and if someone caused us to be separated I was inconsolable ... I really loved my mother. And for me no pleasure could compare to that of finding myself close to her, because God had given her a warm love which knew how to combine goodness with prudence. She easily pampered me, but she could also form me in holiness.

According to the members of my family, when my mother was teaching her children to speak she had the habit of using virtuous words rather than bland jokes. Consequently, my tongue was accustomed to (11) pronouncing above all the names of Jesus, Mary and Joseph. Indeed, from the time that I was able to understand the words that I was pronouncing, I heard myself repeating: 'Jesus ... Jesus, Mother ... Mother, Blessed Virgin, Saint Joseph ...' And when my hand was able to hold anything and when I could easily raise and lower my arm, she did not hesitate to teach me to make the sign of the cross. Perhaps I knew how to make the sign of the cross before I could crawl, that is to say before I knew its meaning. However, I did it because my mother had accustomed me to do so. Following on from that, from the time that I was able to speak more easily, my mother taught me a short prayer which she made me recite before giving me food or breast-feeding me. She made me kneel on her lap, join my hands and say, my head turned towards Mary's picture: 'Blessed Virgin, give me a little food', or 'Give me a little milk', according as to whether I was eating or being breast-fed. Every time, when I had finished, I addressed Mary in the same way, saying to her: 'Blessed Virgin, thank you for having satisfied my hunger.' This practice helped to make me happier so that, very often, I would repeat the words even though my mother was not feeding me.

(12)

In no time at all my mother taught me to repeat by heart the Our Father, the Hail Mary and the Glory Be. She then introduced me to the recitation of the rosary and from the day that I was able to say it, as my mother testified, I became gentler and better-behaved. My mother would add: 'When he was sad or sick he would ask me to say the rosary to make him feel better.' Truly, my Father, at that time, even though I was very small, the Blessed Virgin gave me the grace to feel genuine emotion when I offered her these bouquets of spiritual flowers. Every time that I said the rosary my heart was filled with great happiness, just as if the Blessed Virgin had been close to me, smiling on me and covering me with maternal kisses. And because I experienced this sweet feeling quite readily, I would have liked my mother to recite the rosary continuously, and I regretted the necessity to have to run after her to recite the rosary, since she was always busy. When I urged her too much, she decided to recite it whilst working.*

(13)

When one has such a good mother, how can one bear to be separated from her? One thing is certain; it will only be possible for me to leave my mother on the day when I feel I have found security in life. Yes, it is well known that it is impossible for me to be away from my mother, although this state of affairs is a heavy cross for her to bear. My mother said, in speaking of that period: 'After giving birth to him, I had to look for a maid to look after him in my place, but the opposite happened. During three long years I had to fill the role of maid, and allow her to do the housework in my place. During all that time I was never able to go to the market nor even to make a pot of soup ...'

Alas, for love of me, my mother had to forgo many pleasures, but by that I was able to measure the extent of her goodness and of her tolerance towards me. According to my mother, the maid was not without

---

* Van's mother often said to him: 'If I thought that you did not love the Blessed Virgin, that you did not respect her, I would no longer recognise you as my child.'

good qualities. She was indeed a virtuous person who loved me a lot. Now and again on seeing how tired the love of this child with the difficult character made my mother, she dared to take the offensive by pulling me from my mother's arms to take me to play some distance away. But she never once succeeded. She could hardly get me to the end of the alleyway when, after half an hour at the most, she had to return me to my mother. One day the maid wished once more to take me somewhere. I refused and questioned her forcefully:

'Is Mammy also going?'

'Your Mammy is busy.'

'Then I am not going.'

'So, you are not going,' said the maid. Then she took me away immediately. A few minutes later she returned with me, her face covered with the scratches from my fingernails.

It is my mother who told me this story some time before my first communion. I felt very remorseful and, although this maid had left us some time ago, I begged my mother, when she should meet her again, to ask her to forgive me for this failing.

On seeing my repentance the maid readily forgave me, and she came to congratulate me on the day of my first communion, saying to me in a joyful manner, 'I hope you will grow, and that you will love Jesus (15) more and more, as you have always wished since you were very young.' (Today this person is married and my mother is the only one who knows where she is.)

My Father, allow me to return once more to the time when I was on my mother's lap. Because I was so attached to her I always stayed close to her. But I wonder if this childish attachment has given her any consolation. Alas, I have often felt a deep regret when recalling that I have not given to my mother the solace that she deserved in return for the gestures of love that she has given to me. Speaking of those days, my mother recalls: 'Although very small he was extremely stubborn, domineering and unyielding. In no way did he resemble his brother and sister. On the contrary, he always proved to be a naughty child. I was uncertain what would later become of him.'

That is sufficient, my Father, to let you know what my mother had to suffer because of me. What made her suffer even more was, that, as she says herself, although I resembled little Thérèse by my stubbornness, I (16) was not at all like her in the matter of repentance.

There is one thing that my mother said quietly and with great care for fear that I might overhear her. In spite of these precautions my little ears overheard the secret: 'Fortunately, there is one thing concerning him that consoles me which is that, in spite of all his shortcomings, if I correct him gently, he obeys immediately and does everything that he is told to do.' Although my mother spoke quietly to prevent any uncalled-for self-esteem on my part, if I examine myself I see clearly that then, as always, if she wished to be obeyed she had only to treat me gently, but if, on the contrary, she treated me harshly, I became more stubborn. Because God has given me a sensitive heart, if anyone threatens me I feel fear rather than hatred, but if anyone treats me with love and gentleness, I warm very easily towards him. I had a mother who was both energetic and affectionate, who harmonised with my intimate feelings and who served me as a role model. Truthfully, I cannot find the words to describe the richness of divine love. When I reached my fourth birthday, my mother, no longer fearing that I might overhear, praised me thus: 'Since the age of four his character changed little by little, and I then felt a sure hope for his future growing in my heart.'

(17)

These words are true, Father and do not make me blush, because I also realised that at that time my character had changed completely. I knew how to cherish my mother, and to be gentle and well-behaved. I experienced a great joy when I obeyed her. Is that not the reward that God gives to children who know how to obey promptly?

If I was well-behaved it was also due to my mother, and I wish to affirm that any goodness in me is due to the bounty of her maternal heart. It was already well understood that nourishing me was a difficult task, but bringing me up to be a good man was another extraordinary undertaking that only a virtuous mother was capable of bringing to fruition.

(18)

It is only because I really know my mother that I speak in this fashion. I have not hesitated to call her a saint many times although she is still living on earth. The saying, 'Like mother, like son', is literally true in my case. Although I was not a well-behaved child, my mother succeeded entirely in pruning the faults that were embryonic in me. The season having arrived, the tree of my soul produced, spontaneously, a beautiful foliage, and it could offer to nature fresh and sweet-smelling bouquets of flowers.

Paternal love

My mother's heart protected me with great tenderness during my childhood, and her love has succeeded in making me capable of love, and also of a respectful fear. What fond memories of my mother's heart are imprinted in mine! I have also enjoyed the love and affection of my father which were for me a gentle breeze blowing softly on my childhood to give it more sweetness. If I can affirm that my mother was the person I was closest to, I can truly say that my father was the one who indulged me the most.

(19)

In those days the happiness of the family had a charm so sweet for me that, apart from my desire for heaven, my greatest wish was to be able to live in peace in its bosom.

During the day my father was busy at his work but, every evening after the meal, especially in summer, he would take me for a walk through the village, sometimes to my grandmother's, sometimes to the fields. What I liked most in those walks was that I did not have to use my little feet. For a treat my father carried me on his shoulders with my legs dangling and my hands holding on to his head. Then he would gallop like a horse until I wanted him to slow down. I called this (20) manner of locomotion, 'riding on horseback'.

My father had still other ways of pleasing me, for example, giving me various nicknames. In those days to show that I was a brave boy, a hero, he would call me, playfully, 'the general'. To tell the truth, this would-be general was incapable of doing anything other than playing pranks to which all the others had to submit. He gave me this name, therefore, to make the others more afraid of me. Every evening during our walks, if I wished, he would dress me like a general who would review the troops. It was an imposing spectacle. Then I would regain my father's shoulders. It was a really incomparable joy.

My mother felt sometimes that my father indulged me too much, but my father responded as did Mr Martin to Mrs Guérin,[*] 'After all, he is a general'. Nevertheless, I am sure that my father did not spoil me to the extent of harming me, since, whilst indulging me, he never toler- (21) ated a sulky face on my part. If I sometimes allowed such a shortcoming to manifest itself, my father would show me the cane and naturally order was restored. Before this determined attitude, 'the general', despite his stubbornness, was reduced to silence. Although in fact I was never subjected to this punishment, I readily understood and was genuinely afraid.

The happiest evenings in those days were those of summer when my father took me walking in the fields. The green meadows did not yet give rise to any emotion in my soul. I loved the vastness of the flowering meadows and the yellow paddy fields. I loved to play in the grass, gather the flowers, chase the butterflies. I loved to sing and play in the evening breeze. Ah I loved, I loved a thousand things, but I loved these particularly because they were beautiful. (22)

Concerning spiritual joys such as the union of God in the green meadows, or the heart's voice whispering with the flowers, I was as yet unaware. I did not yet experience any sensitive feelings in the presence of these noble pleasures. Because my soul was still small like a tender

---

[*]   Respectively, the father and aunt of Saint Thérèse of the Child Jesus.

bud, the sun's rays had not yet penetrated it. Its beauty still remained hidden in these natural surroundings.

But it was different for my father. After having deposited me on the ground, he would walk slowly in the fields, arms folded across his chest and, whilst walking, he gazed into the distance following the direction of the wind. Sometimes he stopped to contemplate the rays of the setting sun and the clouds wandering in the vault of the sky. Sometimes I seemed to hear him pray, and very often I had noticed that he seemed to be immersed in the immensity of creation. Sometimes he would recite lines of poetry or describe to me godly things in an enthralling manner. If at that moment I had been able to comprehend what my father understood so well, what sweetness I would have tasted in the heart of God.

(23)   But the evening passed so quickly. When the sun skimmed over the verdant dyke and the Angelus rang in the church tower we returned together, and every time my father carried me on his shoulders in order to return more quickly. Whilst returning I swayed to the rhythm of his step and I sang: *Nhong, nhong, nhong, ngựa ông về; cắt cỏ bồ đề cho ngựa ông ăn.* 'The master's horse has returned at the sound of the bell. Cut fresh grass to feed it with.' Once arrived at the door, I found my mother waiting for me to take me to church. How beautiful were those evenings when I felt my father's love.

Grandmother and grandson

Early childhood is the time when one is loved. It is why I was surrounded with the most tender affection. Both my grandmothers were still alive. They both loved me dearly but each in a different way. My paternal grandmother loved me too much for my physical appearance. Each time (24)   that she came to visit me she praised me in these terms: 'Van has pretty lips, at the same time red and delicate. What regular teeth he has.' Then she would say: 'Go on, smile so I can see.' If I was feeling happy I was able to smile as she wished, and she would hug me closely to her heart, cover me with kisses and give me so many cakes that I could not hold them. Afterwards, if I wanted anything, good or bad, my grandmother always acquiesced. At that time, in imitation of my grandmother, I even learnt to smoke; it was sufficient for me to hold out my hand and she allowed it immediately. Fortunately, there was also close by a mother capable of disciplining me. The excessive praise of my grandmother did not succeed in pleasing her and, after the latter's departure, she took care to (25)   correct things and to prevent my grandmother from indulging me in a harmful manner. For my part, I realised that my mother was right, and in spite of my love for my grandmother I would never dare to contravene my mother's words which were, for me, like commands.

My maternal grandmother's love, on the contrary, was more measured. She loved me with all her heart but she never did anything which could make me too conceited. Being very virtuous, ordinarily when we met she enquired solely of my spiritual health. She would, for example, say to me: 'Van, have you been good? Do you know how to make the sign of the cross? Which prayers do you know by heart? Whose children are we? Where is our homeland? Do you love the Blessed Virgin?' If I knew the answers she rewarded me with a small amount of money. If I was unable to reply she would teach me. But the most precious reward, which she always promised me, was to ask the Blessed Virgin to take me to heaven, our homeland. Every time I was with my maternal grandmother, therefore, as with my mother, I understood the things of heaven more clearly.   (26)

Naturally, both my grandmothers had won a place in my heart, and conversely I showed my love for them in many ways. On one occasion I even wished that my paternal grandmother would go quickly to heaven, as little Thérèse once wished for her mother. I loved it when she wrapped her coat around me to warm me up. I loved it also when she blew puffs of smoke into my face to make me cough since that amused her. And on many occasions I behaved as children do to please their grandmothers.

Briefly, according to my mother, my paternal grandmother loved me for my happy, kind and mischievous personality and called me, jokingly, 'Pierrot', whilst my maternal grandmother called me 'little angel', because she loved me for my pure, simple and virtuous soul. My two grandmothers were still alive when I left my family. One year later God called them both to Him. I was then eight years old.

Brotherly love   (27)

My family then numbered three children. I was the last born. My brother and sister went to the village school. It saddened me that I had to stay at home. However, I was very alert and as soon as I heard the drum announcing break-time I would rush to the school gates to meet my brother and sister. I then received many little drawings of elephants and horses. Although these pictures had no particular significance they pleased me a lot, and I would run quickly to my mother to show her proudly these unusual presents. If my mother gave me sweets I would go at once to share them with my brother and sister.

How our time was filled with warm affection in those days! My

(28)

brother and sister were happy to play with me outside school hours. Every time they called me to play or to give me a present they gave me the pet name of 'little brother'. On Thursday, the school holiday, my mother taught me the catechism, since, despite my young age, I had to follow a programme of study like my brother and sister, the only difference being that they learned handwriting while I studied the catechism, or practised greetings and polite speech. It was my mother herself who taught me. As soon as the time of study was over my sister Lê took me to the table to practise reading and to learn the alphabet. Strictly speaking, this was a subterfuge to keep me close to her, instead of being with the maid. She would, nonchalantly, show me one or two letters: then she would joke with me or show me some pictures. Then the three of us would go into the garden and entertain ourselves with processions, with building bridges, constructing ramparts, digging small lakes, draining fresh ponds or establishing villages. It was all very interesting.

(29)

I have to laugh when I think of the way in which we organised processions. Now and then even the children of the neighbourhood came to join in. Our procession props were very basic. The brancard* was made of clay as was the little bell. Both were sculpted by the nimble fingers of my brother Liệt, and did not lack artistic merit. The flags and fans, made of banana leaves, mingled with the fresh flowers of various colours displayed from one end of the route to the other. In truth, it looked like the thread of spiders' webs decorated with flowers. All of this was the fruit of our delicate, infantile imaginations. Only the picture of the Blessed Virgin had been taken from above the bed. Having finished our decorating, we would imitate with our mouths the beating of the drum and the sound of the flute to summon the crowd around the brancard of the Holy Virgin which was hardly as big as a fist. The proceedings began with a hymn. Then each one was designated his role: one acted as the priest, another as the altar boy and a third the drummer, and finally someone played the trumpet. As for the young girls, they acted as the pupils and as religious sisters intoning the prayers. Sometimes there was a shortage of extras so that the same person had to play two or three different roles. For example, the one who was acting as the priest might also have to carry the brancard and hold the drum. The time had to be divided so that so that all of the different functions could be carried out. Sometimes one muttered the

(30)

prayers and then from time to time beat the drum – *tùng, tùng,* so that all could walk uniformly. When the time came to recite the rosary the brancard came to a halt. Afterwards came the time for Benediction.† As

---

*   The stretcher-like frame used to carry statues in processions.
†   Benediction of the Blessed Sacrament.

we had not got a monstrance we contented ourselves by ringing the bell and inclining our heads before the image of the Blessed Virgin. If the angels in heaven had been able to witness this innocent spectacle they would certainly not have been able to stop themselves from smiling! Moreover, our dear heavenly Mother could not avoid following our smallest gestures. I had then the impression that Mary was smiling on her little children, and who knows if she was not taking part in the procession with us? These processions were very joyful and this happiness, far from being only external, contributed to strengthen the bonds which united us to our heavenly Mother. Our parents never forbade these processions. Only the servant did not care for this entertainment because afterwards she had to sweep the yard.

After these processions my brother would take me some distance (31) away. I could say that he took me hunting. It was very exciting. Wishing to take me along more easily in our quest for birds or mice, he usually employed my father's technique of carrying me on his shoulders. He handled his sling very skilfully. He could find mouse holes very easily. Normally at harvest time when the big fields were dry my brother took Ven the dog with him. The very small mice were very sweet and lovely to look at. I liked very much to amuse myself with these little animals, but this pleasure did not last very long since Madame Cat, being jealous, often came to deprive me of this pleasure. The little birds suffered the same fate, and thus we were deprived of the pleasure of hearing them sing in the house.

However, these hunting expeditions would take the hunters too far away. We were sometimes attacked brusquely on the road by children of a neighbouring village. Their sole aim was to fill their stomachs with cakes or packets of sweets without having to ask anyone for them. (32) Therefore, when they saw some unknown children, to satisfy their appetites they threw themselves upon them and relieved them of their delicacies. But we were not afraid. My brother was very proud of his strength and, thanks to his sling, he had carried off many a victory. It sometimes happened, however, that we had to beat a hasty retreat because of the aggressors' superior strength. Unfortunately, because of these repeated battles, my mother had to forbid the two hunters from venturing too far.

Fights like these can contribute to the bad education of children. This is why my mother imposed this prohibition. It is a fact, however, that on these occasions our fraternal solidarity showed itself to be very strong. My brother would not give an inch until he had recovered from the aggressor the cake or sweets that had been taken from me. He rushed in regardless of danger and sometimes his face was completely swollen after fighting on my behalf. For my part, I also felt very coura- (33)

geous. Although small, I knew how to collect the stones that my brother was throwing, and when it was possible I threw myself into the skirmish like a mad dog, even employing my teeth, especially when I saw that my brother had been wounded. After each of these battles we noticed that our bonds of friendship were tied even tighter.

Even now, in thinking of these things, every wound is like a sweet memory for our two brave souls. But, unhappily, these days of light and joy were suddenly darkened by a thick cloud which came to veil the sun's rays. God made my brother enter early into the path of suffering. From the age of thirteen the cross of disability came to weigh heavily on his shoulders. He was the victim of an eye disease which impaired his vision. Gradually his eyesight declined. Now he is blind. Nevertheless my brother, always brave, did not cease to repeat: 'If God does not wish (34) to cure me, I accept this ordeal cheerfully until the day when I shall see the brilliant light of the eternal home.' O, holy will of God! You keep all the lovely things for the heart which loves God. From this moment my heart will have no more smiles.

Brother and sister

My brother Liệt now living in darkness, my sister Lê will be my confidante from now onwards. She would never give way to anyone in terms of affection for her little, impish brother. Like my paternal grandmother, she also had the habit of spoiling me, and in particular she was expert in dressing me up.

My sister was truly endowed with a generous, sympathetic and even maternal heart. That is why I had great respect for her and called her 'little mother'. In those days, if either of us went anywhere, the other must necessarily follow, and usually when we met anyone they would (35) ask us: 'What are you going to do when you grow up?' My sister invariably replied, 'I am going to be a nun.'

As for me, knowing nothing of the religious life, I replied like her:

'Me too, I will enter religion with my sister.'

'That's not possible, because you are a boy: you must become a tailor like your father.'

'Not at all, I prefer to enter religion.'

These replies would attract the family's attention. They were often alluded to, and everyone waited to see if the little one, so attached to his mother, would find a way of leaving the family. A means of leaving the family? When God wishes to choose a soul, divine power considers as nothing all difficulties, whatever they might be. Later, when I understood the meaning of the religious life I would no longer consider separation from my mother as sad, whilst still being aware that this separation would be a big wound for my heart. But this concerns the future. It is not yet time to speak of it. I am therefore returning for the moment to my sister.

In the evening, after school, we would go together to plant flowers. It is my sister who has taught me how to hold a pick, dig the earth and water plants. Our border possessed an ingenuous beauty. Every (36) morning it overflowed with flowers, their buds unopened, but every evening all the flowers were wilting and faded. The reason for this is that regularly, every morning, in order to give our garden the appearance of beds of flowers, we would go to the fields to collect flowers and then replant them. This account of the transplanting of flowers simply highlights a natural attitude of childhood. In its originality and simplicity it holds a profound meaning for me. It makes me think that one day, after the luminous morning of my radiant childhood, it will be necessary to experience a time of warmth and rain, and then I must become parched just as the flowers I have transplanted have withered under the heat of the day. I look forward only to the tomorrow of my eternal homeland, the only tomorrow when I shall enjoy perfect happiness.

I recall once again those days of May when my sister took me to gather flowers to offer to the Blessed Virgin. Ah, those May days! They were the most beautiful days of my life – those days after the fine rain when the (37) meadows are spangled with flowers and the countryside is wonderful. The breeze blows and seems to bring a delicious fragrance which penetrates man's heart. This display has a compelling charm for me. We were drawn to the fields every day to savour the simple pleasure which the country folk usually refer to as the appealing charm of the Virgin.

The month of May is truly Mary's month, and this good mother has sown happiness and beauty in nature to encourage us to love her with a grateful heart. Nothing could be more appropriate than that the Holy Church has chosen to dedicate this month of May to Mary, since the Blessed Virgin has been called Our Lady of Flowers, the most beautiful of mothers. Following my own personal feeling, I have also called the month of May the month of the 'angels scattering flowers', because everywhere I look I see the fields covered with flowers in bloom.

My sister and I, like two happy butterflies, used to frolic under the (38) pure, mild sky of the countryside amongst the flowers which we gathered with hearts full of happiness as we sang canticles to the Blessed Virgin. This is why our feelings of affection towards her are carved in our hearts. We have been able to gather a warm love for the Blessed Virgin with the flowers in the green fields. I have personally resolved to be a flower without any fruit, so that I can spread my fragrance before Mary's throne during all my life. Thus the thought of entering religion became stronger and stronger in me.

Every evening we placed on a little plate all the flowers we had collected, and we went to the church to offer them to the Blessed Virgin. My sister Lê was a member of the Children of Mary. She put on her dress each evening for the offering of flowers. In this dress which resembled that of Our Lady's she looked like a wonderful queen wearing on her head a crown of flowers as dazzling as diamonds. Following the ceremony of the offering of flowers, the Children of Mary

(39)   had to say prayers, whilst making their offerings to the beat of the drum. It was arranged that at a specific word the drum reminded the young girls that it was necessary to raise their bouquets, to kneel down, and then to genuflect or move forward. They looked like a choir of angels singing joyful chants before Our Lady's throne. It was a very interesting service and I had a strong desire to participate. Unfortunately, being a boy, I did not have the happiness, as my sister had, of offering any flowers. However, I placed a pile of all my good feelings and intentions on my Mother Mary's altar. I looked at her tenderly, waiting for her to accept me like the fragile bud of a little flower still caressed by the breeze of the world. But, fearing that one day it might wither, I opened it from my childhood so that, thanks to Mary's motherly protection, my soul will always keep its freshness until the end of my life. From that very moment I felt an overwhelming joy in my heart. I am certain, therefore, that Mary looked at me and gave me a mysterious smile in my soul. This very joy is the evidence of the Blessed Virgin's commitment to maintain the flower of my soul for ever fresh.

(40)   My beloved Father, I have the feeling that, at this moment, there is hardly any clarity in my mind. I have written in a fairly muddled manner. Furthermore, I do not understand where this disorderliness comes from. Allow me to put down my pen for a moment to recover my senses, and then to turn to another subject.

Virtuous hearts

My dear Father, I have pointed out to you already the love that God has shown towards me in placing me from birth into a privileged family, a family blessed materially, but above all spiritually. It is thanks to the practice of virtue in my family that I have learned from my childhood to turn towards the heart of God. He has given me a tender heart which loves to be happy and to be cared for. Let me say that these were equally the intimate feelings of little Thérèse. Hand in hand with this delicacy of feeling, God has also given to me, as I have already said, a virtuous and prudent mother. It is by the hands of such a mother that I have been fashioned. I once heard her say in speaking of me: 'The more he (41) grew, the happier I was with him.' Yes, that is how it was. My mother never spoke in flattery. On the contrary, she always spoke the truth. As for myself, I recall that in those days the more I changed my behaviour, the more I grew in virtue.

God's action in my soul was becoming more obvious from day to day. Does this mean that I was a saint? No. However, in spite of my lack of stature, my mother never ceased to praise me in these terms: 'He is very small, but very energetic. He does not wish to give way to anyone in the practice of virtue. He demands to do everything for himself and asks to participate like the others in all the family activities. So he never goes to bed before the others, nor rises after them. He never agrees to go to bed until after the evening prayer, and he insists that I wake him up the following day before morning prayers. His pious spirit contrasts visibly with those of his brother and sister. One day, to tease his sister who was (42) giving out nicknames, he said, "Myself, I am Saint Joseph". Hearing him speak in this way someone said to him, "Don't be impolite", but he replied, "How am I rude? If I considered myself like Saint Joseph when I am naughty, that would be impolite: but now, when I am behaving myself, I am sure that Saint Joseph loves to hear me speak in this fashion." On the calm delivery of these words his father began to laugh, and gave him a new nickname, that of "Saint Joker". The question of his entry into religion came up again and again, but that made everyone laugh because he could not leave me,* not even for an hour.

'The funniest thing is that one day, the maid having prepared some food, he did not wish to eat it and he went to prepare his own food. The unhappy maid asked him, drily, "Why are you so difficult? Let me prepare your food as I have to." He replied: "No! In a short time I shall enter religion and I must learn to look after myself." The maid managed not to laugh, slapped him gently and said, "What are you (43) saying? Enter religion! You are still a baby, and still wet behind the ears." And she left him to manage for himself.' At this point my mother burst out laughing and then added: 'Do you know how our little man managed? He ate only a bowl of rice and then furtively filled both pockets, not suspecting that his sister Lê had seen him. She did not breathe a word but waited to see what he would do next. A moment later she saw him go into the garden and then return with empty pockets. He entered the kitchen once again and said to the maid, confi-

---

* His mother.

dentially: "I won't be eating at midday, you know." The tone of his voice indicated prudence. The maid was astonished and asked him:
    "Why is that?"
Embarrassed, he replied:
"I am already full up."
"But at midday you will be hungry again."
"Yes, never mind!" And he disappeared to the bottom of the garden. The maid was unaware of what was going on. Now, that day he had decided to play by himself in the corner of the garden near the bamboo hedge, and he refused to come and eat. It was only later that the mystery was revealed. The previous evening his father had read to him the story of Blessed Tịnh who had fled into the forest to become a hermit. He therefore wished to train himself for the hermit's life.' Having arrived at this point in her story, my mother, instead of laughing, was moved to tears.

(44)

My mother told many other stories of a similar nature. One day I asked her this question: 'Mammy, how do the saints who enter religion give themselves the discipline?'* Before my mother had time to answer, my sister Lê intervened: 'They take a strap and hit themselves on the back. That's all.' She said this because she knew I was terrified of the strap. Then I asked myself: 'If that's how it is, how can I enter the religious life?' Anxiety was written all over my face. Then my mother, in a cheerful manner, consoled me by saying: 'You will then have God's grace.' In spite of that, every time that I thought of the strap I was afraid, and a shiver went through my body.

As I told you earlier, I had the habit of saying the rosary every day. Naturally, I could not give up this practice which pleased me so much because the recitation of the rosary was, for me, an intimate conversation with Our Lady. If I wished to tell her something, or ask for a favour, or draw her loving gaze towards me, the rosary was the only way I knew to do this. There were some unusual favours amongst those I asked for. I asked her that I might grow more quickly, that I might avoid coarse language, hold my chopsticks properly, have a baby brother to carry, and so on. Each time, the Blessed Virgin indulged me by giving me what I asked for. I received in particular the favour of never using coarse speech, no matter what the situation. My mother has recognised this trait of my childhood in testifying: 'He has never uttered an uncouth word.'

(45)

Another favour I have asked of Our Lady, and which she has granted in an obvious manner, is that of never allowing me to be late in church for spiritual devotions. This grace, which I was not aware of, astonished

---

*   An instrument of penance resembling a little whip.

my mother and she had to admit: 'It's strange: he had a passion for games to the extent that he would forgo a meal, but when the time came for the first sound of the bell, I would see him returning. He would ask me to wash his face and dress him for church. This invariably happened (46) every day. Sometimes, not knowing where he was playing, I wondered where to look for him but when I saw him arriving I knew that it must be nearly time for the visit to the Blessed Sacrament.' To tell the truth, I was not paying any particular attention; I had simply asked the Blessed Virgin and my guardian angel to remind me when it was time to visit the most Blessed Sacrament. Afterwards, not knowing why, when it was time I stopped playing and got ready to go to church. You see, my Father, how the Blessed Virgin loved me.

Familiarity with the Child Jesus

The Blessed Virgin, in coming early to possess my heart, brought with her at the same time her little Jesus to unite himself very closely to my soul. At that time I did not yet know to give him the name of Baby Jesus or Little Jesus. I simply called him, in my own fashion, Jesus Child. I learned to love Jesus Child at the same time as the Virgin Mary because (47) each time that my mother told me a story about the Holy Family she would also include a lot of stories about Jesus Child. I could also see a picture of him about to be fed at his mother's breast. This picture was in my maternal grandmother's house. My mother used to show it to me, saying: 'There is the baby Jesus of whom I have spoken so often to you.' Thus, the image of Jesus Child was imprinted in my mind, and my only wish was to possess one to carry in my arms.

Luckily for me, my uncle (Chú Kim)* came back from the town one day and he gave me a very nice puppet and a set of mechanical toys, amongst which was a little motor car with just enough room to accommodate my puppet. I was very pleased and immediately gave to my puppet the respectful name of Jesus Child. I played with it all day and even at night I could not bear to be separated from it. I positioned it every day in my decorated motor car and I walked around the house with it. The places on the route were decorated with flags and flowers. (48) My father helped me sometimes with the decorations because he liked to see me playing in this well-behaved manner with Jesus Child, and thus enabling my mother to go to the market.

---

* Uncle Kim is the husband of Aunt Hiet, the older sister of Van's father. He liked Van and his brothers and sisters very much; thus, they were accustomed to calling him Chú 'uncle' Kim even though he was not so.

Something springs to my mind in speaking of the market. If my mother wanted me to be good during her absence, she had to box clever, saying to me, 'I am going to the market to buy sweets for Jesus Child'. It was on this condition that I allowed her to go, and each time I would say to her: 'Mammy, come back quickly in case Jesus Child cries'. To tell the truth, he never cried; but if my mother returned without any sweets for me to give to him, without fail, I was the one to cry, and I would continue until I got my own way. I recall that on these occasions, even if I was threatened with the strap, it had no effect, so committed was I to die for Jesus Child.

(49)   I also recall that I was not selfish. I divided the sweets that my mother gave me into two portions, one for me and the other for Jesus Child. I knew well that my Jesus never ate, but I was obliged by my friendship to be always attentive towards him. If sometimes there was not sufficient to divide the portions in two, I would take my portion and give him half. Once this was done I would never take it back or cheat by eating it. On the contrary, I allowed no one to eat it: it had to be kept for him. If a poor person came to the house he received it; otherwise, I confided it to my mother so that, in the evening, she could ask my guardian angel to carry it to heaven to have it inscribed in the golden book.

Ah, the golden book! In those days the image of the golden book has stimulated me to direct myself more and more firmly towards God. During the day Jesus and I played together like two little friends. Come the evening, I went to sleep with him clasped to my chest. How sweet was my sleep! However, I do not recall any sweet dreams during those

(50)   peaceful nights. All I do remember is that every morning when I awoke I noticed that the Jesus Child was stretched out beside my pillow. I regarded this as a miracle which, if not the work of my guardian angel, could only have been done by my mother's hands. Without this precaution the Jesus Child would have probably been crushed during my peaceful sleep!

I think that it is in response to my sincere love that Jesus Child has shown me such a generous love. Two years later, in spite of my tender years, he came in person to unite himself to my soul. I will describe later, when speaking of my first communion, this honour which he has given to me. Regarding devotion to the saints, I had not as yet a particular devotion to any of them, except to my guardian angel, since my mother told me that this guardian angel was God's messenger to protect me, body and soul, to collect my good actions and present them before God's throne. In a word, he was the most faithful travelling

(51)   companion, especially charged by God to guide us in this dark place so full of dangers. I therefore loved him a great deal and usually called him by the special name of 'Brother Angel'. When I was doing

anything, I thought above all of him, in order to find help and protection close to him.

I had not yet heard of Saint Thérèse at that time. If I had heard of her, she would certainly have occupied a special place in my heart, and this being so, who knows if there would not have been in my childhood, as in hers, many brilliantly-coloured roses of love? However, Providence has disposed things otherwise. It is only later, when I have experienced misfortunes, when my soul has experienced the crucible of suffering, that this rose of love will show itself to me, that it will come to meet me and make known to me my destiny, and teach me that sacrifice is the obvious proof of true love. This means that if one loves God with all one's heart, one must conform joyfully to his will. But this will of God is very mysterious. It does not bring only happiness, but neither is it always the bearer of sadness. It was at the cost of great suffering that Thérèse became a great saint.

My little sister, Anne-Marie Té   (52)

I was almost four years of age when God, in his great goodness, gave me a little sister. It was an indescribable joy for me but abruptly I had to accept the sadness of separation. Each day when saying the rosary, some months before my sister's birth, my mother would encourage me to pray for the baby which was on the way. As I waited impatiently for this event I fervently asked the Blessed Virgin to give me quickly a little sister to carry in my arms. Not one day passed that I did not ask my mother:

'Mammy, will the baby come soon?'

'Yes, it will come soon if you continue to ask the Blessed Virgin.'

'Is it beautiful?'

'Yes, it's very beautiful,' said she, smiling.

In my curiosity I asked my mother a host of other questions.

'Where has the Blessed Virgin put my little sister?'

'She is hiding her very carefully. When you are good enough she will show her to you.'

'And me, formerly, where did the Blessed Virgin hide me?'

'In heaven.'

'Oh! Then why have I not seen the Blessed Virgin and the holy   (53)
angels?'

'Because you had not yet opened your eyes.'

'In that case, my little sister is certainly in heaven at this moment, and I must ask her to open her eyes sooner.'

And so it was. One fine morning my sister Lê, having just got up, came to me and whispered: 'We've already got a little sister. She's very beautiful.' I rose hurriedly, even forgetting to say my 'morning offering' and, whilst running, I asked my sister Lê:

'Where is she?'

'She is in Mammy's bedroom, but Mammy has forbidden us to enter.'

'Too bad; she's my little sister, not Mammy's.'

Then, head down, I charged into the bedroom. Standing there were relatives and neighbours. They had all come to visit my mother. I asked abruptly, 'Mammy, where is my little sister?'

(54) Straight away, because of the noise I was making, my sleeping little sister woke up and began to cry. My mother quickly covered my mouth and said to me:

'Is it your baby? Be careful! Go and play and let her sleep. I will show her to you soon.'

Determined not to give way and struggling to get free, I replied:

'No! It's my little sister.'

But at that moment a neighbour sent me from the bedroom and gave me two bananas, saying:

'There you are, a present from your little sister. Eat it, and soon she will wake up and you will be able to see her.'

Still agitated, I again entered the room and went very close to my little sister. But I had hardly time to look at her for half a minute when the maid came and took me away forcefully. In the meantime my sister Lê was listening behind the door. She took flight on seeing my expulsion. It was only later that she dared to approach me to ask: 'How is she?' I proudly replied: 'She is rather pretty, but she has not opened her eyes yet.'

(55) From that moment I did not stop asking myself why she had not yet opened her eyes. In this case she had certainly not seen the Blessed Virgin nor the angels. It was such a pity. Now there was no hope of asking her if the Blessed Virgin was really beautiful.

On that very day my little sister was taken to be baptised and, thanks to my paternal grandmother, I had the happiness of getting close to her, and of giving her a kiss when she returned from the church. From then onwards, regarding my little sister, all was beautiful to me except that she had not yet opened her eyes. That was my only disappointment.

It was also from that day onwards that I stuck even closer to my mother. My great fear was that someone might come to steal my little sister; thus, all the plans I had made for us two would come to nought. These plans were simply of this nature: that my little sister would soon learn to speak so that she could say the rosary with me, and that she would soon learn to walk so that during our processions I would no longer have to run to the maid to ask her to intone the prayers. I desired many other things for her. I even hoped to invite her to go a long way away to become a religious as I learned, much later, that Saint Teresa's mother had done.* However, my great daily wish was that she would (56) open her eyes quickly so that I could show her my beautiful Jesus Child and the toys I intended to give to her ... But suddenly, one fine day, I was asked to leave her, no more to live beside my dear little sister. I learned that I had to go to stay with my Aunt Khánh† in the parish of Từ-Sơn. I did not understand why my mother had condemned me to this unjust exile. I rolled on the ground, screaming in a deafening manner and saying to my mother that I would go on condition that my little sister would follow me. Not only did she reject my demand, but she said to me pointedly:

'What little sister would agree to follow someone as unruly as you?'

They said it was my importuning and my rowdiness near my little sister that merited my banishment. That was really a great injustice. I can truly say that I had only affection for my little sister, and that I never intended to trouble her. It is probable, however, that no one (57) could understand my demonstrations of affection. For example, when I received some titbits, I saved some of them for my little sister. I would hide them and then, waiting for the time when I was unobserved, and above all when my little sister was sleeping, I would go quietly up to her, wake her, put some delicacy into her mouth, kiss her and say: 'Eat up so that you can grow quickly.'

Sometimes, wishing that she would open her eyes more quickly, I would separate her eyelids and, showing her my little Jesus, I would proudly say to her: 'Here is my little Jesus, don't you find him pretty?' Sometimes, on these occasions I saw her open her eyes and smile at me as if she were very happy. But it sometimes happened that, instead of smiling, she began to cry, so that my mother ran to her quickly as if my little sister was on the verge of dying. How sad I then was, but if I had not fled quickly my mother would not have hesitated to give me a good spanking. However, this punishment would have been less painful to me than to see my very annoyed mother throw my Jesus Child (doll) to the ground, as happened on one occasion.

It is therefore because of these demonstrations of affection towards my little sister that my mother has condemned me to exile. In other words, from that moment onwards, I have lost my little sister. From (58) now onwards it will be impossible for me to parade as a general: I have, simply, the sad face of a prisoner of Poulo Condore.‡ How I remember

---

* Saint Teresa of Avila (1515–1582), who reformed the Carmel.
† See Van's genealogy in the appendix.
‡ An archipelago south of the Mekong delta called today Côn Đào. The main island is the site of a colonial penitentiary.

having cried a lot and even being angry. I even refused to eat two successive meals. As a consequence the following stratagem was adopted: someone made my little sister cry a little and my mother said to me: 'Now, do you see? Because you are sulking and refusing to eat, your little sister is sad and crying.' As I really loved my sister I had to eat to stop her tears. It was a strange thing: as soon as I began to eat, she stopped crying. In spite of all my efforts the sentence condemning me to exile at my aunt Khánh's had to be executed according to plan.

My new home at my aunt's

A cunning trick was used to get me to my aunt's. Ordinarily, every morning after prayers, I was allowed into my mother's bedroom to see my little sister. On entering the bedroom on this particular morning I could not see my little sister. I began to cry and shout in a loud voice

(59)   for my mother but I could not see her anywhere. The maid ran to me and said: 'Come on, Van! Why are you crying like that? Your mother has already taken your little sister to your aunt's; there's no need to look for them here.'

In fact my mother had taken my little sister to my grandmother's, hoping thereby to trick me into going to my aunt's. On hearing the maid say that my sister was at my aunt's, I was full of joy and cried: 'Then I will go to my aunt's too. Dress me in my best clothes. I want to be dressed in white like my little sister.' Ever since the day of her baptism my mother has continued to dress her in white. The maid rushed to get the clothes to change me. She did this carefully, saying: 'Quickly, quickly, for fear your sister flies away.'

When the maid had finished dressing me I suggested that we run in pursuit of my sister, but there in the yard was a palanche* (shoulder carrier) with two side baskets, one containing boiled rice, and the other empty, ready for me to sit in. A rough peasant† had been hired simply to carry me. Before taking up his load, and following my mother's

(60)   instructions, the man made a thousand threats to scare me so that I did not breathe a word. Then, frowning, he twirled his moustache, clicked his lips several times and in a jerky voice he shouted: 'Be careful, all right? If you wish to follow your little sister you had better be well-behaved. If you have the misfortune to cry I'll throw you in the river.' Frightened and annoyed, I answered curtly: 'Yes'.

---

* A palanche is a shaft of wood which balances across the shoulders with a load at each end.
† He was the younger brother of Uncle Kim who worked as a gardener for Van's parents.

The peasant put the load on his shoulders and shot off like an arrow. The maid followed me with her eyes, clapped her hands and said, laughing, 'Look, Van's travelling by motor car today.' Then she exhorted the porter in these terms: 'You must go quickly for fear that you cannot catch his little sister.' My face beaming with happiness, I looked around at the maid. I allowed myself to sway to the rhythm of the porter's steps. My aunt was following behind with some ladies of her acquaintance. Once clear of the village walls, I looked anxiously towards the dyke and asked my aunt: (61)

'Aunt, where is my little sister?'

'She is already a good distance away. We must walk quickly to catch up.'

Then, addressing the porter, she said: 'When you spy his little sister, tell her to wait for Van so that they can have the joy of travelling together.' Everybody was quiet again. From time to time my aunt spoke up to say the prayers of the Stations of the Cross or the rosary.

My village was already far away. After having crossed the river, all I could see was the church steeple which stood out above the bamboo hedge and finally disappeared completely. I was surprised not to catch a glimpse of my little sister. On thinking of her I felt like crying, but the porter repeated his threat: 'Be careful, or I'll throw you in the river.' I had to keep quiet immediately. After a long journey we took a short cut, passing by little dykes on the borders of the paddy fields. I was engulfed completely by the rice plants. It was impossible to look into the distance.   (62) I could only see the tall, green stems and, now and again, I heard the rustling of the wind amongst the stalks.

As I could not yet see my little sister, I felt like crying and I asked to return home, but my aunt comforted me gently, saying: 'Be patient a little longer. You will see your little sister when we leave this paddy field.' I felt calmer then, and reaching out my hand I gathered a few drops of water attached to the rice flowers to drink, or rather, I amused myself by letting them fall. Then, I don't know how, I fell asleep. I awoke with a start only when I heard a dog barking out loud and I heard voices crying: 'Van, Mammy has brought Van ...' I had arrived at my aunt's house.

All of my cousins gathered around me. One carried me in his arms, another kissed me. These demonstrations of affection made me forget my little sister, but when it was time for dinner I recalled the meals when I sat beside my mother; I thought of her and of my little sister and I asked my aunt:

'Where is my sister then?'

'First of all, continue your meal. Your little sister is probably still on the road. Because she is so small she must go slowly.'   (63)

She winked at my cousins with these words so that they would understand. Unfortunately, I understood the sign better than anyone and, bursting out sobbing, I pushed away my bowl and chopsticks and asked to return home to live with my little sister. My aunt had, once again, to bring everything into play to comfort me and dry my tears. For their part my cousins used every means to get me out of my mood of nostalgia for my little sister. In spite of this I thought of her unceasingly, and every day for a whole week I asked to return home. The week passed, nevertheless, and not being able to do otherwise, I resigned myself to staying with my aunt whilst longing for the day when my little sister would have opened her eyes and I could go and visit her.

Naturally, I did not feel so comfortable in my aunt's house as in my own. On the one hand the family was poor; moreover, my aunt was a widow. When her husband died she had been left with three very young children. These three, however, two boys and a girl, were now big
(64)   enough to work in the fields. In spite of this family situation, far from being left to one side I was, on the contrary, much loved and, dare I say it, sometimes more so than at home. My aunt was always ready to give in to me and sometimes gave me more than I wanted. I am going to give you an example here which will not fail to move you as it moved me.

Being poor, my aunt had to make economies. The family had habitually to eat rice mixed with something else, be it potatoes or maize. However my aunt cooked rice on its own for me. I had, therefore, a special diet at every meal. I saw nothing exceptional in this preferential treatment because at home it was my customary fare. Afterwards, when I was capable of reflection, I saw clearly that I had been the object of an unusual favour. It was because she loved me that my aunt behaved in
(65)   this way, even down to the smallest detail. To this can be added the very affectionate attitude of my cousins in my regard. On every occasion and all the time they would regard me as their most dear little brother. I was given everything I wanted and sometimes I had the feeling that they had to deprive themselves of certain things in order to shower me, their dear little brother, with little treats. I can't prevent myself from being moved to tears in recalling these memories and I have the desire to acknowledge to these generous hearts my grateful love. My cousins, in leading habitually a painful and poor life, did not find these self-imposed sacrifices very hard but I found their behaviour extraordinary and I do not know how to repay them equally. I can only count on the infinite, loving and merciful heart of God.

Having come thus far I feel I have wandered off the subject. I was
(66)   saying earlier that I was less happy at my aunt's than with my own family. The reason for this is that in their neighbourhood there were

few Catholic families, and they had to live in the middle of non-Christians. Moreover, because this parish was only an annexe without a resident parish priest, the people lived more or less in a state of indifference.

The opposite was the case in my own village where the piety of the people was alive and evident. Pious words were heard resonating everywhere. The children were for the most part happy, polite and assiduous in their prayers and at mass. That is why I felt a serene joy everywhere, both in my family and in the village. It was very pleasing for me to share in the happiness that one tasted in a Christian village, leading a simple life illuminated by faith. It was not the same in my aunt's village, although her family was numbered amongst those who were fervent. If it had been otherwise, my mother would not have dared risk sending me to such a place. For a child like me it was a great trial to be always confined in this family, although I found there a thousand compensatory joys.   (67)

My cousins found themselves in the same position. My aunt would never allow them to play with pagan children, for the very good reason that they were nearly all of immoral behaviour, coarse of speech and ignorant of all the rules of polite behaviour. We had, therefore, to content ourselves with living in the house, and being allowed only rarely to visit the village. Nevertheless, my cousins had to work in the fields every day, except for the youngest, who was almost my age and who stayed at home to play with me. However, I did not experience any happiness in playing with him. He lived rather as if he knew nothing of spiritual matters; he did not know the rosary by heart, he spoke in a confused and illogical manner and, worst of all, he used coarse language. Although he did not yet know how to make the sign of the cross he knew how, at the very least annoyance, to speak rudely. This was as easy to him as eating soup.

One day when I heard him for the first time scolding a cat and   (68) finding it reprehensible, I said to him:

'If you speak so coarsely you will later go to hell and the devil will make you drink fire.'

He replied:

'Who told you that?'

'My mother told me.'

'She lied. How does she know? Has she been to hell?'

Unfortunately for him, my aunt was in the kitchen and had heard everything. She called him to her and said, without any preliminaries:

'Open your mouth.'

Then, seizing a stick of burning firewood, she held it to my cousin's face and continued:

'You won't have to wait to go to hell. I will make you taste the fire this very day to see if you can put up with it.'

'Mammy, forgive me.'

'From now onwards you will correct your habit of speaking in a crude manner?'

'Yes, I'll correct myself.'

'Now, do you believe that the devil will force children who speak

(69)   coarsely to eat fire?'

'Yes, I believe it.'

Each time after that when I heard my cousin about to use such words, I threatened him with my aunt, and he was afraid immediately.

During my stay at my aunt's I was allowed from time to time to visit my little sister. I was filled with joy on the first occasion to see that her eyes were open. I proudly took to her all of my toys, including Jesus Child, and offered them to her. However, my little sister, not yet aware, was unable to appreciate the beauty of these precious toys, so much so that she broke them all into little pieces without compunction, even my little Jesus Child (doll). As for me, I was greatly upset and felt very sorry for him. One minute he was in my hands with his smiling face and his hands and legs intact but, after being in my sister's hands, his face was deformed and his limbs completely broken, so much so that he was no longer beautiful. I was very upset and could not stop crying over him.

(70)   Afterwards, my mother had to buy me another, bigger one, but I liked it less because it was made of terra-cotta.

The name Tế was chosen specifically for my sister, because when it is attached to my name Van it has a special meaning.* During the days spent at home I loved to be near my little sister to play with her. I trained her in making the sign of the cross and in pronouncing Mary's name. My greatest wish was that she would quickly learn to speak so that I could say the rosary with her. But the days spent close to my little sister were always too short. I was allowed to stay for a week at most, after which I had again to distance myself and return to my aunt's for one or two months. In the long run, the pleasure of travelling around reduced my nostalgia for my family, and I became as happy at my aunt's as I had been at my own home. At my aunt's I enjoyed climbing the hills and boating in the rainy season. When the weather was fine my aunt allowed me from time to time to amuse myself by following my cousins to the fields, and while they worked I climbed the hills alone.

(71)   I was a little afraid the first time but later I got used to it, so much so that I preferred the highest peaks which extended my view, since these higher peaks seemed to me to be closer to heaven: I wanted to be able

---

*   'Văn Tế': Van means 'prayer' and Tế means 'offering'.

to say my rosary closer to the Blessed Virgin. In those days I did not know how to meditate by looking at the sky, but I was simply happy to look at it whilst saying the rosary. I always had the conviction in my mind that the Blessed Virgin was looking at me more closely than when I was at home.

When I had finished saying the rosary, I sought to entertain myself by imitating the holy hermits. I piled up wood whilst praying out loud, or I collected stones to build a temple to the Blessed Virgin. As I was unable to build a cabin by myself, I was happy to shelter in the shade of the trees. I fixed a cross made out of two pieces of wood to a tree trunk and then, kneeling, I prayed with my hands joined, or I struck my chest like a real hermit as a sign of penitence. Although I played alone, this type of play never tired me. It happened sometimes that the hermit, overcome by fatigue, stretched out at the foot of a tree and had a good (72) snooze. Once or twice someone had to climb the hill to wake me. It was then that I realised that it was meal time.

When my aunt allowed me to play at a distance, on my return when evening came she would question me a great deal on my games and on every word, and I had to recount everything carefully. Consequently, each evening my aunt's family had interesting and amusing stories to laugh at. After making everyone happy I would listen to my cousins reading the lives of the saints. I passionately loved these readings and I retained everything down to the last detail. Once the reading was over, I immediately made the decision that the following day I would imitate this or that saint. My cousins called me, jokingly, the 'pocket' saint, that is to say, a very small saint. For myself, I thought I would never become a saint as I still had a terrible fear of the discipline.

If I told all the little stories I have alluded to I could fill hundreds of (73) pages, but I don't think it is necessary to be so long-winded, so I am summarising everything in these few words. My soul, whilst enjoying the beauties of nature, was also tasting the sweetness of spiritual joys. I can say that I lived with the Blessed Virgin always beside me. She covered me with her motherly protection, inspired me with a love for the peaceful lives of the saints, encouraged me to turn increasingly towards her and removed from my soul any feeling of sadness.

Have I on my part always been faithful? Alas, I frankly admit that I have deserved to go through a time of darkness because during a certain period of my life, though not a very long one, I neglected to say the rosary, the strength of my daily life, because of the everyday distractions and in particular because of my love of games. It seemed to me, naturally, that from that time I had lost all happiness, that joy which in fervent times was like a powerful force giving happiness and liveliness to my existence. This joy disappeared from me little by little from the

(74) time that I had forgotten to say the rosary, so much so that my aunts and cousins were worried, fearing that I was about to become seriously ill. I started sulking again and was once more impatient and snivelling. However, the Blessed Virgin was not slow in revealing to me the reason for my sickness. She encouraged me to renew the intimate links which attached me to her by the recitation of the rosary.

When I had renewed this daily practice the Blessed Virgin gave me once again her sweet maternal glance. Once again she made happy days flow for me. I regained my smile and my joy, and with it an ardent wish to unite myself to God, the source of life after which I sighed unceasingly. When the Blessed Virgin so loves me how can I forget her or not love her?

(75) # My first communion

I was soon six years of age and my little sister Anne Marie Tế was getting close to her third birthday. My exile was over. I had been allowed to return home, and from now onwards I will be able to live always close to my dear little sister. To this happiness will be added that of my preparation for my first communion. This time of preparation lasted for six months. Only Jesus can understand the happiness that flooded my soul at that time. However, as Jesus wished this happiness to be interior, he allowed me to live in a state of anxiety.

In fact, my Father, before tasting the happiness of receiving Jesus, I had to endure a long trial, to such an extent that a miracle was necessary to enable me to receive my heart's desire. The first big obstacle was that in everybody's opinion I was too small, and, consequently, nobody

(76) was sure that I sufficiently understood what was necessary to receive worthily such a great sacrament. Only my mother dared affirm that, despite my small stature, I was very capable of receiving my first communion and in fact that I was already ready. Nevertheless, she was afraid to take the decision herself, so she took me to the parish priest, Father Nghĩa, to put him in the picture.

Father Dominic Nghĩa, after having tested me on the Mass and the Eucharist and having seen that I was able to reply clearly, congratulated me. However, he hesitated to admit me to the first communion which was about to take place shortly, which is why he said to my mother: 'The little one is very intelligent, just like his sister Lê, but I see that he is still very young, and I am afraid there may be drawbacks. Let me try nevertheless. Send him to the parlour each evening with the other children so that he can study the catechism further, and so that I can reassure myself that he knows it sufficiently well.'

These words of the parish priest added nothing to my hopes. I left with my mother and, allowing my concern to be shown, I was unable to (77) hold back my tears thinking that perhaps my wish would not be realised. My mother, seeing my sadness, interpreted the words of the priest in a manner to reassure me. As we were passing the church, she invited me to go in, whilst saying: 'That's enough. God looks after everything. Let us go in to say the rosary and ask the Blessed Virgin to look after this business on our behalf. As for you, always be ready and ask Mary to help you prepare fervently. Promise not to allow any chance of suffering to pass without accepting it joyfully and offering it to her so that, thanks to Mary, your soul will become beautiful and worthy of receiving Jesus her son who will come to visit you and remain in you.' I wiped away my tears and followed my mother in to the church. Having said the rosary, I immediately felt my heart to be unburdened, and I promised the Blessed Virgin what my mother had advised me to do. I even dared to address her in these terms: 'If on the day of the children's first communion my heart remains empty of Jesus, I shall certainly be overcome by a mortal illness and will no longer have (78) the strength to live.' I asked therefore for a miracle from her, begging her ardently to bring Jesus to my soul: if not, she must carry me that very day to heaven, since on that day it was necessary that Jesus and I should be united, either on earth or in heaven. If she made Jesus come down to my soul she would thus avoid having to carry me to heaven.

Days and weeks pass. Sometimes my heart feels joy, sometimes sadness. I can only place my confidence in Mary, going each day to present my supplications to her and offering to her my rosaries said with love and fervour. My hope above all rests in her.

The second obstacle encountered was no less serious than the first. Many times I felt my heart becoming indifferent and as if tempted to abandon everything. I had to go every evening with the other children to learn the catechism. Personally, I did not find this difficult. The diffi- (79) culty arose because of the catechist who, not knowing how to educate children, paid no attention to their needs nor to the thoughts that they might have been able to express freely and openly. What happened was that they recited many things by heart, but understood little of what was essential. All the children assembled there were sitting tightly together, as if in a wine press. Before them stood this worthy,* proud of his

---

* This gentleman, a self-styled catechist, was a widower who had brought up four children. He knew neither how to read nor write, but he had learned the catechism by heart. Because of a shortage of personnel the parish priest had confided to him the supervision of the children during the catechism lesson. This was given without book, board or picture, but consisted in recit-ing mechanically, by heart, the questions and answers the children had to

dignity. Holding a cane in his hand he walked up and down majestically, like a fierce tiger.

If with his piercing eyes he saw a child move a little, doze off, or not open his mouth wide enough in yelling out the catechism answers, he would caress him immediately with the cane. I did not at all like this manner of behaving. Naturally I dared not hate the catechist: however, I felt a terrible fear in the presence of his ferocious majesty. Each time that I heard him strike a child I felt the prickling of itchy spots* all over (80) my body, and I tried very hard to hide my feelings. I must admit frankly that I learned absolutely nothing from this so-called school. All that I have been able to learn and clearly understand is due entirely to my mother, who taught me at home. At the presbytery, on the contrary, he succeeded only in making me forget that which I already knew, without adding to my knowledge. In this situation how can I hope to receive Jesus?

Happily, each evening before we went home, Father came to examine us. He had not the fierce appearance of his lordship, despite his bushy beard. He also used simple words of gentleness and familiarity in questioning us, so that we all loved him and could answer his questions easily. On the other hand, when it was the worthy who questioned us, the child questioned became as pale as a ghost. When the priest saw that a child was answering well, he gave him a reward or encouraged him with words of comfort. If someone answered less well, he exhorted him (81) to be patient. From the worthy there was no encouragement. If one could not answer his questions it was quite simply a matter of stretching out on the ground to receive strokes of the cane. One's subsequent success did not concern him at all.

You think correctly, my Father, that with such a system of education it is impossible to form children and inspire them with good feelings. As for me, the priest rarely questioned me, doing so only when someone gave a wrong answer, and I was asked to reply instead. This privilege put me on the same level as the older children, as I always answered correctly. My sister Lê was also in this special category. Consequently, Father said to us: 'I must take Mrs Mẫu's children† off the register'. (Mau was my mother's name.) This ambiguous remark troubled me greatly. Not knowing too well what the priest meant concerning me, I

---

know. This gentleman was so strict that many persons dared not leave their children at the catechism lessons. His own children had a great fear of him. [This testimony is from Tế.]

*   An eruption of pimples accompanied by itching, frequent in hot and humid counties, due to an inflammation of the sweat glands.

†   Madame Mẫu. To understand Vietnamese names consult appendix.

repeated these words to my mother, who was equally disturbed. However, some days later, during a visit to my family, the priest said to her: 'I never realised that this little one was so alert and so intelligent.' (82) These words reassured my mother who realised that the words he had used concerning me were a form of skilfully-hidden praise.

Six months passed with the speed of flowing water, but the closer the day the more anxious I became, still unaware as I was if I would make my first communion. Nevertheless, I prepared myself very carefully. New clothes had been made for me, and my soul was equally prepared. I only waited for the news of Jesus' coming. I do not know why, but the nearer the time came, the further away seemed the news. I was almost discouraged, especially in the evenings when I had to go to the presbytery to study the catechism. I always had confidence, nevertheless, in the goodness of my heavenly Mother, and I went to her each day to open my heart to hers. Mary understood my feelings well, and she made these wishes come true beyond my wildest dreams.

Father had not yet told me if he was allowing me to make my first communion. He simply told me to be ready, and he would allow me to make my first confession with the other children. The day before the (83) allotted first communion day I went for the first time to admit my faults in confession. It was, also, the first time that I heard my heart palpitate so much that I could hardly speak. Furthermore, I was so small that even when standing up straight with my head up I could not reach the confession grill. The parish priest, easily annoyed by temperament and not suspecting that it was me, thought he was dealing with a mischievous boy who had entered the confessional to annoy the others. He chased me out in a severe manner, and followed me immediately to see what was going on. He understood on seeing me, and sent me for a kneeler to stand on. It was only then that I dared, timidly but with a sincere heart, to confess all of my sins. I confessed everything, even the fault of having scratched the maid's face when I was small. After having heard me, Father gave me a penance and said to me: 'There is not one sin amongst the sins you have confessed which has displeased God. However, you must try to keep your soul completely pure so that you will always be pleasing to God.' He encouraged me to love the Blessed Virgin with all my heart and then, while blessing me, he added: 'Tomorrow, I am allowing you to go to holy communion.'

Tomorrow . . . go to communion. These words struck my ears like the (84) sound of a huge wave. It was like a shining light piercing the darkness of my soul. I was so happy that I forgot everything. I had to ask the confessor twice what penance he had given me, and if he had not asked me to kneel down for the act of contrition, I would have forgotten that also. My mother who was waiting outside for me, seeing that I was a bit confused, thought that something was wrong: but when I turned round, happier than I had ever been, she immediately demanded: 'What's the matter?'

'The parish priest is allowing me to go to communion tomorrow.'

'I told you to have confidence in the Blessed Virgin and everything would sort itself out.'

Then my mother led me to the church to make my thanksgiving. I had sighed ardently for this news of Jesus' coming. Now that I had received it I did not know what words to employ truthfully to express
(85)   my great joy. That evening I said to everyone I met: 'Tomorrow, I can go to communion!' On entering the house and seeing **Vên**, the dog, coming to meet me, I took his head in my hands and said: '**Vên**, tomorrow I can receive communion.'

The news of Jesus' coming had satisfied my hunger. Happiness made me forget it. I did not think at all about the evening meal. I had only one desire, that tomorrow would come quickly. I then made the resolution not to eat anything before receiving Jesus. If I wished to remain fasting, it was so that Jesus coming to me could play freely in my soul, since I had asked him to come in the form of a little child so that I could show him my love more naturally as a child. My mother, fearing I had not the strength to fast until tomorrow, did not cease to insist that I take some food. I was disturbed, feeling my mother's demands too hard. Faced with my stance she had to have recourse to trickery. She said to me: 'Since you do not want to eat, at least take some soup. This will be digested quickly and nothing will be left when Jesus arrives tomorrow.' Finding this reasonable, I obeyed my mother and ate a bowl of fish
(86)   soup. From that moment I played no longer with anyone. I had to stay close to my mother to hear her words of encouragement in preparing me for my communion, or better still I went to the church to recite the rosary and to ask the Blessed Virgin to increase my fervour.

I went to bed that night but I could not sleep. My heart was beating with emotion, and I did not cease thinking of the next day when I would have the grace to go to the holy table to unite myself to Jesus. I rose from time to time to ask my mother: 'Mammy, is it morning yet?' How long the night appeared to me! I only longed for the crowing of the cock to announce the dawn of the day.

Finally, day broke and it was time: the moment which will bring the intoxicating source of love. At that moment, recalling those anxious days when I walked along a dark road, tormented by the fear of having to go to the catechism lessons to face the imposing personage, remem-
(87)   bering also the uncertainty in which I found myself concerning my first communion, I understood that the situation had changed completely. I no longer felt any fear and the trials of the past increased my happiness

and made a wonderful present for me during this day's Mass.

The bell has rung the hour; the much-longed-for moment is here. I walk towards the holy table, my soul overflowing with joy. I never stop reminding myself that Jesus is coming to me under the form of a very small child. I hold the lighted candle tightly in my hand, this symbol of the fire of life burning in my soul. From time to time I look furtively to my right to calculate the number of communicants before me. Finally, Jesus arrives. I gently put out my tongue to receive the bread of Love. My heart feels an extraordinary joy. I do not know what to say. I can no longer shed a single tear to express all the happiness with which my soul overflows. In fact, from that moment it was as if my soul was swallowed up in Love's delights. If I did not speak it was simply because I could not find the words to express myself. More than that, my soul was (88) still enraptured in the presence of God's immensity, before whom I am only an unworthy nothingness, and if I realise that I still exist, my being is nothing other than Jesus himself residing in me. In an instant I have become a drop of water lost in the immense ocean. Now only Jesus remains: and me – I am only the little nothing of Jesus and Jesus makes himself only one with me.

In receiving Jesus, all my wishes had been fulfilled. However, I would have been happier still if I had been allowed to express my intentions freely. But I was obliged, as were all the other children, to recite prescribed prayers of thanksgiving. From then onwards the joy of an intimate heart-to-heart with Jesus was interrupted, and Jesus heard only prayers which were not in harmony with each person's intimate feelings.

Formerly, I had never heard anyone speak to me of a totally sponta- (89) neous intimacy in relations with God. However, at the bottom of my heart I thought that a soul can be intimate with God by using all ways to express its love for him; that it can converse with him by using no matter what sort of ordinary words, according to its needs and circumstances. Of course it is not a waste of time to recite prayers: however, it might be that it is not so profitable as a conversation of the soul conversing gently with God in terms which spring spontaneously from the heart.

It is a regrettable thing that this notion I had of prayer has been for me more than once a cause of torment, and I have finally had to abandon it in accordance with the opinion of many confessors and catechists, who maintained that it was better to recite many formulaic prayers. As for these things that people call the 'voice of the heart', they are only ramblings and useless imaginings. If such a thing exists it is only later, in heaven, that one will be able to converse intimately with God in such a manner. It is necessary to recite many prayers on earth in order to be understood by God and to receive his graces.

(90)   Consequently, in my relations with God, I had lost my unaffected approach since, each time that I spoke to him, instead of saying: 'My God I love you a lot', I had to recite this formula: 'My God, I love you with all my heart, with all my strength ...' etc., as if it was a question of reading a text for meditation. That is why I always felt that there was something lacking in my manner of loving but, whilst knowing that there was this deficiency, I dared not admit it: so much so that, later, God had to send a saint to me to revive in me this notion of prayer that I had been forced to abandon since my childhood. This saint is the little Thérèse of whom I shall have occasion to speak later.

Jesus, present in my soul, has had to resign himself, like me, to keeping silent. He looked at my soul without saying a single word, without making heard the slightest whisper. The only thing possible to us was a mutual understanding, like two little friends still in the cradle exchanging sweet glances. Nevertheless, we loved each other very well, and we loved each other intimately.

(91)   The graces that I asked of Jesus on that day can be summarised by two requests:

1) To keep me pure of all sin so that I could love him with all my heart.
2) To give to everyone a strong and perfect faith.

God has given me this first grace to the letter. As you will notice later, in spite of all of my adventures in life, and despite all the blemishes of the world which I have met on my way, and the scandals which could have led me to serious sin, God's grace has never ceased to envelop my soul and safeguard all its beauty. Although I was obliged to live in the middle of an impure world, my soul has always been directed towards God, just as the heliotrope* is to the sun. God has always been the object of my love, and the appeal that he exerted on my young heart had already all the sweetness that it still has today.

As for the second grace asked for, it will only be later in heaven that I will be able to see clearly if it has been granted. However, I do think my desire to see men believe in God and love him has stimulated me to collect sacrifices and prayers. I still retain today the same wish.

(92)   On my return to the house after my first communion, I met my two grandmothers who had come to see me and offer me their congratulations. Even my little sister **Anna Té**, radiant with joy, came to embrace me and press her head against my chest to see if Jesus, present in my soul, moved or not. Happy as I was myself, she spent the whole day

---

*   Heliotrope. A small shrub with white, blue and violet flowers.

around me to 'hear Jesus'. It was also from this moment that she began to show by her actions her thirst for Jesus. She wished to be as happy as I was, and thus she became fervent and well-behaved, because up till then she had displayed a fairly worrying character. My mother, nodding her head, often awarded this little lady this singular praise: 'She is a terrible child.' And, each time, mademoiselle would repeat 'terrible child'. Formerly she was stubborn beyond words but, from the day of my first communion, she adopted a humble and respectful attitude. She no longer dared to act in an impolite way towards me, knowing that Jesus was present in my heart. Moreover, she loved that I allowed her to press her head against my chest to 'hear Jesus'.

One day, when she was preparing herself to hear Jesus, my mother (93) suddenly asked her: 'Can you hear Jesus?' She answered, 'Yes, I can hear him: he's wriggling inside Van's chest.' We could not stop laughing on hearing this reply. In fact, all she could hear was my heartbeat, but she thought it was Jesus moving inside my chest. Thus it was that Jesus came not only for me, but also for those who loved me. Later, of those who love me, it will be my little sister Tế who will wish to live close to me.

The morning of my first communion passed without any shadow of sadness. The good wishes of my mother and my grandmothers made my heart beat with joy but also made me blush like a daughter-in-law who, for the first time, is receiving congratulations and words of affection from the parents. All I can remember is that after all of these loving greetings I could only lower my head to hide my embarrassment, and I could say not a word in reply.

Exactly at midday there was a banquet. The presence of my two grandmothers produced a greater feeling of togetherness and I sat between them in the place of honour. My little sister Tế was also present. During this happy meal a neighbour who had been invited (94) suddenly spoke up to ask me: 'Van, usually when someone asks you whom you love the most, you always reply, "My mother". Tell us now, whom do you love most?' Without having to reflect I replied, spontaneously:

'I love Jesus the most.'

'To love the most, what does that mean?'

'That means more than my mother, more than any other creature.'

'Then how do you love your mother?'

'I love her just like Jesus, but ... with a different love.'

At these words the whole family burst out laughing because they did not understand what I meant by 'a different love'. I blushed deeply, believing that I had replied badly, but my maternal grandmother rushed to justify me in these terms: 'What he has said is correct. To love

(95) with a different love means, obviously, that he loves Jesus more than his mother. In loving Jesus he can do Jesus' will in all things: but in loving his mother he can obey her in what is good, without ever daring to commit sin because his mother wished it. Is that not so, little one?'

'Yes, Grandmother; that's what I meant.'

And everyone laughed again in approving this attractive point of view which I had not known how to express.

In fact, my grandmother thought I was sad because everyone had laughed before I was able to explain myself. But that did not last very long. Having received that morning the source of infinite happiness, my heart remained immersed in that happiness. How could such a trifling incident make me sad? If I lowered my head it was simply because of the embarrassment which was still hanging over me.

In the evening of this happy day I took all the toys I had received and gave them to my little sister Tế, without keeping the slightest thing. I no longer wished for anything because, from that very evening, I (96) owned a treasure hidden in the bottom of my heart. Jesus alone was everything to me. My feelings were the same as those of Saint Thérèse on the evening of her first communion. This day, passed in joy, gave way to a night of incredible sadness, to such an extent that the happiness of the day gone by was incapable of giving any joy back to me. However, the single thought that I would receive Jesus in my heart the following day gave me a feeling of peace, and I felt the courage to accept this life of suffering.

Father Nghĩa allowed me to go to communion every day. No day passed that I did not have the happiness to present myself at the holy table to receive Jesus. In that was my source of life and each time that I went to receive Jesus my soul overflowed with joy.

In response to my mother's wish my first week of communion was dedicated to prayer for my father who, for some time, had seemed to (97) like the idle* life too much. He worked little, and his only pleasure was to gamble at his friend's house; he became more and more lukewarm and negligent of his spiritual life. One could say that the good God had let her know in advance of all the sufferings that the family would have to endure later, and that is why she worried day and night. She prayed and encouraged us to do penance to ask God to have pity on my father, and to give him the grace of conversion, so that our family's happiness, which was on the point of sinking, could be restored once more.

Having arrived at this point of my story I feel an indescribable bitterness in my soul. I had never before seen my mother so afflicted. Neither

---

* He had not yet got over the trial of the illness of the eyes of his oldest son Liệt.

had I ever felt such a degree of filial devotion overflowing from my heart. In spite of my great love for my mother I saw the need to pray much harder for my father. Thus I have not neglected any of my mother's counsels. I promised God that as a penance for my father I would abstain from wine during my life. This promise explains why, to this very day, I have refused to take remedies containing an alcoholic (98) base. If all the sacrifices and prayers that we have offered to God have not spared us from trials, they have nevertheless been a strength which has helped us enormously to accept them with courage, and to drink to its dregs the cup of bitterness. In fact, the happiness which God gives us does not reside in riches nor in the transient joys of this life, but rather in the acceptance of life's sufferings. He has sent us that which he keeps especially for his best friends.

You can notice today with your own eyes, Father, the distressing picture of our dear family. O my God, can there be anything better than that which you have chosen for us? If in the eyes of the world we are only the poor and wretched, who would dare to despise us before God (99) as people who have been abandoned by him? God understood that we loved him with a sincere heart, which is why he has given us the happiness of sharing with him his chalice of bitterness. Although this chalice is not yet empty to its dregs, we have still today the strength to suffer with courage and even to accept with a smile every day his holy will for his greater glory.

Confirmation

I had the further happiness a short time after my first communion of receiving the Holy Spirit. My little sister Tế was also confirmed at the same time. Words cannot describe her happiness on that day. From the end of the service until the evening she was saying proudly to all she met:

'Today I was confirmed. Monsignor slapped me.'

'Were you afraid of Monsignor?'

'No! he slapped me gently.'

God's grace has not only strengthened my little sister, but it has also (100) transformed her character and made her better-behaved. It is from this day that she lost completely her habit of sulking.

As for me, the grace of God had no other objective than to enrol me in the army of courageous soldiers. From that time, before throwing me into life's battles, God, in his wisdom, has put at my disposal all the effective means to help me gain the victory. Therefore, shortly after giving me his body and blood as my daily sustenance, he has further given me a solid guarantee which is none other than the power of the Holy Spirit.

Today's feast differs in no way from the ceremony of the presentation of the sword. My heart was overflowing with joy when I presented myself before the bishop to receive the sign of the cross traced on my forehead, and to be officially admitted to the band of Christ's brave soldiers. The sign of the cross is the standard of the Saviour's victory, and it is the power and sword of the Holy Spirit. This sign, engraved on
(101)   my soul, can never be effaced. What an honour! I have therefore, this very day, been officially armed as a knight of the sword of the Holy Spirit, and nominated a soldier of Jesus Christ.

Wish to consecrate myself to God: leanings towards the priesthood

My Father, I have noticed, as I have mentioned earlier, that since the day that I was able to reflect and without having a very clear notion of the religious life, I desired to consecrate myself to God. However, from the day of my first meeting with Jesus, this desire has become more and more insistent in my soul. I wished to find somewhere away from the world, whilst being aware that in this place it would be necessary to renounce my father, mother, brothers and sisters, and also all the gentleness coming to me from my beloved family, but I was ready to make this choice cheerfully so as to live alone with Jesus who has intox- icated me with his love. Each time I received Jesus I felt this desire
(102)   ringing in my soul: I responded there and then to his voice without a single thought of resisting; and I took the decision to look for a means of conforming to his will.

I stood one day before my mother and asked her permission to tell her a secret. She smiled, took me to one side and invited me frankly to tell her my secret. Blushing, I grabbed her hand and could only say in a precise manner: 'Mammy, allow me to enter religion, since I think it is God's will.' My mother could not stop laughing at these words, but afterwards she spoke to me gently: 'Because you are so small, once you have entered religion, who will agree to be your servant? However, that's great. If such is your wish, I'll agree readily, but it will be neces- sary first of all that you grow a bit. In the meantime, I shall point out to you some defects that need your attention, such as teasing your little sister too much, or displaying a lack of politeness in your speech, etc. After that I shall allow you to go.'
(103)   Since my mother had agreed, I thought all was in order; but when would I be big enough to leave? That was the only thing which still

worried me. On her part, my mother, not suspecting that, still so young, I could torment myself to such an extent, went to tell the family this interesting secret. Afterwards, although nobody paid it much attention, the news continued to spread little by little, so that even my cousins knew that I wished to enter religion.

At the time of my first communion and of the confirmation that I had just received, my mother allowed me to go for a walk to my aunt's. My cousins availed themselves of the occasion to tease me as they saw fit. One would say: 'Hey, you lot! Van wishes to enter religion, but I have heard that his mother has not been able to find a wet nurse for him, so she must keep him at home to allow him to grow a bit.' Another one continued: 'There's no need for a wet nurse: we can buy him a dairy cow and all will be well. He won't have to wait any longer. Great! Van to enter religion under these conditions! Now, that's very interesting.' I burst out sobbing on certain days because of such teasing. I knew, however, to offer all these trials willingly to God.

There was a non-Christian family in the vicinity of my aunt's house, (104) that of the village mayor who was regarded as an important person. This man and his wife, and above all his daughters, liked me in a special way. These girls got to know me when I was young during my stays at my aunt's. They often took me to play at their house. The man's mother was still alive. She was a fervent follower of Buddhism but she respected other religions. My aunt, although very watchful, never refused to allow me to go there when these girls came looking for me. Besides, the two houses were side by side. It was simply like a visit made by neighbours in the same hamlet. My aunt's only fear was that I might be contaminated by the superstitious practices which ordinarily obtained in non-Christian families. These young girls, however, understood my situation. Each time they took me to their house they left me entirely free. If they gave me cakes to eat they were at pains to tell me: 'You may eat these cakes: they have not been offered to our ancestors.' They never laughed or were scornful when (105) they saw me bless myself before eating. The grandmother especially loved to hear me say my prayers. From time to time she would call me close to her and say to me: 'Let us go and say the prayers of your religion so I can listen to them.' She once praised me in her grand-daughters' presence: 'See how bright Catholic children are! He is hardly five years old, yet he has known his prayers by heart for a long time, and he knows how to speak with judgement. With us, on the contrary, even before knowing how to fasten the belts on their trousers, children speak as rudely as devils, and they know absolutely nothing about religion. To tell you the truth, even though I myself am very old, I consider myself inferior to Mrs Liệt's child.'* One day she said to my aunt: 'Mrs Liệt is blessed to have a child who, although so young, possesses such an unusual wisdom.' Then, calling me close to her, she covered me with kisses and continued: 'Your lips are very pretty. It is certainly heaven which rewards you for never having used bad language.'

(106)   This man's children had also heard people talking of my request to enter religion but they did not understand. They thought that a religious was like an important person who shakes a rattle and has a head shaved like a dried coconut. They would consider this way of life very painful, and beyond the strength of a child like me. They exhorted me not to enter religion. One of them said: 'Come on; if you have any sense, listen to me! It's madness to enter religion. You are still young, well-behaved, indulged by your parents and liked by everyone. Besides, you already have God in your heart now: on entering religion you will not necessarily have anything extra, and every day you will be reciting prayers to God. You can, therefore, be religious at home. Why go far away and sadden your parents? If you enter religion you will eat only salted food, so I am told. Well looked-after as you are, don't be so mad

(107)   as to enter religion where you will suffer a lot.' The only response I could make was to lower my head and say to them: 'Please allow me to do what I wish. I have God's strength to help me put up with all the sufferings and inconveniences. If you ever find yourself in my position you will understand these things clearly, as I do. I shall enter religion and I shall pray that you, like me, may have the gift of faith ...' Nevertheless, they did not cease until my return home from dissuading me to enter religion. This was my last visit to my aunt's before the separation from my family.

The story of my possible entry into religion attracted attention for a while, but little by little it fell into oblivion, and those near me thought no more about it. I was the only one unable to forget this holy wish. Each day I asked God to help me grow quickly so as to compel my mother to keep her promise. I desired ardently to become a priest as soon as possible, so as to preach the word of God to non-Christians. How many villages were there surrounding mine which did not yet know the good God? How many people who knew, only, to complain to heaven without knowing anything about heaven? This state of affairs

(108)   saddened me deeply and made me want to become a real apostle quickly so as to work for the greater glory of God.

---

* To understand the way in which mothers of families are called in Vietnam refer to the appendix.

School

Whilst waiting to grow up I had to start school. However, at the end of two months I fell ill and was forced to give up studying. The sole cause of my illness was, quite simply, that I had to attend school. So that you can clearly understand, Father, the reason for my illness, allow me to tell you the facts, down to the last detail.

My Father, although the good God has allowed this illness, I must first of all blame the school for having made me ill. My illness was not of the body but of the spirit. It was because of this illness that my body also became weak and listless. Let me explain. It was simply that the too-strict method of education practised in this school oppressed me like a cucumber in a jar of salted water.* Judging it only by its methods (109) I could not call it a school but, really and truly, it was a children's concentration camp in which the teacher was no more than a cruel torturer. I repeat, thinking about this school did not inspire any warmth in my regard but, on the contrary, the very thought of it made me detest it even more. My only wish was that it should be destroyed.

In the classroom as in the playground, the master was an obstacle to freedom – I mean that wise freedom appropriate to the discipline of children. In class he always held his head high, his eyes wandering unceasingly from one corner of the room to the other. He usually paced to and fro with his hands crossed behind his back and with a light cane, woven from four others, in his hand. This made walking easier. He had a supplementary stick woven from eight canes, which was longer and heavier, and had wire rolled around the end. He used this one for those pupils who dared offer him 'unappetising sweets'. These consisted of (110) stones thrown at the master's back at dusk, or dirty packets stuffed into the drawer of his desk. It was only the older pupils who dared to offer this kind of 'sweet'.

The sad thing is that when 'Sir' moved around the class he had to try out his cane on one pupil or another. If, for example, a pupil was not sitting up straight whilst writing, 'Sir' straightened his spine with some strokes of the cane. If another held his chin in his hands whilst reading, he called him and claimed to be correcting him by dealing him several blows. It was for such trifles that his hand became tired through striking the pupils. Then he would cry out, rant and rave, bang the table, stamp his feet and insult us by saying: 'Pack of evil-smelling dogs, I am

---

* In order to preserve cucumbers or other vegetables they were put in a jar full of salted water and a heavy stone was placed on top of them to compress them. Van uses this metaphor to explain the state of exhaustion he had fallen into.

wearing myself out in vain trying to educate you.' So we were all afraid: we feared him more than we feared the devil. If 'Sir' was present during playtime no one dared to make any noise, and if the children spied him

(111)   coming they warned one another and moved quickly to play somewhere else, not wishing in the slightest to play close to this grey tiger. It was even more frightening for little ones of my age. Only to see the master hit the older pupils made them greatly afraid and they cried out loud. Some of them even soiled their pants because of their fear.

You may laugh, Father, in reading my description, but these things were the order of the day. It was really pitiful. Often and quite simply because they feared 'Sir's' majesty, many of them dared not ask permission to leave the room, resigning themselves to remain quiet, and to hold themselves until the end of class. They failed many times. What a disaster! What an irony for this 'majestic master!' The older pupils would make use of these circumstances to offer the master less 'appetising sweets'. In spite of all, our master continued to believe that his imposing methods had real value.

And this was not all. He devised many other strange and indecent punishments. For example, boys who did not know their lessons were obliged to crawl between the separated legs of the girls and, corre-

(112)   spondingly, the girls had to slide between the boys' legs: whilst this took place, other boys and girls would widen their legs further and then, cane in hand, they would strike, without stopping, the buttocks of the victims, both to humiliate and at the same time to hurt them. Our master simply stood there and laughed loudly, as if he were watching a very funny comedy. This type of punishment was calculated to cause most shame to the young girls. As for the boys, this did not present any problems for them. The young girls, normally, found it easier to crawl than to allow the boys to slide between their legs. Many of them were so ashamed that they burst out sobbing, but they had to resign themselves, because otherwise he would have made an example of them, and that would have been worse still.

My Father, these are examples of the punishments I witnessed every day at school. I have only been able to describe them in a confused way, but I still think it is too explicit. It is truly ironic that such a method of

(113)   education took place in a school, all the more so because it was known as a totally Catholic school. If you compare the gross behaviour of the master with that of the pupils which I have just reported – pupils who offer excrement as presents to the master, and a master who inflicts immoral punishments on the pupils – which of these is the coarser? If the teacher is uneducated, how can the pupils be well-educated? Accordingly, and following the words of Jesus, 'one reaps what one has sown'. It must be concluded, therefore, that this uneducated teacher is

responsible for the lack of education of his pupils. Even the most accommodating of pupils will never have any affection for such a master. In fact, after having oppressed this group of children for three years, this dominant master fell miserably, packed his bags and ran off after a poor girl. If anyone mentions this teacher up till this day, his pupils can only pull a face and say: 'Don't talk of that henchman of Satan'. There you have it: the words of gratitude inspired by the educa-   (114) tion given by this teacher.*

As for me – well, thanks be to God, I had the happiness of being quickly liberated from the yoke of this immoral education. If I had stayed there for three years I do not know what would have become of me. Happily, I became ill! But what miseries I have endured because of this so-called education. On the other hand I was unable to act against my conscience, and I had to put up with this oppression which was weighing very heavily on my young heart. The school was always on my mind. It was an insufferable agony for me. I was so afraid that I had only to think of it, and this fear so depressed me that I had no more strength to do anything. I became suddenly a lazy child, and this lazi- ness affected not only my work but also my eating and sleeping. When midday arrived my only thought was, This afternoon I must go to   (115) school. In the evening, on my return, I thought, Tomorrow I must go to school again, and this thought terrified me, and prevented me from eating and from sleeping peacefully. I became paler and thinner from day to day. I was stubborn, silent, given to melancholy, and for the slightest thing, I shamelessly shed many tears.

However, I continued to go to the holy table every day to receive the bread of the strong. Each morning I asked Jesus to take me also to heaven with my little brother,† so that I would no longer have to go to school. I am speaking here of a little brother born a few months earlier, and who had lived only two or three months in this valley of tears when the Blessed Virgin took him straight to heaven. He died noiselessly, like a petal falling from a flower, and after his death his face was fresh and pink, just as it was during his sleep when he was still alive. On that day

---

* The teacher, Luân , whom Van describes comes from the village of Tơ, and was looking for work. As the usual teacher had fallen gravely ill, and had had to resign, the parish priest accepted Luân as a temporary measure whilst waiting for a replacement. It was quickly noticed that he was not normal, never knowing how to smile, or to say a pleasant word to anyone. Everything about him inspired fear. He badly treated the older boys above all and they, in turn, tried to get their own back. Van's description is in no way exagger- ated. Even his sister Lê had to be withdrawn from the school because of the bad education which was given there. [This is Tê's testimony.]
† Joachim Tu. (See Van's genealogy.)

(116)

my only wish was to have the happiness to die like him so as to go to heaven with the Blessed Virgin, to play with the Holy Innocents and, above all, to be welcomed into the arms of Jesus and pressed lovingly against his heart. Subsequently, each day when I thought of school, I wanted the torturer of my body to pull out my soul quickly from the miserable life of this world so that it might go to unite itself to God in the eternal life. But death was yet far away from me. Jesus wished that I put up with still more suffering in this world, and the present trial was only a first squall, a portent of future storms. He wished to make use of my body to endure suffering, shame and exhaustion so that the flame of love which devours his divine heart can spread to the hearts of all men on earth.

(117)

My sickness was not mortal and was intended only to highlight the love of God. My parents saw that my health was declining rapidly and, in a strange way, I was showing signs of a bad character. My mother took me to the doctor for an examination. The doctor said I had a nervous illness but I protested, 'Sir, I have absolutely no illness. My only illness is a fear of going to school because of the great cruelty of the teacher.' It was obvious to me that the doctor was not paying any attention to what I had said. He looked at me through his spectacles and then, calling my mother to one side, he said something that I knew nothing about.

On our return to the house my mother took me to see the parish priest and asked him to withdraw me from the school, because the doctor had diagnosed a nervous weakness and demanded that I interrupt my studies temporarily. Oh! how happy I was on learning that I would no longer have to go to school, and I thought: 'Now I shall be able to recite the rosary, visit the most Blessed Sacrament, and play at my leisure with my sister Tế. Above all I shall be free of the torture of having to present myself before this cruel teacher.' That was not all. My mother had promised me that we would avail ourselves of the opportunity to visit Father Nhã in Hữu-Bằng.

(118)

This Father Joseph Nhã had formerly taught my mother, and had then become parish priest of the Hữu-Bằng parish. According to my mother, he was a very gentle priest and kind and very fervent. My mother had even promised to offer me to him to help him in his apostolate and thus he could be my guide and teacher, so that later, God willing, I might become a useful apostle.* For this first visit my mother wished simply that I should get to know Father Nhã. She had not made up her mind to leave me with him. But I personally wished it. If my

---

* Young aspirants to the priesthood were confided to parish priests because there was not yet a junior seminary in the region.

mother would allow me to stay with him, how happy I would be! In fact, I wished to dedicate myself to God without delay, because if I waited until I was big I was afraid that it might never happen. Therefore, towards the middle of May 1935 my mother, accompanied by a cousin,* took me to visit Father Nhã. The aim was also to distract me with some walking. That is why she took me, first of all, to Bắc-Ninh to give me some idea of what a town was like.

Bắc-Ninh

I stayed in Bắc-Ninh for one day only, but I was able to visit all of its districts. It was the first time since my infancy that I had set foot in a town. Even though Bắc-Ninh was only a small town, all that I saw (119) appeared big and extraordinary to me. People moved around continuously in the noisy streets just as on feast days. In the evening especially, the pedestrians were even more numerous. The shop windows were brilliantly lit by means of electric lamps of all shapes and sizes. It was truly beautiful to see. My mother held me tightly in her arms, however, to make sure that these things, beautiful and imposing on the outside, did not seduce my heart, and whilst the rickshaw took us back to the inn, she explained to me that these sumptuous beauties were incapable of giving lasting happiness to a man's heart. On the contrary, if his desires are not maintained at a higher level, they are only capable of making his life bitter. God's love alone is stable, and the most beautiful thing is to accomplish God's will cheerfully.

One thing in particular attracted my attention at that moment. I asked myself how electric lamps could be made so as to bring them into the country. In spite of all my attention, I could not find the place where the oil was put. I reflected for a long time, and even went without a meal, before coming to the conclusion that, for this particular type of lamp, oil was not used. But I asked myself, once again, how the light (120) was produced. It was very strange, even mysterious ... Up till the time of my departure I had not yet found the answer. I interrogated my mother in vain on this subject. She, neither, had the solution. I then moved on to the locomotive. I was inquisitive to know what force gave it such power to make it move. But all of those questioned knew only how to scold me harshly.

---

* Mợ-Sửu. A classmate of Van's mother, when she was taught by Father Nhã. Afterwards she had married a cousin (of the fifth generation) of Van's mother. Van called her Mo, 'Aunt'. [Tế.]

Hữu-Bằng

We travelled by train from Bắc-Ninh to Hữu-Bằng. Although it was my first train journey, I gave the impression that I was an expert. I would have wished to sit with the driver in the locomotive to be able to understand the power of this machine and also, once returned home, to make one modelled on this one so that I would have to walk no more. But my mother, fearing that I might fall, held me close to her. The train having (121) arrived at Hương-Canh station, we had to get off and walk about three kilometres before arriving at Hữu-Bằng.

Hữu-Bằng, whose small population was entirely Catholic, was established as a parish about twenty years ago. Two priests, however, were necessary to do the work because, as well as the main parish, there were four smaller ones with hamlets scattered here and there so that, in spite of the small number of Christians relative to the population of the area, all this represented a considerable task. Father Joseph Nhã was the parish priest, and Father Năng was his curate.

We arrived there wearing the long, fastened clothes fashionable with people of the high region. This is why on seeing us the townspeople, and especially the children, ran in large numbers to stare at us. After greeting the parish priest we stayed with him for more than a week. People who knew us treated us with a great deal of warmth and cordiality. I was so happy that I did not think about my home and my fear-inspired illness disappeared completely.

(122)   During these days I studied carefully the parish situation from the religious aspect. I particularly watched Father Nhã to see if he was as virtuous as my mother had made out. I was not able to get a clear picture of the religious health of the parish, because my mother did not wish me to go everywhere. As for Father Joseph Nha, he pleased me completely, and with his obvious sweet and charitable manners he had really the air of a living saint. He looked upon me as his child, especially after my mother told him of my desire to become a priest, and of my desire to stay with him. He gave me a thousand signs of affection, congratulated me on being an intelligent and virtuous child and then predicted that, later, my priesthood would produce fruits in abundance. Seeing his fondness for me, I liked him even more and I thought to myself: 'If my mother, instead of forcing me to return home, would allow me to stay with him, I would be very happy, and I am certain that in any case I would be able to realise my ambition of becoming a priest.'

(123)   My Father, if the praise which Father Nhã gave me came from an observant perception and honest mind, it was fair and enlightened: but I fear that they were conventional words intended to confuse the sincerity of good people. Perhaps in speaking thus he was sincere, but when

the time came to put his words into practice it was the opposite case. My Father, you will see clearly that the parish priest has not exactly fulfilled my mother's wishes. She confided me to him so that he could work on my education and make a future apostle of me. Not content to give up on me with regard to my intended objective, he abused me further by employing me as a simple 'boy' spending all day at his bidding. I will tell you of all of these sufferings little by little in the course of this account.

Unexpected separation

The days passed with a speed I had not expected. After a week at Hữu-Bằng my mother intended to take me to Dân-Trù to visit Father Joachim Thận who was some kind of relative. But she began to worry (124) suddenly that my little sister might not be happy at home. Moreover, my health being much improved, I could again be called the 'little Pierrot' of my paternal grandmother. My mother, therefore, prepared to take me home. Before our return we went to say goodbye to the parish priest, and whilst we chatted cheerfully my mother teased me in saying, with a smile, 'Van, I am returning with our cousin, and you will remain with Father.' Then, looking and winking at our cousin, she wondered what my reply would be. Perhaps inside she was thinking: 'Van will certainly burst into tears on hearing me speak like this.' At her words, on the contrary, I cried out happily: 'Very good, Mammy, leave me here with Father, and when I am a priest I will return.' My mother, (125) astonished, looked at her cousin, then, turning towards me, she said: 'Van, would you be so brave? I was joking. Come back first to your little sister so that you can grow a little more, and when she is big I will allow both of you to go away.' 'No, Mammy, I am already big enough. You go back, and when my little sister has grown you can send her to me for her to become a religious.'

At these words I slipped away. Thus, when I was being separated from my mother for the first time I did not feel any sadness, any regret … It was the first and only time in my life when I had taken leave of anyone with so much determination. Normally, this separation would have been capable of stopping my heart from beating. For this, the powerful intervention of God's grace was necessary. If at that moment God had not paralysed in me the impulse of feeling, it is certain that I would never have been able to maintain such a determined stance.

I learned that my mother had left that day at nine o'clock, and that the ten o'clock train took her back home. My heart continued to beat regularly, my eyes remained dry and my soul was ecstatic at the thought (126)

that I was following the example of Jesus remaining at the temple ...
But what were my mother's feelings? It was after five years of separation, in meeting me at the house when I had fled for the first time, that she opened her heart to me during an afternoon of intimate exchanges.
'That day,' she said, 'what bitterness tortured my heart whilst thinking of you, my dearest child. I did not pay any attention to the countryside which unfolded along the route because it all brought back to me the memory of my little angel. When I got on the train I could only sit down, exhausted, and say the rosary. I thought the rosary would help me to forget your image but, on the contrary, it brought it back to me in a harrowing manner, because so many times have I told my beads whilst you sat on my knee. Honestly, each Hail Mary was a tear falling on my breast since my empty hands no longer felt the touch of your

(127)   little fingers. I was sighing, "Lord Jesus" ... and I asked God to strengthen my soul. At that moment your voice was heard no longer saying repeatedly, to console me: "Mammy, why are you crying like that? Enough! Don't cry any more, because we are the children of the good God." You were an angel of peace sent by God to console me on days of darkness. Cousin Sửu was very attentive and tried to console me, but I felt more and more alone and could only repeat: "God understands me". I was worried about you, asking myself if you would be able to persevere, or if, once the initial attraction had passed, you would give it all up, which, for me, would be a more painful trial still, since in separating myself from you at the cost of much bitterness and suffering, I wished by these sufferings to please the heart of God: that is to say, to obtain for you the strength to persevere in his service until the end.'
....*

My mother's words were words of good advice given to me.

---

* Van uses many suspension points in his manuscript. These have been preserved.

Photo of identity from Van's certificate of studies, 1940.

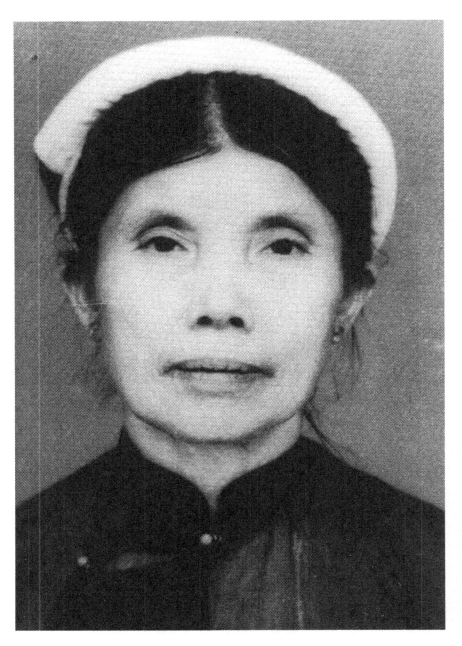

Marcel Van's mother wearing the head-dress of a countrywoman.

The Church at Hữu-Bằng with in the foreground the main gate where the girls and boys met.

The House of God at Hữu-Bằng where Van spent many years. On the left is the room which Van shared with a friend.

Traditional costume worn by Van and other children at the Hữu-Bằng presbytery for processions and other religious ceremonies.

Marcel Van on the day of his taking of the habit at Hanoi, 8 September 1945.

Family group 1946. Left to right: older sister Lê, mother, younger sister Tế,
Van, younger brother Lực, older brother Liệt, father.

Marcel Van and his sister Anne-Marie Tế on the day of his permanent profession at Đa-lạt in 1952.
(Standing at the foot of the statue of St Thérèse.)

Marcel Van and his sister Anne-Marie Tế with Father Boucher on the day of Van's permanent profession at Đa-lạt in 1952.
(At the foot of a statue of Our Lady of Lourdes.)

Father Antonio Boucher at
Đa-lạt in 1953.

Marcel Van serving Mass
said by Father Antonio
Boucher in the novitiate
chapel at Đa-lạt in 1952.

The Saigon Monastery.

Van goes shopping in Hanoi in the spring of 1955.
(This was the last photograph taken of Van.)

The Hanoi Monastery.
The buildings from the left: On the ground floor and first floor are the rooms of the fathers and brothers of the community. The visiting-rooms are also on the ground floor. The novices were on the second floor. The three windows on the left are those of Novitiate chapel. The central buildings include the choir brothers' and teachers' rooms and the classrooms. The building on the right housed, on the ground floor, the communal dining room with the kitchen behind it. Above was the community chapel used for the morning, midday and evening communal prayers. To the left of the monastery is the parish church and to the right is the cemetery. Behind the central building is found the 'rats' loft' where Van lived for three months.

Sister Anne-Marie Tế, a Redemptorist sister at St Thérèse (Canada) holding the folder containing the pages of Van's autobiography (1992).

(Personal dedication written on the back of this photograph of Van)
'I am not looking into the distance nor close up. I look only at He whom my heart loves.'

Van's original manuscript: the prayer written for the attention of his sister to ask for peace for Vietnam (1954).

Beloved Jesus

You know well that your little Vietnam thirsts for the Truth and desires only Peace. So, Lord, we take refuge in You, God of Truth and fount of Peace. Do not abandon us but through your Mercy save us and protect us under your strong arms. Give us Peace, always, your true Peace so that before your gentle eyes we may be worthy to be called beloved children of the King of Love, Jesus. Chase away all those who would harm our good habits. Save us from that most cruel of enemies, namely sin. And, finally, may we become a Kingdom of your Love. You who are the eternal King who reigns for ever and ever. Amen.

Part 2
To Become a Priest
(1935–1940)

The Second Stage

The pious life of the young aspirant to the priesthood (128)

Father, I am now turning to the second stage in my life, which encompasses five long years of trials and sufferings. In the course of this stage the joyful mysteries are transformed into the sorrowful mysteries. The bright spring rose has faded little by little, and the autumn storms have risen with a crash and taken away the detached petals. I had only one thought in embarking on the life of a young aspirant to the priesthood, namely, to live closer to God and to love him more intimately, and therefore the great desire of my heart was to participate every day in the religious service at the Lord's altar. Because I fervently wished to become a priest I knew that, first of all, it was necessary to study the functions of the priest. That is why I paid great attention to the liturgical ceremonies and to my studies.

Father Joseph Nhã, responding to my wish for the priesthood, and in (129) spite of my lack of size, admitted me to the number of young aspirants to the priesthood. He confided me to an older companion to teach me the prayers of the Mass and to take me through the liturgical ceremonies. One week later I was admitted to the ranks of the altar boys (second class), and I had the honour each day of serving in the sanctuary. I served Mass because I knew the prayers by heart and the rubrics very well, although I was no higher than the altar and still too weak to carry the big missal. The thing which filled me with a great joy was to be able to receive Communion at each Mass immediately after the priest had taken the precious blood. I was proud of this privilege and I said jokingly to my teachers: 'I am the most important in this house after the parish priest. Every day after big Father has received Communion, it is me, little Father, whose turn it is to communicate.' These innocent and honest words became later the excuse for a serious accusation against me, because I had offended the pride of the catechists living at the presbytery. In fact, I was the only one in the house to communicate every (130) day; that is why, after the priest, I was the only one at the holy table with Jesus.

After having served Mass my other work consisted in studying the catechism and attending to other scholastic matters. I went to class, therefore, in the mornings, and in the afternoons I stayed in the house to learn the prayers. I found these two areas easy and I was the best at them. The time of study allocated was sufficient for me to learn my lessons, and there remained a little 'special time' to recite my rosary particularly. I offered five decades every morning to the Blessed Virgin to thank Jesus, present in my heart, through her. I offered another five decades in the evening to ask her to prepare my heart to receive Jesus the next day. This was the method which my mother taught me from the day of my first communion. Thus, my days flowed in an unspeakable sweetness. I thought of no one but God. I did not even wish to see my Father's house again. What an extraordinary happiness I tasted in my heart!

(131)   Father Nhã also treated me as well as possible. Every day I took two meals alone with him. Although not eating at the same table, he gave me the same dishes as himself. He had the habit of calling me Benjamin, and presented me as an example when reprimanding the lazy and lukewarm catechists. These nourished a deep antipathy towards me. From then, as much in the presbytery as in the parish, and without being aware of it, I had become a lamp which drew everyone to look at the light.

The Dominican tertiaries were accustomed to calling me 'the little angel' and they congratulated Father, who deserved a little aspirant endowed with such beautiful qualities. But, Father, do you know why the tertiaries called me the little angel? Let me tell you. In the early days, those tertiaries, not knowing exactly where I came from, called me over to enquire: 'Where do you come from? Who is your mother?' And I replied, impishly: 'I come from heaven and my Mother is the

(132)   Blessed Virgin.' 'Then you must be an angel.' From that date the tertiaries called me the little angel. Afterwards, from time to time, they offered me sweets.

Concerning my younger companions, I had gained the confidence of most of them. They liked me because I spoke politely and never repeated coarse language. However, I also knew how to deal with the insolent and console the weak and those who were suffering from illnesses in their minds or bodies. It is for this reason that each morning when I went into the courtyard my companions gathered round me to greet me.

First trial: revenge is necessary

The lamp of my heart was shining brilliantly without stopping. The devil, seeing this, and beside himself with anger, had definitely decided, once and for all, to declare war against this child favoured by the Blessed Virgin.

It was the time of the holy year.* 'The parish priest had arranged

---

*   A holy year is one chosen by the Pope in the course of which the faithful can obtain a plenary indulgence. Since 1475 holy years have taken place every 25 years. In 1933 Pope Pius XI promulgated an extraordinary holy year (2 April 1933–2 April 1934) to commemorate the nineteenth centenary of the Redemption. On 2 April 1934 he extended it for the whole world for one

visits to the churches in the district for the obtaining of the plenary indulgence. At the time of these visits the people of the various parishes (133) heard the story of this child of seven years who had had the courage to sacrifice everything, and whose fervour had touched the hearts of numerous sinners who had come back to God. Everywhere I went I heard people making remarks like this: 'Who is this little one then? Where did he get the courage to dedicate himself to God whilst still so young? Such a puny child and already admitted as a candidate for the priesthood. It's really incredible!' Then those who knew me told those who did not know me, of the fervent life I led in the presbytery.

All of these stories which reached my ears had the blessing of making me blush without awakening in me the least feeling of pride. It is precisely this absence of pride which enraged the devil, since he would consider this attitude as a provocation to the most pitiless combat.

Satan engaged in the decisive battle

Following the military tactic, Satan wished to cut off the route to my soul along which came its spiritual food: a unique food which was none other than the sacred Body of Jesus. Some time had passed when the lamp of love shining in my heart attracted the eyes and notice of a large (134) number of souls amongst the lukewarm catechists of the presbytery, and there was one who particularly hated me. On day, just after I had arrived at the priest's house, he used me to commit an action against the sixth commandment† but, using my will power, I resisted energetically. I avoided that man's presence from that time. I was always regarded as an exemplary child, whilst he was unceasingly reprimanded by the parish priest. This annoyed him and rekindled his hatred for me.

The devil therefore used him to attack me. He had the right as a teacher to call me to his room for correction. He abused this right by continually calling me to his room. Why did he call me? Was it to teach me prayers or handwriting? No! It was to initiate me into the 'perfect

---

more year. It is no longer necessary to go to Rome to obtain the plenary indulgence; it suffices to visit the churches designated by the bishop and to pray there with faith for the intentions of the Pope, after making one's confession and communion. The intentions of Pius XI were: the freedom of the Church; the development of the missions; the return of dissidents to the Church, and the conversion of God's enemies.

† The sixth commandment of the Decalogue given to Moses by God on Mount Sinai forbidding adultery has always been interpreted by the tradition of the Church as the one concerning sexuality.

life'. However, he decided that only he knew the methods used for this initiation. I was forbidden to speak of it to anyone, and above all to the parish priest. If I was unfortunate enough to speak of it I would be buried alive immediately.

(135)   He called me to his room every morning after Mass under the pretext of enquiring about my health. He spoke so loudly that I could have heard him even at a distance of a hundred metres. 'How are you? Did you sleep all right last night? Come, come, why think of your mother? Don't forget that you wish to become a priest.' After having questioned and consoled me in this manner in a fierce voice, he made a sign to me to lie on the ground, and he gave me a volley of blows with his cane, singing all the time at the top of his voice. Finally he gave me a glance which said: 'No crying!'

His big, protruding eyes were even more fearsome than the blows of the cane. I could never look him in the face without feeling the need to detest him. He had a round face, hanging cheeks, big ears, thick lips and a flat nose. His round eyes sheltered under his thick and fearsome eyebrows. Such a physiognomy could have belonged to a member of the retinue of the dictator Hitler. Once, he even questioned me in these

(136)   terms:

'When you look at me, do you find me impressive?'

'Yes, very impressive.'

'Well then, impressive like whom?'

'Impressive like Hitler.'

Slapping his thigh, he burst out laughing and congratulated me on my gift of observation. He really was impressive, but with this proviso: Hitler, the German, made the great nations of Europe tremble, but this new Hitler was capable only of oppressing children. Yet he dared to regard himself as an imposing person. It was the height of nonsense!

Each time, before dismissing me after beating me, he put his finger to his lips, adopted a fierce face, rolled his eyes and ordered: 'Don't say a word!' Sometimes he would say: 'If you say anything I shall bury you alive!' To hear him emphasise each word and to see his frightening physiognomy convinced me he was quite capable of burying me alive in a corner of his room, and that without the slightest feeling of repugnance. I never dared to open my mouth to reveal what he had

(137)   forbidden me to say. He made me learn several answers by heart so that I could respond easily to questions on what I did in his room, such as: 'The master is instructing me in the way of perfection. He is teaching me to speak. He is teaching me prayers,' etc. And I was forbidden to add any commentary to these replies.

Subsequently, in order not to have to call me continually, he arranged the following daily programme for me:

Mornings after Mass. Go to his room for breakfast ... three strokes
  of the cane.
After Class. Aperitif ... three strokes of the cane.
After Lunch. Dessert ... three strokes of the cane.
Afternoon, before class, exercises ... three strokes of the cane.
After Class ... three strokes of the cane.
After evening Prayers. Recreation ... three strokes of the cane.

I must, therefore, in the course of the day receive eighteen strokes of
the cane as training in the perfect life. But these were only the principal strokes. There were also the secondary blows, to which must be
added preparatory strokes, and the strokes of the skin, which
numbered dozens, before each stroke with the cane.

Truly, Father, if I described things accurately to you, you would not
be able to stop laughing, but you would also not be able to stop feeling
pity for the child who was receiving these blows from the cane. This
man laid down many rules for me to observe before receiving the cane. (138)

1. To stretch out stiff like a wooden log. If at the first attempt the cane
   makes a dull sound, it is a sign that the muscles are not sufficiently
   taut. For the muscles to be taut the cane must give a dry sound.
2. There is to be no moaning or moving. If I moaned or moved the
   strike did not count. If this happened on the first strike it sufficed to
   add one more, but if it happened on the third it was necessary to
   begin again. Consequently, if during these fifteen minutes of exercise in the way of perfection I was not able to credit to my account the
   three blows in question, I remained in the master's debt, and the
   following day I owed six more. This multiplied indefinitely, so much
   that by the day when this gentleman was called to the bishop's house
   and expelled from the ranks of the catechists, taking everything into
   account, my debt to him had risen to tens of thousands of strokes of
   the cane. Supposing that he had remained at the presbytery to this
   day, this debt would certainly not have been cleared because, in the
   space of fifteen minutes, he was never able to give me all the blows he
   owed me. Indeed, counting only the trial strokes, which were still
   capable of blistering the skin, the fifteen minutes would already have
   been passed. If one added the complicated conditions, finishing the (139)
   strokes on time was impossible. Thus my debt became heavier day by
   day.

After less than a week of the 'perfect life' regime, my body had become
skinny like a withered leaf. My buttocks were blistered all over as if they
had been burned so that I could neither sit down nor lie on my back. I

had to remain continuously on my knees in the church for an hour and a half. I was obliged to stand to eat, and to sleep I had to lie on my stomach or on my side, and I still spent all night without closing my eyes. Nevertheless, I still had to go every day to practise the 'perfect life' without daring to breathe a word to anyone, so that even the parish priest knew nothing of the affair. However, after two weeks God took it upon himself to denounce this barbarous conduct.

One day the presbytery linen-maid noticed some stubborn stains on my linen. This aroused her suspicion. She was curious and wanted me to admit to having boils. I kept quiet. I refused, absolutely, to speak, fearing to be buried alive and, above all, not being able to go to communion. In fact, the master had forced me, some days previously, to take this oath: 'If I speak of these things I promise not to go to communion (140) the following day.' Such craftiness was truly of Lucifer's invention. He knew well that since my childhood until then I would never have dared to tell a single lie. Consequently, if I abstained from communion on one day, the master would know immediately that I had broken my oath. The linen lady, seeing that I refused to speak, went to report the matter to the parish priest: 'Little Van has boils on his back, but does not want anyone to see them.'

The parish priest called me, and obliged me to undress there and then. He could see that my buttocks were swollen and criss-crossed with cracks from which flowed a yellow liquid. He became angry and wanted to slap me across the face because, being in this state, I had said nothing. But he did not do so. Turning round he called all the boys and catechists to show them this scorched child and said: 'If anyone among you has still a shred of conscience and does not find this appalling, then he is the torturer.' At this the master, Vinh, sneaked away. Naturally afterwards the parish priest knew who the torturer was. From that day, the latter was no longer authorised to call me to his room to train me in the 'perfect life'. However, his hatred did not stop there. The devil's (141) fury will never abate whilst I remain a virtuous and exemplary child in the house.

The parish priest had me treated after the events I have just spoken of, but I was scarcely healed when he had to go to the bishop's house for his annual retreat. Profiting from this opportunity, the catechists, who had been well and truly berated by the parish priest, called a tribunal to examine the case of the little lad who had had the audacity to appear unclothed before them. My master of the 'perfect life' was elected judge of the tribunal, which always sat in the evening after prayers in church. In presenting me before this popular tribunal they stripped me of all my clothes, then gave me a belt of banana leaves, except for certain days when I had nothing. My judges, seeing my shame, said, to make fun of me: 'Hermits of former times did not even have banana leaves to clothe themselves.'

Their sole motive in making up such stories was to amuse themselves by making me act the fool. Each time they startled me by asking me questions on ribald and smutty subjects, I always kept silent or answered them briefly: 'I am still young: I have never heard of such dirty stories.' Finally, I was sentenced. The principal judge of the (142) popular tribunal pronounced sentence in these terms:

'To tell the truth you are not guilty of any crime but, up till now, although you aspire to the perfect life, you have not yet done anything to reach for perfection. So to teach you how to practise mortification, I have decided that, from now onwards, you will have only a bowl of rice with water, and you will eat with the dog to atone for your mincing ways with the parish priest. I have also decided that you must refrain from daily communion but, if you wish to go, I will allow it on condition that you receive three strokes of the cane each day.'

'Three strokes of the cane?'

'Yes, three strokes of the cane. Do you understand?'

'Allow me instead to abstain from food every evening.'

'No, it is three well-directed strokes of the cane.'

I could do nothing but burst out sobbing.

From then onwards, if I wished to go to communion every day I had (143) to receive three well-aimed strokes of the cane. How would I have the strength to live? All the same, I asked God to give me this strength and, thanks to Mary's protection, I would bravely pay the daily tribute in order to have the happiness of uniting myself with Jesus. The devil saw clearly that I always resisted energetically his oppression. He saw that my child's body was supported in its weakness by a spiritual force above the ordinary, and that the source of this strength was none other than the Eucharist. Therefore, he devised new tricks to cut off my provisions completely.

A short time afterwards, my judge, noticing that I continued to receive communion every day, wished to use me once again to commit a bad act. I resisted with all my strength in spite of his threat to bury me alive. Then to intimidate me he said: 'I absolutely forbid you to go to communion every day.' He convened the peoples' committee that very (144) evening to confirm this total prohibition. The committee gave its assent immediately and pronounced this sentence: 'From now on Communion is forbidden.' I protested:

'You have not got the right to forbid me to go to communion.'

'Then who gave you permission to go to communion?'

'The parish priest.'

'Liar! How dare you speak to us in that false manner?'

At these words he seized a cane from the head of the bed and thrashed me with blows that I had no time to count. All I can remember is that I fell to the ground and rolled around to avoid the blows. But the pitiless, indiscriminate cane hit me everywhere. I was no longer able to stand after this volley of blows, so my judges allowed me to sit and, tying my hands to the foot of the bed, they continued to terrorise me with very difficult questions on the Mass and Communion, as if I were sitting a theology exam.

(145)   In spite of all, I answered many questions well, but they compelled me to make digressions in order to trick me. In the end I had to say to them: 'I have never heard of these obscure things. All I know is the doctrine I was taught by my mother: to go to communion is really to receive the Body and Blood of Jesus Christ; consequently, my intention is not to eat a piece of white bread but to eat the flesh and blood of the Son of God. This flesh and this blood will unite themselves to my flesh and my blood to make my soul and body pure and holy like the soul and body of Jesus.'

'Yes, yes: we already know all of that. You need not give us a lesson. We have only asked you how you prepare yourself to dare to receive communion every day and, if you do not know, we forbid you to go to communion.'

'What right have you to forbid me? Only the parish priest possesses this right. Concerning the preparation, that's my business. Jesus is pleased to come to me. That's sufficient. There is no need to say more.'

(146)   'Wham! You question us, you canine specimen? You brazen boy! Wham! You stubborn boy! You dare to contradict us! Wham!'

'I am not daring to contradict you, but I cannot live if you forbid me to go to communion.'

'Come on. Who said you can't live without communion. Look at us, are we all dead?'

'I would not presume to say that you are dead, but it would be better if you could understand what you are.'

'OK. It's understood that I'm allowing you to go to communion tomorrow, but food is forbidden so that we can see if you will live or die. Dare you promise?'

'Yes, I dare.'

The following day I was authorised to receive communion, but come evening I had no strength left. I stretched out on my bed, mouth wide open. Vinh, the catechist, fearing that I was dying, came to my aid and made me take a little soup. I recovered and went to communion the following day, but it was for the last time. That day, after communion, my heart was unusually arid and I was invaded by an indescribable
(147)   sadness. I was extremely troubled by the questions they had asked me.

On the one hand I was extremely tired, and on the other I was confronted by their very difficult questions. I had to admit my ignorance.

During their interrogation the judge strongly emphasised the following points:

1. Is it certain that Jesus is really present under the appearance of bread and happy to come to your heart?
2. Dare you state that your preparation has been truly worthy?

Then, seeking to confuse me, they brought up the lives of the saints from the past to compare their lives with mine. 'In bygone days the saints went to communion on one day and spent the following year in thanksgiving. They spent months in preparation and yet, when the time for communion arrived, they beat their breasts, saying: "We dare not yet receive." But you who do not yet know how to tie the belt of your trousers firmly, and whose mouth still stinks of milk ... etc., you dare to call yourself worthy? This is truly evidence of your great recklessness.' They then read passages from the lives of the saints who, in fact, took communion much less frequently and after having prepared for it vigorously by fasting and great austerity.

Compared with me there was an enormous difference ... I became   (148)
troubled, therefore, certain of having been very rash. I said to myself, however, on reflection, that it was impossible that my mother had misled me. According to my mother, if one is not aware of having committed a mortal sin and possesses sanctifying grace, one can present oneself freely at the holy table to receive communion when one really desires to receive Jesus. My mother spoke the truth without a trace of error but, at that moment, her words were not strong enough to set my mind at rest. I was disturbed and suffered greatly since, not being worthy as the saints were, I had dared recklessly to receive communion every day. The more I tried to unravel the problem, the more tangled it became, and the more painful was the wound in my heart. I did not know who to run to to clear my conscience. I thought all of the time of the false arguments they had brought to bear and, consequently, I dared no longer go to communion every day.

I lost my source of happiness from that moment. I was overwhelmed by an unspeakable sadness and the thought of my family was always with me. This separation was now breaking my heart. I longed to see   (149)
my mother again to tell her of the bitterness in my soul, and to find motherly comfort close to me in those hours of sadness. But my mother was far away, very far, so that this wish further added to my distress.

From time to time I looked for a means of escape, but just as I was about to put my plan into action I felt abandoned like a man lost deep in the forest. Having no more confidence on that score I knew only to put my confidence in God, asking him, even at the cost of my life, never to allow me to fall into sin, because in the presbytery at that moment there was no longer the slightest appearance of chastity. It had become a house of sin where drunkenness, gambling and impurity reigned. As for me, I preferred to shelter myself in my suffering to keep my heart pure rather than to throw myself into the current of muddy water in pursuit of transient affection.

(150)   Reverend Father, God has certainly heard my prayer because he has not given me one day to taste any bodily joy during the five years that I was imprisoned in this house. I have suffered and been oppressed all the time, but I have always felt in my soul the courage to hold out against Satan. I dare to state with certainty that I have never willingly allowed the devil to tarnish the white robe of my purity.

My soul was immersed in an indescribable sadness from the time that I dared not go to communion every morning. I felt a distaste all day and a sort of nostalgia for something which was beyond my reach. I was suffering from a terrible bout of fever because of this inexplicable sadness. I was delirious all the time, and asked to return to my mother. The attack of fever passed quickly, but my sadness never left me for a moment. As a consequence of all this, my body, like my soul, wasted away quickly. I had no taste for food, I slept little, I was easily scared, and my face had become pale and emaciated.

The parish priest, ignorant of the state of affairs, did not know why I was so weak and sick. All he knew was that I no longer went to communion frequently. He also stopped called me by the kindly name of (151)   Benjamin. It was only when I was saying the rosary that I felt my heart become warm and taste a little of the joy taken from the heart of Mary, my beloved Mother. A relentless struggle was necessary, however, to remain faithful to the daily recitation of the rosary. The first thing was, for no reason at all, the confiscation of my rosary. Nevertheless, I found a means of saying it by placing ten black beans in my pocket. At each 'Hail Mary' I transferred one bean from one pocket to the other. When my pocket was empty I said the 'Glory be'. I then continued in the same manner. I thought that this method would be sufficiently unobtrusive but, once again, they succeeded in spiriting away this form of rosary.

I immediately invented another stratagem. I fixed ten knots on the cord of my trousers to use as my rosary. I had to hide it carefully inside and only take it out when I wanted to use it. One day, inadvertently, I forgot to take this precaution. The master noticed it and forced me to tell the truth. Again, he confiscated this very precious cord. In addition, he favoured me with three good slaps, saying: 'How dare you be so

impolite towards the Blessed Virgin as to use the belt of your trousers   (152)
as a rosary?'

Following this, and thinking that no other means remained, I had to use the knuckles of my hands to count the 'Hail Marys'. This method seemed practical because I could thus say my rosary anywhere, undetected. In spite of this, I said to myself: 'Even though I must sacrifice the ten ends of my fingers, my heart will never cease to express its love for the Blessed Virgin by saying the rosary.' It is thanks to this practice that Mary, my Mother, has always come to my aid, forcing the devil to fear me so much that he has never succeeded in overcoming me. Moreover, he has been given unexpected blows which have thwarted his most secret ruses. It is thus that the implacable hatred between me and the devil has never known any truce.

The fate of those who give scandal

Father, allow me to interrupt my story to describe to you the sad fate that God reserves for those who commit scandal. Vinh, after having   (153)
maltreated me in a thousand ways, after having unjustly condemned me to endure hunger and eat with the dog, and finally, having forbade me absolutely to receive communion every day, might appear on the surface to have got his own way completely; but this man did not know that God lived in me in numerous ways. If, each morning, I dared not go to the holy table to receive the bread of angels, my loving thirst for God was sufficient to draw him to me in a secret and mysterious manner. My heart felt his presence in a clear and sweet way although no one saw it with the eyes of the flesh.

The master took it upon himself to go on holiday after all of this had happened and the holidays had arrived, although the parish priest was not yet back from his annual retreat. With his proud demeanour and ample self-sufficiency, he wished to show that even if he did commit a breach of the rules, the parish priest would not dare to reproach him too severely. So he prolonged his holiday beyond the allotted time and returned a fortnight after the reopening of class. Seeing him return so reluctantly, the parish priest asked him: 'Where have you been to have   (154)
had such a good time that you arrive back so late?' Pursing his lips he replied in a stubborn manner: 'I have been for a walk ...'

In view of this obstinacy the parish priest felt impelled to complain to the vicar general. The latter replied that the parish priest had the authority to deal with the business and to impose on the guilty party the punishment he deserved. In accordance with the instruction he imposed this punishment which was to last a fortnight:

1. To lose the title of catechist and be demoted to the ranks of a simple servant.
2. To cook, read in the dining room, eat after everybody else and sit in the last row of the servants.
3. Finally, after this fortnight, to receive fifteen strokes of the cane.

That was all, but 'Sir', because of his pride did not wish to submit. He went so far as to complain to the bishop but everywhere he went, the punishment imposed was upheld. The master decided, therefore, to shave off his moustache and retire. From that moment the majesty of Hitler fell from his face and he became a simple hooligan, capable of all sorts of chicanery. The word spread shortly afterwards that he had disappeared. People asked themselves if he had gone to seek help in Moscow . . .

(155)

Some time after his departure, the curate, Father Năng, changed parish. The number of catechists diminished noticeably and, at the same time, the number of those who gave a bad example reduced little by little. The catechists who had been involved in the business of my unjust judgement were struck by chastisements from God's hands. One had become ill, the other had become a good-for-nothing, a robber and licentious, and had also been chased from the presbytery.

My Father, you must certainly understand that it is not my intention to enumerate these chastisements in order to curse those who have done me wrong, physically or morally. My sole intention is to remind everyone that if I was powerless, God, who is power itself, knew to come to the help of my powerlessness. I did not wish these chastisements on them; but if someone hardens himself, God cannot put up with it indefinitely; he must accomplish his plans.

(156)

Eight years of age

I no longer had to rise up against such bad examples, although the atmosphere of the presbytery remains contaminated by impurity. Alcohol continues to be drunk, gambling persists and young girls come and go to the house as usual. I feel more at ease as nobody obliges me to oppose this state of affairs, and I begin to look for a route which will lead me to the priesthood. I can call this period a short-lived truce.

God, who knows the fragility of his little flower, has calmed the violence of the storm, to allow it to develop and grow strong while waiting for it to be transplanted into his garden. While leading a life full of sorrows I long for the day when I shall taste perfect joy. God has allowed me to wander in a deserted forest and it is in darkness that I look for a route to follow. All my wishes concerning my future as a priest appear absolutely hollow. Nobody is concerned with my studies or my spiritual formation. I notice, on the contrary, that everybody behaves in a manner opposed to perfection. All of these contradictions (157) tear at my heart to such an extent that one day I had come to think that God is just, but men, being sinners, cannot get close to him. So, because they cannot get close to God, they allow themselves to follow the devil.

I feel, here, that there would be very harmful things to say but to avoid them let me assert that in this parish, I have never heard anyone speak of God's goodness, even in sermons given in church, nor of a single sentence urging confidence in God. Nevertheless, this confidence is a very necessary virtue for the souls of Christians.

I felt myself more and more each day a victim of a force which was carrying me far from God. I did not dare to put into practice things as I conceived them in my mind, since I could not find anyone in whom to confide my thoughts. Consequently, I had to put up with everything in silence until the day when I met my sister Saint Thérèse on the hill at Quảng-Uyên. This was five years later. It was because of this fear that I dared not communicate every day. Yes, in my spiritual life I was domi- (158) nated increasingly by fear. As for my studies, nobody cared. If I had remained at my parents' house it is certain that, at my age, I would never have become the abandoned child that I was then.

The parish priest, totally absorbed in the repairing of his church, had completely forgotten the living temple that I was, and the responsibility that he had assumed to build an altar in it and to light there the flame of love which would, day and night, ascend towards God. In a short time he had even forgotten the plans for the future that my parents had formed for me. He placed me in the ranks of the servants. This was convenient for him and pre-empted the necessity to pay a wage. Having become a little servant of the parish, it could be said no longer that I had entered God's service. My priestly future was, therefore, plunged into a pitch-black night.

Return to suffering

I would never have suspected that Father Joseph Nhã would forget me so quickly. He thought of me from time to time when he received a letter from my family, but he contented himself with a few vague (159) promises to reassure me, only then to forget me as if I had been nothing but a meaningless dream. I soon became thin and stubborn, oppressed by the hard and unfair work. Every day, after having quickly learned my lessons, I had to spend the rest of the time in the service of the parish priest and his interests. With my diminutive stature, underfed, not sufficiently warmly clothed and under ten years of age but forced to accomplish the same work as a male adult, it was, quite simply, a glaring injustice.

The poverty was even greater in the year in which I became ten. Because of the flooding, the whole of the region where I was, lost its harvest. People suffering from hunger roamed in the forest every day to find something with which to feed themselves. The situation was worse still in the presbytery. People argued over every grain of rice ... The spirit of charity had disappeared without trace. To tell the whole (160) truth, in a house of twenty people, only two had their hunger satisfied. One must first of all point the finger at the parish priest who, during the entire famine, agreed to do without a meat or fish course at each meal. That apart, his little cooking pot of rice was always full and accompanied by savoury seasonings. Above all there was the bottle of alcohol and on the sideboard the always-full jar of grilled groundnuts. Secondly, there was the parish procurator, the parish priest's nephew. He went to receive his portion at meal time like the rest of us but there was always something 'black' hidden under his bed or again something 'white' hidden in his blanket. To tell the truth, there was connivance between the catechist-procurator and the cook, but it was impossible to hide these things from ten pairs of hungry eyes. Naturally, no one dared to complain since, if the parish priest was satisfied, that made the size of our sacrifice more obvious and if the procurator ate in secret he showed that his Christian spirit had been replaced by selfishness.

Even in the distribution of rice there were those who cheated, so much that, afterwards, uncooked rice had to be distributed. I do not know how it was for the others, but I received about one hundred (161) grams of rice each day and a quarter of a litre of soya sauce which was often diluted with water. With that I was able to prepare my food as I wished, in order to live for one day. Usually, I had to use all of my free time to collect some herbs to add to the other ingredients in the preparation of my soup. There was no fixed time for meals; each one ate as he wished, but work had to continue as normal. I cannot find the words to describe them, now that these sufferings have passed, and in speaking of them, I am afraid of hurting someone. The distress which reigned in the Hữu-Bằng presbytery made my stay there more and more unbearable. The young boys whose families lived close by were sent home. But I, who was the furthest away and, at that time, the most badly treated, would also have wished to profit from this opportunity to return to my parents. Unfortunately, the flooding had not yet finished when I received news that made my heart bleed. The dykes were broken in the Ngăm-Giáo region and to cap it all my family, reduced to the most dire poverty, had to borrow money and feed on soup to stay alive.

This news astonished me as much as if I had heard of the death of my (162) father. All I could do was to cry secretly and confide my hurt to the Blessed Virgin. I felt that my current sufferings were no longer so bitter. I forgot them as if they had never existed, so as to think at that moment only of my family. All I could imagine was that immense waves had flooded all of my village, allowing only the bamboo clumps and the thatched roofs so dear to me to appear. I even thought sometimes that my mother and my little sister Tế were dead. Oh, what tearing there was at my heart! I sobbed from time to time and I had bouts of dizziness.

It was only three months later that I learned that all my family were still alive, and that it had been enriched by a little brother called Joachim Lực. He lived, and enjoys better health than his brothers and sisters although he was born in a time of famine. However, being the youngest, he has not had the happiness of seeing the cheerful appearance of the house as it used to be. He has grown up in a cramped and unclean environment. The whitewashed walls are now covered with a very black moss, the flower beds have become a vegetable garden, and the stone-paved courtyard has been transformed into a trellised area for pumpkins.

My Father, in speaking so summarily you are going to think that my (163) family's situation was suddenly changed because of the floods. In reality that was not so. What led my family from being comfortably-off to poverty was my father's passion for gambling. If, after the flood, my father had known how to repent, how to apply himself to the work of reconstructing the dyke of family happiness which was on the point of collapsing because of the flood, my family would have known in a short time the comfort of former years. On the contrary, he had used all his strength and all his talents to destroy all that which could again be called family happiness. He competed with his friends at gambling, and the day came when it was necessary to sell the paddy fields, to pawn the inheritance, and even to sell the slabs in the courtyard, to satisfy his passion for gambling and to buy rice. My mother, brothers and sisters lived more on their tears than they did on rice ... In spite of this, my father always remained calm, getting upset less than anyone and my (164) mother's greatest sorrow was not the loss of the inheritance but, much more, his lack of love. Afterwards my father, no longer knowing how to reflect, gave himself over to alcohol, began cursing and lived among us like a man without any affection.

We surrounded our mother every day with thoughtfulness, sharing her sorrows and her joys. She remained, always, the column which supported the family, but more than anyone she felt numerous wounds in her heart. She was very brave, never complained, and always wore a smiling face, so well that, apart from us her children, no one knew of her sufferings which she hid with great skill. For example, once – and this is the most sorrowful memory of my life – I had to see with my own eyes a drama which could not be more cruel and, in my powerlessness, I could not find a means of protecting my mother. The author of this cruel drama was none other than my father. Allow me to tell you

(165)   frankly what I felt in my heart on that occasion. My father's fury terrified me on that day, and I could no more imagine that this man was my father. I would have rushed forward to aid my mother and, had I been a boxer, I would have been capable of killing my father on the spot. But I was powerless and this fortunate impotence helped me to avoid a crime. O my God, I cannot say more! My throat tightens and my eyes spill a torrent of tears each time that I think of this frightful drama . . .!

After this scene my mother's face was purple and swollen. Nevertheless, from morning till evening and from evening till morning, she remained calm as if she had not endured any physical suffering. There was not a word of rancour, although in the darkness of a corner of her bedroom she must have sobbed secretly many times. We used to visit her to comfort her, but her only response was to encourage us to

(166)   think of our father and to pray a lot for him. She never allowed us to allude to her sufferings. She was so reserved and so discreet that outsiders did not know who had caused the injuries to her face. If anyone questioned her on the subject, she replied with these words: 'I am sick.' That's all she said. If I continued to speak of our dear mammy I do not know when my story would stop. All I know is that I have allowed myself to wander off the subject.

My family, finding itself reduced to this state of poverty, could no longer provide me, as it used to each year with clothes, money and other things I needed. I must, therefore, from now on, rely entirely on the parish priest. However, he no longer had for me the tender affection of the early years. He no longer loved me, for the very reason that he should have loved me, especially after receiving from my mother a letter couched in these terms and giving me entirely to him: 'Our family's situation no longer allows us to put to one side the

(167)   least sou for our distant child. We are therefore counting entirely on you. From now onwards, Van will be more your child than ours; living or dead, good or bad, we ask you to look after him.' From then onwards Father Nhã had no longer to fear my parents. Previously they were considered as his benefactors, but now . . . they have become very poor . . .

Father, I have no need to expand on this subject. You will be able to understand yourself the change which had taken place regarding the parish priest. He no longer considered me as a candidate for the priesthood, but as a simple servant who was nimble and useful. Therefore I had to accept the status of slave, but the type of slave who is still treated with a little humanity; that is to say, no one has the right to put me to death, but as for the rest – the insults, the affronts, the hunger, the cold, the blows, the injustice – I have to put up with all of this, not daring to open my mouth in protest. For the parish priest, my studies counted as nothing, rather, he looked to obstruct them with a thousand tasks. My (168) new teacher, a man who knew my family very well, praised me for being an intelligent child, and took steps to send me to study at the provincial school, but the parish priest turned a deaf ear, saying: 'Do not make him too able, because if he becomes too clever he will go so far as to insult me, and that will be even more dangerous.'

Therefore, I devoted almost three times more of my time to work than to study. During the winter, on opening my eyes as soon as it was dawn and before having been able to even wash my face, I had to go quickly with the copper kettle and heat up the water so that the parish priest could wash himself. In summer I had to take a basin to the well and draw water so that the parish priest could wash himself in fresh water. Afterwards I served Mass, I served at table, I helped in the kitchen, I cleaned his spittoon and his chamber pot. I had to change these unclean bowls every day and rub them to make them shine and if, by chance, a stain remained, the obligatory punishment, which varied according to the programme, followed. Frankly, I found nothing more repugnant than to have to put my hands in this dirt in order to clean them. During the winter, although my hands were very clean, they (169) were covered with chaps and boils which sometimes gave them the repulsive appearance of lepers' hands. In the afternoon, once lunch was over, I had to work in the garden until half past six. Winter was the season when the vegetables were planted and it was necessary for me to spend any of my free time in the garden. On holidays all day was spent in the garden. On Sundays I could rest only in the morning in order to go to Mass and work in the house. In the afternoons, again, it was the garden.

The really inhuman and unjust practice was that it was never permitted to reveal to the parish priest or complain about one's lot, no matter how unjust the treatment. The catechist-procurator was, as I have told you, the parish priest's nephew, and in terms of avarice they were mirror images. Wishing the work to be done quickly and profitably, they behaved injustly, for no matter what reason, provided that it was lucrative. They exploited a group of children separated from their parents in selfishly making them work for them. The procurator, not

(170)   wishing to spend money on a gardener, worked himself and forced the children to dig the ground in order to save money. Wishing the work to be done quickly, he apportioned the ground between pairs of young children whose job it was to weed and water the ground. The procurator alone planted in it what he wished.

Another completely unjust thing was that he obliged us to work without giving us the necessary tool. We lacked everything, from a bucket to carry the water, to a hoe for weeding the ground. It was a good distance from the pond to the garden and transporting water was very painful. Two children of my size carried, with difficulty, fifty litres of water from the pond to the garden. In winter and summer I simply wore shorts and I worked bare-footed. My 'shirt' consisted of bare skin. There was nothing to moan about in summer, but in the cold season it was agony for me. Each time that I went to get water for the vegetables my feet were paralysed from the ankles downwards. I had difficulty walking on ground or on stones and I felt absolutely no sensation, either of pain or sweetness when walking on thorns or through water.

(171)   There was also the problem which arose if I happened to break a basin or damage a bucket. In this eventuality it was necessary to present oneself to receive some blows from the cane and be rewarded with extra work. If the bucket was damaged, the guilty one had to make do or find another with which to continue the watering, or borrow one. This was not always easy. It was no problem with the well-disposed children but if one came upon an unscrupulous type, before borrowing his watering can, it was necessary to work for him, that is to say, to water his portion of the garden before one's own. I noticed that my life, so dominated by work, had become very hard, and this situation had killed any spirit of charity.

It was the same for work done in church: we were subjected to the same regime. The person employed for the care of the church must see to the lamp and the oil himself. The parish priest gave only a limited

(172)   amount and if, unfortunately, there was a shortage, the boy responsible had to find the money and buy some. The parish priest even skimped on the matches! Consequently, seeing that being so parsimonious he was considered as a miser, he ended up by no longer giving any matches and thus he avoided being regarded as miserly and could thereby use the matches for smoking. He threatened us unceasingly: 'Be careful! If the sanctuary lamp goes out it means the cane ...' The cane! We were used to it, but the sad thing was that the parish priest had an abundance of light for smoking and gambling, whereas Jesus, alone in his tabernacle of cracked wood, was deprived of the light and remained all day plunged in darkness. There was indeed a sanctuary

lamp but there was no wick to draw up the oil nor light to shine ... It was truly sad!

If I compare Jesus' situation with mine, I notice that they are identical. In the presbytery with its depraved morality the only example for me to imitate was Jesus in the Blessed Sacrament. The tabernacle veil, torn and dirty, invariably of the same colour, half white, half brown, (173) reminded me that I must accept poverty and discomfort cheerfully. If Jesus was ignored, then, for all the more reason, this little Van counted for nothing. My only friend was Jesus in the Blessed Sacrament. My loving heart would never separate itself from him. However, one thing tortured the soul of his little friend; it was that he no longer dared to receive Jesus every day, victim as he was of a false opinion, worthy of being stamped upon, namely, that Jesus is not so accommodating as men. How wicked is the person who has led me to have such an idea of Jesus! In those days all I knew was to offer myself, me, his little friend. I could only express my feelings towards him by a loving glance, filled with an ardent desire to be liberated from the yoke of this cruel idea. I had very often such a wish to unite myself to Jesus that I would burst out sobbing, not understanding why I was always told that I was not worthy, and Jesus was not happy. Jesus was the only one able to understand me at that time.

Robber   (174)

My Father, I have just summarised for you the life full of injustice that we led at the Huu Bang presbytery ... But, so that you may know how this impoverished life has effected changes in me, allow me to speak frankly to you of certain reprehensible acts that I have been obliged to commit in order to live.

Formerly I was the best-provided-for child at the presbytery regarding both clothing and money. I do not know how many clothes my mother would send me each year when my family was comfortably off, clothes which came sometimes from my grandmothers and sometimes from my aunts. The clothes which I had received during those two years would have been sufficient to last me during the six following years. In fact, I gave the largest part of these clothes to the poor. The (175) poor boys at the presbytery received some of my finest clothes and each time that I received a parcel of new clothes, I took my old clothes, even if they had not been used, to the laundress for her to give them to the poor.

I felt a special sympathy for the poor which went back to my childhood. My mother gave me many striking examples of charity towards poor families when I was still at home. Each year, on the big feasts, my parents had the practice of giving clothes to poor families.

Subsequently, this custom has stopped since my family have themselves experienced poverty. If a poor person came to the house, no matter at what time, he was never refused anything. Often when these poor people arrived at meal times, they ate at the family table and, once satisfied, they received a little rice or money to take away with them. I admired, sincerely, my parents' generosity. Their good example gave (176)   birth in my heart to a special sympathy for the poor and since then this sympathy accompanies me everywhere. Wherever I am, I love to give alms, and my intention is to give it to Jesus himself.

My mother often said to me in the house: 'Each time that you give something to a poor person, think that you are giving it to Jesus. Pay no regard to the value of what you give, but rather to the love that you feel for the one who receives. That is to say, in giving something you must also give your heart. Consequently, never scorn the poor but, on the contrary, if it is an old man, respect him: if a child, have pity on him, and if it is a sick person, support and help him. It is necessary that they are members of the mystical body of Jesus and also our brothers.'

Following this maternal advice, my little sister and I were prone to tease the poor, especially my little sister. Each time that a poor person came to the house she ran to meet him and greet him with these words: 'Good day, Jesus! Good day, Jesus!' ... And if it was a woman: 'Good day, Blessed Virgin! Have you come to visit us?' One day, seeing a (177)   beggar with a club foot, she ran to meet him and then called me: 'Van, come here, I have something to tell you ...' I ran to see what the fuss was about. Then, laughing, she pointed to the old man and whispered in my ear: 'Jesus has a club foot ...'

Another time, meeting an old lady with conjunctivitis, she burst out laughing and said to me: 'Look, Van, the Blessed Virgin has conjunctivitis!' Another day, seeing a little one who had no trousers, she ran to get my father's trousers to give them to him; then, laughing helplessly, she said to him: 'Little Jesus, I have given you a really big pair of trousers ...' The child's mother accepted the trousers, but, not knowing how to dress the child in them, had to ask for another pair. This other pair, naturally, was mine. My little sister Tế, just like her brother Van, was very inclined to imitate those with disabilities. However, we did it in a careful way so as not to offend anyone, but rather in a manner to cause the victims to hold their stomachs with laughter at our would-be (178)   impersonations. We never allowed ourselves provocative or insulting airs in their regard, and we never scorned them.

I often met many poor people at the Hữu-Bằng presbytery, who ordinarily were rebuffed and sometimes even beaten. On seeing such a thing I looked spontaneously for alms to give to them, but the more spontaneous my action the greater the opposition. In spite of that, each time that I saw a poor person arrive, I tried secretly to give him something or other. Most often I had only a few coins or some clothes. If I wished to give clothing I had to have recourse to trickery to carry them from the house to the garden gate. That is to say, I put the clothes on myself and then, arriving at the place, I hid in a corner of the wall, took off the clothes and gave them to the poor.

Ordinarily, I very much liked to talk to the poor and to console them even if they were not of my religion. In these conversations I always had the chance to hear instructive words from their mouths which reminded me of my mother's words on conformity to the holy and mysterious will of God. I also had the impression that only the poor can (179) easily discover the will of God. Their words are as sincere as their hearts, that is to say, they can only say what they feel, and only know how to complain or to implore because they are suffering. God has declared the poor blessed, and I find that this beatitude conforms completely to the truth and it is worthy of the hearts of the poor.

One day, fortuitously, I also became a poor child. God has wished that I also experience this beatitude. That is why he has permitted me to become poor and needy. I did become poor, very poor. I have had to make use of all that I possessed to make up for the injustices allowed at the presbytery. I have had to sell my clothes to get the wherewithal to buy the tools necessary for the service of the parish priest and his assistants, and also to get pen and paper for my studies ... In this situation and not receiving any more help from my family, I had to live empty-handed. Each year the parish priest gave me only two suits of very thin (180) tulle cloth. Even in treating them very carefully these clothes lasted no more than three months. I had some very bizarre wishes brought on by the hunger and cold but I succeeded in overcoming them ...

Once or twice only, and in my obligation to do my duty well, I have had to submit to spying in order to take some coins from the parish priest; for example to buy a packet of matches to light the sanctuary lamp, or to not to have to ask for a light each time that I had to heat the water ... etc. It was evidently in the service of the parish priest, and I profited in no way from the small amount stolen. In my opinion the meaning of the word 'theft' in this instance meant nothing more than this: the asking for money to buy these necessary things but without daring to let it be known to the parish priest. If one asked him directly one usually got nothing more than a humiliating scolding. Assuming that I was surprised by the parish priest in the attempt to get money in this way, he would have treated me as a thief but, before God and my (181) conscience, I was not guilty of any fault.

I had at the presbytery the reputation of being a past master in deceit. I was the only one given such a name. As for the others, past masters in cruelty, who had stripped me of my human dignity, no one dared to say a word against them. I have been educated from my childhood by a perfectly sincere mother, so that I have never known how to tell a lie, even playfully. It was only because of circumstances that, later, because I was unjustly compelled to, I had to commit any reprehensible act. If I had been beside a soul such as my mother, despite the worst circumstances, these reprehensible things would never have arisen. Unfortunately, I was lost, far away from this loving mother. There was no shortage of thieves in the presbytery and I can say bluntly that the parish priest himself was a thief. The thefts that he committed were ones for which he will have to render an account before God. On this (182) subject allow me to give way to my beloved Jesus who can speak for me.

Often it was not easy to steal from the parish priest. Usually I had recourse to the Blessed Virgin. After having gone to her and made clear to her all the misfortunes of my life, I approached the offerings box and looked for a means of extracting some coins. If I had been caught in the act I would have been dealt with as a robber, but in the eyes of the Blessed Virgin I was innocent, since it was with her permission that I dared to take this money. Each time that I extracted money from the Blessed Virgin's box I found it easy and all passed smoothly.

One day I had neither paper nor ink for my class, while I had to study doubly hard to prepare for my exam. In this situation I would have been condemned to spend three long days seated in class staring at the blackboard without anything with which to write up the lesson. I asked the parish priest for some paper but he replied: 'You are studying for yourself, not for me, and yet you have the effrontery to come and ask me for paper.' These words hurt me more deeply than if someone had cut off my head. In class the master threatened me: 'If (183) you have no paper tomorrow, I will dismiss you!' What could I do? All hope was lost. I ran crying to the feet of the Blessed Virgin and, my heart full of bitterness, I told her how unfortunate I was compared to other children. After the prayer a thought came, gently, to my mind. I approached the Blessed Virgin's offerings box with the intention of withdrawing something, and there it was. I had reached the box when I noticed something sticking out of the opening. It was a twenty sou note, much more than was necessary for buying paper and purple ink. It is thanks to this note that I was able to gain my primary certificate!

From the day that the Blessed Virgin had given me, indirectly, twenty sous from the offertory box, I no longer lacked anything important. She inspired people, in a natural manner, to think to give me money. On one occasion I needed to do my duty quickly in order to prepare for an examination and I did not know where to find five sous with a view to hiring someone to water the vegetable garden in my place. I had to go therefore to ask the Blessed Virgin. I had hardly left the church when I met a lady who knew me. She stopped, looked at me and then signalled me to come closer, saying: 'What makes you so pale and thin these days? No doubt you are studying for your exam.' Then, (184) taking out her purse, she handed me five sous, saying: 'This is to buy sweets.' I had enough time that evening to prepare for my exam.

How can I praise worthily the goodness of Mary's maternal heart? Truly, I shall never be able to forget her favours. She is my mother. I have never during my life seen Mary under the form of an apparition, but I have felt with an extreme sweetness in my soul and in my body the favours which have come to me through her hands. My soul is dumb with feeling at this moment and my spirit is submerged in the abundance of graces she has given to me. I do not know what words to use to express it. All I can say is, 'Mary is my mother and I am her child.' All is there. What meaning could my witness have for her mother's heart beyond that? Mary is always my mother. Although I am distanced from my bodily mother, the figure and the sweet gaze of my heavenly mother will always be with me. Yes, Mary looks lovingly on me and (185) protects my every step. Please allow me, dear mother, to sing eternally of the deep love of your maternal heart! ...

A charitable widow

I received from the Blessed Virgin a consolation which deeply moved me. I had reached nine years of age and it was a moment when I was more and more overwhelmed by sadness and suffering. I had to accompany the parish priest that year when he went to give the retreat at Bảo-Sơn. It was there that I was the victim of an accident which gave me the privilege of being helped by a hand as kind and caring as that of a mother for her child. The accident happened simply because I was obeying faithfully an order from the parish priest.

Towards the end of the retreat he had invited two priests from neighbouring parishes to come and lend a hand with confessions. Now, during their stay at Bảo-Sơn, the parish priest gave me the order not (186) to allow any young girls to enter the presbytery during the time of siesta. Why this prohibition? I do not know. All I noticed was that at Bảo-Sơn, as at Hữu-Bằng, as in all of the other parishes, people were accustomed to visit the parish priest at midday during siesta time, and in the evenings after the prayers in church. These visitors consisted solely of young girls, the biggest of whom were amongst those who intoned the prayers in church. One saw younger people only very rarely and in small numbers, except at the arrival and departure of the parish priest. This practice has given rise to many things that I have no need to speak of, not because they were good but ... infinitely bad.

These young girls would often come in the evenings to visit the parish priest from the end of prayer until midnight, and often they even slept (187) in the presbytery ... In truth, I was pleased with the visits of these girls at the appointed hours, since I gave them the job of waving the fan for the parish priest and massaging him, which allowed me to use the time for sleeping. Each time that these young ladies came to the parish priest, the latter gave me leave for the duration of their visit. Personally, I preferred this because since my childhood, and without really understanding why, I blushed easily and felt uneasy in the presence of young girls. This did not, of course, include my sisters or other relatives.

I did not like, therefore, remaining near these young ladies that the young people called 'carpenters' mallets'.* They were of doubtful character and in the parish priest's presence they respected no one. They clipped me over the head even in the presence of the parish priest and he, instead of objecting, encouraged them and gave me more himself. I found this shameful on his part. In their presence I was afraid to say a (188) disagreeable word. I had to give them the respect I gave to the parish priest. I avoided them as one would avoid a carpenter's mallet!

On the occasion in question the parish priest would have done better, perhaps, to have had a quiet word with these girls rather than to give me, a young boy, an order which obliged me to oppose a custom which had already been in existence a long time. In spite of this, I decided to carry out the priest's command. I had anticipated that the young ladies would not be slow in making a great fuss at my refusal to allow them to enter but, with a certain cunning, I prepared the materials to disinfect them well and truly. They did indeed come knocking at the door at midday. Fearing that they might prevent the priests from sleeping, I rushed out and asked them to go away, saying that if they did not, they would have me to deal with.

'Ah! Van, the little monkey. Have you gone mad? You'd better be careful. Do you understand?'

'I'm not afraid of any of you. Go away, otherwise I'll crush your (189) bones, all of you, now.'

'Van, the dog with the little eyes. You would dare to break our bones? If you value anything, open the door so that we can crush you.'

'Band of she-devils! You make fun of my little eyes? They are still more beautiful than yours, with your red eyelashes.' (Most of the girls

* A slang expression to describe a despicable person.

of Båo-Sơn suffered from conjunctivitis.) 'Take care, otherwise I'll show you what I'm made of!'

'We challenge you.'

'Fair enough! If you are smart, wait here to challenge me.'

I went to look for a catapult whilst filling my pockets with little fruits of Indian lilac to serve as projectiles. As they stood at a distance beyond the wall they easily avoided my missiles, and they riposted by throwing stones at me. Perched on top of the wall, and being incapable of avoiding the stones, I had to withdraw and have recourse to another tactic. I returned to the house and came back with a basin of chemical water* of my own concoction, and a big syringe made from the stem of a bamboo to project the water; I climbed the wall, trying very hard not to laugh, and I made fun of them in these terms: 'All right! I'll open the door for you to visit the parish priest but, before entering, allow me to spray you with perfume to make you more elegant.' At these words they guessed   (190) the nature of the perfume. Irritated, but unable to stop themselves from laughing, they did not suspect that I was capable of playing such a trick. They gathered round again to threaten me: 'If you squirt that water on us we will beat you until you are ill.' Whilst they were uttering these threats I sent a jet of water from the top of the wall. This reached their clothes and obliged them to flee. One of them, having received some water in her sore eyes, raged and rubbed her eyes as she fled. After waiting for a few minutes I saw that they had withdrawn behind the church. I was then certain that with their tunics impregnated with such a strong odour they would not come back that day to visit the parish priest. Satisfied, I said to myself: 'If they come back tomorrow I'll do the same thing.' I returned to the house with my syringe and basin of water. The silence was total. Everyone was asleep, unaware of the victory I had just won. I sat down for a moment to calm the pounding of my heart. I had to try very hard not to laugh.

As I was about to go to the well to wash my hands I suddenly heard   (191) whispering beyond the wall, then knocks on the door, and finally a young girl's voice crying: 'Father, we were coming to visit you but Van does not want us to enter and has thrown foul-smelling water over us.' I knew well that their intention was to make trouble again for me. I went back with my syringe and my basin which, this time, contained only ordinary water and not my 'chemical water'. When I climbed the wall the girls created a clamour and, seeing me brandishing my arms, they fled.

I was feeling happy when my basin, falling accidentally outside the wall, broke into pieces and splashed water all over the wall. The girls

*   Urine

came immediately on hearing the noise and, seeing the broken basin, they approached to challenge me.

(192)   'Now you've got us to deal with. We are going to call the parish priest to come and see.'

'Oh, I'm not afraid if the basin is broken. There is no shortage of them.'

Then I struggled to get down to look for another basin but ... heavens! My foot slipped on the wet moss which covered the wall and I fell where the basin had fallen. The girls thought at first that I had changed tactics to hand-to-hand fighting and fled. But hearing my moans and cries for help they gathered round me. I then lost consciousness for a few seconds. On opening my eyes I saw the girls gathered round me. Some scolded me pitilessly:

'He has got what he deserves. We'll leave him to die.'

Others, on the other hand, asked me gently:

'Let's see, Van. What's the matter? It's really our fault. There, there, don't worry.'

(193)   'Why do you comfort him like that? Let him die without being sorry for him! My clothes still reek of that devilish smell.'

Those who were sympathetic towards me wanted to lift me up but I said to them:

'Leave me alone. I don't wish you any harm but I must do my duty. I am going to stay stretched out here to prove to the parish priest that I have carried out his orders faithfully.'

In between times the clock sounded half past one, and the parish priest called me to fan the priests as they read their breviaries. The boy who helped me in this duty, noticing my absence, looked for me, calling loudly all over the house. The young girls all slipped away ... Then the boy, while passing close to the garden door, heard me moaning from the other side of the wall. He opened the door and saw me recumbent on the ground, huddled up with a pale face, holding my left knee in both hands and crying copiously. He lifted me immediately to carry me to my bed and asked me what had happened so that he could alert the parish priest. I told him, frankly, all that had happened.

(194)   He urged me to lie still and he went to warn the parish priest. At four o'clock, cane in hand, the parish priest arrived close to my bed. 'Allow me to cure your foot,' he said. Then, standing close to me, he shouted at the top of his voice: 'What have you done, monkey, to cause yourself to fall and hurt your foot?' He raised his cane to hit me on my back. Fortunately, a servant who was standing there held his hand and pleaded on my behalf: 'Father, I beg you. This child is very feverish.'

'What fever? Why are you interfering in my business?'

He then hit her on the back with the cane. She grimaced with pain, crying 'Jesus' and threw a look of silent anger at the priest as if quietly reproaching him for having committed this injustice. I was moved to tears on seeing this woman's gesture, which was full of pity for me. Although burning with fever and extremely concerned about my own situation as an abandoned child, I hurriedly stretched out my hand and said frankly to the parish priest:

'I have done wrong: hit me but don't strike an innocent person.'   (195)

'Be silent! Is it your job, little lout, to tell me what to do?'

At these words he again raised the cane to hit me. I was ready to turn my back to receive the blows but the servant, extremely annoyed, threw herself at him, seized the end of the cane with both hands and, looking the parish priest full in the face, said to him: 'You can't do that. Because you have not fathered this child you have no mercy for him. This child has a mother. What will you do if he dies?' She then brusquely pulled the cane from the priest's hands and threw it into the courtyard. At that juncture I lifted my hand to intervene and say to her, sobbing: 'Let him do it ...' Then I continued: 'When my parents gave me to the parish priest, they gave to him all of me: my life, my death. He has therefore the right to kill me, as he has the right to allow me to live. Please allow him to exercise this right as he sees it ...' At these words, the parish   (196) priest, purple with anger, softened a little and went out in silence to the veranda where he remained a very long time.

After his departure the servant came close to my bed, and whilst drying her tears and mine she said: 'You were very daring. Don't you know that when he is in a temper the parish priest is quite capable of killing you?'

'You are right. Faced with a tiger the only outcome is death.'

'What did he just say?' asked the parish priest, his head in the frame of the door.

I had not suspected that he was still there. The servant quickly put a hand over my mouth and turned the conversation round.

'His head is so burning he is going to die ... What is to be done now?'

'What is to be done? Leave him there. If he dies I shall bury him. If he remains sick I shall return him to his father.'

He left with these words. I then said to the servant: (197)

'My only fear is that he dare not return me. If he would allow me to leave I would get up and go right now ... My greatest wish is to return to my parents, to see my mother again ... and to be able to die on her breast.'

Then I began to sob again and then cry profusely. Once calmed down I was able to say:

'But here I have the Blessed Virgin. She is my Mother. That's enough for me ...'

'That's enough, little one. Rest yourself and stop thinking about what is going to happen. Perhaps, after the priest's anger has died down, he will reconsider and will take care in looking after you.'

'All I can do is trust in the Blessed Virgin.'

The servant got up to go to the kitchen and she added: 'You are right. All we can do in our trials is confide in God and the Blessed Virgin. As for me, I'm sure you understand my situation.' She pronounced these last words in a choking voice whilst looking at me as if to make me understand that she would really like to help me as much as she could, but she was only a poor and unassuming servant, to whom nobody paid any attention except to order her to do a hundred and one things.

(198)

As soon as she left I intended to say the rosary to beg the Blessed Virgin's help in my sadness. But the fever began to rise again and my left foot became entirely paralysed and incapable of movement. A moment later I became delirious. I had the feeling I was being pulled up and down like a pebble in swirling water. This and the shivering through my body made me very afraid. I wanted to cry out from time to time but then I woke with a start, covered completely in sweat. When I regained consciousness I asked the Blessed Virgin once again to help me.

(199)

At six o'clock I received a visit from the servant who then went to inform the parish priest of my condition, and to ask how to obtain medicines for my foot. I do not know what she said to the parish priest, but she returned with a sad face about fifteen minutes later. She said to me: 'That's enough. Since nobody cares about you I shall look after you myself.' She made me stand up and she carried me on her back to the house of a bonesetter. There we were told that this person was on her way to Mrs Sáu's house which was very close to the presbytery. The servant took me to this person's house so that the bonesetter could attend to my bad foot, while she went in search of medicines. Unfortunately, the servant had hardly carried me to Mrs Sáu's house when the bonesetter, before even saying a word, had a blackout and had to be carried home on a palanquin. Mrs Sáu's family, still in shock at the weakness which had overtaken their visitor, now had to feel compassion for the misfortune of a little lad, the victim of a serious accident, who had ended up in their house. At that moment, a lady with a bony body and sticky eyes, and who was dressed very simply, said, laughing, to the parish priest's servant:

(200)

'Today my house is indeed a house of bad luck. Misfortune gathers here like ants. If I were a heathen there would be a lot of people deriding me.'

Then, coming close to me, she touched my poorly knee and said to the servant:

'What have we here? Does that hurt him very much?'

The servant, pulling a face, replied:

'Obviously, he has had a high fever since early afternoon.'

Then, after several shakings of her head she added in a low voice in Mrs Sáu's ear:

'And to think that the parish priest still wanted to cane him!'

If I had not been there to see the respect that the servant showed to this lady much younger than she, I would still have realised that Mrs Sáu was an honourable person. The servant expressed her disappointment that the bonesetter was ill, saying:

'It's a great shame. Let's go back to the presbytery and tomorrow, if she's better, we'll go to see her. Goodbye Mrs.'

Mrs Sáu then intervened:

'How can you take this boy to the house now? He's burning with   (201)
fever. He won't be able to stand the draughts. Leave him and if you have to go back, let me look after him instead of you.'

She went to prepare a bed for me whilst saying:

'But Mrs. If the parish priest asks for an explanation, what shall I say?'

The lady thought for a moment and then replied:

'That's not important. If the parish priest asks questions, say that the child is incapable of walking.'

The servant giggled and said:

'I will also say that you have adopted him.'

'Don't say that. People will make fun of me ... A child of the parish is like my own child. The parish priest is not looking after him, therefore, I shall do so in his place ... Don't mention adoption.'

I was still feverish as night fell. Since the servant's departure, I was invaded by a strange feeling which further increased my sadness. The servant came close to me before leaving to embrace me and comfort me: 'There, there, little one, stay with the lady, and if the parish priest wants explanations, leave it to me.' I made an effort to smile in gratitude and I said to her in a low voice: 'I understand.'   (202)

Mrs Sáu had prepared another bed for me whilst I was lying on the camp bed in the middle of the house. It was the one she usually used herself. She came to me and said: 'How are you? Move now to this bed which is south-facing, where it will be warmer for you, won't it?' She moved me to this bed. My clothes were soaked in sweat. I had not yet had the opportunity to change them. It was difficult to put up with, but I tried to do so cheerfully. Since the time that the servant had brought me to this house, if the lady moved me, I had to maintain the same position without being able to make any movement, without saying a word, not even to the lady who was caring for me. She tried to talk to me, on no matter what subject, and to attend to me as she wished but I remained completely dumb, unable to say a word, not even a simple 'Thank you'.

(203)

It was not that my heart was insensitive but, finding myself in a new environment, I was asking myself if this lady was harsh and authoritative as are many rich ladies. If this were so I would have found my new situation even more frightening than that of being abandoned in a corner of a bedroom in the presbytery. I was more or less unconscious because of the fever. This made me lose all feeling. The lady came silently, from time to time, to feel my brow and wipe the perspiration which was flowing down my face. She was really surprised not to hear me moan nor complain despite the unhappiness which tormented me. Then, having accidentally touched my back, she said: 'It's important that you change your clothes. Your shirt is drenched with sweat.' She sent someone to bring my clothes from the presbytery, and once I was changed, I felt more comfortable. The lady smiled on seeing me a little happier and asked: 'Do you feel better? You'll eat something now, won't you?' I tried to express my gratitude by smiling and replied: 'Yes.' She rushed to prepare something for me but, unfortunately, when she brought the food, I was once again seized with a violent fever.

(204)

Evening prayer at the church was finished and for a fairly long time I could clearly her the curfew bells. I became delirious from that moment onwards. From time to time, terrified, I called my mother and asked for a drink: 'Mammy, Mammy, give me a drink ... It hurts a lot ... Jesus, Mary, come to help me ...' But, when I opened my eyes to see my mother, and did not see her anywhere. I burst out sobbing and did not stop asking, as at home, 'Where's Mammy? ...'

After the prayers in church, people invaded the house to come and see me, but no one could soothe the pain in my foot, nor comfort my heart of its nostalgia for my mother, nor of my desire to see her again. The more the night advanced, the greater was the fever. I had the feeling that my foot was crushed between the teeth of a fierce beast or thrust into a blazing inferno. Mrs Sau watched over my bed searching

(205)

for any means to ease my pain. She went into the garden from time to time with a lamp in her hand to collect some leaves to massage my foot. But in my delirium I called my mother. She whispered gently into my ear to comfort me: 'My child, your mother is sitting here beside you. Sleep in peace.' These words sometimes brought me out of the delirium. I would open my eyes, look at her and smile fondly at her. She on her part looked on me lovingly and lavished me with caresses. But it was a great sadness for her because, in spite of all her efforts, she could not stop me shivering nor stop the tears which this excessive pain provoked. She could only look at me tenderly in her helplessness and ask me quietly: 'My child what can I do for you?'

From that time she would often use the word 'child' when talking to me when we were alone. In company she used the word '*Câu*'* like everybody else, because she did not want to lay herself open to criticism of her manner of acting towards a child who had been offered to the 'house of God'. It was only at times when I was alone with her that I felt sufficiently at ease to make my wishes known to her. For her part she was very fond of me, and helped me with all her heart, without heed for her tiredness.   (206)

This woman was a widow. She had given birth to six daughters, five of whom were already dead when her husband died in his turn, leaving her alone with the last of her daughters who had just reached seven years. Before the birth of this child she had really wanted and prayed for a boy to continue the line. She had even made a pilgrimage to Our Lady of Perpetual Succour and prayed for this intention, but she brought into the world a frail and disabled little girl who, without the miraculous intervention of Our Lady, would not have survived to this day. This lady's heart, because of this hardship, had become an abyss of bitter sufferings. Instead of acting haughtily towards others as most rich ladies do, she was, on the contrary, rich in sympathy for those who suffered. She welcomed into her house after her husband's death a family which was still pagan. Not content with giving work and the necessities of life, she also helped this family to become children of the holy Church of Jesus Christ. She was loved by all the people of the village. Indeed, most of them at one time or another had benefited from her generosity. As for myself, it was quite natural that she wished to help me, given the wealth of feeling and all the love that was in this lady's heart. She was following quite naturally the attractions of her sensitive heart, without the ulterior motive of finding in me a son who would be later a sort of compensation.   (207)

Did the parish priest deceive himself by thinking that this lady acted in this way so that, in spite of her fatigue, she would, later, gain some consolation? He was not averse to criticising her. People have told me about these criticisms. 'This is not your child; why do you bother yourself with him?' Later, not happy to leave me at her house, he threatened to send me to the house of the wife of the district official. Overwhelmed with sadness as she was, Mrs Sáu had not the heart to look at my sickly body. She did not want to sadden herself more and uselessly. She was also waiting for the parish priest to put his plan into effect. It was already midday and no decision had been taken. If anyone went to remind him about it he could only repeat: 'It's my business. Leave him there. Let him die so that I can bury him. If he's disabled, I'll send him back to his father. It's a strange thing. The people of Bảo-Sơn have   (208)

* The term 'cậu' was used to indicate an aspirant to the priesthood.

different traditions from us. It's strange that for a little brat who has fallen and hurt his knee all the parish is moved. I have been head of this parish for more than ten years and have seen all sorts of handicapped people, and yet no one has shown the slightest pity.'

(209)   That very day at midday, despite all the parish priest's insults, the lady went again to see him and said to him directly:

'Little Van is on the point of dying. He has already lost consciousness several times and is continually delirious. I beg of you to administer to him. If you do nothing to cure him and you allow him to die in such an unjust manner, on your head be it.' Troubled, the parish priest said: 'All right, what do you want to do with him?'

The lady accepted responsibility to care for me until I was cured completely. There was one thing that she dared not say directly to the parish priest, but on her return she allowed the words to escape: 'I believe that the behaviour of this parish priest is totally unjust. Another person's child is not a lump of earth. Even supposing that he deserves to be hated he is not, by that, a stranger. This child's parents, through respectful love for the parish priest, have shown confidence in him in offering their child to him so that he can watch over him, instruct him well and give him sound advice. On the other hand, the child helps the parish by serving at the altar. It is obvious, this being the case, that the

(210)   parish priest should love the child, in place of the parents, with a deep love, even more so after the accident, even supposing that the child was at fault. He has the duty to provide the necessary care, as the parents would, who have handed their responsibility over to him. Who would have suspected that the parish priest could go so far as to treat him as he has done? I find this conduct completely reprehensible. If I have been so affected through pity for this child, imagine how sorry, and with much greater reason, his parents would be if they learned what happened?' She then hid her face and cried. I burst out sobbing myself on seeing that, and I cried with her. People rushed round us to comfort and calm us.

After having taken it upon herself to care for me, the lady sent someone immediately to collect sap from a fig tree for me to drink whilst another went to look for some bear's venom. She sent for a bonesetter who observed that I had a dislocated knee cap and who put my knee back in place. As for the lady, she was at my side every day looking after everything. She noticed, because of the bad treatment I had received from the parish priest, that my interior sorrow caused me

(211)   more pain than my physical suffering. So she always spoke to me very gently. She often asked me: 'Are you still sad?' I was deeply moved each time that she asked me this question, and with tears flowing from my eyes I replied: 'Yes, I am sad ... I am missing my mother.' She caressed

me and tried to comfort me with funny stories.

My Father, it is impossible to describe to you at this moment the feel-ings of sadness and joy which followed one another at that time in my soul. I felt that God would never distance himself from me. He gave me the chalice of a bitter potion, but he did not forget to bring me at the same time some lumps of sugar. He proportioned the suffering to my weakness, mixing it in the tenderness of his love.

An emotional evening   (212)

I spent six months in this lady's house before my leg was cured. My convalescence was so long because the parish priest, not liking to leave me with this lady, obliged me to return to the presbytery to send me afterwards to the bonesetter who had attended to my knee. But in both of these places there was a lack of remedies, and above all there was missing the sweetness of being loved. The result was that my leg did not get better, and to this illness were added still many other 'pains' which reduced me to an extreme scrawniness. Seeing this the parish priest, to get some peace, had to return me to convalesce at the lady's house.

All the time I was at Mrs Sáu's house, she treated me as her child and tried really hard to respond to my slightest desire. If there was a fruit I liked in the garden she allocated the tree to me. It was my privilege to enjoy it and if anyone took a fruit from it, it had to be with my permis-sion. Among all the fruit trees my favourite was a grapefruit tree planted near the house. This tree which produced crossed fruit, half sweet and half sour, had a very special taste and was also very juicy. It was loaded and had I been the only one to eat grapefruit, I could never (213) have managed to eat them all, even during the length of the season. I therefore gave the servants permission to eat them as they wished. Apart from the lady who looked after me, there was also a servant whose job it was to keep the house clean, but ordinarily I had recourse only to the one who had dedicated herself to being my servant, the most venerable, the most loving Mrs Sáu. She once asked me:

'Would you like to tell me why you like the crossed grapefruit so much?'

'Because Mammy, in this fruit as in my life there is a mixture of sweet and sour. The good God knows how to join joy and bitterness in order to make life easier.'

'You are very smart.'

I noticed that when I was happy and called her 'Mammy' her happi-ness seemed complete.

*   *   *

One evening, at the end of autumn, I was overtaken by sadness at the sight of the countryside. I thought of a thousand things of the past: of the time of my childhood with my parents, of those gentle years when I was surrounded with the loving smiles and caresses of my dear Mammy. I thought again of those beautiful, moonlit nights when I played with my little sister Té under the areca palm trees or hid in the clumps of the banana trees ... How beautiful and pleasant all of those (214) things were ... But little by little painful memories came to mind: the moment of separation; the dark days spent in the presbytery; my life as an aspirant to the priesthood, a life full of humiliation and work. There, instead of finding affection, I found only miserly hearts, sullen faces and cruel hands. Very often, and simply for following a higher ideal which contrasted with the bad example of those around me, I have been an object of ridicule, beaten and abandoned by my companions. Oh! what sadness for my heart, whose beating mingled with the rustling of the leaves of the banana trees shaken by the autumn wind from the other side of the veranda.

Moved to tears, I succeeded in calming myself and looked for a means of clearing my mind of these sad thoughts. I turned towards the camp bed nearby where the lady was preparing some medicine for me. I never suspected that this sight would move me further. It is true to say that all her attention, all her heart was concentrated on the bottle which (215) she was holding in her hand. She stopped from time to time to pour some liquid and then plugged the neck of the bottle with her finger and gathered the smallest fragments of leaf which remained on the filter. She then continued the process. This action touched me deeply. I thought to myself: 'If my own mother were doing this for me, I am certain that she could not do it with more care than this widow. My God! Why does this woman love me so much?' I would never have found such a tender love if God had not put in her heart a little of his merciful love! Being unable to control myself any longer, I burst out sobbing and lowered my head to cry. The lady came close to me and asked me, gently: 'My child, why are you crying?' She asked me the same question three or four times, but the more she questioned me, the more I cried; so much so that her words of comfort were drowned in my sobs. Perhaps she thought I was very sad. Seeing that I could not reply she kept silent. She was standing and looking as if to discover the reasons for my tears and then, sitting beside me, she held my head (216) against her breast, comforted me and offered me these words of consolation: 'If you are in pain, why don't you tell me? Are you suffering because there is something which displeases you, or because you miss your mother? Whatever it is, why don't you say?' I was unable to hold back my tears to reply to her in spite of her repeated questioning.

However, understanding her feelings very well, to each of her questions I could only shake my head and say: 'No.' Later I succeeded in controlling myself to say to her: 'I would have liked to express my feelings, Mrs, but I could not speak.' 'In spite of everything,' she said to me, 'it is not appropriate to cry. It is not too good that a boy who has been given to God should be always snivelling. If Sáu* knew this she would make fun of you.'

Then, getting up, she took me from the bed, saying: 'That's enough! Don't cry any more. Your foot will soon be cured. You will be able to run and jump as you please. Your sadness will disappear, you will begin again your studies, and later you will become a priest. It will be marvellous!' At these words she leant forward to press her cheek against my forehead. After getting me out of bed, she smiled, patted my cheek with her hands and returned in silence to her medicaments. I continued to (217) cry and even sobbed occasionally.

That evening when lowering my mosquito net, she alluded to what had happened in the afternoon. I asked her to wait until the following day to speak about it because there were many visitors present. We were alone the following day at midday at the time when everyone was working in the fields, and the children were playing outside. She brought up the subject and asked me why I had cried. Seeing that she was really very good to me and afraid of hurting her by not telling her everything, I told her frankly what had so moved me the previous evening. She listened to my words with the greatest attention as if she were listening to a very interesting novel. She sometimes looked at me tenderly and I saw that there were tears flowing from her eyes. I read in this her astonishment in noticing that I was not an ordinary child. She would often say, afterwards, to people who came to visit me: 'I find it very strange. I have never seen a child with so much vigour, and yet so easily moved.' On seeing my (218) conduct and piety she could not doubt that I had a very wise and virtuous mother. She asked me questions now and again about my family, and I was happy on each occasion to speak of the so-sweet times of my early childhood when I was loved and indulged by my parents. I spoke to her of the little amusing stories of my infancy close to a loving mother. I spoke to her many times and above all of the tender and compassionate love of the Blessed Virgin for me. I said to her, proudly, 'My mother loved the Blessed Virgin very much. She taught me, from the day that I was able to speak, to recite the rosary ...' This moved the lady very much, and she said to me: 'Truthfully, I must consider it as a special favour that the Blessed Virgin has given me the happiness to welcome and provide for you for some months.'

---

* Her daughter.

(219) Father, I would be happy to speak unceasingly of the tender love which has come to me from the heart of this widow. I noticed the day that I saw the film *Marie Louise*,* about a young French victim of the war who was a refugee in Switzerland, that her sad fate was similar to my own, but her misfortune enabled her to enter into surroundings no less happy than those of her family. My Father, at that time it was also given to your humble child to leave a place of sadness to live in happier surroundings. My life as an aspirant to the priesthood would not have known a single day of consolation without that, and if God had not sent me a kind hand to support me, those days of suffering could have made me unhappy for all my life. I offer to God a 'Thank you' overflowing with love, to praise without end the tenderness of his merciful heart. Each step that I take today reminds me of the charitable hands and generous heart which helped me at that time. I offer these steps to God so that they may become a perpetual 'Thank you' before his throne.

(220) This lady loved me with a motherly love which I responded to with the love of a child. This two-fold close love showed itself all the time, so much so that people called us 'mother and child'. In fact it was reasonable to refer to us in this way. Today this dear mother has already left for heaven, but my heart overflows no less in gratitude. Each time I think of her, I see again in my mind all her marks of affection, the gentleness of her delicate hands, and I have the feeling that her voice still resonates in my ear. In a word, all these engaging souvenirs remain deeply engraved in my memory ... Oh! my dear Mammy, when I shall be in heaven with you, I shall make known to you the depth and the sincerity of my love for you, and the pain I feel in being separated from you. However, I am certain now that you are in heaven, that you understand me better than anyone; you understand that I must belong to God more than to the world, and you will no longer be sad to hear me say: 'I must follow Jesus.' On the contrary, you must be pleased, since I have gained the mastery over those lively attachments which seethe in my puny body. Mammy, this exile is really sorrowful. Please help me before the throne of God to fight with courage to the end.

(221) ## Running away

Regarding my studies, all I possessed at the age of twelve years was my certificate of primary studies. Father Joseph Nhã, the parish priest, thought that that was sufficient for me. He no longer authorised me to continue my studies. From then onwards he obliged me to spend all my

---

* A film directed by Leopold Lindtberg in 1945.

time in manual work to make up for the time he had allotted to me to go to school. As I said earlier, there was nothing more unjust than this forced labour ... The parish priest therefore paid no more heed to my priestly future. All he wanted was to profit from my services for such work as cooking the rice, washing the dishes, sweeping the house, cleaning his spittoon and chamber pot, washing the linen, brushing down his horse and, from time to time, accompanying him when he was going somewhere and carrying his pipe*, etc ...

I found this shameful and hurtful, because in these circumstances my priestly vocation was nothing more than pure irony. I made so bold therefore as to ask the parish priest to send me back to my parents. This was my reasoning: 'I entered God's house not to be a servant boy, but to follow God's call which has resounded in my soul. I want to become (222) a priest, and it is solely in this hope that my parents consented to our separation and to confide me to you. Why do you now force me to break my back in your service?

'If you think I have not got the aptitude to become a priest then allow me to return to my parents: there is no shortage of work for me in my own house. Why should I stay to work here?' Not only did the parish priest not agree to my demands but he gave me such a volley of blows that I believed that my buttocks had been completely skinned. From that moment he demonstrated greater cruelty towards me, considering me as being inferior to a house dog. It was from that moment that I began to draw up plans to escape from this presbytery of Hữu-Bằng.

First escape

I had taken the resolution to run away for the sole purpose of return-ing to my parents to let them know of the life of forced labour that I was leading in the presbytery at Hữu-Bằng, and to ask them to send me to another parish where the parish priest was not given over to alcohol, (223) and where the rules would be carefully observed. I realised that the name 'house of God' was meaningless when applied to this presbytery. This holy place had been made into a place which had an ambience of alcohol and impurity. The personnel of this house had no longer any respect for law or personal dignity.

I noticed that after the inauguration of the parish the parish priest in effect devoted himself every day to alcohol, gambling and allowed himself too close relations with women and young girls. He became a new Solomon ... allowing the bad example from the presbytery to

---

* Water pipe; an earthenware or lacquer container.

spread further and further, and thereby creating improper customs which were a source of discord and jealousy. I also observed that the more the parish priest had affection for young girls, the more cruel he was towards us, and above all to those who did not like to allow these young ladies to come freely to visit him, even in places forbidden by the rule concerning women and young girls. Those who did not respect these 'pretty ladies' were considered by the parish priest as enemies.

(224) Moreover, those who had accidentally surprised him in unworthy behaviour with these young girls were regarded as Satan's spies, and he absolutely forbade them access to his bedroom. Hard luck to anyone who dared to show disrespect to these girls in his presence! They were cursed as being unworthy to wash their skirts.

But, Father, among the fifteen boys living at the presbytery, there were those brave enough to stand up and disapprove of this reprehensible behaviour. As for me, I can proudly state that I showed my total disapprobation and disagreement regarding these uncalled-for actions. It is for this reason that, amongst the young boys at the presbytery, nobody deserved less than me to be dragged through the mud. From time to time I further received a volley of blows for showing a lack of respect for these young girls. As regards the insults, it is impossible to reproduce them. The parish priest never used bad language, as many people do, but his reproaches were no less gross and scornful.

(225) I do not know why I more than anyone else had witnessed at the presbytery the bad deeds between the parish priest and these girls. Normally I would not have seen them, because I would keep out of sight and would not spy on the behaviour of anyone. I also think that the parish priest knew that I wished to be discreet. I believe therefore that God wished to show these things clearly to me to make me understand priests better, to lead me to suffer cheerfully and to pray a lot for them. I am not a priest and never shall be; however, it is not certain that among the ordained priests there are many of them who understand their dignity as well as I do. God has awarded me, for this reason, the role of colleague of priests rather than the dignity of the priesthood. I speak here in harmony with the ideas of little Thérèse. In truth, God has also made me to understand that to help priests is a very necessary role. Indeed, once a priest is lost, the world can only fall into a pitiable

(226) state. Consequently I prayed especially, every day, for my parish priest. I offered to God all my work, and all the insults I had to put up with from his hands, so that God would give him the grace of conversion. On the other hand, I earnestly begged the Blessed Virgin to do everything to help me escape from this disreputable place. Having to suffer a great deal at the hands of the parish priest I was very tempted, because of my displeasure, to give way to anger and to make known all the evil

concerning him that I had seen with my own eyes. In those difficult times it was as if my Mother Mary had been there to comfort me and make me forget. I felt the grace of a force in my soul which extinguished completely the fire of anger. I said to myself: 'What good would it do to speak? It is necessary to put up with everything, so that his priestly dignity can be safeguarded and produce fruit in souls. If because of one word his authority was despised, it would be better to ask God to destroy the world. How could I then wish to go searching for souls to bring them back to God?'

There was meanwhile a squabble at the presbytery between the parish priest and a young man. The only reason was, again, young girls. (227) This young man was in love with one of those who assiduously frequented the presbytery. She was the parish priest's favourite,* and she was normally considered as the most prominent in any meetings. Unfortunately, the young man's ambition was reported to the parish priest. The latter then used his status to denigrate the young man so that the young girl lost all respect for him. This process brought to light the jealousy of the parish priest, who loved this girl as the 'child of the house', the expression used by people to indicate in a delicate manner, an attentive interest that a priest cannot allow himself with his spiritual children. Our young lady was liked simply for her physical appearance. To tell you the truth, to me she appeared boorish in her words and behaviour. She also had this characteristic: she was as stupid as a donkey!

When I was admitted to the school at Hữu-Bằng, I saw her seated in the last row of the Infants' class, and until the day when I sat the examination she was still sitting in the same row. Seeing this, her father (228) obliged her to look after the buffaloes. This girl's family often had the honour of receiving the parish priest who went there to gamble and, each time, the girl stood beside him to wave the fan and bring him drinks. When she was small the parish priest probably liked her for her ingenuousness, but now that she has grown up and knows how to bewitch, it is less probable that it is still for her naiveté that he continues to like her. The parents were respected by the parish priest because they joined him for card-playing, and the young lady was spoiled by the parish priest. So it was no surprise that she adopted a proud and threatening air, that of a queen. She even defied the parish priest. In all circumstances she had only to give the parish priest a furtive look and it reduced his grandeur to nothing. I have no need to invent anything. I am telling the whole truth. I even saw her once smack the parish priest. Although this happened in a corner of the bedroom, it suffices

---

* She was the daughter of a village dignitary.

to prove that he who had allowed himself to be so intoxicated by such a beauty had really fallen low.

(229)   Because he had been deprived of his friend, the young man, furious, decided to revenge himself well and truly on the parish priest. He spoke up in protest against the unjust conduct of the priest towards the boys of the presbytery. He strongly encouraged them to agree among themselves to complain to the bishop's house about the abuse of alcohol, and the relations with girls who visited the presbytery, which I have already alluded to. I then truly felt like someone desperate for sleep who had found a mat to stretch out on. I decided to organise myself this time so that the parish priest would be suspended from his functions, and I would be able to escape easily from the house. It is not necessary to think that the complaints against the parish priest could be summarised on one or two pages. All being angry with him, each one tried hard to report all of his actions, all of his words. To tell the truth, there were fifteen reports, as many as there were boys, carrying accusations against the priest. I myself, annoyed and inflamed, drew up a long report relating, amongst other things, that I had twice seen the parish priest allowing himself improper actions with young girls. Finally, I asked Monsignor absolutely to forbid young girls to have

(230)   access to the presbytery. I also cited the names of corrupt boys who knew how to flirt and become infatuated with girls. Once the reports were finished, each one signed his own; all were put into a big envelope and one of us was delegated to take the document to the bishop's house.

Without really knowing how, and before we realised anything, someone who was spying on us grabbed the secret letter and took it to the parish priest. We were very worried, anticipating that in no way would the parish priest miss the opportunity to create problems for us. It was therefore decided to organise ourselves for an escape that very day, and we were quite prepared to use force against anyone who would obstruct our path.

Running away did not appeal to the large number of boys who lived in parishes nearby, since they were afraid of trouble once returned to their homes, but because the leader and his council were obviously in favour, and because they were smart and resolute in their decision, they

(231)   advanced tempting reasons which dragged the others along. Personally, I was not feeling too happy. For some unknown reason I now felt a lot of sympathy for the parish priest. I regretted having made my report. This regret did not stem from any fear resulting from the seizure of the documents and their reaching the priest's hands since, even before that, I felt a kind of unease. I was sorry for the parish priest. I feared he might be punished.

After the whole business had been revealed to the parish priest the ringleaders took the decision to run away without delay. I anticipated that things might become more complicated, and I wished to lie low for two or three weeks at my adoptive mother's at Bảo-Sơn. I would wait there and see how things unfolded. From there I intended to return to my parents. The leader of the opposition who came from Tử-Nê, a village close to my own, promised to accompany me to my home to explain to my parents why it was necessary to come home. Finding his reasons attractive, I agreed to the suggestion. He then said to me: 'It is absolutely essential that before we leave we find a means of retrieving (232) the accusations which are on the table in the parish priest's bedroom, and then we must decide what to do with them.' In the event, some days later we were able to recover the envelope, thanks to the parish priest's favourite young girl. We were very pleased indeed, and I do not know why the parish priest had not opened the envelope which was still completely sealed. No matter: the moment of decision had arrived.

The parish priest threatened us forcibly when he noticed the disappearance of the letter. He even engaged the imposing presence of the old catechist of the presbytery to intimidate us and bring us to our senses.

Speaking of this old catechist, I must admit frankly that we feared him more than anyone, not because he had an impressive personality, but because of his legendary cruelty, with cane in hand. Once the catechist was angry, the victim became like a lump of inanimate and insensible earth that he would hit and hit without counting the blows, until he himself had no strength left. We had a lot of respect for him (233) because he followed the rule to the letter: that is, even if he drank a little too much, he always behaved correctly towards the young girls. On the question of young girls visiting the presbytery, he was in disagreement with the parish priest.

Who would have suspected that, one day, this man would become the prey of the devil of impurity? It was, without doubt, alcohol and the loose life led at the presbytery which led to his downfall. The parish priest invited the catechist to his room for a chat. We called this interview 'the meeting of Herod and Pontius Pilate', and with good reason. Formerly these two men did not get on: they were now allies in perfect solidarity against us, the little hooligans. The parish priest said to the old catechist: 'I have lost a considerable amount of money, and some very important papers which were in an envelope addressed to Monsignor. Make enquiries among the boys to see if one of them is the guilty party ... Personally, I suspect Van ...'

Heavens, why did he conclude it was me? Having heard this from our (234) espionage committee, I was shaken, not knowing why the parish priest had accused me of such a large theft. I thought that I would be interrogated and thoroughly beaten because of the affair, but I prepared to put up with everything. I was able to understand, later, the parish priest's secret motive. He had wished to drive me away many times, especially after I had twice seen him embracing a tertiary and young girls. It would be too shameful for him to advance this reason for getting rid of me. On the other hand, if he sent me away without a reason my parents would demand an explanation and he would not know what to say. In fact, to dismiss someone from God's house is seriously to damage the family's reputation. He tried therefore to bring this accusation of theft into play, with the secret motive of showing me the door and getting some peace for himself. Subsequently, if my parents came demanding explanations, he could answer them: 'It is because he has stolen.'

(235)   The parish priest continued: 'I notice that, at present, they are very badly-behaved and have no respect for anyone, sometimes I am ashamed of them ...' These words upset the old catechist who was responsible for our education. It was an indirect reproach to him for not knowing how to educate us, and for allowing our recalcitrant behaviour. The old catechist was not slow in protesting immediately: 'If that's the situation it is largely our fault. If the superiors are not unjust, the subordinates will not revolt. I notice that in many respects their behaviour is good, whereas you regard it as being impolite. Nevertheless, their stance is an honourable one. Why do you oblige them to submit, even to young girls for whom you have a particular affection? I am in total disagreement with you on this point and I reject it. The fault is yours alone.' The parish priest blushed considerably. The young girls present withdrew, little by little, to the back. Only those two remained, except for the spy who was hidden under the camp bed. A moment later the parish priest turned the conversation round to the subject of alcohol, and he brought out a big bottle which he offered to the catechist. The atmosphere became friendly but there was no more

(236)   question of little hooligans. The catechist, before going to his bedroom, said to the parish priest: 'I'm with you. The business that you have just spoken to me about, I will look into it.' He flicked his nails, touched his ear and added: 'Little Van? ... I am very suspicious of him myself because he has villain's eyes ... Perhaps? Nevertheless, during my time here, I have never found anything reprehensible in his regard ... Naturally you mention him to speed up the process ... Of course. Let me deal with the matter ...' Then he left, carrying with him his large bottle of alcohol.

The old catechist called us to his room that very evening, first for a general inquisition and then for individual questioning, where each one under his searching eyes would have to answer concerning the sum of money and the document stolen from the parish priest. The former was pure chicanery. He had introduced the element of money to give more importance to the affair, and with the intention of more easily conceal-ing the accusations levelled against him and avoid having to discuss them. But we were still more cunning than he. 'The crafty old man has more than one trick in his bag.'* But the old man must know the saying: 'Those who are born after us must be feared.' We met together first of (237) all, before responding to the call to the catechist's room. Our leader gave us this order: 'If the catechist questions us together, let me answer the questions. If he questions you individually, reply that you know nothing.' Then, walking in front, he led us to the old catechist's room.

The parish priest came down slowly and stood behind the house, impatient to hear what was going to happen. The old catechist, with a serious demeanour, walked among us with a questioning glance before getting down to business. The silent atmosphere became heavier and heavier. Although we were all well up to date in the affair, each one of us was curious to know what clever trick the old catechist was going to pull. After walking for about ten minutes, he began by insulting us in a thunderous voice, and then harangued us for fifteen minutes on the house rules which forbade this and that. It was all presented in a monotonous tone and in an angry voice, which was very disagreeable. Then he came to the matter of the stolen money. He said, still with a (238) serious demeanour and in an angry tone: 'The parish priest has just lost a large amount of money and some important papers ...' Then, after a short pause, he continued: 'I already know all about it. I only need a quick glance at the guilty one's face to know who it is.' And whilst speak-ing he directed his piercing gaze on us. We looked at him steadily with both eyes without showing the least sign of emotion.

After this indirect questioning our chief stood up, angrily, to say to him: 'Sir, allow me to reply. If the parish priest has had money stolen, kindly question the young girls who usually frequent his bedroom. As for us, it is such a long time since we set foot in his room that we cannot be implicated in the matter. Our reply is, therefore, that we know nothing about it. As for the important papers, why should we have taken them? If the parish priest has lost them, again, interrogate the young girls. For us, we have only our own personal papers.' At that (239) exact moment the parish priest, who was standing hidden behind the house, shouted at the catechist: 'Enough, enough ...' Then, running in front of the house, he entered the old catechist's room and dismissed us with these words: 'What's the good in speaking to this pack of dogs? Enough! Get out!' We went out very noisily into the courtyard. The

---

*   Vietnamese saying: *Lão mưu đa kế ... Hậu sinh khả úy.*

parish priest again stayed a long time in the catechist's room, but I do not know what they talked about.

After the episode of the stolen money and the confrontation of the opposing parties there was even greater need to hide. When we saw the shadow of a young girl come to visit the parish priest we got together to shout: 'Thief! Dirty Thief! Go away, otherwise, when money disappears, you will again put the blame on us.'

Where, therefore, was the money? Had it really been stolen? Any money there was had already been used on alcohol, or in the pockets of the young girls, or on the card table. What remained to steal? The parish priest again overwhelmed us with heavy work, but we decided to do nothing about it. Rather, we demanded to be treated according to (240) the regulations for candidates to the priesthood. We demanded that the presbytery be purged of the gang of girls, otherwise, we would leave. The parish priest, through his intermediary the old catechist, asked us to lower our voices for fear that these serious accusations might be heard by some Christians, to his great shame. The catechist, once again using his imposing authority, threatened to strike us. But we were exasperated and shouted: 'Down with the catechists!' On hearing this the parish priest in his turn threatened us: 'If any one of you succeeds in running away, I shall have you all put in prison.' The parish priest was very important at that time, and prison was a hand he could have played. That is why we dared not leave openly: but we had to find a means of escaping freely. It was therefore decided: we would leave the parish one day, but before our departure we would give the girls a lesson they would never forget. The suspicions which had fallen on Van were forgotten. We had even discovered the parish priest's spy. (241) Because he was sorry for his crime and cried bitterly, instead of condemning him to death or throwing him into the pond with a stone around his neck, we had pity on him, and condemned him only to obtain a sufficient number of batons for us which would serve as weapons to attack the young girls. He was made conversant with all our secret plans but with this condition: if our plan was uncovered he would have to submit to the punishment decided for his first betrayal.

Father, do not think that this band of boys was incapable of murder. Truly, those that our major-general had condemned to death had good reason to fear. Orders were given and carried out with fear for no one. That is why our company became stronger and stronger, and that of the parish priest was weakening. Our chief had drawn up a plan of escape with Ngọc-Bảo as the rallying point. We would leave in the course of the afternoon, and after having spent a night at Ngọc-Bảo the group would disperse the following day, each one heading for his home village. The secret letter was in our leader's hands, and he would give it to Monsignor when passing through Bắc-Ninh.

We were all satisfied with this well-thought-out plan. Our man had   (242)
anticipated that this stratagem would divert any pursuit by our adversary, and even if he sent someone after us, it would be difficult to find
the leader, and thus everyone's escape would be guaranteed. The
farewell to the young girls had been carefully prepared. Our arma-
ments were entirely home-made. One had made a rubber catapult,
another had collected a pile of little stones as projectiles. Every evening
there were preparatory exercises in a corner of the forest which served
as a parade ground. I was given the job of making a water-jet, and the
preparation of chemical water to supply it.

I must mention here one of my jobs at the presbytery. I specialised in
looking after the ducks, and so I was honoured with the title of 'admiral'.
There were fifteen ducks under my command. Each day after Mass, the
admiral went to the farmyard, opened the door, reviewed the troops and
then chased them towards the marsh where they could find food. Come
evening, about five o'clock, the admiral had to change into his sailor's
uniform, all provided by nature, and lead his flotilla of ducks to the
moorings. He was so poor that he had only his sun-tanned skin but, being
responsible for such a large troop, the admiral should have been given a
small craft by his superiors to make his work easier. But he had received   (243)
nothing. It was therefore necessary to paddle unclothed every evening to
lead the ducks to their shelter. In summer there was no problem but in
winter ... all the admiral could do was snivel. It was understood that if
the admiral lost a duck he was summoned to appear before the top brass
to have a medal pinned on his hindquarters.* Today when I think of the
title of 'admiral' I have to laugh, but in reality it was blameworthy that
they obliged me to work naked in this manner. From my infancy until
now, it was only in the presbytery at Hữu-Bằng that I was forced to lead
such a life, and I frankly admit that I felt totally ashamed when someone
saw me in my nudity. I often cried because of it. I can never understand
why children find such a state natural. I was much more modest. Perhaps
this was due to my tendency to blush easily.

So, in the offensive against the girls, our chief well understood the
efficacy of jets of chemical water. That is why he encouraged me in my   (244)
work and gave me a reinforcement of four men from the cavalry so that
the work could progress quickly and efficiently. Normally these four
lads were employed in cleaning the bicycles so, in the village, they were
known as the 'cavalry troop'. They were under my orders during the
battle. When everything was in place we issued this ultimatum to the
girls:

---

* 'Pinned on his hindquarters': to be punished.

1. Henceforth, no visits to the parish priest during forbidden times.
2. If you break this prohibition your backs will be broken.

The young girls, always counting on the parish priest's affection, did not stop threatening us. Their reply to our ultimatum was to become outraged, and they challenged us: 'All we have to do is give you sweets, and not one of you would dare to do anything.'

Without saying more, we decided that that very evening we would give them a good hiding and make our escape the following day. Even if the girls were defiant, they thought it prudent to remain on their guard. Among the five best known there were two who went to the pres-

(245)   bytery every day to give the priest a massage. The other three paid two to four visits per week. Usually, apart from the parish priest, there were still a few adolescent boys who received these girls in some corner of the presbytery. But the movement afoot to purge the house of these girls proving very strong forced them to turn tail and follow us. The five young ladies arrived that very evening. Their arrival usually coincided with the commencement of evening prayer in church. One would carry chicken soup, another a bottle of alcohol, a third some cakes, etc. They came to serve the parish priest. I say to serve the parish priest, but it was also to eat with him. This service lasted late into the night, after which they returned to their homes. On those evenings when there were only one or two of them the parish priest allowed them to sleep in the presbytery. When there were priests visiting they arrived later and left earlier, according to a prearrangement. I do not know if this partic- ular evening they had informed the parish priest of the threats they had received, but we knew in advance that they intended to return late to their homes. We went as usual to pray fervently in the church, and then

(246)   we made our preparations. After the prayers the leader assigned each his responsibility. In one hour, everything was in place and, in accor- dance with the command, each one had to remain at his post and wait for the girls to come out and then attack them without warning. The place of ambush was no more than fifteen metres square, but it was very dangerous, and the girls would have needed wings to escape. The passage from the church to the presbytery had two doors, an external one between the church and the parlour, and an internal one between the parlour and the presbytery rooms. According to the rule, women and young girls were forbidden to go through this door. There was a solid wall round the parlour which made the place even more danger- ous. No matter what prayers to heaven, once between these walls escape was impossible.

It was only at eleven o'clock that the girls thought of withdrawing. As they walked they spoke in loud voices. As soon as they had cleared the

interim door a rope device quickly closed it. Then a very sturdy boy,   (247)
armed with a stick with nails attached, posted himself to block their
passage. The young girls on seeing the door close in such an unexpected manner, exclaimed faintly, 'Heavens!' They were afraid to speak
loudly. The leader gave a brisk order: 'Attack!' At that moment a hail of
projectiles hit the girls, while the water hose sprayed their clothes copiously, without neglecting their faces. Unfortunately one of them,
opening her mouth to cry out whilst neglecting to protect her mouth
with her hand, was hit full in the face by a strong jet of water which
respected no one in the darkness. She had just been eating peanuts,
and had not had time to rinse out her mouth. During these initial
moments the young ladies would have very much liked to have cried
out for help, but of necessity they had to keep their mouths closed.
Those who had already tasted this indefinable liquid felt like vomiting
and spat loudly, which caused us to laugh so hysterically that we had no
strength to fire. Our leader, who was directing operations, spotting the   (248)
danger of this situation gave the order for a new attack. He opened the
door so that the girls retreated towards the church. Our young ladies,
thinking that everything was over, cried out and cursed us as they
guided each other to the door. But they fell over the trap of ropes
which had been stretched by this 'pack of dogs' which they had been
cursing so loudly. Their legs were tangled in the ropes and they fell
backwards, hurting themselves on the thorns which had been scattered
all over their route. Our leader cried: 'Charge!' The infantry faced the
girls calmly, and with their short sticks delivered a volley of blows. It
was not easy. The girls crawled forward, tried to rise, and shone their
torches into the eyes of the attackers to blind them and stop the blows.
Then three torches were shattered and the other two were seized.
Deprived of light, the young ladies could no longer offer resistance. We
had two electric lamps, and by shining them on our victims' faces we   (249)
were able to see in what a pitiable state they found themselves. Their
faces were filthy, and they were impregnated with chemical water from
head to foot. One of them was shedding many tears as a sign of repentance, as if the day of judgement had arrived. It was a really sorry
sight . . .!

Nobody had the heart to break their backs. We were waiting for only
one thing: that they ask for forgiveness. Nevertheless, the admiral
arrived with the cavalry and, pointing the hose pipe in their direction,
threatened them: 'If one of you makes a sound, you will be made to
drink this fragrance immediately.' They maintained total silence, not
daring to move. Then, panting, they tried to rise. Our leader, in his
turn, said: 'If one of you tries to escape she will be lamed immediately.'
They got up and stood together to await sentence. The chief delivered   (250)

a short speech in a statesmanlike manner on the subject of respect towards the personnel of God's house at all levels. He forbade them from then on to visit places forbidden by the rule. Then, shining an electric light in their faces, he obliged them to kneel down and recite 'penitential litanies', that is to say, one of them mentioned successively the names of the boys of the presbytery, and the other four replied: 'Forgive us our sins.' When they had finished, our leader gave them a 'plenary indulgence' and gave them leave to go. They dispersed.

They had hardly left when we heard these words: 'The parish priest is coming! The parish priest is coming!' We opened the doors as quickly as possible, and passed by the brick-paved courtyard to the dormitory. The parish priest, certainly understanding that his dear girls had met with some misfortune, came to the door with his stick in his hand. He demanded in a loud voice: 'What are you rascals doing, not yet in bed?'

(251)   He also noticed the disagreeable smell which filled the place because in covering his nose he continued: 'It's too strong! What have they done to . . .?' He was without his lamp, which had been broken by the attackers when in the hands of the young girls. He did not know what to do to get some light.

The young girls dared not yet return to their parents. They remained hidden somewhere near the church. Since their persons gave off such an odour what explanations could they give? It was impossible. Once they realised that the parish priest had come out, they returned to knock at the door, calling him with loud voices: 'Father, Father, they have half killed us! These devil's henchmen have done a terrible thing.' The parish priest opened the door to listen to the stories of the young ladies. They poured all their vexation and anger into the ears of their dear parish priest, to such an extent that the latter, furious, ran to the house to summon us to the yard to give us a thrashing. But all to no avail. Father broke two canes, but only in striking the bricked sides of

(252)   the veranda. However, we all moaned, begged for mercy and cried. In truth, when the parish priest called us to the yard to whip us, some boys reacted by proposing to beat him up and then escape without delay. But in respect for the dignity of the priesthood most rejected this idea. On the other hand, slyly availing ourselves of the opportunity, we went into the courtyard and each of us stretched out below the brick veranda to deaden the blows. As it was dark he struck out blindly at anybody he saw stretched out, but before having finished beating the seven boys, he had already broken two canes. He was out of breath and trembling violently. He was unable to say a word. He stood there for a moment, his hands on his hips, breathing painfully. Then he ordered those who had already been beaten to go and find another cane. They said 'Yes' and then withdrew to the dormitory. Those who had not yet been beaten also

withdrew, but in an orderly fashion by the back way. There remained before the parish priest the admiral escorted by two cavalrymen.

We could not stop laughing at that moment, because from outside we could hear the cries of the girls: 'Father, beat this pack of dogs to death, especially Van.' Everybody asked themselves, spontaneously, why these (253) young ladies hated Van so much. They also all competed to demonstrate their sympathy. Deep down they all knew the reason for this animosity. He was the one who had invented the chemical water weapon which had made them lose any enthusiasm for the combat, and especially had prevented them for crying for help during the most difficult times. To tell the truth, in this victory gained over the girls loved by the parish priest, nearly all of the credit must go to Admiral Nguyễn-Tân-Văn and to the four cavalrymen under his command. The young ladies had been overcome by courtesy of the nauseous water squirted on them, rather than by the sticks which had beaten their backs. They hated the one who had launched the water more than all of the others. The parish priest was still waiting, but saw no one bringing him a stick. He noticed also that the number of those who had not yet been caned was reducing little by little. He called me in a loud voice in response to the demands of the young ladies: 'Where are you, Van? Van, come here!' 'Yes, I'm here already.' The admiral, both legs of his trousers still (254) rolled up, went to stand before the parish priest. He had not yet had time to unroll them. He had had, naturally, time to slip a fan of palm pods into his trousers to deaden the blows of the stick in anticipation of tomorrow's escape. Standing before the parish priest, I excused myself:

'Father, I did not strike those girls.'

They shouted from outside:

'He did not hit us but ...'

'You are lying. I had no wish to beat you, you bitches.'

We burst out laughing again. The girls were even more furious, but they did not really know what words to use to describe the indefinable water without embarrassing themselves. It is probable that the parish priest guessed their thoughts and, taking the initiative, he said to me:

'If you did not hit them, what are they moaning about?'

'I assure you I did not hit them.'

The boys behind me and those in the dormitory were all giggling. (255) Finally, perhaps because he was so ashamed, the parish priest rushed towards me to slap me with all his strength, but he only managed to brush the top of my head since I suddenly threw myself to the ground, pretending that I had fallen. I made several twists and dodged into the dormitory. The parish priest almost fell in trying to hit me. The admiral's two aides, seeing the parish priest stagger, cleared off and ran into the dormitory.

It was past midnight, and the families close to the church already knew what had happened. Early the next day, people began to comment in the church grounds about the tale of the boys from the presbytery who, the previous night, had beaten the young girls who used to go and play in the night with the parish priest. The mothers of these young girls gritted their teeth and uttered terrible threats against them, so much so that this episode led the parish priest to pay us a little more respect. We gathered together in the dormitory after our victory to see if anyone had been hurt. We had all escaped from the struggle totally unharmed. On our side there was no damage done but on the side of the parish priest and the girls there was considerable damage:

(256)   three lamps broken in pieces, two lamps seized, and a parish priest out of breath and exhausted for having tried to defend the girls.

The battle continued until the following day. In the morning, no one wanted to get up to beat the drum to announce the angelus. We told ourselves that we were all sick, for the good reason that during the night the parish priest had beaten us so cruelly that we were unable to get up. At the time for Mass there was no one to serve it. Our leader's reply to the request of the parish priest was: 'Call last night's girls to serve it for you. As far as we are concerned, our bones are broken and we can't get up.' It was finally the old servant, the doorkeeper, who had to go to serve the Mass. As for us, it was only later in the day that we got up and said our prayers.

After his Mass the parish priest, armed with his cane, came again to say to us: 'Who among you dares to claim to be ill?' We had closed the door securely to stop him entering. Powerless, he had to take his cane

(257)   back to his room, not daring to tell us off too loudly for fear of being heard by people, and thus losing his reputation. The old catechist, who had been away for a few days, returned towards the middle of the morning. He initially expressed his annoyance with the parish priest when he was made familiar with the events, but after a one-to-one conversation, and recalling the big bottle of alcohol of a few days previously, he changed his mind and sided with the parish priest. He immediately called the old cook and with the intention of frightening us he sent him to cut a bundle of canes as thick as a thumb. He gave us this warning: 'Whoever is not up by midday will not eat. Any reasonable person will go and apologise immediately to the parish priest. Anybody who stays in bed will 'eat eels'.*

We were given until two in the afternoon to accept these conditions. No one wanted to respond, the door remained locked and we slept until half past nine. Those who did not sleep kept guard for those who

---

*   This is a figurative way of describing strokes of the cane.

did. At half past nine we went as usual to the refectory. Seeing the only place laid was that of the old catechist, we asked the old servant in a harsh manner:

'Why is our meal not ready?' (258)

'The parish priest says that those who don't work don't eat.'

'The parish priest really said that?'

In the meantime the parish priest and the old catechist arrived. The parish priest shouted at us: 'Now that they are hungry, this pack of dogs is no longer ill. You who are sick, go back to bed. You who are not ill must first of all clean out the stable, and then I will feed you.'

The parish priest had hardly finished this sales talk when, all together, we returned noisily to the dormitory. There we each grabbed a stick and returning to the refectory, we banged on the table saying, as far as I can remember: 'We must be fed! We are not a pack of dogs who can be treated as you like, and fed or killed as you wish ... We have left our parents and have come here to become priests. If you can feed us, do so. If you can't, allow us to return to our families ... You have not got the right to treat us as you do. We have already done a great deal of work for the presbytery. Now that we are ill you must look after us and give us medical help. Why do you still refuse to give us food?' Then our leader gave us this order: 'My friends, don't be afraid! Let's take (259) this cooking pot of rice and throw it into the well, so that they can have a go at sleeping without food.' The pot was grabbed immediately and thrown noisily into the well. There was a real scrum of bodies. After having made a mess of the kitchen we rushed to the parish priest's kitchen, and we even threw his little cooking pot of rice, and the other pots on the fire, into the pond. The old cook and his assistant, being threatened with a beating, fled to the parish priest's bedroom.

This destruction over, we intended to go to the old catechist to give him a beating until his bones were broken. But after having first locked his door, he had entrenched himself in a corner of his bedroom. We knocked on the door, threatening to kill him. Some among us, normally calm, had become furious and threatened to set fire to the house if the catechist did not agree to come out. Sitting against the bottom of the wall, he began to laugh stupidly and to apologise. He said to us: 'Come (260) on, calm down. Why are you getting so worked up? The parish priest spoke as he did for a joke. If there's no rice ready, some can be cooked. Nobody is forbidding you to eat ...' Whilst saying this, he handed us the key to the store room through the window slats and continued: 'Here's the rice store-room key. Ask the servant to take some rice and cook it. Try to calm down, otherwise ...' Luckily for him, he knew how to speak self-effacingly, otherwise we would have crippled him that day. As for the parish priest, he maintained a total silence, no more adopting a domineering posture and ranting and raving against these mischievous lads who had become almost dangerous.

Honestly, I would never have thought us capable of carrying out our leader's orders with such enthusiasm. Most of us were twelve years of age at most: I was only ten. The five oldest were between sixteen and twenty years. However, once enraged, any force would have retreated (261)   before us: otherwise the only thing left to us would have been death. In truth, we still had right on our side. Furthermore, no matter what the consequences, we feared nothing.

The meal had been delayed that morning until eleven o'clock. Once it was finished, the leader gave us the order to pack our bags. There was a total interdiction on anyone, no matter whom, going to the village to say goodbye to parents. It was agreed that, after the benediction of the Blessed Sacrament in the afternoon, we would leave incognito for Ngọc-Bảo. Peace reigned. Neither the parish priest nor the catechist raised his voice against us. Our luggage was deposited secretly in the sacristy before Benediction and, once it was over we entered the sacristy one by one, and, taking our bags already packed, we left as a group, without the knowledge of anyone in the priest's house. As we arrived at the front of the church, we met some nuns talking about the story of the young girls who had been perfumed and beaten the previous night. (262)   Seeing us looking rather suspicious, they asked us:

'Where are you going like that?'

'We are going to Ngọc-Bảo.'

'There's obviously some anniversary tomorrow.'

'Yes.'

It was very difficult for us to reply. Anyway, our leader cut short these questions from the nuns, pretending to scold us: 'You are silly. Let's get a move on. When we get there we still have things to do.' So everyone took to the road quickly, and the sisters understood nothing.

Among the chatting sisters there was one who was very fond of me. Every time she met me she called me over, gave me a cuddle and a few sous. On that day, as I was escaping from the priest's house to return home, it was difficult on meeting her to pretend not to see her, and not to greet her. I decided, therefore, to walk a little slower and, once my companions had disappeared along the path which leaves from the (263)   village, I would retrace my steps and give her at least a greeting. But I did not realise that our leader saw me slowing down in a suspicious manner, and turning round he slapped me saying: 'Quick! You must keep up with the others otherwise when they are far away, you will be snivelling.' The sisters, feeling sorry for me, cried:

'Hey, you there! Why are you hitting him like that? He's very small. Wait for him and then walk together. That will be better.'

'Better? What's with better?'

And, turning towards me, he took me by the elbow and said, to cheer me up: 'What an admiral! As slow as a tortoise! Let's go quickly. If the gang at the house knows what's happening, it's bad luck for us.'

As we ran together I, one of the boys who formerly could keep up with the parish priest's bicycle, on that day I had two leaden feet and I don't know why, but I ran very slowly.

We had already travelled about a quarter of the way to Ngọc-Bảo when, on the point of arriving at the village of Bá-Cầu, we saw some adults running after us and waving their hands to indicate to us to turn back. That convinced us that our flight had been discovered. The leader, still holding me, encouraged us all to run faster. I felt my feet (264) getting heavier. I had already fallen twice, head first. Nevertheless, I forced myself to follow the others and, so as to escape more easily, I resigned myself to sacrificing the bundle of clothes that I was carrying on my shoulder, and I threw them to the side of the road. The leader encouraged us from the front to go faster. Behind, our pursuers called us with loud cries and terrible threats. Out of breath, exhausted, my view obscured with sweat and dust, I could do no more. I was the first, unfortunately, to fall into the hands of our pursuers. They saw me there, trying to raise my head and breathing like a man in agony. Then I lost consciousness. When I regained my senses I felt a new vigour and I began shouting to be released so that I could return to my parents.

That evening, little by little, they had succeeded in capturing all of us (265) but if we had proceeded as the situation demanded, only one or two with weak legs would have been caught. The others could have escaped but because we wished to remain as a body better to defend ourselves, those who had not yet been captured returned voluntarily to the presbytery to join those who had been led there already. When we were taken before the parish priest we did not allow ourselves to show any fear because we were determined to leave. The parish priest was shattered by the turn of events and he announced a change of attitude towards us. He regaled us that evening with peanut nougat, a delicacy that normally the young girls received in abundance, but for us it was on rare occasions, such as this day.*

---

* This account corresponds exactly to what people knew. His parents, not knowing the reasons for his running away, were very unhappy. All Van's father did was to make threatening noises, saying: 'He's nothing but an unruly, badly brought-up boy. Not only does he not want to study but he loves to wander with his friends. I would not be sorry if he were beaten to death. If he comes home I'll cut off his head!' Van got to hear of these words and they plunged him into a deep fear ... [Te.]

Hunted

(266) Our situation became more worrying because of our abortive flight. The promised change of attitude meant that the parish priest became even more cruel in our regard. His unjust behaviour made our relations even more fraught. The oldest packed their bags and demanded to leave. It would gain a reputation for them as 'unfrocked' because, in the minds of Christians of that time, to leave the house of God without a good and evident reason was a sign of failure and dishonour. Moreover, through respect for the dignity of the priesthood, Christians dared not pay attention too readily to wrongs committed by priests at that time. Priests have profited greatly from this respect of the faithful, but as for the faithful who were the victims of wrongdoing, they dared not open their mouths. This has encouraged regrettable abuses by some. But, my Father, be so kind as to dispense me from speaking more of this here, and if it is necessary I shall return to it at another time.

(267) Therefore, those who asked to leave got themselves bad reputations with people of their religion, because it was impossible to convince them that it had been necessary to leave because the parish priest's behaviour was questionable ... The parish priest gave permission immediately to those who asked to leave, but they left in a state of extreme destitution. Do not believe that he gave them sufficient money to return to their families: far from it. Whether this family was far away or close by, they received a few sous, sufficient for a cup of tea. Consequently, those leaving had to sell clothing to obtain a little money for the journey. After a few departures and accompanying problems the parish priest agreed that the older ones who were sensible should be sent immediately to their families. Of fifteen, eight only now remained. Of these eight, three others left a few days later. Now there were only five. Some time previously Father Joseph Nghĩa, the curate of the Thái-Nguyên parish, had written to Father Nhã to ask for the assistance of some boys. The parish priest had promised him four, but now that the 'war' had reduced his numbers by two-thirds, he had to reduce this number by two, and my name did not figure among them. I had wished very strongly that it would, because all the scandals of this disorderly parish were weighing heavily on my soul, (268) and I could no longer resign myself to living always like this. All I could think of was escaping, and I asked the Blessed Virgin each day to come very quickly to help me leave this place of licentiousness. To this end I had even made a novena to Our Lady of Perpetual Succour, asking her to arrange things so that I might go to Thái-Nguyên. The Blessed Virgin granted my prayer by facilitating a completely unexpected and fortuitous opportunity. I considered it as

a blessing to be able to go to Thái-Nguyên, but to enjoy this happiness, I had to put up with many snubs.

The day of the departure of the two boys chosen for this parish coincided with the day when the parish priest took me to serve Mass at Tam-Lộng. That particular day was the feast day of the apostles Saints Peter and Paul, the patron saints of Tam-Lộng, and I had to accompany the parish priest there. It was usually an exceptional favour to accompany the parish priest to a neighbouring parish, and everyone, including me, enjoyed the privilege. The food, and the manner in which one was (269) treated there, was ten times better than in the presbytery, no matter the financial state of the parish. On leaving one could always get some six sous to buy soap, pen and paper or whatever. This time, as always, I was happy to go but, unfortunately, I had to refuse. I had no trousers! At that moment in time my belongings consisted of a single pair of trousers and one tunic. And misfortune was again added to my poverty. The previous afternoon I had to look after the ducks. It rained, and I returned with my clothes completely soaked. It was therefore necessary that I borrow a pair of trousers, the condition being that for two weeks I heat the water in place of the lender. As for my sodden trousers, I washed them and took them to the kitchen so that they would dry more quickly.

I have a foolish wish to laugh in recalling the time when I was so reduced that I had to borrow trousers. But to avoid going naked, it was necessary to put up with all the inconveniences imposed by those who speculate on their trousers. For your amusement let me digress in telling you a story of speculation on trousers. In truth, I could never (270) have imagined a house of God corrupted to such an extent. The priest's house in Hữu-Bằng had become a school in selfishness where no one could rely on anyone, no matter who. Those who had a modicum of humanity, of charity or of virtue were ignored. They were no longer paid any attention. They were repulsed at every turn, which made them selfish and unhappy like everyone else.

Among the five boys remaining at the presbytery, I can say that there were three who were wearing trousers of mine. I never dreamt that they could be so ungrateful. Some months before the adventure of our escape, two groups were formed amongst the boys. There was one which sided with the parish priest, in order to have the chance to receive visits from the girls they liked, and the other included boys who liked to climb the wall to look for 'love' during the night outside the walls. These two groups did not agree. They did not get along and this (271) remained so until they merged to instigate the 'purge' in the presbytery. At the time when they were opposed, the two groups tore each other to shreds in an unspeakable fashion. Then the business of the clothes surfaced. Those of one group would take the clothes of members of the other and use them, not to wear but to use them as dusters for cleaning purposes. In a short time, boys of both groups no longer had any clothes to wear. At that time I was the most stubborn of all and firmly resolved not to submit to either group, and if anyone dared to come and force open my trunk and take my clothes to clean the parish priest's bicycle, he knew that he had me to deal with, because I was neutral. Truthfully, being neutral was the unhappiest state of all for me. Because of the state of affairs many little ones had no clothes and I loaned them some and even gave them away, quite simply to gain a little friendship. It was thanks to this sympathy that I was able to group around me eight young ones from both groups, and from a neutral group. This new group little by little became powerful, and inspired fear in the other groups consisting of older boys.

(272)   Later, the group opposed to the parish priest's group converted to a normal life, and stopped going out with the young girls. It was only then that I accepted its merger with our group to launch together the movement to boycott the girls who visited the priest's house. But in the neutral group, most of the young boys had been scarred by inhuman treatment and, above all, crushed by the yoke of duress which held sway in the presbytery. Their hearts had therefore become dry, hard and selfish. I considered this a consequence of the bad example they were exposed to. This is why I do not blame them. They who deserve the blame are those who knowingly allow this base and vulgar behaviour.

So, many boys have used my kindness to spirit away my inheritance, that is to say, my clothing. At the beginning, clothes were borrowed, then asked for brusquely, and after demanding them they, in their turn, loaned them to others for payment in money or work. To raise the price they would point out that the borrower had scabies or lice or had

(273)   suffered from diarrhoea during the night. I never thought that from my former state of comfort I would be so reduced as to have to borrow a pair of trousers. But since the day of my frustrated escape, I had lost my entire collection of clothes, and had been further punished by the parish priest who refused me any clothing. All I had, therefore, that year was one set of clothes. As a result, in order to wash my own I had to hire a pair of trousers on a weekly basis. Those whom formerly I had helped willingly saw my painful situation but, seeing themselves harassed continually by the parish priest, far from showing me any gratitude, only added to my sufferings by making me hire their trousers like everybody else . . . and O! Please dispense me from saying any more about it . . .

On that particular day, the boy who had hired out his trousers to me hoped very strongly to accompany the parish priest to Tam-Lộng, since his home village was close by and it would be a good opportunity to visit

his mother. But when he saw that I and not he had been chosen, he was
not happy, changed his mind and asked for his trousers back. 'Not at   (274)
all,' I said to him. 'I have agreed to heat the water for two weeks and I
have therefore the right to wear them until mine are dry.'

'Out of the question. I need my trousers.'

I understood his plan immediately and to please him I replied:

'All right, I'll ask the parish priest to take you to Tam-Lộng, and me
– I don't mind staying here.'

I therefore went to the parish priest and asked him:

'Father, please allow Tôn to go to Tam-Lộng.'

'And "General Van", why should he stay at the house?'

He paused, rolled his eyes, looked at me sternly and continued,

'I've made my decision. The one I've chosen must go. Why do you
wish to give Tôn your place?'

'Because Father I've ...'

'What?'

'I have no trousers ...'

'What a miserable creature you are! Where have you put all your
clothes? Take care! Get ready to leave, otherwise you'll be beaten sick.'

'But Father, Tôn wishes to go also.'   (275)

'That makes no difference. I've said you'll go, and you'll go.'

'But I have no trousers ...'

'If you have no trousers, wretch, then you can go naked.'

Then he stamped his foot on the floor as if to threaten me, but I
raised my head, looked at him and said:

'I am not a pig.'

'You are a dog from Ngăm, that's what you are. Don't act the rascal
with me. If you want to live, take this pipe immediately. Otherwise, get
ready to taste the cane!'

I knew it was impolite to argue with the parish priest, and anyway I
decided to remain silent. Wiping my tearful eyes with the hem of my
tunic, I went to the ground floor. I removed the hired trousers to put
on my own, still damp, then, taking the parish priest's pipe, I followed
him. The continuous rainfall had given rise to a great sadness in my
aching heart. Because of the rain, my damp trousers, and the cold wind
which was blowing, I had hardly reached the exit from the village when
I had a violent stomach-ache. I forced myself to go on nevertheless,   (276)
hoping that thanks to the warmth of my body, my trousers would dry
quickly and my stomach-ache would go away. But after a few steps my
pain became so sharp that I could no longer walk. I had to sit by the
side of the road and hope that the pain would lessen so that I could
continue. Thinking of my sad lot at that moment, my tears would not
cease to flow. Suddenly the parish priest, already well ahead, turned

round and, seeing me crying at the side of the road with my head lowered, retraced his steps, came up to me and said:

'Wretch, why are you not coming? Why are you sitting there?'

I got up, crossed my arms and replied:

'Father, I have a very bad stomach-ache. I sat down, hoping it would get better, and then I could continue.'

'Oh, so you've got a stomach-ache. You are very good at playing the fool.'

And lifting his stick, he gave me two blows on my back. Then with the muddy end of his stick he hit me on the head, so that I stumbled and almost fell.

(277)   Father, you can guess the extent of my suffering without my needing to tell you. You can realise how I was boiling with anger. To satisfy this anger I would have loved to have thrown his pipe in his face and said to him: 'Father, you are crueller than a dog!' I do not know how I was able to restrain myself. I was trembling all over, as much from my stomach-ache as from the blows I had just received. I was sobbing, and covered in sweat. After the beating the parish priest chased me to the presbytery and, whilst following me, he told me that someone else would go to Tam-Lộng in my place. As for me, he dismissed me and sent me to Thái-Nguyên with the other two. He said to the person who was taking us to this parish: 'If, when you get there, Father Nghĩa won't take Van, all you have to do is send him to his father. He really is an uneducated brat.'

The bitterness in my soul came to my throat, but as soon as I heard the parish priest's words sending me to Thái-Nguyên, I was so happy

(278)   that the smile came back to my face despite my stomach-ache which was still there. I said to myself interiorly: 'From now onwards I will not have to breathe the depressing atmosphere of this sinful presbytery.' I did not forget to thank the Blessed Virgin for having obtained such a great happiness for me. I got ready to leave for Thái-Nguyên that very morning. I did not neglect to advise Mrs Sau and to make my farewells to her whom I called, 'my very dear adoptive mother'. I left in the greatest dishonour, with nothing other than the reproaches of the parish priest for consolation. He did not even give me a sou, under the pretext that I had already stolen enough. In spite of that, the thought of being able to escape from this house made my heart sing for joy, and no further humiliation could sadden it.

When I got in to the train I sighed deeply and began to sing: 'My

(279)   dear mother, I thank you ...' My two companions, seeing me so unperturbed, said to me: 'How can you be so calm after all the insults you have received?' I did not reply. They continued: 'You are someone who no longer knows how to get upset, someone with a

"thick face".'* It is true. If I had not had a 'thick face', it is not certain that I could have endured all the humiliations that people had over-whelmed me with, but because if I had a 'thick face', even if someone had slapped me, joy and peace would have continued to reign in my heart.

Then my two companions left me to go and eat sweetmeats. As for me, it was only after my arrival at Thái-Nguyên that I was able to eat a bowl of Chinese soup, bought with the five sous given me by Father Nghĩa. I did not take offence at my comrades who, because they had some money, ate some sweets, but what made me cry was that whilst eating in a disgusting manner, they said: 'If he wants some, we can give him a pebble.' That hurt me more than not being able to share a bit of the cake which they held in their hands. A short time earlier, Father, these two boys had asked me to share my clothes with them ... But, after having won the favour of the parish priest they had no more grat- (280) itude for the one who had given them their clothes.

There you have love as the world knows it. Luckily, God made me understand from an early age how superficial men's hearts are. I discovered among them a nastiness both deceitful and detestable. But the more I understood the superficiality in worldly love, the more I felt impelled to delve deeply into God's heart. I knew only how to put my faith in God's love, and life was, for me, only a lesson in greater confidence in this love.

Running away for the second time

I had the idea before arriving at Thái-Nguyên that in this parish, having as its head a Spanish priest as acting parish priest, I would prob-ably find a place where discipline reigned with great charity. After several days, I realised that the opposite was the case. The worst thing (281) was the segregation practised by the Europeans. Here is a little example to illustrate the certain distance maintained by the Spanish priests. A young boy adopted by a Spanish missionary took precedence over the rest of the group of children adopted by the Vietnamese curate, although the former had only joined a short time previously. Now, we had entered two or three years before him. According to the rules, the first arrivals took precedence, were they the children of the acting parish priest or of the simple curate of the parish. Here the opposite obtained. From the beginning I had to submit to all of the abuses imposed by the superiors. This is a small example, which will enable

---

* A Vietnamese expression meaning impassive.

you to understand the segregation practised by the Spanish against the Vietnamese in the most important matters. It was very painful to witness. From this time I began to hate European missionaries, and my sole desire, if ever I became bishop, would be to send all the Spanish fathers back to their own country. On another tack, I had also noticed that everywhere there was a catechist, there were conversations about impure love. These catechists, being from the town, were in the habit of talking about dirtier, more awful subjects than catechists from the country. This parish left a stench in my nose and I looked for a means of getting away. I asked the Blessed Virgin to provide me with an opportunity to escape and to return to my own house when, one day, the episode of the cinema came up.

(282)

That particular day Father Xuân, a Spanish Dominican, came to visit the house of the parish priest Father Trong. I do not know if there was an interesting film on that evening. The two fathers always agreed to go to the cinema. Father Xuân, seeing that we were from the country and therefore ignorant of the cinema, asked us:

'Would you like to go to the cinema?'

And we all replied enthusiastically: 'Yes Father! Yes Father!'

'But, first of all, have you any money for tickets?'

The boldest of us replied: 'You will give us some . . .'

'No, I don't give money away for nothing. I'll give you some if you agree first of all to "eat some eels".* It's five sous per eel. Three eels equals fifteen sous which is the price of the ticket.' At these words he lowered his head, smiled reluctantly in a sweet sort of way and glanced at us to ascertain our thoughts. 'Eat eels!' I said to myself. 'I won't go to the cinema. I shall stay at home and sleep. That will be more relaxing.' I was going to withdraw when the other boys grabbed and threatened me:

(283)

'Don't do that. The Europeans can't stand such postures. If you are not happy, say so openly. If you go like this they will say you lack frankness.' Straight like a European! The boys had just reminded me of an expression I have often heard from people's mouths. I made an effort to contain myself and to stay where I was, but I also replied: 'Straight like a European. I don't think so!'

The others replied: 'If you don't want to be, the rest of us do.' While we were arguing, Father Xuân went to look for a cane and, holding it in his hand, he questioned us again:

'Now then: what do you say?'

'Father, we want to eat eels.'

(284)

I looked across at the one who had replied and, nudging him with my elbow, said to him:

---

*   Receive cuts of the cane

'All you do is interrupt. Have you got my agreement so that you can speak like that?' Because I was not speaking loudly, Father Xuân could not hear my words clearly, and he asked the others:

'What did the little chap say?'

'He says he agrees also, Father.'

Then without warning the priest took me by the hand, brought me to the middle of the room, and gave me three strokes of the cane. I was so afraid that I cried out. Seeing me cry so much, he gave me an additional five sous but, with my eyes moist with tears, I looked across at him, murmuring: 'But this European missionary, with the reputation of being as gentle as a lamb, is as cruel as the devil!' He did not understand my words, but seeing my fear he allowed himself to laugh, and congratulated me on my skill in receiving blows from the cane.

So we went to the cinema with the two priests. Unfortunately for my (285) first visit to a cinema, I landed on a film which contained nothing worthwhile. I do not remember very much, neither did I understand a great deal since it was in French: but it seemed to be about a beach where people bathed in the sea. After the film, when recalling the images, I felt a little ashamed and unhappy at having gone to the cinema. I blushed easily at the sequences when Europeans, men and women, were dressed as children do here, with bare legs etc., which was indecent behaviour for adults. I had never before seen men and women so naked since my childhood. I was ashamed of it all, and ill at ease. I must thank God with all my heart that the images did not remain in my head for very long. They appeared as if in a dream, and once out of the hall, I remembered nothing.

In looking at the screen my attention was focused on only one thing, and one question came back unceasingly to my mind: 'What do people do to reproduce in this way these moving pictures?' I thought about it a (286) lot without coming to any conclusion. I then said to myself: 'I will study the cinema later.' I always felt within me, whenever I saw anything, the need to know more deeply about it. I wanted to study and examine in detail any machine that I saw – an electric light bulb as much as a locomotive. It was the same regarding the way to perfection, but apart from my dear mammy I was never able to meet in my family anyone who could answer clearly the questions I posed in my search for God. From the day that I left my home, moments of enlightenment apart, I have been completely deprived of the happiness of hearing my mother speak to me of the love of God, and the joy to be found in doing his will.

The projection of the film came to an end just as my attention was (287) caught by the ray of light which was projected from behind me, right on to the screen. I tried to puzzle out how the electric current produced the light and the sounds of the deafening music. I felt uncomfortable, my nostrils were slightly blocked, my head was hot, and all I wanted to do was lie down. We were accompanied by the two Fathers as we returned to the presbytery. It was dark on the road, except for here and there an electric lamp which shone at face level, and blinded us so that we did not know where to put our feet. I walked in front with a young companion. The two priests followed, and behind them were the older boys. They spoke of the film they had just seen. It was not, however, to pose questions of a scientific nature but to dwell on passages I thought it was inappropriate to speak of. My young companion had thoughts similar to my own. We walked in silence, but from time to time one spoke up to ask his companion: 'How do they make the images move?

(288)   It's very strange. Do you understand?' But neither of us could understand or give an explanation. Sometimes I asked myself, hesitatingly, if there were not actors behind us whose shadows were projected on to the screen. But my companion objected: 'If that is so, where do the mountains, the forests and the vast oceans that we saw come from?' Shortly afterwards I turned towards the older men and asked them: 'What do the men do to be so skilful?' But my questions interrupted their conversation, and each time they silenced me by saying: 'We'll speak of this business another time. You are no bigger than a jacquier seed, and you want to know everything.' They burst out laughing at this. I did not understand the meaning of their reply, but I was very upset to hear them make fun of me in comparing me to a jacquier seed.

(289)   Just as we were about to arrive at the presbytery, Father Trong turned suddenly towards us, and asked us in an aggressive manner:

'Who gave you permission to go to the cinema?'

'You did, Father.'

'Not at all. Nobody came to ask my permission.'

'But you questioned us and gave us the money.'

'Don't be cheeky. I gave you the money, but you did not ask permission: so why did you dare to go? When you get to the house, come to my room.'

I understood that to go to his room meant receiving the cane once again. I was still sore from the recent beating and I began to cry. I thought: 'It's a waste of time arguing. All I can do is ask Father's forgiveness and he will forgive me.' So I ran to ask his pardon. He did not reply, but as I reached his room to be beaten he told the old servant, the doorkeeper, to take me to the dormitory. The other three had to stretch out to receive their beatings. The next day, unhappy because I had not been beaten, they told me to keep out of their sight, and

(290)   refused to play with me. One of the bigger boys, a favourite of the parish priest, reproached me:

'You went to the cinema like us: how come you managed to escape a beating? You are extremely selfish.'

'Why do you call me selfish? You knew you were going to be beaten. Why didn't you ask the priest's forgiveness straight away? Would that not have been the better thing to do? It's because you were proud that you were beaten. You are wrong to complain.'

The parish priest's protégé, hearing me reply in this fashion, clenched his fists and came towards me with a threatening glare to say to me:

'Who did you say was proud?'

Not being big enough to fight, I remained on the defensive and replied to him:

'I was talking about you.'

Seeing my resolute demeanour, he lowered his hands and, pulling a face, he again threatened me:

'Scoundrel! Don't think that Father is still not watching you.'

Then, lowering his voice in an intimate manner:

'Listen, the Spaniards are really nasty, but because you are new, (291) Father is bending a little. But see what happens if you put another foot wrong ... You'll get a double beating. I'm warning you. Keep on your guard.'

Then, addressing the other boys and still threatening me:

'My friends, let's play somewhere else. Who would want to play with this selfish specimen?'

With these words he began to sing in a loud voice:

'*Còn trời, còn đất, còn mây...; còn thằng ích kỷ lằn mây vẫn còn...;*'[*] 'It's unbelievable. You were able to get away with it once, but from now on if he catches you doing anything wrong, he will take you to his room and give you a good hiding.'

My two companions from Huu Bang also bombarded me with criticism, to such an extent that it was very difficult for me to hold back my tears.

To tell the truth, the threats of the parish priest's favourite did not frighten me at all, but since yesterday evening it was impossible to believe any more in the gentleness of Father Trong. I had already tasted his cruel games. From now onwards, even if the European performed miracles and raised the dead as evidence of his sweetness and charity, I would consider it all as a trick, as a complete lie, so I felt (292) the boy's warnings well-founded, and I was afraid that one day I might do something wrong. This was inevitable given human carelessness and weakness. Consequently, I looked for an immediate means of escape.

---

[*] 'As long as heaven, earth and clouds remain, the marks of the blows of the cane will remain for the selfish man.'

The next day, at midday, I ran away. I went to the church before leaving to pay a visit to Jesus, to consecrate myself to the Blessed Virgin, and to place myself under the protection of the holy souls in purgatory, so as to arrive home peacefully. I had only been travelling for two days when I arrived home. My heart had mixed feelings of joy and anxiety. I had reflected deeply, and I did not know what to do to alleviate the seriousness in my parents' eyes of my running away. I chose, therefore, the following course of action. If, having arrived home, the situation seemed favourable, I would frankly admit that I had run away. If, on the other hand, things were not looking good, I would say that the parish priest had given me permission to visit the family. Before I could make a calm decision, the worst happened. I had hardly crossed the threshold when my father saw me. Seeing me as I was, sad, dirty, my

(293) face soiled, my hands and feet tanned by the sun he guessed immediately that I had absconded. He scolded me in a loud voice, and pushed me away as if I were a rough beggar. Happily, Aunt Khóa,* was in the house that evening, and she intervened. Without her, my father would have given me the father and mother of a hiding. She held me to her breast, caressed me and urged me to stop crying. Just at that moment my mother arrived from the market. I threw myself into her arms, hoping to be comforted by her, but she stepped back, gave me an annoyed look as if she had no pity for me, and then reprimanded me with these words: 'You have dared to run away? You miserable creature. Misfortune on you ...' She then gave me a long lecture ... as severe as my father's. I felt rejected. Seated in a corner, I had only my tears to plead my innocence. I really wanted to admit that I had run away but instead, for fear of a beating from my father, I tried to excuse myself by saying that I had permission to visit the family.

(294)   'Look at the state of your face! and you still say you have permission to visit the family?'

'Yes, it's true, but on the way I was threatened, and all my possessions were stolen.'

In spite of this, no one in the family believed I was telling the truth. To find out the truth my mother got my uncle Nhượng to write a letter to the curate, Father Nghĩa, to find out all the details.

I now recall a friendly gesture of my little sister Anne Marie Tế. I experienced an unspeakable joy on seeing her again after such a long absence. When I ran away from Thái-Nguyên, I still had in my pocket the five sous remaining after the film show. I had taken from this amount one and a half sous to buy five cakes, the size of five big toes, to give as a present to my little sister. That apart, I had to beg along the

---

* Aunt Khóa was Van's maternal great aunt.

route and travel at the expense of others to make my escape. These five cakes represented a big sacrifice for me because I had to travel on foot from Bắc-Ninh to the landing stage at Hồ-Tiên. This meant twelve kilometres in the scorching sun. I was many times tempted to use this (295) little amount to refresh myself, but the thought of my little sister made me forget the thirst I had to overcome to bring her this little present. My sister was probably unaware of these painful circumstances, but she was very hurt to see that, only just arrived, and in such a pitiful state, I had still been scolded so mercilessly. She did not dare to be separated from me. She held me tightly in her arms, caressed me, covered me with kisses, and encouraged me not to cry any more. I must admit that, without the affectionate behaviour of my little sister, I could not have imagined that I was among my much-loved family.

My little sister's attitude did not succeed in drying my tears, which continued to flow all that day and even during the following days. My sister would leave me only to go to school for the holiday lessons. I felt an extreme tiredness after the scolding of my father and mother. I began to sweat and shiver, and I stretched out on a bamboo deck chair and slept (296) until four o'clock in the afternoon. It was only then that I felt more comfortable, and I felt the need to eat. My mother prepared a bowl of soup for me although I had not dared ask for anything. She placed it on the table with two little breads and invited me to eat. On seeing my mother and hearing her voice, I felt again a certain shame. I lowered my head to cry, saying that I was not hungry. My mother gave me another sermon, but this time speaking gently, she reproached me for not having told the truth. That evening I went out to make a short visit to the Most Holy Sacrament and afterwards I went early to bed. I did not want to speak to anyone and if anyone questioned me, I answered briefly. Apart from that, all I could was cry. For three days I ate very little and that only when my little sister Tế invited me, otherwise I was not hungry. After (297) three days I was unable to dry my tears, and my eyes became very swollen and were seriously sore. I was condemned to remain in bed for a whole week in a dark corner where no ray of light could penetrate. The least beam caused a sharp pain, a feeling of burning. Even the small oil lamp that my mother brought to chase away the mosquitoes in the darkness was sufficient to make my eyes run. The sole cause of my illness was my deep sadness. I returned repeatedly to the same thought: Since they know that I have run away, why don't my parents question me to find the reasons why I was forced to do so? I could then explain to them in a few words the circumstances which led me to do it. But absolutely nothing was said on the subject. I had not even had the time to greet them before I was severely reprimanded by my parents. They had the right to punish me for running away, but also they should have tried to understand something about their unhappy child. No one runs away from a place where he feels loved. So there was at least one reason which may have prompted my running away.

(298)   In fact I was not allowed to supply any information to my parents which might have helped them in forming a judgement. As I have told you in all sincerity, after having acted with the best of intentions, I had been misunderstood, so that I felt a great pain, to such an extent that I could not hold back my tears. I understood also that it was very meritorious to put up with injustice for the love of God, but I was still far from such a high level of virtue. My soul, like a young plant which the wind blows in all directions, had not yet the strength of such self-control. In listening to all the rebukes of my parents since my arrival home, I thought of her who some months previously had been my adoptive mother, and I would have wished to meet a heart like hers. Above all during my sickness I said to myself, 'If only my adoptive mother were here, what a comfort that would be for me.'

It was not possible that because of my running away my parents would lose all affection for me. The tears that I had shed for three days, and the terrible eye ache because of it, had calmed their anger and had led them to try and to understand me. From then, instead of scolding me and being indifferent towards me, they comforted me and took care

(299)   of me. Perhaps the word indifferent is a bit too strong, because my mother has never been indifferent in my regard. Since the day of my running away she has taken care of me, down to the smallest detail, but what saddened me was that she believed nothing of my story. She prepared my food for me with her own hands during my illness. I had to abstain from many things, following the prescriptions of the old lady who was looking after me, but my mother was even stricter, even forbidding people in the house to make any allusion to my absconding. Moreover, she did not cease to utter affectionate words to me, so much that it was impossible to continue crying. Thanks to this, my painful eyes improved very quickly, and when I was cured she prepared some pick-me-ups for me.

On the other hand, she made preparations to return me to Father Joseph Nhã to apologise to him, and to ask him to take me back. I had to follow my mother's will completely, but personally I was completely opposed to it. I wished no longer to live in this corrupt presbytery ... My mother, on her part, could not believe that Father Nhã would toler-

(300)   ate the bad behaviour that I spoke of. She did not stop repeating: 'The priest is holy. He is God's representative. It is impossible for him to do such things. It is only because you are a scoundrel that you say such things and you don't wish to be corrected.' I was obliged therefore to follow her to Hữu-Bằng, to be once again a prisoner in this presbytery.

Escape from prison for the third time

I want to say that for those young people who entered it with a view to the priesthood, the presbytery at Hữu-Bằng was a prison. There was there only sin and punishment, but it seemed that the punishments were reserved only for those who did not wish to follow the path of sin. That is why I still wish to call it a prison. My mother remained some days at the presbytery at my request to see if the situation really was as bad as I had described. After three days of careful observation I heard my mother say discreetly but reproachfully to the parish priest these (301) very simple but deep-meaning words: 'Father, I notice that your presbytery has changed a lot in the last five years ...' In truth, physical appearances had changed a lot, but what my mother was getting at was less the outward signs, but rather the personal feelings of the parish priest. I accompanied my mother to the jetty on the day that she returned home, and it was only then that she made known her desolation to me, since she had never expected that things would come to such a pass. While walking with her along the deserted road, I sobbed and begged her to allow me to return with her. Seeing my tears, which mirrored my sorrow and my worried face, she wiped them and then wiped her own ... We walked slowly, sharing our mutual grief. Then my mother pressed my head against her breast and gently said to me: 'Can you understand a little of my helplessness? Are you aware of the bad situation because of your father? If you are, I am asking you to share it with me. Try to remain here for a while, then I shall try to find (302) you another place where you can prepare for the priesthood. Accept willingly all the difficulties you will meet in the parish, and offer them to the good God. As for me, I will ask God and the Blessed Virgin to look after you, so that you don't fall into dangerous situations which are numerous here, as I have noticed. In any danger, maintain a strong confidence in God and the Blessed Virgin and you will come to no harm. You must also understand this; if after having brought you here, I then took you home, people would immediately gossip unceasingly and I should therefore be obliged to speak of the evil I have noticed concerning Father Nhã. You must understand we have a duty to safeguard the reputation of priests. So I am asking you to make an effort to stay here, and put up with this painful life a little bit longer. I shall try to find a better situation for you when I get home.' My mother kissed me on the forehead with these words, and asked me to go back to the presbytery whilst she walked quickly in the direction of the station. I watched her move away and it was only after seeing her disappear in (303) the forest of Nội that I resigned myself to return to the parish. My heart was torn apart.

I spent that day thinking of my mother and I was sorely tempted to follow her but, recalling her advice, I resigned myself to remain. My mother had scarcely left when the parish priest called me to his room to question me on the subject of my running away from Thái-Nguyên: 'What did they do to make you run away like that? I heard that you had stolen money from somewhere and, afraid of being caught, you absconded. That does not surprise me. I have known from the time when I was robbed how deceitful you are. There is no doubt that it was you because you were the only one who came into my room. However, I will still put up with you, which I would not do for anyone else.' He took some tobacco, filled his pipe and continued: 'Don't believe that I want to take you back. It is only due to your mother's insistence that I have agreed to keep you. Personally, I would never dream of taking

(304)   you back a little thief like you. You are fully aware of the situation. There's no need to dwell on it. You also understand your family's decline. It is only through pity for your mother that I have accepted you. Now try to behave in a worthy manner. You must agree to work in living here. I have already supplied you with your certificate of primary studies. That's sufficient. I guess that any further study would be a waste of effort. Besides, you show no interest in study, spending all your time as you do in amusing yourself with this and that. Therefore I am putting you in charge of the ducks. Feed them, and I will feed and clothe you.'

I had to stand, arms crossed, and listen to these words for a whole hour. They broke my heart and reduced me to tears. I wanted to challenge what he had just said and ask him to send me straight home but, recalling my mother's words, I resigned myself once more to submit

(305)   and agree to what he said. He made it completely clear, quite openly, that he despised my family. He called me a thief and asserted that, because my family had no rice to feed me, they had to bring me to him ... etc. Briefly, he could not have dishonoured my family more. He was, incidentally, wearing an ample black silk soutane, which had been made by my father's hands, and which had been given to him by my mother. I was totally exhausted after his speech, but I forced myself to smile and thank him before leaving the room.

I took up once again my role as admiral in charge of the ducks and of any additional work usually reserved for occasional labourers. It would have been some consolation if I had received just one sou each month, but I did not, as all the money was used on alcohol and gambling. For two months my work went well. Then once again I was

(306)   the victim of unjust oppression which led me, once more, to run away. It could be said that, on this occasion, I was guilty, but I was not judged fairly by anyone who had the authority to do so. It was an older boy who

took advantage of certain circumstances to oppress me. And this to get his own back because I had answered him in a displeasing manner.

It was after the harvest. The smell of drying straw and rice was still on the ground. Availing themselves of the parish priest's absence after the midday meal, the old catechist and the bigger boys went to the village to the families of young girls they loved. The remaining group consisted of seven of the younger boys, including those who were at the presbytery to study without being students for the priesthood. Our group managed to enjoy a rare free afternoon of fun. We agreed to play a war game. We divided ourselves into two opposing camps. The bigger   (307) ones put themselves into the French camp and the smaller, more puny, joined the Japanese. Naturally, I immediately took my place amongst the Japanese heroes. I was given the rank of general because I had the candid look of a Japanese. After each side was assigned its territory, a pile of straw was taken from the yard to act as a frontier. We began to draw up rules of engagement for the commencement of battle. There were three soldiers on the French side, and a general whose cap was decorated with twelve stars. On the Japanese side there were only two soldiers and their much-loved general. As well as being his soldiers they also served as his horse. For his part, the general loved them as he loved himself. When he saw that they were tired from running, he offered to act as the horse to carry them but they refused this gesture on his part. Seeing their general so decent towards them, they responded even better to him. On the French side everyone wanted to be on horseback and fire the rifle so that they never stopped quarrelling. We had   (308) wooden swords for arms, and fire-crackers to act as rifles and machine guns. The two sides opposed each other without wilting. The aeroplanes, flying in formation, consisted of only one but bombed everywhere. The spluttering of the rifles enthused the army. At the beginning the battered Japanese retreated to their capital, that is to say, to a corner of the yard. Then, luckily, two enemy planes, on exploratory flights, were brought down. Venturing too far over enemy territory, they were pursued by the general's plane, and in spite of all their strength they had to surrender. The Japanese general, short on personnel, did not take them prisoner, but allowed them to go free, and they in their turn asked to join the Japanese troops. This meant an increase in the general's forces, and the counter-attack was fierce. The French, overcome, abandoned their arms depot and flew into the forest. The Japanese general, taking time only to put on a turban by way of helmet, scorned his sword, jumped on his horse and gave his soldiers the order to hurry after the fleeing soldiers. The French general had to be   (309) captured alive or forced to surrender – a condition for the termination of hostilities. Just at that moment a solitary Japanese aeroplane, flying at great speed, penetrated into the forest and was taken by the French. The Japanase general, annoyed, roared with all his strength. His soldiers, like tigers, gritted their teeth and roared in imitation of the sound of aeroplanes and tanks in order to frighten the opposing camp.

We were playing the game with great pleasure and gusto when unfortunately one of the boys who had gone to the village came back earlier than the others. Seeing us playing in this foolhardy manner, he approached, incensed, towards the piles of straw on the edge of the forest and scolded us in a loud manner. I thought it would be a good idea to ease the tension by cracking a joke to make him laugh.

'Ah, has Sir missed his meeting with his lady to have such an angry air?'

The Japanese soldiers burst out laughing. Our man laughed also but, becoming serious again, said to me:

'You are just a cheeky so-and-so.'

'Cheeky? You speak of cheeky! I don't know which fellow had his arms wrapped round the shoulders of a certain person last evening in a corner of the entrance to the parlour ... and you still speak of (310)   cheeky?'

The Japanese group in the grass roared out:

'Ah! Caught in the act, caught in the act.'

'Van, you are nothing but a monkey. Do you think I am going to play with you like a child?'

I raised my eyebrows, jumped off my horse and, taking a false moustache out of my pocket, I placed it under my nose and answered him:

'Let us see. I'm not sure that you have as many whiskers as me, and you dare to call me a child?'

He burst out laughing on seeing me with this strange accoutrement but, composing himself immediately, he dashed towards me saying:

'How dare you address me so familiarly?'

'Who called me monkey and was familiar with me first?'*

'I did.'

Not allowing me any time to reply, he threatened me:

'You'd better be careful. Give me the crackers and the matches.'

'Are you serious, or are you joking?'

'Do I look as if I'm joking?'

'OK! Then I'm also speaking seriously. I'll give you neither the crack-(311)   ers nor the matches.'

'Really!'

'Really. And on whose authority do you ask me to do so?'

'Mine.'

---

*   The Vietnamese are very punctilious about hierarchcial procedure. Even in the family, the oldest and youngest are not addressed in the same way.

'Your authority extends no further than the stables.'

'You dare to say that?'

'Yes.'

'Ngăm, you dog! You are walking on ice. People keep telling you but you still act stubbornly.'

'What are you on about? If you want to play with the crackers, ask, and I'll give you some but if you are going to act like the great "I am" to frighten me, you could kneel down before me with your hands joined and I would not give you any. Where do you get this conceited idea from, that because you are big you can boss anybody around?'

With these words I turned round to my troops and said: 'My friends, let us continue.' The French, seizing the opportunity, secretly retook their base position. The Japanese army had to regroup for battle but their general gave the order not to use guns any more, which deprived the game of a lot of its interest. Meanwhile, our man, annoyed by my firm responses, withdrew with a scowling face while threatening me: (312) 'Fair enough. When the old catechist returns I'll denounce you.' A moment later, seeing that he was supposed to be looking for the French general, the Japanese general mounted his horse and followed his soldiers to the capital. From there he sent the following communiqué to the French: 'Starting from now, the army whose soldiers shelter in the forest will be defeated.' The war recommenced. Once again, little by little, the French withdrew towards the forest. They were on the point of being overcome when our man of the moment returned to make trouble for the Japanese general.

'Van, I warned you, and you are still stubbornly playing.'

'What do you mean, "stubbornly"? I'm no longer lighting crackers. As (313) for playing, we are playing because nobody is going to stop us at this hour.'

Without replying, he ran in a furious mood to find a drumstick and then approached me. Panic-stricken, the Japanese army took flight. The general alone remained standing there, quite determined to maintain his dignity as a general. Our man provoked me with the stick in his hand:

'Now, if you are able to, act stubbornly while I watch.'

'Why do you speak of stubborn? When you speak reasonably, I'll listen to you, but who has given you the right to abuse your authority by forbidding us this and that? Don't act the part of the big fish eating the little one. If I look at my status, I have as much authority as you.'

'Who is this big fish which eats the little one?'

'You are. All you know is how to oppress others.'

'Are you accusing me of oppressing others?'

And he swung his arm and dealt me two blows on the calves with the stick. So much for the general's dignity! I immediately collapsed on the spot and no longer looking for good reasons to stand up to my persecutor, I remained stretched out, holding my leg and moaning. After this exploit, the older boy withdrew with his stick, murmuring: 'That'll teach you ... Japanese general! Just look at you with your lame leg!' Then he repeated his threat to denounce me to the old catechist.

(314)   He went to the old catechist that very evening to relate the incident, adding and leaving out certain details so that the blows he had dealt me had no serious consequences for him. In beating me as he had done, he had broken the rules and committed a serious fault. But did rules exist any more for the old catechist? Since the day of his joining forces with the parish priest to take to task the band of little brats, he had succumbed to temptation, and shown himself as attached to the girls as was the parish priest. He liked that they came to massage him and speak to him, and he liked to talk in a dirty manner, especially when his glass of alcohol was almost empty ... Furthermore, the older boys who had been expelled from the *probatorium** worked with him, so that they could do whatever they liked concerning the young candidates for the priesthood, who had become some kind of plaything for them.

The old catechist already hated me, and knowing that the parish priest was going to be away for the annual confessions, he waited for the time when he would be lord and master of the house, to place on the agenda the subject of the crackers let off in the middle of piles of straw, and to judge the guilty. He hated me more than anyone else for one reason: each time that I passed his bedroom, as a joke, I imitated the Chinese vendor of remedies by crying: 'Who buys extracts of tigers'

(315)   bones mixed with pure alcohol ... a *lông* a jar.'[†] He would clear his throat and moan: 'Brat! ... Monkey!' At midday, when I saw young girls whispering in his room, I used to sing:

> *Con cò trắng bạch như bông.*
> *Lấy ai thời lấy, chờ trông nhà thày;*
> *Nhà thày làm biêng đã quen.*
> *Hễ mó đến cái chổi thì ho hen khừ khừ...*[‡]

---

*   Junior Seminary or house of formation for catechists.

†   The exact word is 'Đồng' i.e. piastre (a coin) but the Chinese cannot pronounce the letter Đ correctly and pronounce the word 'long', and this is how Van pronounced it!

‡   Translation: Stork, white as cotton wool
                            Marry whom you like
                            But expect nothing of a lazy catechist
                            Who, if he touched a brush would moan.

By this popular refrain I hoped to warn these young girls, already at the age of puberty, to remember the unhappy lives of other young girls who allowed themselves to be deceived by thinking that these well-dressed men had only to cough or to speak to produce rice or money. Once they had become their husbands, they knew only how to eat, drink, dress well, become lazy, and hurt their wives a great deal.

It is not surprising that the old catechist had a grudge against me. I well understood that, one day, by some means, he would seek the opportunity to revenge himself. I was, therefore, on my guard, but the sad story of our imprudent game surfaced. I spent all night wondering, (316) weighing the pros and cons and asking for the grace of inspiration. I knew that it was cowardly to run away through fear of a beating. Furthermore, though not greatly liked by the older boys of the presbytery, I had gained the friendship of the majority of the younger ones, and I sometimes felt that my presence among them was necessary. I was afraid, in spite of this, when thinking of the heavy cane and the hateful face of the old catechist, and once again I came to the conclusion that I must flee this place, that I must find for myself a genuine house of God where I could aim for perfection, and my desire for the priesthood could take shape once again. This was my prayer: 'O my God, if it is your wish that I should become a priest, I would like to be a priest of a parish to make known to souls your merciful love. I long to become a priest. I thirst for your name to be glorified and this thirst impels me, like the thirsty deer, to look for a spring of pure water . . .' In this house, however, they have deliberately buried the most beautiful wish of my life. Instead of preparing me for the priesthood, they have forced me to (317) expend my energy looking after ducks and the needs of the parish priest.

Outraged by this state of affairs I decided to run away, but not to my parents' home. My sole object was to find a real house of God. At that particular moment my mother's words rang in my ears. Nevertheless they were not strong enough to shake my resolve to go elsewhere to prepare for the priesthood. Where to go? Where will I find a real house of God? I have not yet found one. I will run away and confide myself to Providence who, I hope, will lead me to the very place I am looking for. I got up and rubbed my calves with a Chinese painkiller to ease the pain. My left leg especially was hurting; the one which had been dislocated at the time of a previous fall. However, after much rubbing, my muscles began to soften. I tore up some old clothes to wrap around the calf. I stood up to practise walking and running. Shortly before dawn the pain was easier and I was able to rest. I said I was sick when (318) morning came, but once everyone had gone to church for prayers I got up, knelt down and said my morning offering, putting myself once more entirely in Our Lady's hands, and I asked her to protect my flight so that it would succeed without mishap. I also prayed to my guardian angel to show me the route to follow, to avoid danger from those who would wish to catch me. Finally, I thought of the souls in purgatory and I asked their protection.

Before I got up, the two small altar boys, while waiting the arrival of the parish priest, came to visit and comfort me and asked me to think no more of the events of the previous day. I answered them: 'Yes, I've forgotten it already, and I've forgiven the one who hit me. I am no longer resentful. Anyway, I know I'll no longer be here today.'

'Jesus! Van, are you serious? Are you joking?'

(319)   'Perhaps I'm just saying it to make you laugh. No, I am serious. You know how our life here differs in no way from that of prisoners condemned to hard labour . . . We are treated here according to everyone's whims . . .'

One of them cut me short:

'You have got to be joking. How could you run away with your bad foot?'

'Don't let it worry you.'

Hearing the priest coughing on the veranda, the two boys ran quickly to the sacristy.

I never hid my intentions from the younger ones, but I acted this way only with those who were particularly friendly towards me. As for those who spied for the parish priest, and the older boys, I never revealed the slightest thing to them or, if I did, it was only to play a trick and guarantee that their denunciation had no basis. Among the boys that I had just spoken to, there was one who particularly flattered the parish priest, and who was the main source of information between the girls and the bigger boys. I made him aware of my intention in spite of this,

(320)   so that my escape might succeed. I had devised an amusing and skilful plan of escape which demanded that the pursuer would run in front of the pursued, and the latter would hide behind the pursuer's back. I took the precaution of hiding in the house until the people went in pursuit of me; then I escaped, walking behind them. It was necessary, therefore, to tell of my escape in advance to the informer, who, seeing me no longer in bed, would immediately signal my departure.

The parish priest went to say Mass. I went quickly to the kitchen, bringing absolutely nothing with me. I had left all my clothes in a locked trunk. I left a note to a boy in whom I had total confidence, asking him to take care of it. I hid a key below his bed and allowed him, if he had need of anything, to help himself. I wandered up and down in the refectory, waiting for the farmers to leave the yard with their buffaloes. I then opened a cupboard and collected a small amount of rice which remained from their meal, and I ate it with some soya sauce. There still remained enough to fill my pockets. That was my food for the day. I felt more reassured thanks to this little rice. When Mass was (321) over the two altar boys left the church and rushed to the dormitory, and not seeing me they ran out horrified, crying: 'It's true, Van has run away ... He's run away!' I slowly withdrew to the side of the forest and hid in a thick bush. A half hour later all the presbytery was agitated by Van's escape; all the boys rushed to the forest to look for him. The parish priest was in a foul rage. I was very much aware of the little ones searching for me and I said my rosary fervently, asking Our Lady to prevent me from falling into their hands. Something unexpected happened. A small boy that I would call my pal was determined to find me at any cost so that I would remain, and he would have a friend. He came right up to the place where I was hiding as if he had already seen me. I was afraid and lay on the ground, trying to get deeper into the bush, but once again for no obvious reason, he came right up to me, (322) even treading on my tunic. Once more step and he would have trod on my head. However, and it was a strange thing, he stopped and murmured a few words: 'It's strange! My friend Van?' ... He then retraced his steps.

When he had reached a sufficient distance, I quickly climbed a high and leafy tree. From this vantage point I could see very far without the danger of being seen. The young boys had not found my hideout after looking for some time, but they had guessed correctly that I was still in the forest, and that I could not have escaped so soon in the direction of the station. They became discouraged at being unable to find me, and they withdrew one by one. One or two who were my friends continued to look further and searched everywhere in the bush, anxiously but without success. They then threw to the wind these words of farewell: 'Van, we are saying goodbye to you.' They then left the place as the drum signalled the time for class.

After the younger ones had left, I spied the one who had beaten me (323) the previous day. He was walking alone towards the forest looking for me. He had a really sorry appearance. I was told later that he had just confessed his fault to the parish priest, who had threatened him: 'If you don't find Van this very day, I'll show you the door.' He was an orphan, having neither father nor mother. Where would the poor fellow go to? ... Looking down on him from high in the tree, I felt very sorry for him. He was crying like a child, and from time to time he picked up a stone and threw it into the bushes, saying in an irritated manner: 'Van, Van, why are you making me so unhappy? Take care! Come out from where you are hiding, immediately, otherwise ...' At that particular moment he no longer seemed worthy of my pity. After a long period he went away. In the precincts of the presbytery all was quiet as usual. The sun was rising little by little and its rays were projected through the branches on to my face. The birds were chanting their morning prayers. My heart was suddenly filled with a great joy which chased away any feelings of sadness from my mind. I had the feeling that I had escaped from unhappiness ... I made the sign of the cross and said my morning prayer.

(324)   After my rosary I joined my hands and raised my eyes to beg for divine protection, and to put myself in Our Lady's keeping; then, looking towards the pier, I saw someone on the road heading towards the station. I guessed, immediately, that it was my tormentor of the previous day, and that he was running to prevent me from getting the eight o'clock train to my village. However, having reached the jetty, he stopped, chatted for a moment with the ferryman, seemed to hesitate as if wishing to come back, and finally got into the boat to cross the river. I slid down the tree without delay, sped across the fields to regain the road and calmly followed our man heading for the station. Having arrived at the jetty, I asked the ferryman in a nonchalant manner:

'Sir, have you seen a young chap of about my size running away along here?'

'No young man, but a moment ago a boy, not too big, passed this way. He also questioned me about a runaway but, honestly, I have not seen one.'

Whilst speaking, he took his pole and placed it on the jetty and then, putting his hands on his hips, he continued while looking at me:

(325)   'Anybody else might be deceived but not me ... I am very perspicacious. I have only to look at someone to know if I am dealing with a runaway ...' I had to make a big effort to control my laughter on hearing him speak in such a pretentious manner. I said to myself: 'That's enough, you've been deceived already. The runaway's face is under your nose, not anywhere else ...' I walked on to the jetty, and affecting a puzzled expression, I let these words slip out: 'It's very strange'. Then, turning towards the ferryman, I said to him: 'Can you take me across straight away so that I can catch up with the boy in front of me?' 'Sure; but the boy went so quickly that you will be lucky to catch him. Once across the river, he flew like the wind.'

Having reached the other side I thanked the 'perspicacious' ferryman, rolled up my trousers to my thighs, took off my tunic and folded it to make a hat and then, disguised as a crab collector, I began running, apparently to catch up with the other boy. When I was a few hundred metres away from him, I went off at a tangent along the dyke of a paddy field, walking slowly and from time to time going through the motions of looking for crabs. When he had reached the station, I immediately

edged along the shelter of a dense hedge, the length of the railway line   (326)
behind the station. From there I could observe all the actions of my
bloodhound. Panic-stricken, he enquired here and there if anyone had
seen a young twelve-year-old lad waiting for the train. He asked the
station master to warn his staff that if they saw such a small boy, they
must be careful to retain him. Unfortunately for him, the train heading
south that I would normally take was late that day, and the train
heading north arrived first. I realised that the boy intended to watch
only the train heading south. I boarded the train heading north
without delay. It began moving off just when the train was arriving
from the other direction. I had escaped the surveillance of my pursuer.

I had no ticket when I got on the train but that did not worry me. I
immediately looked for a carriage containing a lot of Japanese soldiers
so that I could mingle, because, in these carriages no employee dared
to check the tickets. I wandered through all the fourth-class carriages
but I could not find any Japanese. I reached a third-class carriage with   (327)
a tightly-closed door. I opened it forcefully, entered the carriage and
noticed that all the passengers were Japanese. I closed the door as
required, turned towards the passengers and standing up straight, I
saluted them in a military manner, '*O-hai-yô*'. (Good day, gentlemen!)
These were the only Japanese words I knew and I used them to greet
all Japanese, whether approaching or taking leave of them. The
Japanese soldiers, seeing such a gallant little chap, stared at me and
then burst out laughing. I sat on a bench in the middle of them. Those
who were near me tapped me on the shoulder, stroked my head and
chatted quickly, and I understood nothing. They were probably replying to my greeting and asking me where I was going. Their attitude
reassured me and I was no longer afraid. I lowered my head and gave
them a big smile to let them know that I did not understand the
Japanese language. Noticing this the Japanese seated next to me
stroked my head and asked me in Vietnamese:

'Where are you going to?'

'I am going to Vĩnh-Yên, sir.'   (328)

Opening his eyes wider and making a slight movement of the head
he repeated:

'Vĩnh-Yên. Good, good.'

From then onwards, they left me in peace. Nobody spoke to me
again.

A group of soldiers got off when we arrived at Đình-Ấm, which was
a town where arms were manufactured. All who passed by me laughed
and gave me a good handshake. On thinking of yesterday's game when
I acted the part of a Japanese general, I was all the more excited that
they were so well disposed towards their general. When the train

arrived at Vĩnh-Yên station, I stood up, saluted again as on my arrival, and shook the hand of every soldier, among whom there were probably some officers. They, equally politely, stroked my head and opened the door to allow me to get out. Once off the train, I waited for the carriage to pass, and I then slowly entered the station. Naturally I regretted the presence of Japanese soldiers, but, although they were

(329)   foreigners, strangers and even enemies, I was touched by their kind demeanour and delicacy. Having left them, I felt alone again as if I had lost a protector.

I wandered for a time behind the station and then I caught the train to Yên-Viên. Not finding any carriage with Japanese soldiers, I had to take a place with other passengers in the fourth-class carriage. My ticket was asked for once we were past Phúc-Yên but, not having one, the ticket collector locked me in the toilet. However, as soon as the employee left, the other passengers opened the door for me. He returned again shortly afterwards and questioned me, but several passengers intervened to testify that I was not a thief. 'There is no reason,' they said, 'to associate this sweet and friendly child with a gang of robbers.' Moved by their testimony, the collector let me go free, whilst forbidding me to leave the carriage. When the train arrived at Yen Vien station, he helped me to get off, and even told me the route to follow to reach Bắc-Ninh.

Captured

(330)   Unfortunately at Yên-Viên, I found myself face to face with two women, Dominican tertiaries who had been with me in the parish at Hữu-Bằng. They were taking the same train as me, to go to the parish of Đạo-Ngạn. On spotting them I wished to hide immediately, but they forcibly held me and asked me why I had run away. I was angry, and I embarrassed them by telling them bluntly the reasons which had forced me to abscond. Being unable to deny the truth of my words, they had to lower the temperature, and mollify me with sweet words. They then went to buy some sweets, and gently asked me to eat some. I accepted their invitation gladly, because I must admit that by this time I was hungry. On the train heading for Bắc-Ninh they suggested that I should get off with them at Đạo-Ngạn, promising that if I did not wish to return to Hữu-Bằng they would find another parish for me. Since their words appeared totally sincere, with nothing suspect about them, I accepted their proposition, but, once arrived at their residence in

(331)   Đạo-Ngạn, I realised they had deceived me. The two tertiaries handed me over to the head of the house and encouraged her to maltreat me

and to make life difficult for me, so as to compel me to return to Hữu-Bằng. I had to labour as an agricultural worker for three days, while the two women overwhelmed me with insults which made me cry. Fortunately, there was a lady there who was related to me (Ngắm)* and who, seeing me so badly treated, spoke up for me, and vigorously confronted her two companions. She asked the superior to allow me to go free to a parish of my own choice, or to my parents' house. She added: 'To restrain this child is to stifle him against God's will.' Although the superior was not very happy, she gave me my freedom and rewarded me with a payment of twenty-five sous.

Two weeks of adventures

I left with a sum of money which was insufficient even for one day. Miss Ngắm added to it a further twenty-five sous, so that I had fifty in total. Having such a small amount, and because everything was so expensive, I did not know what job to seek to survive; so I became a young tramp on the streets of Bắc-Ninh. It was my intention on leaving the house at (332) Đạo-Ngạn to return to my parents, admit my guilt, and ask them to send me to another presbytery. Then I remembered my father's threat when I was leaving with my mother for Hữu-Bằng: 'You are now leaving, and if you ever dare to run away again I will chop off your head.' The tone of his voice and the accompanying gestures convinced me that my father would find it as easy to chop off my head as he would to utter the words. Each time, therefore, that I recalled these violent words I was terror-struck, and I had the sensation of losing consciousness, and the feeling that my head was detached from my neck. I saw in a dream from time to time my father cutting off my head, and people mourning me as a martyr. I often thought during the day of the unjust death which awaited me, which probably prompted these dreams. Whatever the possible eventuality, I dared not return to the house because of this threat which was a source of unspeakable bitterness for (333) my soul throughout my wanderings.

The idea then came to me to go to my Aunt Khánh in the hope that she could find some place where I could continue my studies and achieve my ambition of becoming a priest. Unfortunately, bad luck was with me, allowing me twice to miss the bus going in her direction. My fifty sous had melted away after two days of wandering around the town of Bắc-Ninh. On the third day, I was in time for the bus, but I had no money left. I begged the inspector in vain to allow me to travel free as

---

* A niece by marriage to Aunt Khánh.

far as Từ-Sơn, which was only fifteen kilometres away, but he refused adamantly. I then decided to walk to my aunt's, following the direction taken by the traffic, but again there was more trouble. I had hardly walked half a kilometre when I came across a band of young buffalo keepers. They began intimidating me with a thousand questions, and (334)   then asked for my tunic, trousers, etc. They were too numerous for me to stand up to, so I had to turn tail and go back to Bắc-Ninh.

Once there, I wandered around the market place looking for work. I transported water by cart, and I washed dishes in the inns. I worked one day here and one day there, and when I had time on my hands I went into the church to visit the Blessed Sacrament and to say the rosary. I led this life for three days without acquiring a sou because the owners of the restaurants, not wishing to give me money, gave me the leftovers to eat. Because they saw that I was a good worker, they wanted to keep me as an employee. Not knowing where I was from, they took me as a child who became lost when the Japanese entered Lạng-Sơn. If I was asked about my past I simply replied:

'I have run away from the hill country.'

'Where are your parents?'

'I have not yet found them.'

'How old are you?'

'Twelve.'

'Have you done any studies?'

(335)   'I have my certificate of primary studies.'

Fortunately, I was not asked about the Japanese invasion of Lạng-Sơn. They were happy to take pity on this well-educated child who was lost and far from his parents. Some of them even wanted to adopt me, promising to help me continue my studies. I refused, because these people were not Catholics, and I was afraid that they might advise me, or even force me, to abandon my religion.

On the afternoon of the third day I was working for a lady who sold Chinese soup. She was friendly towards me because I was hard-working, polite, well-behaved and obedient, and she indicated that she wished to adopt me, promising to send me to learn a trade with her older son. From her manner of speaking I was almost certain that she was a Catholic. She was not like other employers; she spoke gently to me, as a mother to a child: 'Young man, I believe that you are the child of a family which is a cut above the norm. I don't know where you come from but one thing is certain, you have not yet been able to find your (336)   parents. Here is something for you to think about; a child must have a father and mother. Now, if you have to wander here and there, in the end how will you manage? I must admit, honestly, that being of the same religion as you, I admire you a lot because you treat your religion with respect. Those who wished yesterday to adopt you, I know that they are rich in material things but they are wanting in charity. They are Buddhists, and hate us Catholics a lot. If they like you, it is only because they have no children. They make you believe that you will be free to practise your religion, but once in their hands I doubt you will enjoy this freedom. I have nothing to hide from you. I feel sorry for your unhappy life and, living as you do now, don't imagine that you will always be able to live in peace. The day will come when these people will let you go and will no longer need your services. How will you live then? The best thing you can do is learn a trade. I am ready to help you. You can come to live with me if you agree, and go with my son every day to learn the trade of metal worker. He is fourteen and, like you, he (337) has his certificate of primary studies. You could then learn a trade together, and later assist each other.'

To reassure myself I was bold enough to ask the woman this question: 'Mrs, it may be impolite to ask, but I have the feeling that you, yourself, are a Catholic.' She looked smilingly at me and, moving her hand to her neck, she pulled out a string to which a little copper crucifix was attached, and a few well-worn aluminium medals. I looked at them carefully, but I could not identify which saints were depicted. Then, looking admiringly at her, and to be polite in my turn, I said: 'Thank you, Mrs.' She shook her head while replacing her medals and said to me: 'Don't be mistaken. When you come to me, you know who I am. I am poor, very poor, but I pay great attention to the spiritual and bodily needs of my children.' Here I interrupted her and apologised: 'I would not dare to doubt you, Mrs. If I ask such a question, it is to have more confidence in you. Your assessment of my situation is accurate, conse- (338) quently, I can do no better than profit from your concern and advice and, one day, should I succeed in life, I shall remember you with gratitude as one of my great benefactresses.'

I thought to myself: 'I shall go to her house and evaluate the situation. I shall speak honestly to her about my desire for the priesthood, and I shall rely on her to arrange the continuation of my studies, which has always been my fervent wish.'

When evening came the woman took me to her home. She lived in an alley which stretched deep into the suburbs. Her dwelling was hidden behind a row of clean houses of several storeys. The apartment she showed me as hers was really awful. I would never have imagined that in any town there could be apartments so poor. I have never seen such a type of construction. To tell the truth, it was a house made of stone but repaired in three or four places with old, woven bamboo. The door apart, which was simply a hole serving as an entry and exit, there was (339) no other opening, not even a window. The tiled roof was also patched up with straw in five or six places. Around the house, drains full of fetid water flowed into the paddy field and gave off a foul smell which was hurtful to tolerate. This woman made me cross a bridge made of a thick plank about two metres long. The entry to the house was one step from this bridge.

We had hardly entered when the woman shouted: 'Come on, children, where are you?' The children, who were behind the house, exclaimed: 'Hooray! It's mammy, it's mammy!' Three kids rushed into the house: a boy of about five years, and a little girl of eight who was carrying her little brother who could have been eighteen months old. The sight of the children made the situation even more pitiful: they were covered with purulent scabs, their clothes were dirty and in tatters, and they gave off a smell as foul as that which pervaded the house. The mother gave the two older children a cooked potato, took (340) the little one to be breastfed, and invited me to sit down near the bed. The two children looked at me with curiosity but the little girl, bolder, asked her mother, whilst eating her potato:

'Mammy, who is this boy?'

'He's your brother,' said the mother, smiling.

'What! . . . You are joking.'

The noise of a bicycle was heard in the alley. The little girl thought no more about quizzing her mother about this stranger who had been brought into the family, but ran to the door and cried:

'Ah, my brother Đinh is here.' The little boy went to join his sister.

Looking around me at that moment I saw, clearly, the state of abject poverty in which this family lived. The interior walls were of the same construction as the external ones. Here it had been necessary to cover a section with a bamboo mesh, there, stained and protruding bricks presented all kinds of imaginable shapes. The unpaved floor was damper than a fish-counter at the market. There was neither a chair (341) nor a cupboard in the entire room. The square bed was the only place on which to sit. Opposite the bed on which I was sitting, in the other corner of the room, was a stone fireplace about a metre in height which served as an altar for the family. In fact, a wooden crucifix was hanging on the wall next to the fireplace with a picture of the Sacred Heart on one side and a picture of Our Lady of Perpetual Succour on the other. All was darkened by smoke, so much so that the images were hardly visible as such. It seemed to me nevertheless that this was the most suitable place for hanging these pictures, because everywhere else was worse still.

While I was pondering the circumstances of this poor family, the little one who had just been fed, gave me a huge smile. From time to time he moved his hand to his head to scratch his suppurating spots, but it seemed that mammy was more interested in the child she had just 'adopted' than in her baby. I then spoke up to ask the woman: 'Mrs, where does your husband work that he has not yet returned home?' She replied calmly, without moving and without showing the slightest surprise: 'My husband has already been dead for over a year.' I was (342) surprised by this reply, because there was no evidence to support it. If her husband had been dead for just over a year, why were she and the children not in mourning? I was going to ask for explanations when she continued:

'My husband disappeared when the Japanese invaded Vietnam.'

'So your husband had to join the army?'

'No, but because of the unrest which reigned in our province, my husband ... was taken away somewhere.'

She stopped for a moment as if to control her emotions; then she continued: 'At this moment I do not know whether he's alive or dead.'

Đinh, the older boy, placed his cycle in a corner of the room, and as the two little ones had already told him that his mother had adopted this boy, he ran towards her, took the baby in his arms and asked, hurriedly: 'Mammy, who is this boy?' She told him what had happened, after which Đinh, full of joy, cried: 'Good, now I will have a friend at (343) the workshop.' Then he began to wave his arms about like an orator: 'Mammy,' he said, 'do you know that at the workshop there is not a single Catholic apart from me. I have to listen all day to my workmates swearing like troopers. It's really painful.' With his little brother in his arms he came to sit beside me, tapped me on the shoulder and said to me, happily: 'Be patient and stay with my mother. We will study together and, later, when we have a trade ... it will be marvellous ... won't it?'

'Yes. In this matter I trust you and your good advice.'

Đinh gave the baby to his mother and went to prepare the meal. The two little ones were playing marbles all the time in the alley near the house. The street lights were shining in the town, even before the people had need fof them.

Đinh took me to the church that evening and, thereafter, we became like real brothers. He was full of affection and kindness for me, and he told me many of his intimate feelings. When we returned to the house after evening prayers, we had our arms on each other's shoulders and (344) he began calling me 'little brother'. He was only fourteen, but he seemed as mature and hardened to his task as a man of thirty or forty. He loved his mother, brothers and sister very much. It is probably for this reason that, like them, he cheerfully put up with the itching scabs that he had to scratch unceasingly as soon as his hands were free. On our return home from church he prepared a bed for me to sleep on.

The only bed was reserved for his mother and the two little ones. Đình and his little sister slept on mats on the floor. Đình's mother had to go, after evening prayer, to help her brother who ran an inn, and they were particularly busy with clients taking meals at that time. Before going to bed, Đình assembled his brothers and sister around the fireplace to say three 'Hail Marys' in honour of Our Lady and to ask that his father might still be alive. The children obeyed him reluctantly, without daring to let escape an impolite word or action. I admired this fraternal

(345)   intimacy and I felt a great joy every time I heard Đình call me his little brother. When the prayers were over Đình invited me to settle on my bed on the ground. I suddenly felt a chill because the ground was so damp and gave off an odour which was painful to breathe. I feared that Đình might notice my distaste and be offended, but he was too busy choosing a log from the wood pile to act as my pillow to pay any attention to me. My pillow had already been found. Đình, pointing to his left arm, said to me, 'Here's your pillow.' At that moment I was still sitting on my bed laughing at Đinhs joke. He then put the two little ones on the bed and, turning his shoulder towards me, he said, cheerfully, 'That's enough little brother, let's go to sleep. Usually when my mother returns we must be asleep, otherwise she's not happy.' The little girl, not waiting for her brother's invitation, rolled herself in her mat and slept deeply. To sleep on the damp ground continued to be abhorrent to me, but in following the maxim of St Augustine to conquer my

(346)   repugnance, I said to myself: 'If Đình can sleep on the damp ground, so can I. I won't die because of it.' I had to raise my head, however, from time to time, to try to get rid of the saliva which I could not swallow because of the horrible smell from the drain. As soon as I stretched out on the matting, Đình put his left arm under my head, and with his right hand he did not cease from scratching the scabs from his armpits to his feet, which prompted both my pity and a strong urge to laugh. I asked my guardian angel to prevent my friend's scabies from migrating in my direction, because I had a fear of itchiness. Since we were so close together, I was certain that I would not be able to escape this voracious microbe. Happily, I was in no way contaminated.

Đình told me about his family situation while we were waiting to fall asleep. I was quite astonished at his honesty with me because we had only known each other for a few hours. It is thanks to this sincerity that

(347)   I clearly understood his family's circumstances. This is what he told me. 'Formerly, our family was far removed from the poverty it now suffers. Dad was a teacher at the school at Bắc-Giang but, because he was a member of the revolutionary party, the French government gave him the sack. He was also spied upon so that he had to move to different places to earn a living by giving private tuition. As regards my mother

and the children, she had a little business in the provincial market and managed well enough. My dad joined the revolutionary army [Phục Quốc] raised by Trần-Trung-Lập to overthrow the French in the year when the Japanese invaded Lang Son. Because of this, spies in the pay of the French often came to question my mother. For the sake of some peace my mother would give them a little to eat and drink. It was on this condition that they agreed to leave my father alone. In the long run my mother finished in poverty because of these spies. When Trần-Trung-Lập had been defeated and his army broken up, Dad secretly rejoined the family, and he intended to earn a living by selling Chinese soup. He received a secret letter, hardly a month later, hidden in a paté of pork meat that somebody had given to him. The letter said: "On a given day, two Japanese soldiers will come to take you." Recognising   (348) the letter as coming from the army, he prepared himself and waited for them. Indeed, on the appointed day, two Japanese soldiers arrived at our house in a military vehicle and spoke to my father in French. They invited him to get into the car with them. My father, dressed as a Japanese soldier and carrying a small case, followed them. We have not seen him since that day … Two months later, we learned that the French spies had tricked him in this way to capture him. My mother was distraught, but after living for a few days as if she had lost her mind, thanks to her great confidence in God and the Blessed Virgin she regained normality, and busied herself with bringing us here. She bought this dirty shack to protect us against the rain and the sun and began working with my uncle in order to feed us.'

He also confided in me that when he was young his parents sent him to a presbytery as a candidate for the priesthood but, after a short time, because of the bad example he was witnessing, he had asked his parents to bring him home. Because he was so sincere I intended to tell him my   (349) story but, and I'm not sure why, I did not yet wish to say anything. Instead of speaking about myself I questioned him on the revolutionary life led by his father. Thanks to this conversation I was able to form a good opinion of the revolutionaries whom I had considered, until then, in accordance with popular opinion, as the emissaries of anti-Christ. This opinion did not correspond with the truth.

The revolutionaries are people who love their country and respect their fellow-countrymen, but when they see their country dishonoured and despised they suffer greatly and look for every means of liberating them. To obtain this freedom for their country they are prepared to sacrifice their own, and they are often forced to go into hiding from the invader and even to sacrifice their lives to accomplish their ideals. I suddenly felt a warm affection for the revolutionaries. I cried for those who had died although they had pursued an objective opposed to

(350)   religion like the friendly revolutionary Trần-Trung-Lập. During that night, remembering this man who had failed in his plan to reconquer his country, my eyes filled with tears and I allowed some poignant words to escape: 'O Trần-Trung-Lập, may it please heaven that you had faith in God. May it please heaven that you never chased God from any of your activities which deserve to be remembered. Why did you hate the Christians, these faithful children of God? Yes, it is quite possible that you deceived yourself. Nevertheless, if your intentions were good, I now ask God to deliver you quickly from purgatory ...'

Đinh, seeing my floods of tears, and hearing my jumbled words which he did not understand, was suspicious and asked me, abruptly:

'So you like Trần-Trung-Lập then? It's not ... O Van! You aren't Trần-Trung-Lập's son?'

'No! You know Trần-Trung-Lập wasn't a Christian, whereas I've
(351)   been one all my life.'

'Then why do you cry when you speak of him?'

'Because I like him for being a revolutionary who was killed by the French. Furthermore, I am moved because he so hated religion. I have heard it said that at the time when he was being taken to his execution, a priest came to him, but, instead of expressing any gratitude, he insulted him, called him a pig and an emissary of the French invaders ... I like Trần-Trung-Lập very much. I do not know if he has lost his soul.'

'Come on, our friend is not lost. If he's not in heaven, he's in hell! How then could it get lost?'

I burst out laughing in spite of myself on hearing Đinh's little joke. He, seeing me laugh, scratched himself in a satisfied manner and then added:

'Van, you are really generous, but why do you cry for this man as if you were crying for your father?'

'I am very sorry because I know, from the example of your father, that revolutionaries live under very precarious conditions.'

'That's enough of that, Van. If you love them, pray for them because, as my father used to say, there are a good number of revolutionaries
(352)   who only know how to rise up for a group which pleases them considering all others as anti-revolutionary enemies.'

'Well, Đinh,' I interrupted him, 'why has your father, who is certainly a good Christian, followed Trần-Trung-Lập?'

'If my father followed him, it was simply for opportunistic reasons.'

With these words he kept silent. Then shortly afterwards he continued, hesitatingly: 'Naturally, I am not very well informed because, usually, my father was very discreet.'

But talk of the revolution had to end there because the mother had arrived. She asked us why we were not yet asleep. Without waiting for any reply she put down her shoulder carrier and went to bed. Not daring to chatter any more, we thought only of sleeping … Nevertheless, I found it difficult to close my eyes … In fact I had hardly any wish to sleep with all these notions of the turbulent life of the revolutionary still twisting around in a frantic manner in my head. Afterwards I had the desire to be a revolutionary myself. I wished to fight to create a good future for the Church in Vietnam. I wished to reform the parishes, I wished that all candidates for the priesthood   (353) could enjoy real freedom in an ambience conducive to piety where they would be supported and assisted in a spirit of charity … etc. In brief, I longed for many, many things: to so arrange things that the parishes could really be called parishes which were one hundred per cent Catholic; where priests would stop abusing alcohol, stop beating people etc. I was thus really finding myself in the role of a real missionary … However, on reflection, I asked myself if young revolutionaries in a situation like mine had ever attracted anyone's attention. Then, overtaken by a feeling of helplessness, my tears began to flow once again. I was both hurt and outraged that no one was interested in getting a full knowledge of the facts of the lives of these children who, with sincere souls, were preparing themselves for the priesthood.

I heard a cock crowing in the distance and I suddenly realised that the night was almost over. I felt very tired. Sitting up, I said some prayers to dissipate the dark thoughts which haunted me. Then I lay down again. I had hardly closed my eyes when the church bell sounded. Định's mother called us to go to Mass. Although half asleep, I forced myself to get up and follow Định to the church because I was afraid that   (354) I might have to accompany him soon to work.

Dissension

Unfortunately, my luck changed. That very day after breakfast, Định's mother suggested that on his arrival at the factory he should suggest to the owner to take me on as an apprentice. She invited me to accompany her to help her in the morning's work at the inn, but when her brother learned of her intention to adopt me so that I could learn a trade, he immediately opposed it and chased me from the inn, not wishing to give me any work. At first the lady thought that her brother, in the habit of drinking and of talking in a hard manner, would soften once the drunkenness had passed but, at midday, noticing that his sister continued to give me various jobs to do and show me how to proceed, he became furious, threw down his knife and disappeared. Where to? I did

(355) not know. It was only at two o'clock in the afternoon that he returned. His eyes were red and his breath smelled of alcohol. He spotted me, stared at me and then, grabbing his knife, he came towards me, grabbed me by the throat and then, raising his arm, he threatened me in a most cruel voice: 'Do you want to live or die?' Everybody who was there was stunned at this spectacle. They ran to overcome the man and drag me from his hands. His action caused me to freeze with fear as if I were deprived of all feeling and unable to utter a word. My face was full of tears as I breathed painfully like someone completely exhausted.

Đinh's mother was probably more afraid than I was. She held me in her arms and comforted me by saying: 'Don't be afraid.' But her voice was croaking as if she were breathing her last and her face was as pale as if she'd seen a ghost. Just then, two policemen arrived with a summons to take the drunken man to the police station, but thanks to the concern of his friends at the inn, he was treated leniently and avoided a spell in jail. Đinh's mother, realising that she could not protect me at her house, took me to the market to recommend me to (356) other people. On leaving this lady's house I missed the happiness which reigned there in spite of its great poverty. That is why I could not hold back my tears as I took leave of her to begin again my life as a vagrant in the market of Bắc-Ninh.

Up for sale

Towards the end of the evening all the women of the inn were talking about the little lad who had almost had his head cut off. They were all horrified and full of pity for this lost child but none of them was prepared to take me in, for fear of a husband with a bad temper. All I knew was to place myself under the protection of the Blessed Virgin. However, when the market was over, I saw a woman aged about thirty who was wearing clothes redolent of both town and country and who was wearing on her breast a little crucifix with a gold charm. She followed me and showed an interest in my story. Once or twice when someone spoke of my unfortunate circumstances she tut-tutted or made some sad comments while looking at me with pity. She went from one stall to another without buying anything, but continuing to look at me (357) very carefully. When everyone had dispersed and the market was deserted she came to me and said, coaxingly: 'Listen, little one, it's nearly night time. It's better that you come and spend the night at my house' ... Her words were marked with concern and the words, 'It's nearly night time', brought to my mind the freezing night that I would have to spend in the market, so exposed to the winds. I lifted my eyes towards this woman and then immediately lowered them to the ground to allow my tears to flow. Instead of replying, I tapped the cemented paving stones in the middle of the market. Seeing this, she once again insisted: 'Come to my house, and I will feed you and make you do the study you need to.'

Frankly, impressed by her crucifix and her gentle and kind words, I was certain that she was a good Christian, just like the lady I had met the day before, and without questioning her further I accepted her proposal, and followed her to her house. This was in a district at a distance from the suburban area; there were only straw huts, and it (358) resembled a hamlet in the country. It was more than a kilometre from the town. It was not a busy place. My suspicions were aroused the moment I set foot in the place, and I did not wish to take a step further because the style of decorations of the apartment made me realise that this lady was not a Christian. I looked fixedly at the altar of the ancestors to make her realise that I had noticed it and then, affecting a surprised air, I asked her:

'Is this really your house?'

'Yes.'

'Then it would be right to say that you have no religion.'*

She forced a smile and replied:

'Why that uncalled-for question? Everybody has a religion.'

'Yes, but the Catholic religion is the only true religion. That was the meaning of my question.'

'Come, come. All religions are good.'

'I am certain that you wish to deceive me.'

'Not at all ... and if you wish to go to Monsignor's house to pray, I will let you. Nobody will stop you.'

With these words she went into her room to change and prepare the meal.

At that moment there was a great sadness in my heart, but because it (359) was already night I resigned myself to wait for the next day before coming to a decision. When the lady came out of her room I noticed that she was dressed as country folk dress. The cross and chain had disappeared and only an amulet on a string hung from her neck. On examining her then, I felt there was a dreadful and malevolent air about her. She looked at me from time to time with her dark eyes as if weighing up my dissatisfaction. She probably understood my profound sadness and guessed my intention of not staying there. She was searching for words to welcome me. She would even adopt a virtuous demeanour and say to me: 'You will ruin your life if you would roam

---

* He meant by this, 'One could say that you are not a Catholic.'

around as you do.' Then followed some words of warning: 'You never know, but in these uncertain times a large number of unfortunate children like you have been seized, sold and even been sent to China. These Chinese love to buy children to pronounce magical incantations on them, before burying them alive so as to make their spirits look after their belongings. I took pity on you and brought you here to look after you, fearing that you might suffer this cruel fate ...'

(360)

All that this woman said to me neither moved nor frightened me. I was convinced that a child like me would never allow himself to be caught and sold. Besides, even this woman's mischief which sought to deceive me could not escape me. Once I had unmasked her deceitfulness, all the sweet things she poured out for my ears had no more effect than that of water on a duck's back. The more she spoke, the less confidence I had in her, and the better I understood her intention to keep me for her own profit. She spoke non-stop like a wailing gramophone, until the moment when, collecting a packet of bindweed, she got up and went into the kitchen to prepare the meal. She added, on rising, 'If you don't believe me, ask my husband when he returns shortly. He is as honest and as good as those of your religion.'

(361)

As soon as she left for the kitchen, I made the sign of the cross and began discreetly to say my rosary. The sky had changed outside and in the distance, towards the town, electric lights were twinkling like stars. I had finished two decades of the rosary when I noticed a very skinny man pulling a handcart into the yard. The woman shouted to me from the kitchen: 'Here is my husband coming.' The man put the cart under a thatched roof in front of the house and came on to the veranda. I stood up and greeted him politely: 'Good day, sir.' He was astonished, but replied in like manner and then asked: 'Who is this little fellow?' His wife answered from the kitchen. 'He is the little one who was wandering round the town market, and I don't know why, but he almost had his head chopped off by the owner of an inn whom he was working for, who was in a drunken state.' Then, as if she did not want her husband to question her further, she cleverly called him into the kitchen, saying: 'Oh, who does this belong to? Come and see a minute.' The husband could have been about forty, but looked much older with his weed-like arms and legs, his bony face and his sunken eyes. But the worst were his bushy eyebrows and his dishevelled hair, which gave him all the appearance of a very drunken man. He went out to draw water from an earthenware jug at a very slow pace, washed his face, combed his hair with his fingers and entered the kitchen to listen to his wife speak to him concerning what she called 'this thing'.

(362)

As I greatly doubted their sincerity and I was unable to contain my curiosity, I tiptoed to the kitchen but I could not catch clearly the words they were whispering to each other. Apart from that, I understood well from their demeanour that they wished to hide something from me. In order to interrupt their conversation and affecting a serious manner, I entered the kitchen whilst vigorously tapping my heel against the ground and I asked, innocently: 'Mrs, is the rice ready? Let me help you.' They immediately stopped their hushed conversation when they saw me enter, and the wife pretended to say something inconsequential in her husband's ear in a manner calculated for me to hear. Presuming from my question that I did not know what they were talking about, she turned towards me and said, quite normally: 'Go and rest. The rice has just been put in the pan. It is not ready yet. You go and relax, and I'll prepare the food for you.' The couple did not give me a courteous sign before the meal began. On the contrary, when I carefully made the sign of the cross and said my prayers, they looked at each other and giggled. I ate very little, afraid that they had mixed some potion in the food which would make my escape difficult. Once the meal was over I went to sit in a corner to say my evening prayers and the rosary before lying down. I did not sleep a wink that night although I was stretched out on the bed. I was incapable of closing my eyes but I did not hear the husband and wife talking about me. (363)

(364)

I got up early and said my prayers while the couple were still deeply asleep. As it was still dark I lay down to sleep until it was light. They were already up when I awoke, and the meal was ready. The husband sent me to the water basin to wash my face and then invited me to eat. I had hardly sat on the stool, and had not had time to bless myself, when the husband said to me in a scoffing tone: 'Steady on, young man! Before eating you must first make a sign to drive away the devil, otherwise he will enter your stomach, and hard luck on you ...' Then, laughing, he looked at his wife. They made fun of me but it did not upset me. Whilst laughing also, I in my turn, asked him, teasingly:

'And you, sir, have you never made a sign before eating to drive away the devil?'

'It's different for me.'

I laughed triumphantly and added to his words: (365)

'Yes, it is different ... which means, quite simply, that your stomach is full of devils.'

His wife, seeing that I had gained the upper hand, roared with laughter and, tapping her husband on the shoulder, made fun of him, saying:

'Well, there you are! Beaten by a child!' The husband swallowed his mouthful greedily and, not being able to hide his shame, lowered his head with the air of a beaten dog.

The sky was very dark that morning, as if foreshadowing the sufferings that I shall soon describe. The woman bade me to remain in the house to rest after the meal, while she went to the town to buy things needed for my studies. The husband did not go to work, saying that he would stay at home to keep me company, fearing that I might be sad. Since their first meeting with me, this couple had shown me none of the affection one would to a child. They considered me simply as a friendly, passing guest. The woman only returned with her shopping basket towards the middle of the morning, and I noticed that she had not brought any books. However, a woman with a friendly manner, aged about fifty, arrived as if she had come for a chat. While speaking she scrutinised me from head to toe. The woman and her husband intro-

(366)   duced me so casually to her that I assumed they were related, but after a moment of friendly discussion, I saw them withdraw to the kitchen to argue over the question of price, and I immediately understood that this woman was there to buy me, to make me her adopted child or her servant. Having reached an agreement on the price, (I do not know how much exactly) the stranger, whom the couple called Mrs Hương, came out of the kitchen and spoke to me in these terms: 'How are you little one? I have been told that you come from a good family and that you have finished some studies, and after chatting with you for a while, I have noticed that you have some good qualities, and I for my part will hide nothing from you. These people really wish to be kind enough to give you to me as my adopted child, because in my family there are very few children. You should think about it. It is true that the family of this rickshaw driver, where you find yourself currently, have no children either, but they are very poor. It would be much better if you came with me. I will take the responsibility of making a man of you, and I shall

(367)   treat you as my own child. What do you think? Do you agree or not? . . .'

I did not answer her but, realising the bad motives of this couple, I began to sob. They had made me wonderful promises: they would attend to my studies; they would feed and clothe me as necessary, etc. Now the reality was staring me in the face. All their false promises were simply to trick me to keep me at their house so that they could sell me and make money for themselves. I remained seated a long time after Mrs Hương's exhortation without moving or saying anything, although she repeated her question many times and leaned towards me twice so that she was almost touching my face. I kept an obstinate silence with my head lowered as plentiful tears flowed on to the bottom of my tunic. I then thought, this man and this woman have deceived me. How do I not know that the nice words of this other woman with her bourgeois ways are not equally deceitful? I lifted my head abruptly and asked her:

'Mrs, have you any religion?'*

---

*   That is to say, 'Are you a Catholic?'

'Well, I never! What a question! But everybody has a religion.'

'I was obviously talking about the Catholic religion.'   (368)

'Oh all religions are good, but if you wish to keep yours nobody will stop you.'

I lowered my head and cried silently without answering the lady. I said to myself: 'Who knows if she is telling me the truth? Who knows if, once I'm in her hands, she will not employ the cruellest means to make me lose my faith? O my God, what a torture it will be for my heart if I lose my faith one day! But what can I do now? A price has already been agreed to sell me to this person and she, after having paid over this amount of money, even if it is only one sou to buy my freedom – she has full authority over me. I belong to her completely, just like a slave, and I must obey her orders and do all she wishes. How can I keep my religion and fulfil my much-longed-for ambition to reach for perfection and become a priest?'

The husband, seeing me in tears, spoke up to comfort me:

'Come on, why are you crying? What are you afraid of? It's not so   (369) bad, is it? Religion can be practised everywhere. God is everywhere. He can be worshipped anywhere, there's no need to ... provided that one has food and a trade ... that's really something.' I became angry and pressed him:

'If you believe that God is everywhere, why don't you worship him?'

'I was speaking according to your religion. As far as I'm concerned, I don't believe that God is everywhere to be adored.'

'Is that why you both believe that telling a lie is not a sin and deception is an act of virtue? I will never believe anything you say since you admit that you do not believe in God.'

On hearing me, the woman got angry herself, and as if to eradicate the words I had just spoken, she said in a loud manner:

'That's enough! The business is done! Well and truly! Mrs Hương, you may go and tomorrow you can come back and take him ... If one believes or not, too bad!' ...

The woman accompanied Mrs Hương into the street whilst talking in a low voice. And me, I was still seated with my head bowed, and I cried. (370) The man went to the kitchen to get his bamboo pipe. He took a puff and then, going on to the veranda, he sat on his heels while looking at the sky. He looked as if he was on guard near me. The weather became gloomier, and the torrential rain seemed to sympathise with the profound unhappiness of this lonely child.

Escape

It was still pouring down when dinner was over. I decided to escape before the couple received the proceeds from the transaction. I maintained a calm demeanour, nevertheless. Even more, I adopted a stupid air so that they could not guess my intentions because, at that time more than ever, they were sensitive to my least movement. After having eaten my fill as usual, I stretched out on the bed and slept like a log. When I (371) woke up I saw the couple crouched beside my bed, talking, unaware that I was awake. I intended to sleep further to gather my strength because, who knows, when night has come I will have to remain awake to be on the look out for a chance to escape. But it was impossible to sleep any more. I remained still, therefore, as if in a deep sleep. A moment later I heard the husband give a long yawn, stretch himself and say to his wife: 'It's very gloomy weather ... I'm going to lie down.' He stretched out on my left and in five minutes he was snoring away ... The woman lay down on my right but, before doing so, she leant over my face and said, softly: 'If this little one could marry little Tí, the daughter of Mrs Hương, how happy he would be.' I immediately felt disturbed, my face became very hot and I felt very ill-at-ease. I do not know if the woman noticed the change in my face which her words provoked. Probably not, because she fell heavily on her bed which creaked and shook.

(372)   It was certainly not the greatest of pleasures to lie thus between the woman and her husband, but anything else was impossible. About five minutes later I thought that the woman, like her husband, was deeply asleep, so I got up and stepped, quietly, over the husband to get out of bed. He suddenly stopped snoring. I was momentarily afraid, but he soon recommenced, louder still. I sat on the camp bed in the middle of the room and I looked into the yard. The rain had lessened but the general ambience remained sad. I had not even decided to run away at that precise moment. Nevertheless, I felt impelled by a mysterious voice which told me to flee immediately. I guessed it was probably a pressing invitation from my Mother Mary because, since I had been put up for sale, I cannot describe how homesickness for my family was breaking my heart. The picture of my much-loved mother especially was always on my mind and if I cried a lot, it was simply because of the thought that I must be separated for good from all those whom I held most dear. If I did not manage to escape from their hands, once the lady had paid the agreed sum, any so-longed-for meeting with my family would (373) be no more than a prolonged torture.

Thinking of all this, I begged the Blessed Virgin to come to my aid to help me to escape before this lady came to pay the money and take me to her home. This was therefore the favourable time that Our Lady was giving to me. Reassured to see the couple sleeping so soundly, I decided to follow the promptings of my soul and flee without delay. I blessed myself and said three Hail Marys to ask Our Lady's protection. I then stepped out of that house. Once through the door I felt overcome by a great anxiety. I turned round to see if anyone was aware of my escape but, seeing no one move, I moved resolutely along the main road to run without stopping to the market of Bắc-Ninh.

The owners of the inns, who had already noticed my absence, supposed that I had already found lodging somewhere but, seeing my return, looking afraid and drenched to the skin, grouped around me to question me. They listened to my detailed account of the story of the (374) rickshaw driver's family who intended to sell me. They found it a dreadful state of affairs, but no one thought of coming to my aid. Shortly afterwards, as I was sitting near the fire of a seller of Chinese soup to dry my clothes, a man of about fifty appeared holding a big meat knife in his hand. I realised then that he also sold Chinese soup. He came up to me and tapped me on the shoulder in a friendly manner and he greeted me by bowing his head as if I was someone important. I understood that he was playacting. Then he tapped me on the chest and in the middle of the market proudly introduced himself: 'I am a Catholic myself ... My God! it was really too bad for you. I have just heard folk telling of your adventure, and I was greatly moved. Why don't you come with me? I will feed you and teach you a trade so that you can earn a living.'

Once again someone was promising to care for me. How I hated these fine words from peoples' mouths. That is why, in spite of his (375) declaration and his crucifix exhibited dangling from his chest, I did not believe in the man's sincerity. How could one believe the words of such people? So I answered him immediately:

'Thank you kindly for your sympathy, and your offer to teach me a trade so I can earn a living, but I cannot stay at Bắc-Ninh. I must find a way of returning to my parents, or at least to people who know me and can look after me. All I ask of you is that I may work for a little while, so as to earn some money to go to one of my aunts.'

'Where does your aunt live?'

'At Từ-Sơn.'

'Từ-Sơn! That's very close to here. Why don't you just go there?'

'Yes, I know it's very close, but I have not got a sou for the bus.'

'Go on foot. It's only fifteen kilometres.'

'I've already tried that, but a gang of youngsters, buffalo herdsmen, blocked my way and tried to intimidate me. They even took my white coat.'

(376)   'Curse that ignorant lot! But did you not ask for a seat on the bus?'

'Yes, I did, but the driver made fun of me – "Come off it, you expect to go on the bus without paying?"'

'Then come along with me. You can work for a few days, and then I'll make sure to send you to your aunt's.

Unfortunately, as I learned very quickly, the man was dominated totally by his wife. He spoke at the market with the self-confidence of a general but, once at home, he became a lamb and feared her as if she were a tiger. This woman had embraced the Catholic religion with a view to marriage, which was celebrated on the same day as her baptism. She had had two children, but unfortunately the first-born died very young, which plunged the woman into a deep sadness and, from that moment, she abandoned all practice of her religion. Shortly afterwards, and without her husband's knowledge, she went to the pagoda of Lim to ask for the gift of more children. She even consulted a soothsayer to find what the future had in store. A short time afterwards she gave birth to a second boy, just as beautiful as the first, but this time, she was determined not to take him to church to have him baptised, although the

(377)   church was only fifty metres from her house. She was afraid that this child, like the first one, would die if he were baptised. The poor husband had to agree. She ordered him to take down all the statues and pious pictures in the house, and to discontinue saying his prayers. The poor man had to obey his wife's orders.

I realised immediately on entering the house that the wife did not like me for the simple reason that I was a Catholic. She showed her unhappiness as soon as her husband introduced me, and when I began to do some work in the house, she treated me very harshly. She moaned at her husband all day because I asked to go to Mass in the morning, and to the church again in the evening to say my prayers. Before the day was done she had already asked her husband on two occasions to show me the door. What annoyed her most was that each time that she handed me the baby, I tried to teach him the sign of the cross. He was not yet one year old, but he was very bright, and after several practices, when I asked him to sign himself he raised his hand immediately, and did so correctly. Of course, he could not yet say the words as he was not yet able to speak.

(378)   The husband, despite the wife's insistence, would not agree to dismiss me, because it was profitable for him to retain me. He satisfied himself by trying to tempt me saying:

'You know, it's sufficient to believe in God, so why burden yourself by going to Mass and saying your prayers? It would be nice if you could listen to me so as to not sadden my wife. From now on, my friend, stop going to Mass. It is sufficient to keep one's religion in one's heart.'

'As far as I'm concerned, I don't agree that it is sufficient to keep one's religion in one's heart. I say that we must also adore God externally.'

In my enthusiasm I gave the husband and wife a sermon, and the first question I posed to the husband was this question from the gospel: 'Do you light a light to put it under a bushel?' I then gave this warning: 'If you don't keep God's law, God will certainly punish you.' I then advised the husband to remind the wife of the obligation she had to baptise the infant as soon as possible. Seeing that I was right, the husband agreed and said to his wife: 'Don't you see? Doesn't this boy speak as well as the (379) missionary who preaches in church? You see, everyone says so. The little one must be baptised, but you . . .'

'Baptise! Baptise!' the woman said, and then flew into a rage and well and truly abused her husband. Not knowing what to reply, the husband muttered something and then, getting up, he discreetly withdrew to escape the wrath of the 'queen' of the household.

The following day, at midday, seeing her husband bless himself before eating, the wife began to sulk and refused to eat. What exasperated her even more was to see the little one also make the sign of the cross like us. She hit him on the head immediately, and cursed him with these words: 'Wretch! Are you imitating your father in punishing me?' She then withdrew, not wishing to eat any more. Her husband ran after her to mollify her, but his wife, the 'queen', was so angry that her face was purple with rage. What ensued was typical. The husband, who normally spoke fluently, began to stammer as soon as his wife told him off. I had to make a big effort not to laugh when I saw his efforts to (380) speak while his wife showered him with insults. He had to leave the house every time. This time, her husband having just left and not having anyone to argue with, to soothe her anger she began to cry in vexation. Then, taking advantage of her husband's absence and without giving me as much as a sou, the lady of the house immediately evicted me. I left without even bothering to ask for any wage, and I hurried to the church to confide my life, once again, to the Blessed Virgin. I said the rosary and then left, and like Saint Alexis, I sought perfection by begging on the streets.

I did not go again to Bắc-Ninh market, but from then onwards I would ply the trade of beggar by holding out my hand to the passersby as they moved from the church to the station, and from the station to the church. My life was uncertain. When the sun shone, all was well, but there were also rainy days, typical of this changeable season of autumn. Sometimes I was full, but sometimes I was starving, so that sadness left me only fleetingly. I lay at night under the shelter of big (381) trees or under the canopies at the sides of the streets. Had someone seen me once and then seen me five days later, they would not have recognised me. I was aware of the change which had taken place in me: my hands and feet were skinny, my skin was tanned by the sun, and when I touched my cheeks, I felt only the bones of my emaciated jaws. My hair was very long and, probably, very dirty ... I realised, even without a mirror, that my body had changed a great deal. I was wearing the same clothes as at my absconding and they had not been washed. They had, obviously, lost their original whiteness and had become very yellow, blending with the colour on the ground. One could add the oil-stains and the marks of the remnants of food. Apart from these, the only other garment I possessed was a potato sack which I had picked up in front of Bắc-Ninh station. This served as cloak, headgear, scarf, and also to collect the leftovers which people gave me as alms. When night came it was a useful blanket, covering me from my stomach to my feet. Nevertheless, I found no hardship in this life as a beggar. I felt, on the contrary, a peaceful joy in suffering for God. I knew that by running away I had fled sin, I had fled that which was offensive to God's heart. In spite of the very painful aspect of my situation, I put up with it willingly without being afraid of suffering although it could stir my heart and move me to tears.

(382)

At this time when I had to struggle unceasingly to survive, my desire for the priesthood did not weaken, but how could I achieve it if I continued to live on the streets as a beggar? I would have really loved to meet a priest to explain my situation to him, but where could I find such a priest who would be able to understand me? I often thought of presenting myself to the mission at Bắc-Ninh in order to meet a priest to whom I could open my heart, but I was afraid of being held and sent back to the parish of Hữu-Bằng. This thought frightened me. I was resolutely determined never again to stay in that parish.

(383)

I also had a great desire to see my family once again, and to feel once more the support of my mother. She would understand me, and find a place for me where I could continue my studies for the priesthood. Unfortunately, my father's words were still embedded in my mind. The words, 'I will cut your head off', still struck my heart like a flash of lightning every time I thought of them. The thing I found most painful was that, whilst walking along the road from the station to the church, I had to pass where the road for motor cars began which ended up at my village and with my much-loved family. My desire to follow it and return to my parents' home was always a sad fight. Sometimes, unable to resist, I set off down that road, but once my feeling of exaltation had passed I turned back, full of sadness and regrets, terrified again by the thought of my father's threats.

(384)

Meeting people who know me

The sadness which agonised my soul sometimes made me behave foolishly. I cried when I was given food, and on the other hand I laughed when I was slapped, but in critical situations I was clear-sighted and never deceived. I could even respond in a mischievous manner. I found myself twice in the presence of people who knew me. On the first occasion it was at a Chinese soup vendor's, for whom I was working. I met a pupil of the catechism school who had stayed in the same presbytery as myself. On the evening of this meeting the vendor had pushed his   (385) cart right up to the churchyard to sell his wares. He even allowed me to go in to say my prayers on condition that I returned afterwards to help him. Clients would arrive until eleven o'clock. We were on the point of leaving when five high-spirited youths arrived and asked for food.

I immediately noticed three that I knew very well. Only one of them, however, had lived with me in the Hữu-Bằng presbytery and he was standing close to me. It was hardly three months since we had left each other. Afraid of being recognised, I searched a means of avoiding them by saying to the merchant: 'That's enough. It's late and we have already put everything away.' But, seeing customers, he did not reply. He ordered me to poke up the fire, to heat the broth and to lay the table to give these gentlemen a good meal. Their words and laughter burst out like fire-crackers while I was preparing things. I understood by listening to them, that they had been to a modern play, even though the rule of the monastery forbade going out at night for amusement. I worked   (386) with my head down from the outset without saying a word, for fear of being recognised by the one who had been with me in the presbytery. This could have been dangerous. My boss commanded me from time to time to do this or that, and I was happy to signal my comprehension simply by an inclination of the head as I worked with the speed of lightning. The vendor's cart by good fortune was parked far enough away from the electric lamps that the light was too weak for an individual to be distinctly recognised. An oil lamp was also hanging fairly high up in the cart, but I hid my face by standing behind a piece of meat which was hanging at the side.

Once the meal was prepared, I went to sit at a distance, tapping my foot rhythmically on the pavement. The boss walked here and there chatting with his customers. Suddenly, the boy who had lived with me at Hữu-Bằng asked him:

'Who is that little chap who looks like Van?'

I jumped, but pretended not to understand anything. Just at that moment, one of his companions from Tử-Nê who was a nephew of Father Cương asked in his turn:

(387)   'You are doubtless speaking of Lê's little brother?'

'Yes, Lê of Ngăm-Giáo; you know.'

'You are very vulgar. You think of nothing but Lê.'

'Don't be cheeky. I answer your questions and you ...'

Then they jostled each other whilst laughing in a satisfied manner. A moment later Đông continued:

'It's true, anyway. This young chap does resemble Van. It's weird! Van, is it you who is sitting there?'

Pretending not to understand him, I replied:

'Me, Sir? Do you want something?'

'You are Van, aren't you?'

He was convinced it was me. My heart was beating harder and harder, but I forced myself not to give way, and feigning a silly manner I asked him:

'Sir? ... Van? which Van?'

'It's strange. You are the spitting image of Van of Hữu-Bằng.'

Hưng, of Tử-Nê reproached Đông:

'You are really silly .... You'd mistake a chicken for a fox.'

'You are getting on my nerves. Attend to your own business.'

'As you please, but all you think about is Lê ...and when you see a young lad, you assume it's her little brother Van.'

Once again they punched each other on the shoulder while laughing noisily. The boss, who was standing on the pavement on the other side,
(388)   seeing his clients question me and noticing my uncomprehending attitude, came close to me and asked:

'Gentlemen, is something missing?'

'Who is this young chap that one does not ordinarily see around here?'

The boss, speaking confidentially as if he were knowledgeable of my situation, said: 'Ah, yes. This young fellow comes from Lạng-Sơn. He was lost at the time of the Japanese invasion, far from his father and mother, and seeing him wandering around the market a few days ago, I brought him with me to teach him a trade so that he could earn a living.' Falling over backwards, Đông began to laugh, to hide his embarrassment and said: 'Well, who would have believed it? He doesn't half look like a little lad I know from somewhere! That's why I posed the question, to see if it was really him. As a matter of fact, I learned recently, that he had run away. That is why I was wondering whether it was him or not.'

Well, what a happy outcome! I felt as if a heavy load weighing on my heart had been lifted off me. From then onwards the boy paid me no
(389)   further attention. Eight months later, on meeting me again at Hữu-Bằng, he told me this story and he asked me if it was really me who was

there. He thus proved that he had a good but uncertain memory. Had this not been the case, he would have been able to recapture me near the soup vendor's cart. As for me, I listened to this interesting story, being careful not to admit that I had worked for a soup vendor.*

Some days after this adventure, while still begging on the street, I met Hạng, a cousin of my mother's. I was standing on the Hồ jetty, where the road comes from Bắc-Ninh, when I was lucky enough to meet a bus which had just arrived. I was standing there, holding out my hand to every passenger when suddenly I found myself face to face with my cousin. My God! Should he recognise me it was bad news for me! ... Blessed Virgin, help me! With this prayer in my heart I strode boldly towards him to ask him for alms as I had done the others. Just at that moment I pretended to lose the sack which was covering my shoulders. I bent down to recover it and put it over my head so as to hide myself (390) a little and to change my face a little. I moved towards him pretending to shake all over as if I were feverish.

My Father, you must understand that in those days people said that I had caught malaria at Lạng-Sơn, which was understandable, because the appearance of my face and exhausted body would help them to believe that I was a refugee who had left Lạng-Sơn following the Japanese invasion, but it was curious. The attitude of the passenger in question was really bizarre. Twice I put out my hand, to him, but he did not even reject me with a look of compassion. He neither offered nor refused me anything. Holding his bicycle, he looked at me for a long time with an astonished expression. Knowing that he was looking at me, I withdrew my hand and went elsewhere. Suddenly he questioned me: 'Hey, you there, Van! I heard that you had run away from Father Nhã's house a few weeks ago, and that you had not returned to your family. You little toad! And now you're a beggar!' On hearing again the words 'I heard' I felt calmer, because these words spoken by my cousin meant that he had no definite proof. He could well have heard that I (391) had fled, but he was not sure of the fact. I returned, therefore, and putting on an act, I answered him:

'Excuse me, sir! What did you say?'

He was flabbergasted. He thought he was speaking to Van personally, but here was this little beggar interrogating him in his turn.

'Are you Van, by any chance?'

'Sir? Van? But which Van?'

'Come, come! Van, Father Nhãs protégé who has just run away. Nobody else.'

---

* To tease Lê, whom he loved a lot, he told her that Van, her little brother had become the 'boy' of a Chinese soup merchant. Lê was very hurt. [Tế]

Sighing deeply in a cold manner and shaking my head, I replied, 'It's strange, sir. You are asking me something I don't understand.'

On witnessing this amusing scene, the passengers were astonished by the strange attitude of the traveller, and asked themselves what question he had just asked to cause the boy he was speaking to to complain in this way. Slightly embarrassed and believing that he was indeed mistaken, he hurried to push his bicycle, murmuring: 'If you don't understand, fair enough.'

(392)   Before getting on to his bicycle, he turned round to apologise, saying to someone: 'I thought it was my little cousin. That's why I questioned him, to make sure.' He jumped on his bike, turned his pedals to get going and then, turning round, he looked at me again carefully, and said: 'How can he look so much like Van?' Then he disappeared quickly.*

Meeting him at home a month later, he told me the story of the little beggar he had met at Bắc-Ninh, and he asked me if it was really me. To save my family's reputation, I did not wish it to be known that I had been a beggar, so this secret remains a secret to this day.

On other paths

Following this double encounter I had to leave Bắc-Ninh to go and beg elsewhere. I thought that the best means of avoiding such setbacks was to beg on the trains. This would allow me to change my location several times a day. I put this new plan into execution, choosing as my usual route, Bắc-Ninh–Hanoi, Hanoi–Bắc-Ninh. I slept at night at Gia-Lâm in empty carriages.

I tried to save a small portion of the alms I received, to buy a coach ticket to take me to my aunt's. She was the only person in whom I had any special hope at that particular time, the only one capable of helping me and looking after me in my parents' place. Concerning myself, I thought of my family every day. This caused me great suffering since my family remained the ones the most dear to me, but there was this

(393)

---

* Some days later, cousin Hạng went to Van's parents to tell them that their son was begging on the streets of Bắc-Ninh. His mother went crying into her room. His father did not stop cursing him, saying: 'What a wretch! He's run away again; too bad for the scoundrel. If he comes to the house I'll cut the nerves in his legs [so as to stop him walking]. Cousin Hạng did all he could to calm him, and advised him to try to find out what had pushed Van to act in this manner. But the dishonour was too great and his father was ashamed and wanted to chastise his son come what may. [As told by Tế.]

persistent fear which deprived me of all the comfort I could find there
... I did not lose hope of reaching my aunt's, but it was impossible to
save a sou. I had hardly enough to live on from day to day, and sometimes I had not enough. It was not easy to beg on trains. One had to
take care to avoid the ticket collector, and if by mistake one got caught,
one could expect to receive at least some slaps with a few kicks on the
backside, and even the possibility of being sent to prison. In spite of this
I had to live, and continue this kind of life while waiting for the day   (394)
when it would be possible to go to my aunt's.

I had once taken the last train from Lạng-Sơn to Hanoi with the
intention of getting off at Gia-Lâm. I got out to find some empty
carriages but I could not find any. I entered the station warily when I
realised my mistake. I found myself in the Hanoi station. I hesitated for
a moment, and my hesitation attracted the attention of an employee.
He came towards me and, suspecting I was a robber, he slapped me
several times. I fled quickly with him in hot pursuit, threatening to
hand me over to the stationmaster. I was frightened, and even threw
away my precious sack before disappearing into the darkness. I lay
down on the pavement in order to regain my composure, and then I
stood up to inhale some fresh air. The further the night advanced, the
more abundantly fell the dew. I was cold and missing my only coat   (395)
which I had allowed to fall. I almost decided to return to the station to
search for it, but I was afraid of falling into the hands of the station
employee. A last train left for Gia-Lâm about eleven o'clock, and I
climbed aboard with the intention of sleeping peacefully in that station.
I was probably the last passenger to catch the train. Someone inspected
the carriages on our arrival at Gia-Lâm. I was seen but escaped unpun-
ished. The stationmaster even allowed me to enter the station to sleep
inside, and the next day he directed me to the train which was leaving
early for Bắc-Ninh.

I return to Hữu-Bằng

That day was a Saturday. Two weeks had elapsed since the morning of
my running away. I had experienced everything during this time of
wandering, even hunger. Nevertheless, if I compared all the sufferings
with a single day of imprisonment in the presbytery of Hữu-Bằng, the
latter was infinitely worse. I found it much easier to practise virtue
whilst begging than whilst stretched out beside a pile of superfluous rice   (396)
at the presbytery, where people were much wickeder and more dangerous than people in the world outside. It could be said that they wore a
mask of virtue to devour the inheritance of people of good faith. I

begged all day at Yên-Viên, and it was only in the evening that I thought of the following day, which was a Sunday. I intended to return to Bắc-Ninh in order to hear Mass, but there was no train going in that direction. The only remaining train was going to Lào-Kay. After reflecting for a while, I decided to return to Hữu-Bằng that very evening, while asking myself how I could guarantee that the parish priest would know nothing about it. I would take advantage of the occasion to collect all my clothes still at the presbytery. I seemed to remember that in the trunk containing my clothes there was also some money, less than five piastres, which had been put by for a long time.

If I had thought of taking it with me at the time when I ran away, I would not have experienced those days of adventure. I took the train for Lào-Kay and I arrived at Hương-Canh at six o'clock in the evening. On the train I spotted Father Sự, the parish priest of Trang-Lan who knew me very well, since I had served his Mass many times. He was a very serious priest. He was embarrassed on seeing me; he seemed to want to question me, but I felt that he was afraid that I might not be 'little Van', so he did nothing. However, he looked at me a long time without being certain of recognising me, because my torso was bare and because I was begging ... On the way from the station to the presbytery I met some women who were returning late from the market. They were asking on the way where Mass would be said the following day ... Thanks to them I learned that the parish priest had gone to Tam-Lộng, and that he would say the Mass there on Sunday. My mind was put at ease to such an extent that I was no longer afraid that my return to the presbytery would come to the ears of the parish priest.

If my plan succeeded I still intended to use my money to get to Phúc-Yên by the morning train. I would hear Mass there, and then continue my journey by the ten o'clock train. In this way I would not miss Sunday Mass, and my return to Hữu-Bằng would be known by only a small number. But once again my plans and God's will did not coincide. My arrival at Hữu-Bằng that evening was achieved with many difficulties. I had to wade through the paddy fields and grope my way in the presbytery at the time of evening prayer in the church. Hungry and tired, I had only time to run to the sacristy and signal to the boy who was looking after my trunk, so that he could give me a garment to change into. I then stretched out on the bed to have a good sleep. I advised this boy to keep everything secret, and to alert me when the prayer was about to finish so that I could avoid any groups of young boys. But, I do not know why, he allowed me to sleep until after the prayer. At that particular juncture I saw myself, in a dream, wandering the streets of Bắc-Ninh or holding out my hand in the trains to beg for some sous. Suddenly I heard ringing cries and I saw myself surrounded

(397)

(398)

by a group of young buffalo guards who grabbed hold of me. One banged my head, another stripped me of my clothes and a third, seizing my legs, threw me to the ground.

I awoke with a start, to find myself facing a group of young boys who were thrilled at the return of their 'general'. Alas, they really exasperated me. I would gladly have given all of them a smack or two. But the (399) general must concede, bow before them, and ask them to wait until the following day to hear of the ruse which made possible his escape.

The cat has been let out of the bag

The next day I had to appear before the old catechist to ask forgiveness. Afterwards, everyone left to hear Mass at Tam-Lộng. On the way, I had to tell my companions all the stratagems I had to employ to facilitate my escape. They showed their annoyance at having allowed their general to flee, and they informed him of their sadness during his absence and of their happiness at his return, but without understanding why he had come back. However, they were smart enough to guess that I had come to take what was necessary, and that I would again depart with all my luggage. They were not wrong. I tried to be as discreet as possible, but they followed me everywhere without leaving me for a moment. Thanks to my skill in changing the subject, I managed to hide from them all that had happened to me during the period of over two weeks which had just flown by.

Once Mass was over, despite myself, but forced by the old catechist, I (400) had to go and ask the parish priest's forgiveness, who reprimanded me in a very humiliating way by saying: 'So you returned home and were beaten by your father, so you came back here again. Of course, there's nothing to attract you at your parents' house, reduced as they are to such abject poverty. It certainly must be because there is no more rice left that you have come back to me looking for something to eat. That's no great surprise!'

In fact, I had not yet returned to my parents' house.

On my return to the presbytery at midday, I devised a new ruse to run away. The most difficult thing was to divert the attention of my young companions, who followed me very closely without giving me a moment's respite. Fortunately, with fifty sous' worth of sweets, I was able to get them together in the parish priest's room. I invited them to eat the sweets and look at some magazines. I joked for several minutes with them as politeness demanded, then I excused myself as I had to go (401) and write an urgent letter. I went to the parish priest's office and I wrote a long letter of farewell to my little comrades. I explained the reasons why I no longer wished to remain at the presbytery. Meanwhile, the little chaps, tired of reading magazines, had stretched out and were sleeping soundly. I went out for a moment and I saw the porter* asleep against a tree. He awoke at my approach. I said to him: 'Very good, my friend: I'll keep an eye on things while heating water for the old catechist.' The porter thanked me and went to take a rest.

I then went back to the parish priest's room, and opened the door of his bureau to get an envelope in which I would put the money for my journey. It was also an act of foresight, since I said to myself, 'If during my journey I meet someone who recognises me and suspects that I have run away, I shall show them this letter for posting, to reassure them that I was going to post a letter'. While opening the drawer to take the envelope, I saw there 2.90 piastres. I thought for a moment, and then I placed this money with my own in the envelope. It was really a good opportunity to claim what the parish priest owed me. Yet this small amount was insignificant compared with all the time I'd spent in the

(402) service of the parish priest.

It was shortly after two o'clock when I had carefully finished my work, including what I had promised the porter. I went out slowly, and before leaving I put on a truly elegant tunic, but it was impossible to bring away all of my belongings, because had I met someone, they would have suspected that I wished to escape. I went to say goodbye to Tân, my dearest friend among my young companions. I then went straight to the station so as to be on time for the train.

I had to try again not to laugh on meeting the so perspicacious ferryman. On my request to cross the river, not only did he not move, but he adopted a threatening attitude as if he knew that I was a runaway. Although I was a bit anxious, I was sure that the fellow was not so discerning. So I got a grip of myself and I said to him, calmly, but in an uncompromising manner: 'Can you take me across quickly so that

(403) I can catch the first train?' While speaking I let him see the envelope. There was no need to say more. The perspicacious ferryman got up quickly and grabbed his pole to get me across the river, saying: 'I suppose you are going to deliver a letter.' I took twenty sous from my pocket to pay him and I said to him: 'Don't wait for my return, because I'm going to Ngọc-Bảo, and if anyone enquires about me, please let them know.' In truth, I was not lying, because the train from the south did pass by that village. I had barely arrived when the train entered the station. This time I bought the requisite ticket without having to hide as on previous occasions.

The next day I reached my aunt Khánh's. At Bắc-Ninh, I kept only

---

* The porter was one of the candidates for the priesthood.

sufficient money for my bus journey to Tử-Phong. With the rest I bought some toys as a present for my little sister. One of these, a porcelain tooth-pick holder, can still be seen. This was the finest of the presents. This souvenir of my warm affection for her has, fortunately, been spared. A short time after my return to the house, I was accused of having stolen a large sum of money from Father Nhã. Te immedi-   (404) ately on hearing of this, collapsed and she broke into pieces the toys I had bought for her, thus showing her rectitude in not wishing to accept the fruits of a theft.

Sufferings at the hands of my family

I had been at my aunt's for two weeks when I heard of my mother's demands that I be brought home. This news was not calculated to please me. I begged my aunt tearfully to keep me with her, and to find a place for me to prepare for the priesthood. She made it clear that she had no authority over me, and anyway she had to consent to my mother's demand. On the day when she took me to my parents' I cried during the entire journey, while begging Our Lady unceasingly not to allow my father to kill me. In fact, he did not cut off my head, but he nearly beat me. If my aunt had not intervened, he would have showered me with blows. The next day, however, I regretted not having had the happiness of dying the previous evening, because, supposing that   (405) my father had cut off my head or beaten me to death on that day, I would have avoided having to endure, for many days, sufferings worse than death. The day before I had feared death, but the following morning, instead of fearing it, I longed for it.

. . . .

My Father, I wish I could put to one side this part of my story and be dispensed from speaking of it! But I recognise that obedience is the key which opens the door to happiness, so I am no longer afraid to speak, and I will tell things clearly just as I remember them.

As soon as I returned to the house, my parents treated me as a degenerate son. My family was poor; half the paddy field had been pawned. My father was indifferent to this, and continued to lead the life of someone comfortably off. He always had money for gambling, whereas the children had not enough to live on. Everyone in the house had to work to feed him and get him money which went on gambling. My little brother Lực was still young, and his childhood had been deprived of   (406) much sweetness because he was born at the time when the family's happiness was broken. My little sister Tế was still going to school, but she was making little progress in her studies, first of all because my family was poor, and also because the method of teaching employed by the teachers left much to be desired. They liked to grow their moustaches and use the cane a lot.

It is not necessary to say that my mother was the backbone of the family; while she was there the family subsisted, the family lived. The family's survival depended entirely on her ... but given the lack of sufficient material means, it was at the cost of many tears. A mother's hearts remains always a mother's heart, but I noticed that, being very unhappy about my running away, and in order to make me expiate my crime, she treated me as if I were no longer her child ... From that moment my heart's door was hermetically sealed. I dared not open my mouth to

(407)   say a loving word to my mother. All that remained for me were long nights of tears expressing my profound sadness. After a month I no longer had the courage to live with my family, and this time my sister Lê understood well my situation. She also saw how sad was the family environment, and she wished to find some place where she could enter the religious life. We both agreed to leave, but without knowing precisely where we would go. On leaving on the agreed date, our only thought was of fleeing the family; as for the rest, God would provide. Then ... after confiding to God the helm of my boat, I knew that his will would lead me to victory, but before gaining the victory I had to pass through a period of uncertainty and suffering.

We had not had the pleasure of one peaceful day when there was disagreement between us. Having arrived at Bắc-Ninh, we no longer knew where to go. Behind us we were being pursued by our father on his bicycle. We had seen him from the Hồ jetty, but he had not spotted us on the bus. Uneasy, my sister asked me:

'Van, where shall we go now?'

(408)   I answered her in a resolute manner:

'What are you afraid of? You can ask for temporary admission at the Đạo-Ngạn convent.'

'And you?'

'Me? Let the good Lord look after things. You have seen that on running away from Hữu-Bằng I stayed away from my family for more than two weeks, and I was able to survive.'

'Van, don't be conceited.'

'I can be because I still have faith in God.'

'Daddy is about to catch us up. We must take the bus quickly to Đáp-Cầu.'

My sister was still very anxious as we sat on the bus.

'Van, how can I ask permission at Đạo-Ngạn? I have no reference from the parish priest.'

'Oh, you are a pain!'

I, in my turn, became more anxious than my sister. After a moment's reflection I continued:

'All right. Do this: go to the superior for temporary admittance, and then ask the parish priest for a reference.'

She sobbed.

'Van, I can't do that ... O heavens!'

'Me, I'm ... having nothing to do with it.'

The bus stopped near the cinema at Đáp-Cầu. We got off and ate in (409) a restaurant, and afterwards we walked aimlessly around a military training ground which was beside the road. Just at that moment my father passed by us on a bicycle but, once again, he did not see us, but continued with his head down to ride straight ahead towards the bridge. My sister was so afraid on seeing him that she became white, and dragged me near the cinema door so that we could both hide behind a thick bush, but, would you believe it, just at that moment when our hearts were pounding hard enough to break our chests, a huge French dog dashed barking towards us from the house. Terrified, I cried out, not knowing what to do. Fortunately, the 'boy' came out of the house holding in his hand a chicken ready for plucking. Seeing it was only two children from the country, he asked us some questions without scolding us, and then made us go and sit at the front of the house.

We went to hide under a tree at the side of a road. We were full of indecision: on the one hand we dared not go to Đáp-Cầu because our (410) father was already there; on the other hand, we dared not return to the house. Unhappiness was staring at us from both directions. My sister, overcome by nostalgia, cried from time to time. I also thought about the house but, come what may, I did not feel any regret. There was no longer anyone in the family who loved me. My own feelings for the family had become dry and empty, probably because I had too much self-esteem. It was a great trial for me when I loved someone and my love was not welcomed, and naturally I wished to distance myself from it. Because of that, the memory of my family did not draw a single tear from me.

My sister continued to cry, but her tears did not stop me. My sole interest was to watch the soldiers playing ball in the exercise yard. It was very different for my sister, who was overcome with sadness, and wore a very thoughtful demeanour. For a long time we did not exchange a single word. However, whilst I was absorbed in the soldiers' play, my sister said to me, slowly:

'Van, let's go home.'

'But, Lê, why go back?'

'It isn't possible for me to enter religion.'

(411)   She lowered her head and continued, while crying:

'Perhaps mammy's waiting for us at the house.'

'No. You go back if you wish, but I'm not going back. If I return now, mammy will beat me to death.'

'No, she won't. Mammy is very gentle, she won't beat you.'

'Mammy is very gentle towards you, but not towards me, as you well know . . .' And I began to cry.

'No, Van, it's because you don't understand her.'

'I understand her very well. I understand that if I return she will beat me before you. I'll say it again. Go back if you wish. As for me, I'm going to find some place where I can become a priest, and if the good God does not want me anywhere, I would rather be a little tea salesperson than return and live at the house with . . . You understand what I mean?'

'If you don't go back, I can't go back either.'

'As you please, but I beg you, don't torment yourself because of me. But that's enough. Go back if you wish.'

And I went under a tree opposite. My sister hid her face and cried,
(412)   and I – I cried also. Sometimes the memory of my family became very strong. I thought: 'We have both run away, but now we must separate since my sister will go back.' Tired because of my crying, I said my rosary. A moment later my sister came to sit beside me and she encouraged me once again to return home. I replied: 'No, you are free to return, but I am staying here:' and I went to the other side of the road. Once more she came back to tackle me, and once more I crossed the road. We had stopped crying, but were unable to talk together because my sister wanted me to return and I did not, for fear of being beaten by my mother. That was all I feared. After having spoken gently, my sister began to get annoyed and she said some harsh words. At the end of the discussion she began sulking and decided to leave for good. She began walking with her bag on her shoulder, leaving me free to go where I wished. But fifteen minutes later I saw her coming back to persuade me to return with her. As I was really sorry for her, I made this suggestion: 'Listen to me. I agree to go back on condition that we go to aunt Khánh's rather than to our house.' My sister agreed immediately and,
(413)   once again, we took the road to Bắc-Ninh.

We were just about to arrive at this town when, suddenly, behind us, we heard the sound of someone falling off a cycle. We turned round. 'Heavens! It's daddy! . . . Poor daddy . . . he's fallen!' . . . However, we were not sufficiently in control of ourselves to stop and sympathise with him on his misfortune. As soon as we saw him, we began to run as fast as we could to escape him. His fall had certainly no serious consequences, because he got up immediately to run after us, leaving his cycle at the side of the road. My sister Lê was the first to fall into his hands, because she was carrying her bag. As for myself, had I run with all my strength, my father would have had difficulty in catching me up because I was not carrying anything. However, seeing that my sister had been seized and was being slapped by him, I was sorry for her, turned round and gave myself up. He was exhausted; his face was white and he was breathing with difficulty. I was hardly within reach when he lifted his hand to slap me, but he missed and tried to hit us no more. My sister was crying. I went to hold her in my arms but she, embarrassed, told me to release (414) her as we were being watched by a lot of people.

My father went to get his bicycle, and after having taken away all our money and clothes, without even leaving us a *sapeque**, he ordered us to return to the house. He got on his bicycle and rode in front of us, stopping now and again to make sure that we were following. We had hardly started when I began to cry. It was now my sister's turn to console me. We had to walk more than twenty kilometres. It was almost nine o'clock when we arrived at our house.

My father, who had arrived before us, had made all the preparations to give us a good beating and make an example of us. We noticed that our mother's voice was hoarse, and not her normal one. She had certainly cried a lot, but that did not prevent her from giving us a brief lecture, after which our father in his turn reproached us for our crime, and intimidated us by hitting the camp bed with the cane. Shaking all over I said to my sister: 'Let's save ourselves.' She refused and dissuaded me saying: 'Enough's enough, Van! Let's put up with it, and then it's done with. Don't be scared that it will do you a lot of harm.' My mother spoke up in my sister's defence, but for me she said: 'Hit him until he's raw!' I leant (415) my head on my sister's shoulder and said to her, weeping: 'Now you see that I did not deceive myself. Mammy hasn't the least pity for me.'

My father, cane in hand, came shouting towards us: 'Tie them by the neck for me. Stretch them between two posts! If they die this time, I won't be sorry for them.' I rushed towards the garden gate which, by good fortune, was wide open and my sister followed me ... My father dashed after us, but once through the gate we had each taken a different direction, so he did not know which way to go, all the more so because the darkness was now total. So, that night we escaped the beating. My sister returned to the house the following morning to do her normal work. But I, I dared not return because of the words of my mother which had made plain that she had stifled any feelings of affection for me.

I wandered around the church until midday. My little sister Te began (416) to despise me and called me wretch. She no longer recognised me as

---

* Coin of almost no value which was in circulation in the Far East.

her brother and treated me as someone worthy of scorn. I shed tears every time I met her. Midday came and although I was asked more than once to return to the house without being afraid, I still hesitated, fearful that once inside, my father would hit me in accordance with my mother's injunction until my flesh was raw. Finally, when my sister Lê called me at the church to promise me, in my parents' name, that I would not be touched that day, I agreed and followed her to the house.

During a whole week no one alluded to the punishment that we must endure, but not a day passed that I had not to wipe away my tears and, in my opinion, the insults that I received during many days would have sufficed fully to make amends for my running away. But it was not so ... My parents were not able to dispense me from a beating ... One evening when we were talking cheerfully in the bedroom, my father, arriving suddenly, carefully locked the door and took all necessary

(417)   precautions to make escape impossible. With cane in hand he then began to rant and rave to frighten us as on the first occasion. He drank some alcohol and then, in order to correct us, he gave the order to tie us to the camp bed. I began to shake and my heart was beating as if it was going to burst. I thought of running to my mother for her to defend me, but unfortunately, she spoke up once again to protect my sister. As for me, there was only one thing left: a beating until my flesh was torn and then, if I died, to bury me as soon as possible.

My sister remained calm as if she was not the slightest bit afraid; this evidently because my mother had padded her with many extra clothes to deaden the blows. As for me, I began to cry as soon as my mother had spoken up. I felt alone and helpless. My mother's words were echoed from time to time by my brother Liệt and my little sister Tế. 'Hit Van, the good-for-nothing, until his flesh is torn. Nobody will feel sorry for him if he dies!' My father, he himself was the torturer. Who was left to

(418)   have a little pity for me? This total desertion made me look to heaven. I raised my tearful eyes to the picture of Our Lady and invoked her aid, hoping that she would come to my aid or, at least, give me enough courage to put up with, that night, the blows from the cane. In fact, after raising my eyes to this good, heavenly mother, these deplorable events became sweet to endure ... My father's blows became faster and faster, but each blow fell on the frame of the camp bed, which was higher than the canvas I was stretched out on, so that I did not feel any pain. Nevertheless, I cried all night because, deep down, I felt a great sadness which was impossible to contain.

From this moment I felt even more distant from my mother and I felt that she, also, understood that I would never dare to show any mark of affection towards her. I tried to avoid all the members of my family, including my little brother Lực.

But that was not all. The weight of my sufferings was getting heavier (419)
from day to day. Less than a month later, Father Joseph Nhã came to
visit my family. After having maligned me in listing the enormous
crimes I had committed at the presbytery at Hữu-Bằng, he finished
with a calumny, saying that, before running away, I had stolen thirty
piastres of Mass stipends from him. When I heard this news I was
husking rice. I had to down everything and I staggered into my
bedroom and stretched out on my bed. I did not say a word to declare
my innocence, but if I had said what I wanted to say, my words would
not have appealed to Father Nhã. I consoled myself by telling myself:
'God knows the truth: that's enough for me ...' And in the bottom of
my heart I accepted the derision. I expected another beating was being
prepared for me after Father Nhã's departure but, thanks to Our
Lady's intervention, I was left in peace.

. . . .

From then on my life became sadder still and bitter days did not stop
piling up. In writing these lines, I feel I am reliving those terrible days.
My heart tightens and my eyes flow a torrent of tears. This happens every (420)
time I recall this period of my life, and the only way of suppressing this
deep sadness is by thinking of the days of my childhood and the affection
given to me by my family. But at the same time I am speaking of, I was
considered by my family as a nasty creature... Everyone was in two
minds whether to speak to me, and if I was spoken to, it was only to add to
my hurt. Everyone was on their guard for fear of being stolen from. If
anyone noticed me touching anything in the house, even if the object was
not lost, the slightest suggestion of movement sufficed to have me
suspected of wishing to steal it. I was given a string of nicknames: sometimes 'swindler', sometimes 'young Hương' (Hương was the name of a
well-known robber in the Mão-Điền market), and instead of treating me
as a child of the family, I was relegated to the ranks of robbers.

One day my little sister Tế had lost a picture which served as a book- (421)
mark. After having searched for it unsuccessfully, she suspected me
immediately and she followed me all that day, moaning and demanding her picture: 'Rogue, give me back my picture.' Then, a moment
later, changing her tune, she continued: 'Little Hương! Give me back
my picture. If you don't, I am going to tell mammy to beat you until we
can see your bones.' Not happy with that, she then went to accuse me
before her little fellow Crusaders,* so that everywhere I went I had

---

* Following the Eucharistic Conference of 1914, the Eucharistic Crusade was
founded so as to encourage children in their spiritual formation which was
centred on the Eucharist. It comprised three sections: the pre-Crusaders for
the 3 to 7 year olds being prepared for their first communion; the Crusaders
for the 7–12 year olds; the Knights and Messengers of Christ for the 12–15

these young ladies at my heels demanding my little sister's picture. The story of the money stolen from the priest went the rounds of the village in a short time, so that everywhere I went I was the object of scorn. In the house everyone made fun of me, outside, everyone pulled a face on seeing me and cursed me as a ne'er-do-well. The pious little Crusaders regarded me as a bad person who was not worthy of their prayers.

(422)   During this time I practised a secret apostolate among a group of young children who hired out their services. That is to say, I played in a friendly manner with them, and I encouraged them to follow what I understood and practised in my Christian life.[†] Having lived a life similar to theirs, I was familiar with their circumstances and the scorn which focused on them. I felt a natural kind of joy in playing with them and they, for their part, showed that they understood and also that they liked me. Although I never believed it worthwhile to exonerate myself before them, neither did they ever behave as if I were a robber, as other people were saying. When people saw me mix in a friendly manner with these children, universally regarded as illiterate and uneducated urchins, I was all the more reviled. It was the only pleasure remaining to me and, lo and behold! my mother absolutely forbade it. Each time she saw me chatting with the young buffalo herdsmen, she took me straight back to the house and hit me several times on the head with her hands. The first time this happened I reasoned thus with my mother: 'We are all God's children, and we are all brothers in this world'. The more I reasoned, the more I received blows on the head, and the more (423)   my family detested me. I had to keep quiet, therefore, and in obedience to my mother I had to abandon my visits to these scorned and rejected children.

My father rarely spoke to me but each time that he did it was in such a manner as to leave me in no doubt that I originated from nothing other than a pile of manure. The meals consisted of family prosecution sessions against me. When it was not my father it was my mother who was the president of the court, and every time that I was accused I had to listen to a sermon which lasted for the whole meal. Consequently, I cried more than I ate. The sermons were supplemented by several

---

year olds. It is spread throughout the world. The Cadets of Christ follow the Messengers of Christ, and it was Pope Pius XI who asked them to be 'the soul of the Catholic Action of youth'. The movement continues today under the name of Y.E.M. (Youth Eucharistic Movement).

[†]   These young people were orphans of the village, abandoned and left to themselves. They were regarded as dangerous, vulgar and without education. The children of 'good families' must not play with them. Van's parents were very strict on this point and they forbade Van to see them under threat of the cane. [Té.]

warnings from my little sister Tế which was like adding salt and pepper to the pure vinegar, which made me cry even more than my parents' long lectures. Usually, I did not dare object to my little sister; I understood that she was still innocent and was only repeating what she heard. Sometimes, however, I would look at her with my eyes full of tears and beg her, with a glance, to be silent and soothe the sadness of my heart. My little sister would sometimes catch my glance and read in it the state of her suffering brother's soul.

I never had the desire to eat in community with my family. I wanted (424) to eat alone or at another time but I did not have the choice; it was either eating with the family or going hungry. I had to resign myself sometimes to being hungry, and then to find a means of eating secretly. Happily for me, my sister Lê saw to it that I ate secretly, or furtively kept something for me. But that did not last very long. Shortly afterwards she gave up on me ... And so every time I ate secretly, it was considered a crime worthy of the cane. My Father, as I said earlier, ascribed to me all the lapses which occurred. Of course I would not suggest that I was blameless, because I was a lazy and sullen child, but I do not understand why I was so lazy. Quite simply I felt that I no longer had the strength to work, not even the strength to wipe away my tears. And if I was so lazy and in such a sorrowful mood it was only because I was lacking in virtue since I had no respite from my suffering.   (425)

I even had to carry the whole responsibility for the adventure with my sister Lê. At that time, at the presbytery in my own parish, just as at Hữu-Bằng, one witnessed shocking behaviour. The catechist in charge of the Crusaders liked very much to chat alone with the oldest of them. I do not know exactly what was said at these meetings but people reported the most awful things. It was when these rumours were most rampant that my sister and I had run away ... and people had concluded that the leader of the Crusaders had ordered Lê to 'go to the country' and that she, afraid of going alone, had dragged Van along for company. My mother found this gossip really insufferable. She forced my sister to tell the truth openly and declare it before everybody. Faced with my mother's demands, my sister blushed and, not daring to admit that she had intended to run away, said: 'It is Van who urged me to enter religion.' To tell the truth, Lượng the catechist had not ordered my sister to run away, and neither was it her little brother, who had encouraged her to enter religion. I had only put her on the path which leads to the religious life, and it was Lê who left willingly for this end. (426) We both had the same intention: to run away to enter religion. I am not the one who forced her. It was only because she was ashamed that she dared not tell the truth and allowed me to endure long days of painful suffering.

Personally, I told everything as it was. I did everything to defend my sister when she was accused of having been with a boy, and if the speaker was a Crusader, boy or girl, I did not hesitate to give them a good slap to silence them. But because I was not liked at that time by anybody, even when I spoke the most patent truth, nobody wanted to believe me; credence was given only to my sister's words. So she was accustomed to blame me for everything. If something happened to prompt my mother's intervention, my sister would reply: 'It's definitely Van. What a queer fish he is!' I was being led away to be punished very (427)   often without knowing at all what it was all about. In view of this, I got into the habit of admitting my guilt. Whatever the crime, whenever my mother wanted to know who had done it, I took the initiative and said: 'It was me, mammy.' If she forgave me, I thanked her: if she punished me, I put up with it. In my opinion it was neither a lie nor a miscarriage of justice. This was my reasoning: a misdeed is obviously a misdeed, but if no one committed the fault it does not exist. Once it does exist there must be, necessarily, a guilty person. However, if it happens that this person does not dare to admit the fault, consequently, I will admit it in their place. Concerning brother and sister, if one is punished instead of the other, it can be considered that the other is already punished.

However, my brothers and sisters did not understand it like this in my regard. In their self-love everyone maintains that they are acting correctly. One day, my sister Lê was carrying a basket of rice which, inadvertently, was not covered. Placing it outside, she entered the kitchen to do some shelling with me. Unfortunately, a flock of hens, grabbing the opportunity, jumped into the basket and, while scratch- (428)   ing, scattered the rice all over the place. Suddenly, my mother, coming back from somewhere, saw what had happened and cried out: 'Who has been so careless?' My sister, realising that she was guilty, remained silent. My mother repeated the question a second time. My sister still remained dumb. My mother then went to look for a brush and while gathering up the spilled rice, repeated the question for the third time. My sister remained still like a stone statue. I realised that she was afraid of being punished so I replied for her: 'Mammy, it was me.' 'I knew it! ... Nevertheless you've let me ask three times before admitting your guilt ...'

My mother had hardly finished scolding me, and I was still expecting the cane, when my sister Lê rushed towards me with a very red face and gave me three hard slaps. She scolded me thus: 'Good-for-nothing! I did it. You knew it was me ... Why didn't you say so? Do you think you are acting virtuously? ... So I'll admire you? You devil! All you know is how to lead others into sin. Go away! Go where you want ...'

(429)   Outside, my mother knew nothing of what was happening. Noticing

that we had just been squabbling, she held her brush by the head, came into the kitchen, pushed down my head violently and, grinding her teeth, she scolded me, saying emphatically: 'Monkey! Anything sinful in this house, and you are the source of it ... It happens to everybody. You upset everybody!' I began to cry and answered: 'Oh, I know very well that if anything goes wrong I get the blame. That's why I loyally accuse myself beforehand.' My sister said, cruelly and ironically: 'It's amazing! We've got a saint here ...' My mother, raising her broom handle, threatened me: 'Shut up, otherwise I'll hit you with this brush here and now.' My sister added: 'Give him a good one, mammy!' I dodged below my mother's arm to flee outside.

It was only at midday the following day that I dared to return to the house. I was so exhausted by hunger that having arrived at the garden gate I had to sit on the ground. I felt I was losing consciousness. I soon regained my senses, and a moment later I met my little sister Tế who was coming back from playing. She had intended to go and look for me. (430) Seeing me, collapsed at the garden gate, she ran to alert my parents and, having brought me a bowl of rice with brine and a glass of cold water, she said to me: 'When you have eaten it, go somewhere else' ... Her intention was to treat me like a beggar. I felt full up even before eating, and so that my sister might understand, I had no better argument than to shed some tears. With a suffocating voice I said to her, indifferently: 'Thank you, little miss.'

At these words Tế immediately understood her scornful attitude towards her brother and, with a regretful air, she took the bowl of rice back to the house. My parents scolded her and said: 'Drag him here by the scruff of the neck.' Fearing another misfortune, I felt a shiver right through my body. I made the effort to get up and stagger on to the road to get to the church, my hiding place from evening until morning. Tế ran to the door and seeing me leave cried: (431)

'Daddy, Van's leaving again.'

'Where's he going to?' my father asked and my mother added:

'Where's he going to? Drag him here by the scruff of his neck.'

My little sister ran to bar my route.

'Van, come back.'

'Come back where?'

'Come back home.'

'My home is across the road.'

I meant to indicate the church.

'No. Do you want me to tell mammy to come with a cane?'

'If you think it is necessary.'

She began to cry.

'No, Van! Mammy is sad because you have left the house.'

'If I come back she'll be sadder still, because she'll have to put up with all the crimes I commit.'

'No, you must come back. If not ...'

She pushed me gently towards the house. Suddenly I fell backwards. Frightened, she went to report everything to my mother. The latter came out a minute later. I was still sitting on the ground. She ordered (432) me to get up and come into the house. I got up but stayed where I was. I no longer knew what to say to my mother. I was trembling all over as if seized by an attack of fever, my eyes were dazzled and I was about to fall. My mother, seeing that I was not moving, took me by the hand and dragged me along while scolding me: 'Good-for-nothing! Half-dead with hunger, you are told to come back, and you don't budge.' After having taken a few paces, I fell head first at my mother's feet but she continued to drag me to the house. My father grabbed the cane with the intention of hitting me but, I don't know why, on seeing me he did nothing.

. . . .

Afterwards I had to run away several times without daring to go back to the house. Every time it was the church which served as my refuge. My bodily food consisted of the remains of the wax which I found on the altar, and when there was no one at the community house I went there to collect the paper in which the cakes had been wrapped, or again the snail shells so as to eat the small pieces which were still stuck to them.

(433) ## My soul is terrified

My soul has been transformed in experiencing these ordeals and sufferings. I came to regard myself in a short time as a creature worthy of abomination. The devil made this bitter thought grow in my mind: 'If men can't stand me, can God put up with me any more? I am going to die soon and I will go to hell. God's judgement has already punished me here below.' This thought came to add to my fear. I was afraid of a sudden death and of being dragged by the devils into hell before I even wanted to go with them. In spite of all this, I maintained a firm confidence in the Blessed Virgin. And each time that the devil put the idea in my mind of the terrible punishments which were waiting for me in hell, I rushed to my Mother Mary, moaning: 'Oh Mother, you know that I shall have to go to hell, but that is something I do not want. Whatever happens, if it is God's will, I accept his holy will readily. But (434) I still believe that God will never wish to make me go to this place of torments. I feel, however, that all I deserve is to fall into this place of darkness and humiliation. I see that in this world there is no longer anyone capable of loving me. Even my parents who are God's representatives on earth, curse me. How then can God love me? O Mother, whatever the outcome, help me nevertheless to persevere in God's grace to the end. Help me to accomplish perfectly the work which God wants to see me realise in this world, namely, to follow his will in everything. My life, no matter how I look at it, is only one of continual suffering. However, if such is the will of God for me, I readily accept everything and if, one day, by my fault, I am found lacking, displeasing to God and deserving of eternal punishment, I ask you still to help me to endure eternally this chastisement to glorify the holy will of God.'

I think the devil is very afraid of this prayer, and when I am feeling troubled, I never fail to repeat these words many times and Our Lady   (435) always answers me with a supernatural consolation whose mysterious strength it is impossible to describe ... I made an examination of conscience afterwards, followed by general confession. I made known to my confessor, Father Dominic Nghĩa, all the sad circumstances of my life. At the time of my first confession he had told me first of all: 'There is nothing which has given pain to the good God among the faults you have confessed.' This time again, he said to me in God's name: 'Accept all these trials cheerfully and offer them to God. You must believe that if God has sent you a cross, it is a sign that he has chosen you.' Peace returned little by little to my heart, and when the feast of Christmas came that year (1940), my soul had recovered all its vitality.

Part 3
Filled with Joy in Love (436)
(After Christmas 1940)

The Third Stage

During this sorrowful winter external circumstances had deprived my soul of any joy. I was like a plant which, when frost is around, can grow neither leaves nor flowers. Nevertheless, the time will come when the plant will produce flowers of an incomparable beauty. The second stage of my life was a very severe winter, and to bring this cold season to an end God has allowed that I live the saddest days being badly treated in the bosom of my family. But it is also there that the source of divine consolations made itself known to me. The season of great joys will begin with the third stage of my life, precisely, at Christmas night.

The grace of Christmas night

This most sweet recollection is graven in my memory for ever, even down to the last detail. I do not know if, on that day, Saint Thérèse had intervened in any way. The favour I received that blessed night differed (437) in no respect from the one that, formerly, Saint Thérèse had received. There was nothing different in my situation. Christmas is coming, and my heart cries out with joy when it thinks of it. I think of the moment when I will have the gift of contemplating the sweet face of the Child Jesus smiling at me in the night. Just to see him in my mind moves me, and my heart overflows with joy. That year, as Christmas draws near, I no longer thought of the presents I received at the time of my child-hood. I understood that, this time, my Christmas present had been prepared by the tears and sufferings of the months I had just lived through. But the mysterious meaning of suffering escaped me completely and, therefore, the reason for which God sent it to me. Consequently, instead of taking delight in suffering, I was naturally distressed by it. God will make me understand, therefore, that suffering (438) is his holy and mysterious will, it is the present of Love. My heart is still overwhelmed by fear of suffering; I suffer, but instinctively I run away from suffering, although now I am not so cowardly.

Midnight Mass begins. My heart prepares itself carefully to receive Jesus. In my soul it is dark and cold as in the depths of a winter's night. I no longer know where to look for a little light and a little love to warm up the empty dwelling-place of my heart. At that moment, Jesus, alone, is my only hope. I long for his coming ... and for that only. The much longed-for time arrives ... and, lo and behold! I clasp Jesus present in my heart. A great joy has taken possession of my entire soul; I am outside myself as if I had found the most precious treasure I have ever met in my life ... What happiness! And what sweetness! Why do my sufferings appear so beautiful at this moment? It is impossible to say. It (439) is impossible to describe this beauty in comparison with an earthly beauty. All I can say is that God had given me a treasure, the most precious present of Love.

My soul has been totally transformed in one moment. I feared suffering no longer; on the contrary, I was delighted and took pleasure in finding opportunities to suffer. From now onwards my flag of victory will fly on the hill of Love. God has given me a mission, that of changing suffering into happiness. I am not abolishing suffering, but I am changing it into happiness. My life from now on, in drawing its strength from Love, will be only a source of happiness. I have, above all, been able to conquer myself. It is my too-sensitive nature which, many times, has made me suffer, much more than regrettable external events. I now felt I had a lighter heart and I could stand up to all suffering.

First battle

(440)

After my thanksgiving I wanted to read one or other of the fervent prayers I had chosen from my missal but, not being a Crusader, my place was quite far from the lighted candles, so I could not use my missal during the Mass. I had, therefore, to wait until the Crusaders had left, in the hope of getting closer to a candle which would give me a little light to read by. It was necessary to wait until almost the end of the second Mass before finding a place where there was some light. I approached quietly and opened my book. Naturally, I did not dare consider myself as a Crusader. I had to be circumspect, and I said to myself: 'If some young Crusader comes to move me on, I have not got the right to object.' After a few moments of silence a member of the family* came suddenly to extinguish the candle which was providing me with light, while saying to me, 'Are you a Crusader to be sitting here?' Formerly I would not have been slow in grumbling but, that particular night, something had changed. I closed my book calmly and went to sit

(441)

close to a pillar. There I offered to God my tears and my victory.

There you have my first battle over self; quite trifling and which does not deserve to be compared with the bitterness of many other trials; but for once I had known how to suffer joyfully for love of Jesus. I then went to the crib to offer to Jesus the present I had just received. On my return to the house I met the person who had extinguished the candle near me and I wished the latter a merry Christmas as if nothing had happened. From the time of this victory, each time that an opportunity to be humiliated presents itself, I will usually emerge the victor. And from now onwards, the flowers of Love will blossom abundantly in my

---

*   Van's brother.

soul and I shall welcome with a smile the bad behaviour of my family towards me.

From the other side of the river

From this moment I enter another phase of my life. The road to travel is still long and although I am not at the end of my sufferings, my soul had been transformed on entering this period full of light, of beauty and of gentleness. I begin to live again a spontaneous life. Once again, as at the time of my childhood, I see opening out in the bottom of my heart, wonderful dreams, dreams which, alas, were blurred during the (442) dark days I had just gone through.

Shortly afterwards God even changed the surroundings of my exterior life. At the time of Têt (1941)* my aunt Khánh came to visit the family. Noticing that I was very pale and looking tired, she certainly understood the cause of this change which had taken place in her favourite nephew. She felt sorry for me, and asked my mother if she could take me to stay with her. My mother did not hesitate in allowing him to go who was the cause of so much trouble in the family. I understood very well that this was the case, but I was very sorry for my mother because the family was very poor ... Anyway I had to accept the situation. She said to me on my departure, while tapping me gently on the head: 'Try to be good at your aunt's.' I thanked her with two streams of tears and my mother, without my knowing why, cried also. She put a yoke on my shoulders with two baskets that she asked me to carry to my aunt. I succeeded in carrying them, painfully, until the end (443) of the village but I felt such a pain in my shoulders that my aunt had to relieve me of this burden. The sight of the natural world that day made me cry. It was completely different from previous years when the road to my aunt's was so joyful. This time the weather was sombre, it drizzled all the time and the north wind cut right through to the bone. From time to time, feeling very emotional, I cried again and my aunt, thinking that I was missing my mother, turned round to scold me: 'You were treated like a dog at home and now you are sorry for having left.' Then, changing her tone: 'That's enough! Stop crying! You will stay with me for a while, and then I will attend myself to what you want to do.' From that moment I felt as close to my aunt as if she had been the only mother in the world. I opened my heart to her without holding anything back. There were things that I was careful to hide from my mother but with my aunt I had no secrets. I was happy when she called (444)

---

* Têt is the first day of the Vietnamese year. In 1941 it fell on 27 January.

me her child and when she pressed my head against her breast to see if I had any lice. Although I never had any lice, this was for my aunt and me a favourable time for talking intimately together.

My aunt's house had an altogether different aspect from before. The former rather low-roofed compartments had been replaced by others, more elevated and cleaner, although covered with thatch. The earth courtyard was now paved with cement and everything was orderly. It was the exact opposite of what I had witnessed in my own family. Where my aunt's had improved mine was deteriorating.

My cousin Khánh had taken a wife, and my cousin Đào was also preparing for marriage. She was carefully rearing pigs and chickens as a small capital that she would later take with her to her husband's. As for the other cousins, Lan and Dư, they were going to school at Ngăm. Dư, being more intelligent and alert, had been sent by my aunt to help (445) Father Bảo, the curate of the parish of Ngăm. I therefore found myself without a companion of my own age. I was the youngest. My cousins, as well as my aunt, still loved me in a special way as at the time of my childhood and amongst them my new cousin Dê, the young wife of my cousin Khánh, appeared the closest to me. The reason for this closeness was that we two were in fairly similar situations and we both had, equally, a deep spirit of piety. I noticed that when I suggested something concerning the spiritual life she agreed immediately with me, but most of the time I learned much more from her than she did from me.

I noticed an astonishing thing. My aunt, who was quite a virtuous lady, had a very harsh manner towards her daughter-in-law. She could not be more friendly towards me but towards her daughter-in-law sometimes she did not even show a bit of affability. I knew there was a lesson there for me. God wished that I could observe the example of this cousin Dê so that I might imitate her patience. In addition, she (446) would choose a life of the saints for me to read whilst I took the ox to graze. My work at my aunt's consisted, first of all, in looking after this ox and then, on my return, in carrying water to fill the big jar. I had, also, to sweep the yard in front of the house and to work in the kitchen to prepare the meals. I was also proud, when evening came, to be the only one to start the family prayers and to have the privilege to read aloud the lives of the saints. If my aunt reserved this privilege for me, it was, she said by way of congratulation, because my voice was clear and reached right into the ear.

The task of leading the ox to graze was, in the beginning, rather painful for me because this work was normally considered by everyone as rather repugnant. I had to swallow my pride. Personally, I found nothing lowly in it. I shed some tears on the first days because I was made fun of. Then I had to practise getting on the ox's back. It was only after repeated practice that I managed this, and to make him stop willingly when moving. I fell off several times. Fortunately my aunt's ox was gentle, because without that I would have been trampled on more than once.

The most difficult thing was that in order to graze the ox I had to join (447) forces with the village children, who mostly belonged to pagan families. This made me feel uncomfortable. Even if these children dared not criticise religion their conversation was coarse. Most of these boys, hardly older than me (thirteen) were already married. It was even the case that some of them, still wet behind the ears, and who had not yet lost all their milk teeth, had drawn false moustaches and had had their ages increased by their parents so that they could marry. However, their wives were all older girls, so that if a stranger met them he could have taken them for aunt and nephew. I dare say that among the boys I knew, not one of them knew the meaning of conjugal love. They knew only how to treat their wives arrogantly, and they would sulk for the slightest thing, throw themselves on the ground and wriggle about at their feet like eels covered with burning cinders. It was really ludicrous, and personally I thought an injustice had been done to these girls forced to take such husbands. Nevertheless, the boys knew how to talk so coarsely that it made me blush, and I had to get away from them.   (448)

I went, therefore, to graze my ox at a distance, trying to pass the time with Our Lady. Alone with my ox, my greatest pleasure was to organise a new kind of procession. I divided the field into several parts at a certain distance from each other and I decked out the ox as well as possible with the most varied flowers which I fixed to his horns. Then, kneeling on his back and holding a picture of Our Lady in my hand, I made the ox graze slowly beside the paddy field whilst I said the rosary out loud. If I had recited a decade and the ox had not yet reached the point for the following decade, I stood on the ox's back and sang a hymn in honour of Our Lady. These processions ordinarily would last two or three hours, but I never felt tired. When the ox had eaten his fill, I would interrupt the procession to lead him to the stable.

Do you think, my Father, that Our Lady would be able to stop laughing before such innocence? One day I met a Christian* who, seeing me amuse myself in this way, told me off for lack of respect towards the (449) Blessed Virgin in daring to recite the rosary on the back of an ox. 'Don't you think,' he asked, 'that acting like that insults Our Lady's dignity?' I retorted without delay: 'Where's the lack of respect in this? I love my mother, the Blessed Virgin, and I love her everywhere. On her part, she loves me also: therefore, what place cannot be dignified?' The fellow,

---

* Phan, Miss Ngắm's brother.

dumbfounded, walked away, saying: 'This lad is really a terrible child.'

You see, Father, how many souls in their relations with God still fear him as someone very exalted and distant. Deep down, such people dare not allow themselves any intimacy with God because they do not yet understand the nature of Love. They are happy to regard God as a king above all kings, and possessing an incomparable authority, so that any intimacy with him appears as something totally impossible. As far as I'm concerned, each time that I have known how to throw myself at the heart of the Blessed Virgin, I have felt that this mother brought me closer to God. Yes, I felt that God was close to me just like the flower in the fields, the murmur of the wind in the pines, the magnificence of the (450) break of day or the bird's song ringing out everywhere in the air. No, God has never been a distant being for me. Without ever having seen him with my senses, nevertheless, all his creatures are like a voice, like a sign which is part of him and which impels me to admire him. The fields appear to me from day to day dressed in a great splendour, and make me reach closer into the heart of God.

My Father, I would really like to show you here all the feelings which the beauty of nature gives rise to in me, but I realise that they are only minute details, and I am sure that you would find nothing extraordinary in this admiration which rises quite easily in a soul like mine. Allow me, therefore, to move on to another subject.

God wants me to return to Hữu-Bằng

I worked at my aunt's for five months and after the Ascension I returned to my parents', since at harvest time, the ox being needed for (451) the work, there was no longer any need for me to take him to pasture. My aunt wished, however, that I should have time to rest. My cousin Khánh found this unnecessary. Not being of a happy disposition, he disliked above all to see my aunt pamper me. His attitude towards me had created a tense atmosphere for several months, although he dared not hit me for fear of my aunt. Harvest time was therefore favourable for asking his mother to send me home. I understood very well that my cousin, having started a family, had to think above all of his future. That is why I had to ask my aunt many times to allow me to go, for fear that, by remaining, I might upset my cousin, even though, naturally, it would make me unhappy. But each time my aunt, while tapping me gently by way of caress, said to me:

'Stay here! Why go back home just to suffer?'

'But,' I said to her, 'if I cause suffering for others, that's even more hurtful for me.'

Shortly afterwards my aunt went one day to walk to my house. My cousin, who had remained at home, used the occasion of a meal to speak of my family. He knew that I was a very proud child, so, when he (452) mentioned some things which were not very honourable concerning my family and especially about my father, I burst out sobbing and then, standing up immediately, I answered him: 'It is true, my family is very poor: but you have forgotten how, some time ago, you yourself were dependent on my family. You should take more care not to be unfair.' After my reply, I had the feeling that my cousin wanted to get up and slap me, but his wife got up first and restrained him. I left the table and set off for home that very instant. When I met my aunt on my return to the house, she, seeing me also return suddenly and with reddened eyes, guessed that something unpleasant had occurred. She gave me a good ticking off, reproaching me for acting in such a way and not recognising the affection she had for me. She then added: 'Why did you not wait for my return before leaving?' The next day I returned, alone, to her house. Some days later she also returned and dealt with the matter in a (453) just manner.

A month later I was preparing some rice pudding which was not cooked enough. I was cruelly made fun of. I was annoyed and refused to eat for several days, being happy to nibble from time to time at some raw potatoes. I must frankly admit that I was habitually spoiled by my aunt which explains the several victories won by my self-love. Later, I was sorry and embarrassed at such infantile behaviour. My aunt, witnessing my stubborn refusal to eat, was obliged to take me back to my mother. Today, my aunt has already forgiven me this serious fault, and each time that the story is alluded to she rushes to my defence in a friendly manner, saying: 'You have to be stubborn to become a hero. When he says "no" he means "no" and when he says "yes" he means "yes".' She then expressed this wish: 'If you can always be as strong in the way of truth, that would be really splendid.'

A month later I spent some happy times in the bosom of my family. (454) My parents no longer had towards me the indifferent or aggressive attitude they formerly had. My brothers and sisters also showed themselves much more welcoming, except my little sister Tế, who still refused to be on good terms with me. She treated me from time to time as if I was a robber, and she ordered me to do all sorts of things as if I was a servant. She would say, sometimes: 'If you don't do what I say, I'll go to tell mammy to send you away.' I longed to give her a good slapping by way of reply on hearing her speak like this, but I said to myself: 'Tế is still my dearest sister in spite of everything.' So, instead of hitting her or showing my displeasure, I tried to put up with everything and to pray for her, hoping that, one day, she would understand me better than anyone and consider the words she then said to me as shameful. It is a fact, however, that when I heard her speak like that, tears came to my

(455)   eyes. Perhaps my sister has now completely forgotten these things of the past which caused bitterness between brother and sister. If later, however, she gets round to reading these pages and is sorry, she must remember that her brother forgave her long ago, and he has forgotten everything as if he had never encountered, in her regard, the slightest hint of contradiction.

One day Father Nhã came to visit our parish priest. His motive in visiting him was to come to look for me to get me to return to Hữu-Bằng. I would never have thought it possible but, in a surprise move, Father Nhã came personally to ask my parents to allow me to return to his place to help him. Things were now in the open. When I understood what was happening I wanted to refuse, reasoning thus: 'If formerly at Hữu-Bằng, I was good only for committing crimes and stealing as Father Nhã had asserted, why was he now looking for me?

(456)   During the many years I had lived with him I had been downtrodden like a slave, to such an extent that at a certain point, not being able to put up with this life any more, I had to run away. But he had tarnished the honour of my family by alleging that I had fled because of a theft I had committed ... No! I decided not to return to his house even if my refusal meant death. Faced with my determination, my parents expressed their displeasure at what Father Nhã had said at the time of his previous visit. In her reply to the parish priest my mother emphasised my feelings: 'My child has already run away many times, but I did not understand why he behaved in this way. Since the day when you stated that he had stolen a large sum of money, I was outraged and considered it a stain on the good name of the family. Now I see that he is really innocent; he has been honest with us and with everybody. Because of his shyness he was suspected of deceitfulness, whereas in reality he was sincere. If therefore through weakness he has stolen thirty piastres, allow me to give this sum back to you. Concerning his return to the presbytery, I dare not force him because I know well that he does not at all wish to do so.'

(457)   Father Nhã had to ask my parents' forgiveness and beg them to allow me to return to the presbytery, because he had need of a boy like me in the parish. He frankly admitted that all the boys of my group had left him, and it was now necessary to get new recruits and someone to guide them. After a discussion my parents allowed things to clam down, and I was then called to see if I would agree to Father Nhã's request. Once again I obstinately refused. Seeing this, Father Nhã stood up to return to his presbytery, asking my parents to sort things out. My mother called me immediately after his departure and gave me some words of

advice and even some words of warning. I replied to her: 'Am I now a girl whom you can require to go where and when you wish? I can feel my heart tremble at the thought of having to go back to that hateful presbytery.' Not daring to insist, my mother told me, simply, to ask for divine light in order to come to a decision. I spent all that day in the (458) church praying, asking God to enlighten me to make a decision in conformity with his will and acceptable to my parents. I went to communion the following morning and I begged God, once again, to help me to know his will so as to find peace. At that moment I was hesitant, only wishing half-heartedly, still affected by fear. After my thanksgiving I went to Our Lady's altar where I had the feeling of hearing a voice encouraging me to leave in accordance with my parents' wishes. I understood immediately that it was a divine inspiration. Full of joy, I ran from the church and went directly to the house. I looked first of all for my mother who was in the kitchen. Seeing me return, radiant with an extraordinary happiness, she scolded me gently: 'Where have you come from? Where have you been wandering? Go and eat and then ...'

'Mammy, I am agreeable.'

'In agreement with what?'

'I'm willing to leave for Hữu-Bằng with Father Nhã.'

Smiling, my mother asked me,

'Who has coaxed you into this?'   (459)

'Absolutely no one has been able to coax me. I am agreeing to leave because ... because ... Well, it's a big secret.'

'Very good, if you agree to go, go; but if you ever come back here you will have me to answer to.'

'That's enough. This time, to my dying day, I will no longer wish to abscond. With God, I no longer fear anything. I will do whatever he wishes me to do, absolutely. However it will be necessary to pray for me, mammy, every day, asking God that I may become a priest.'

I said my farewells to my parents at midday that very day, and I left. Nobody shed a tear, because I chatted happily like a magpie until my departure. The cause of my joy? It was God's grace which had filled my soul since morning.

A twelve-year-old warrior

I felt immediately, on returning to Hữu-Bằng after an absence of nine months, that I was entering an environment polluted by impurity and selfishness. The evil was grave. The presbytery deserved no longer the (460) name 'house of God'. There was licentiousness, irregularity and scandal. Obscene words were heard and regarded as pious words coming from everybody's mouth. People still believed in God but worshipped only the bottle of alcohol, gambling and many more things. I repeat it, the presbytery of Hữu-Bằng had now reached such a pass that it no longer deserved to be called 'house of God'. Yet why had God driven me to go back there and for what purpose?

On the first day I cried and shivered as if I was coming down with fever. What more could I do? During three months I did nothing but pray and mortify myself. I acted in this way because I thought that it was appropriate to do so, since it had been given to me to know in advance what God would wish of me after this time of fasting and prayer. This lasted until the month of October of that year. I usually

(461) designated this month solely as the month of the holy rosary. One day, it was a miserable afternoon, and escaping from everyone and not agreeing to play with anyone, I went to sit alone in a corner of the sacristy to gather my thoughts. It was an unusual thing, since on other afternoons when I wished to pray, I went, as it was appropriate, to the church. But on this occasion, and I have no explanation why, in getting away from the group of children I went and huddled against a corner of the sacristy without the intention of expecting anything whatsoever. I do not know what supernatural force compelled me to sit there, and I understood nothing.

I was sitting, therefore, near the jar of holy water, when a film began to unfurl in my mind. The first tableau depicted the distressing spectacle of my life. However, the most frightful period was the one in which I was then living. I saw displayed before my eyes a world full of sins, above all sins against chastity. What frightened me the most was to see sincere children like myself falling and covered in stains ... I was so

(462) afraid in just looking at the picture that I was almost covered in sweat. I was startled, and it seemed to me that my entire body was covered with the leprosy of sin. I had not yet sinned; I had never even wished to do so, but the scandals which were flaunted at the presbytery plunged my soul into disgust. The thought of fleeing the place came once again to my mind. How could I do so since God wanted me there? I lifted my head; my eyes were moist and my lips were trembling, and I asked God this question in the form of a prayer: 'My God, what do you want me to do here?' No voice replied to me. There was no sign either which would make his will known to me. I lowered my head silently ... Only my fear and my tears remained.

Then the film unfolded little by little, and introduced me to another world consisting solely of saints preserving their virginity and leading, in the main, simple lives. But what has protected them that they could lead a life so pure and beautiful? Such was the question that I asked my

inner self. I lifted my head and, slowly, the film came to its end. I (463)
reflected on the question I had just asked myself and I came to this
conclusion: if the saints had been able to keep their hearts perfectly
pure in this manner it is certainly because they had made a vow to the
Blessed Virgin of remaining virgins. It will therefore be the same for
me. I also wish to preserve my virginity like the saints, and I must
commit myself by a vow, like them, in spite of all the hardships and
sufferings.

With dry eyes, beaming face and peaceful heart, I rose quickly and
entered the church. I knelt there before the picture of Our Lady of
Perpetual Succour and, with my two hands placed on the altar and my
eyes fixed on my Mother Mary, I pronounced the following words: 'O
Mother, I am making the vow of keeping my virginity, like you, for the
whole of my life.' I had hardly said these words when I felt my heart fill
with a joy that no pen could describe. Unable to contain myself, I had
to go out of the church straight away. I was confident that from this day
the Blessed Virgin would be the guardian of my virginity since it was to
her that I had made the vow of perpetual virginity. My life from now
onwards will be her life; my sorrows will be her sorrows, and my (464)
personal role will be to remain always huddled up under her immacu-
late mantle. On leaving the church, I began to run and jump in all
directions like the white foam which dances at the foot of a waterfall.

I began to reflect again, from this day, on how to find a means of (465)
resisting these examples of bad behaviour. Was not this the new mission
that God wished to confide to me and for which he had prepared me
during several months?

I did not hear the good God speak to me but, within myself, I said:
'Even if only one man remains in the whole world to be saved, I would
still act and use all means for his salvation.' I was far from being the only
man of good will at the Hữu-Bằng presbytery. I knew many others,
especially among the group of younger ones, who also wished one day
to free themselves from this life of constraints in which they were being
kept by the 'big heads' who had the authority to oppress them. By their
attitudes they compelled everybody, in a manner of speaking, to give a
bad example by riding roughshod over the regulations, and above all
by engaging in unwholesome conversations. They persisted with the
strange practice of making us give the name of 'big sister' to the young
female friends of the catechists, the teachers and even the young boys.
It was necessary to accept 'love slaps' from time to time from these
young girls, and complaining was forbidden. On the contrary, one had
to thank them, because they were 'love' slaps. In spite of all of this, none (466)
of these young ladies dared to touch Van because he did not appreciate
their signs of love. That is why I was the first to stand up and protest.

On a particular evening when everyone was talking, seated round an oil lamp, the catechists, while slapping their thighs, exchanged unsuitable words. One was praising the beauty of his little female friend, another, the sweetness of his, and a third concluded: 'Mine is very intelligent.' And while they gossiped in this vein, we, the younger ones, had to sit quietly and pay attention as if we were in a catechism lesson in church. They provoked us from time to time to see if any of us understood the slightest thing about love. Annoyed, I got up and left immediately in an angry mood. The old catechist understood from my demeanour that I did not appreciate these stories. To save face and, also, to tempt me to enter into the spirit of things, he made me come back and, smiling, asked me:

'Van, where are you going like that? Come back so that I can ask you a question.'

(467)　　'I am going because I feel uncomfortable.'

'What, uncomfortable? Come on, it is necessary to make an effort to learn the tricks of love. Later, when you are older, you will understand how to choose a little female friend.'

I could not help smiling but I closed my mouth quickly, which provoked silly laughter among them, and they continued chatting:

'Van is a saint and he will never want to marry.'

I lowered my head and left straight away.

'Van, you are a blockhead,' said the old catechist, who called me back and continued in a manner which could not be coarser: 'Tell me, Van, do you know the size of Miss Ngoạn's breasts?'

Everybody burst out laughing, even the younger ones. Blushing, I replied: 'They are as big as your head ...'

I thought that because I replied to him in an equally rough manner he would get angry and send me away to have some peace, but no, he began to laugh, and scornfully make fun of me:

'Ah! That's how it is! So you know that Miss Ngoạn's breasts are as big as my head. That's what I call knowing!'

(468)　　Everybody burst out laughing loud enough to bring the house down. I was angry and I left, murmuring: 'Ignorant lot! I don't want to stay any longer with you.' The old man called me back again but I'd had enough. I did not go back.

The group of younger ones had gone into the yard with me. I was going to speak discreetly with some who were closer to me, and I decided, with them, resolutely to oppose this attitude of the catechists, even if it meant dying in the process. At midday the following day I called together, at the edge of the forest, the group of younger ones of which I had become leader. We were six in number. I did not hesitate to indicate to them my intention of breaking completely with those amorous stories woven in the presbytery without consideration for anyone. God commands us to love all men but he also forbids us to commit sin. We must love, as is necessary, with customary considera-tion, but we must not join anyone in evil. I explained things to them to help them better understand their situation and their duty as young aspirants to the priesthood; then I added: 'From now on, the pres- (469) bytery rules must be respected. If the bigger ones are degenerate and have rejected the rules, it is not our duty to imitate them. If they do not change, they will all be subject to God's punishment.' I cannot summarise at this moment in these few words the discussion of fifteen minutes I had with them. Afterwards, and spontaneously, everybody raised their hand as a sign of perfect agreement and with one voice they repeated after me: 'From now onwards, we are determined to sever all connections with evil and to protest against all that is sinful in this house'. I then suggested to my little companions that we found together a company which would provide us with mutual protection, both from a spiritual and corporal point of view. All gave their assent and it was agreed that, in the evening after supper, we would meet beside the pond and there we would make our decision. I was happy and prayed a lot.

That evening, thanks to God, I succeeded in establishing a company which we called the 'Angels of the resistance'. I chose the name inten- (470) tionally to honour our guardian angels and to ask their protection. It was for this reason that the first article of rules stipulated that we have a great confidence in our guardian angels, and the obligation of think-ing of them every day and begging their help for the success of our venture. We voted that very evening to elect a leader. Out of six, five ballot papers bore my name. Naturally, I gave my name to another but when the votes were being counted my companions even took my voting paper with someone else's name on it and replaced it with my own. From that moment they called me chief.

Every day we held a secret meeting in the forest to deliberate on the subjects necessary to protest against. There were some things it was appropriate only to avoid but others it was suitable or necessary to keep. Normally, the subjects which engendered most resistance were those concerned with the older boys withdrawing themselves from the regulations of the presbytery and using force to oppress us. Here are (471) some examples: sending us to liaise with their little girl friends in the village; making us do certain work outside our own duties, such as cleaning their pipes, buying alcohol, waving the fan etc. All of these things had become normal practice for a long time among the cate-chists, who loved to give orders and be waited upon. These customs had been successfully established only because those people abused their strength in order to subdue us. The house regulations never authorised such abuses. I therefore banned them completely. Also still necessary to avoid was this: if, while speaking, anyone said a dishonest thing, this must be condemned by standing up and withdrawing in silence to make him understand that we did not approve such words.

Above all it was necessary to maintain a spirit of charity. Charity had disappeared entirely from the presbytery. It was our duty to re-establish it. Everyone must try to help others and come to their aid by all means possible. I also asked my companions to reduce their expenditure on tit-bits and to put into the common purse the little amounts they received so as to use them to help those of us who had need of (472) them. This amount, although very modest, was growing day by day and we made good use of it for different charitable causes, such as buying medicines, papers or pens for our poorer comrades. It was also my intention, funds permitting, to keep hens to make some money which would allow us to have made woollen jumpers for the winter. Unfortunately, and it was a terrible thing, the quite passable hens that we had already been able to procure were taken away by the gang in order to eat them whilst drinking alcohol, and, at the same time, swallowing our woollen jumpers.

In less than three weeks these children who formerly had been timid, dirty, lazy and quarrelsome, had become gentle, caring, clean and very energetic. They had become elite soldiers in the 'Angels of the resistance' company. During the same period, the influence of the good spirit of the company had moved beyond the walls of the presbytery to (473) reach right to the school and even to the little Crusaders of the parish. But, alas! Mr Satan was not happy!

Satan's counter-attack

The flower had blossomed for scarcely a day when the wind of hatred was unleashed during the night to crush it in its beauty. That very evening when the company 'Angels of resistance' was founded, I thought that the secret had been well kept, since all were in agreement that, outside the six then present, nobody was aware of what we were doing. Unfortunately, one of our company had betrayed us. It was Đoán, one of my close friends. His action was attributable only to his excessive timidity. Fearing that he would not be able to put up with the beating which would follow if our plans were exposed, he decided to withdraw before the event and, to avoid being suspected, he went to denounce our organisation to the old catechist; to make a greater (474) impact he laid at our door many other false tales, such as that we had given him the name of 'pig' and 'drunkard'. The old catechist called us to his bedroom to question us after evening prayer. I thought that no matter what, he would not neglect to give us a good beating. I therefore decided to take all responsibility on myself so that if he was going to beat us, I alone, would receive the blows and the others would be spared. Happily, he did not hit anyone. He satisfied himself with a sharp reprimand, in which, above all, he attacked that 'dog' Van, the worst of the lot, and he then dismissed us. He thought that his speech would influence the malleable souls of these children, since hitherto he had only to open his mouth and everyone would bend before him.

But this time it did not work. His skill as an aggressor remained powerless against the brave lads of the company of the 'Angels of resistance'. Even though he threatened us, our duty was to continue to function. Should he beat us, it was to dominate us but we decided, (475) unanimously, always to react as agreed. He could never have imagined that this 'good-for-nothing' Van would dare to stand up to him. He had been my teacher. He had beaten me many times until I was black and blue. How many times have I turned pale when he looked at me, rolling his terrible and piercing eyes? Now I had become an obstacle who, by means of a strict rule, was preventing him from sitting freely beside his most beautiful girl friend. This girl who was, a short time ago, one of his snotty-nosed pupils. Hardly a year ago he was still tying her between two posts and with the help of his cane was giving her lessons in feminine behaviour, good deportment, chaste language and modesty. He was still forbidding her to frequent the presbytery during the night; and he did that because he liked her, and wished to make her a pupil worthy of him, 'Sir', the teacher, Nhân.

But today he loves her in another way. He no longer wants her to call him 'Sir', the teacher, as he had formerly taught her to, but now he makes her call him, 'brother teacher', and to call herself, 'little sister'. (476) He no longer forbids her to enter the presbytery at night but, on the contrary, if a night passes without her coming, he cannot sleep a wink and the next day he has to send a boy to see how she is. Now he can no longer act in this way. 'Sir' must obey the rules. Since the formation of the 'Angels of resistance' the doors have been well and truly closed at the hour stipulated by the time-table. Sir was, therefore, a little out of sorts each night, condemned as he was to sigh all alone. But when morning came and he called one of us to send us to enquire after the health of Mrs Teacher, we replied that the regulations forbade us to go out on business outside our remit, and if he intimidated us in any way, we relied on the parish priest's authority.

As regards himself, the parish priest's relations with the young girls had much improved. He only mixed now with his bottle of Vietnamese alcohol and his jar of peanuts. It was his only pleasure. He kept silent on the subject of women. Furthermore, the young girl that he loved the most had moved on to the old teacher. He allowed this without rancour. Concerning the younger boys, he no longer concerned himself with them. Each one could like whom he wished and if, during the night, someone opened the doors to let young girls enter to have fun with, he no longer took any notice. From time to time he was even victim of the malice of these gentlemen, to the extent of having to provide them with hens for the preparation of soup intended for their female friends hiding in their bedrooms. Then again, he would sometimes bring them alcohol to drink. In spite of this, the parish priest was a little closer to the group of younger ones. Normally he would listen to us and allowed us to act as we wished; that is to say, he always came to our defence if we kept the rules.

(477)

Nevertheless, it was not always sufficient to engage the authority of the parish priest to succeed, since the old catechist had no respect for the parish priest or, if he had, it was a respect based solely on reason. Đoán, who had betrayed us, was the only one who remained to liaise between the old catechist's group and the young girls of the village. He had to be on the road unceasingly, to carry a letter to this one, or to invite that one to come that evening to such or such a corner to meet such or such a catechist. It was a real muddle. And his reward? To receive, now and again, when the young girls came back from the market, perhaps a few sweets or a piece of soap or some blue soap flakes so that his suit would be a bit cleaner than the others'. He was, at the same time, a spy working for the old catechist. We found him at our heels everywhere, but we did not give him much recognition and we never allowed him access to our meetings.

(478)

A short time later we devised a plan which made it impossible for him to go outside the church property – one which worked so well in fact that communications with the young girls of the village were interrupted. We found a means of getting in touch with the young people outside, letting them know that the old catechists were like this or that, that they kept company with such and such a girl, and that Đoán was their liaison officer. The young people did not need anyone to speak to them on this subject. The feelings of these young people had been for a long time: 'The village boys keep the girls of the village, not allowing the bees and the butterflies (lovers) to violate the frontiers of our village.' Even if these young people were more or less licentious, they had at least this saving grace, that they were safeguarding the reputation of their village. Now this good reputation resided precisely in the virtue of the young girls of the village. That is why if a young man of another locality came to marry a girl of their village, they would not

(479)

object on condition that it was done lawfully and faithfully, but, if anyone was careless or inconstant, they would beat him to the bone. These young people had a lot of respect for those who lived in a religious house, but they came to detest them when they learned that these same people allowed behaviour unworthy of their status. They would never have pardoned our catechists for their conduct.

I let the people outside know what was taking place in the presbytery. It was a clever way of making Đoán stay in the house. In fact he dared not go anywhere because the young people had threatened to beat him up if they saw him going alone in the village. Inside, we barred his way, not allowing him to go beyond the boundaries we had marked. Đoán (480) searched for any means to communicate with the young girls, but most of the time we guessed his intentions so that he could do nothing.

The older catechists were full of resentment and took their revenge in different ways. We were called to question for the slightest peccadilloes e.g. sleeping during prayers, sounding the signal for class a minute late, etc., and cruelly punished. In spite of our vigilance we were often found wanting in matters of this nature, so we were often beaten; but what was more painful was that if any of us committed a fault, we were all punished. We were, nevertheless, happy that such was the case, since our enemies acting together against us helped us to tighten the unity of our spirits in the company. We fought together, rejoiced together in our success, and suffered our pain together. My Father, is there a greater happiness in this world than the unity of hearts?

One day, at midday, a fit of madness exploded. The old catechist (481) determined to use all the weight of his authority to bring down the wall built by the company of the 'Angels of resistance'. This wall consisted of 'the timetable and the rules'. When the bell rang at midday, the door of the garden was closed, and in the evening, at nine o'clock precisely, all doors communicating with the outside world were locked and, following the established rule, nobody, including men, could visit the presbytery. If something arose obliging someone to go out, two boys only had received authorisation from the parish priest to do so. The door key was confided to one of these two, but it was he who kept guard who had the key to the main entrance, and it was he also who had the privilege, when the order was given, to go out alone on business while everybody was resting. The young ones had to keep guard in turn for a week at a time. This was a long-established rule, and had it been kept faithfully in all the presbyteries, one would not have seen these houses of piety transformed into temples of the vice of impurity. At Hữu-Bằng the company of the 'Angels of resistance' had begun to re-establish this restriction. It was a difficult task and one surrounded by bitterness.

So, on that particular day, at midday, the old catechist, in a furious (482) mood, had delegated Đoán to go to the village to invite his girl friend to come and visit him. The parish priest was taking a siesta in his bedroom. Đoán left but, arriving at the main gate, saw Van's shadow seated, his back leaning against the door flap while he was learning his school work. Hesitating, he was going to turn back when, changing his mind, he went straight up to the door and stretched out his hand to open it.

'Where are you going to at this hour?' I said to him.

'Where am I going? What right have you got to ask that question?'

'I have the right to ask because it is forbidden to leave for the village at this hour.'

'I have some business for the old catechist,' he replied in an arrogant manner.

I shook my head.

'No matter what you have to do, no matter for whom, even the most elevated catechist, he has not the right to act in this way ... this hour is my hour of duty, and if anyone has business which requires going out, I am the one with the authority to do so.'

There was a moment's silence between us and then I continued:

'It's not important. Go back and rest, and if anything happens I will help you.'

Đoán protested:

(483)   'The old catechist has told me to go out and I'm going out. If you can do anything about it, do so.'

'Fair enough. Go! I'll do nothing, but you'll have to be patient and stay outside until the bell for getting up. Only after that will I open the door for you to enter.'

Without answering Đoán returned immediately to the old catechist's room. Still leaning against the side of the door flap, I felt a little uneasy since the old catechist, in his fury, was capable of beating me to death on the spur of the moment. However, I immediately got a grip on myself, and I was very determined not to relax the surveillance so as to safeguard the purity of this place of perfection, even if it meant dying. A moment later Đoán returned to call me once again: 'Van, come here! The old catechist is calling for you.'

'Are you telling lies to frighten me, or are you telling the truth?'

'It's the truth. Come on, there's no need for threats ... this time you will be sick.'

While following Đoán to the old catechist I consoled myself by saying: 'It won't take more than a thousand strokes to kill me once and for all. It is not worth being afraid.' I begged Mary and my guardian angel to come to my aid and to give me an increase of strength. For no appar-

(484)   ent reason, the catechist did not give me a single blow. Perhaps he was

afraid of making a noise during the time of siesta. He allowed himself a long speech to curse and threaten me: 'I'm warning you, be careful!' Then he dismissed me. I was not yet out of the door when I saw Ðoán climbing on the bed and lying down beside the old catechist, who embraced him tightly and stroked him as if he were a little dog.

Revenge

I did not suspect that revenge would be exacted that very afternoon. I had expected it to take the form of a good beating. When arriving in class that afternoon, I was astonished to find that my pen had disappeared from my satchel where I always left it. It was nearly time for dictation. I was annoyed and I thought that perhaps I had taken it to the house to do my work and had, afterwards, forgotten it. But I remembered very well that I had arranged everything in my satchel before going to keep guard at the door whilst learning my lesson. Anyway, I had to go back to look (485) for it. I got up and approached the teacher's desk to ask permission to go and look for my pen. He probably heard my request but he kept his head down and continued writing without saying a word or making any sign to give me the permission requested. I said more loudly: 'Sir, please allow me to go and look for my pen.' He made no movement. I renewed my request for a third time but he remained impassive. I took this as permission to go. Searching for my pen took fifteen minutes so that there was only a quarter of an hour left to hand over my work at the time appointed by the teacher. There was one thing I could not explain: how was it that my pen could hide itself in a crack below my bed? A hand was obviously necessary to have stuffed it there. Now, who was in the house? I could only suspect Ðoán. He no doubt wanted to get his own back for what had (486) happened at midday. Nevertheless, having recovered my pen I did not utter a word of complaint, offering everything up to the good God. I went back to class quickly and took my customary place. Just at that moment the teacher said in a loud voice:

'Who has just come in?'

'Me, sir.'

He rolled his eyes and said:

'Good-for-nothing! What were you doing to make you arrive so late? Were you sleeping?'

'No, sir. I have just asked your permission to go and look for my pen.'

'Is that true?'

'Yes, it's true.'

As a matter of form's sake he asked the pupils sitting on the back benches:

'Is it true that Van asked permission to go and look for his pen?'

They all stood up and replied:

'Yes, sir. We saw him go to ask your permission.'

Then, changing his tactics:

(487)   'You can protest your innocence but you dared to go out before I gave permission. Rude specimen!'

Then, with a change of mood he shouted:

'Come here! Lie on the ground!'

'Sir, if I have done anything wrong, please forgive me this time because, truthfully, I did ask your permission but you were not paying any attention to what I said. That is why I thought you were allowing me to leave. Please excuse me this time.'

'You? Forgive you, dog from Ngăm ...'

Then, seizing a cane, he beat me black and blue.

Not the slightest sound was heard in the class except the blows of the cane and the curses of this out-of-control teacher. I no longer wished to beg forgiveness since I was not guilty of any fault. He hit me simply because he wanted to, simply to appease his anger. He paused to take breath.

He then looked towards my young companions. His eyes were fixed and staring like those of a madman hell-bent on vengeance. He made (488) them come to him, and he caned them just as he had me. It was really pitiful for these little ones, all completely innocent, but not one allowed the slightest complaint to escape. Personally, seeing them hit so unjustly, I wanted to cry out in protest there and then, but it was useless. He hit them all and without respecting any part of their bodies. Whilst admiring them, it was impossible for me to contain myself. I felt inside me the desire to die in protecting them. Without saying a word, I threw myself towards them. I forced them to the ground and under the table, so that the blows would fall only on me. I no longer felt the pain as at the time of my first beating, but each blow which landed gave more endurance to my body to hold out until the end.

I had not counted the blows which were intended for my young companions in the corner of the room but which I received, but I put (489) out my hand to grab the end of the cane. This action made him madder still, and he inflicted on me I do not know how many more dozens of blows, which left their marks to such a pass that the young pupils seated at the back of the class were terrified and began to cry. Revenge was reaching its last gasp. The teacher, out of breath, his forehead covered with sweat, threw his useless cane into a corner and slumped heavily on to his chair. He stared at us with his bloodshot eyes and continued to shower us with insults. Recovered from his fatigue, he stood up once more, picked up his broken cane and, seeing that it was no longer any use, threw it out of the window and sent a boy to find another one. Three beats of the drum rang out to announce the time for recreation. He made the pupils remain in class for a few more minutes. He looked very annoyed and called the boy, too late in bringing the cane, a dead dog. He gave the signal for recreation after waiting for five minutes without seeing the boy come back. Then, boiling with anger, he returned, head down, to the house without saying a word, probably because he had no strength left.

The younger pupils, hardly out of class, came to me and, crying, held (490) me in their arms. All my body, at first quite limp, became stiff, little by little, like a piece of wood. My hands were so swollen that I could not close them, but the most painful areas were the muscles of my shoulders, my elbows, my back and my hips. I was exhausted and unable to fold my arms. I had received several violent blows to the head. One had hit my left ear which was bleeding and very swollen, so much so, that I could not hear with it. Fortunately, my eyes were left untouched. My classmates lifted up my clothes to count the marks of the cane and encouraged me to report the affair to the parish priest, but I knew well that if I started proceedings against this teacher, they would only result in further tarnishing his reputation and, beside, because I was his pupil, I did not wish there to be any hatred between him and me. For his part, if he hated me it was because he saw me keeping faithfully to the regulations he had formerly laid down himself.

I sat down in the class to rest for a moment and then I went into the church, exhorting my companions not to make too much fuss about the (491) events, but from the afternoon of that day all the village of Hữu-Bằng knew that the teacher had taken his revenge on the leader of the 'Angels of resistance' by giving him a terrible beating. And everyone spoke of it with a great deal of excitement.

Up till then I had been able to hold back my tears, but when I entered the church and observed the picture of Our Lady of Perpetual Succour, her so gentle gaze made me burst out sobbing. I went to sit on a bench before Mary's altar, and all I could do was repeat these words: 'O Mother, this is my victory. Suffering is my victory ...' And I began to sob as if there was no one in the church, but it was nearly time for Benediction and the tertiaries were already there. Seeing me crying, they came to me to interrogate me. I felt a bit awkward and I answered briefly: 'I'm not crying. I was just having a bit of fun' ... Leaving my bench I left the church to lie down. I felt a sweet comfort in my heart which softened my suffering, and I had the feeling that the Blessed Virgin had placed a discreet kiss in my soul to reward me for my victory and to give me extra strength for the sufferings ahead.   (492)

The story of the old catechist also reached the ears of the parish priest but the latter seemed rather uninterested. However, after some days, seeing all the fuss people both inside and outside the presbytery were making of the story, and especially when he learned that the old catechist was infatuated with a junior Crusader and that he had been frustrated in seeing her by a group of young ones and, furious, had played a trick on them to get his own back in a cruel fashion, he called him to his room to warn him, quietly, to take care and to be more watchful. The young people from outside the parish asked the parish priest to get rid of him from the presbytery. On the afternoon when I had been beaten, my friend Tân came to visit me with another young man. They forced me to tell them everything so that they could join me to purge the place of that scoundrel, the old catechist, and his gang.

(493)   I never suspected that this story would become so big. But the only person responsible was the imbecile with the big head who had brought disgrace on himself even though no one had attacked him. When he hit the children, who asked him to make incessant allusions to his little girl friend? He thought she was very beautiful but the pupils made fun of him, saying: 'Where does this nasty character come from, who, having entered the house of God, still entertains himself with girls?' After having been forced to spell out in detail the circumstances which had led me to act in opposition to sin, I asked Tân, through friendship for me, to let the young people know of my wish that no one lay a finger on the old man and his gang. The best possible outcome would be the prevention of the young girls visiting the presbytery during the night. In fact they did as I asked, but it lasted for only about a week. Afterwards, nobody was heard crying out on patrol around the church because, among these young people, many were related to the young friend of the old catechist. The situation was even more tense because she was the daughter of the senior official of the village ... That is why even the young people of good will, through fear, had some consideration for the other side.

(494)   Some days after the beating my wounds were healed completely. I had hardly any pain. A village family* who were still friendly with my parents, learning that I had been beaten severely, cared for me and made me take some pick-me-up. Thanks to this care I quickly regained my strength and I felt stronger than before.

The old man never mentioned me but, on the days when I had to stay in bed, he had to keep his distance away from everyone. On the one hand, he dared not show himself in public since the young men had threatened to beat him up; on the other hand, his little friend was followed by the children of the village who mocked her all day, so that

---

*   The family of Madame Tiết.

she no longer dared show herself in the street. The young girls of her group had received an order from the young catechists not to visit the presbytery any more, but to wait, for fear that they might lose their reputations.

First of all, let us wait

I understood only too well the ruse of the old catechist and his friends who wanted to wait for the departure of the parish priest on his tour of confessions in adjacent parishes before acting. Being alone he would be   (495) in sole charge at the presbytery and could easily find a means to force my departure. I went immediately to point out this possibility to the parish priest, saying to him: 'I want to leave before I'm forced to do so. I'm asking you to confirm that it is because I was faithful to my duty that I have been unjustly expelled.' The parish priest comforted me and promised me that from now onwards he would, by all means, forbid these young girls to frequent the presbytery. In spite of his promise, how could the parish priest dare to forbid access to the presbytery to the daughter of the principal official who was still his great friend? He still went to his house to gamble, and if he forbade his daughter to come to the presbytery, she, in her turn, would be able to forbid him to go to her house to gamble. Then what would happen to him? It was a tricky situation. Therefore, in spite of his promise, even if he gave her titbits, he would never dare to sustain this prohibition. He had, nevertheless, found a means of getting me away from the presbytery for a while, and thus to soothe the sadness caused me by the old   (496) catechist, by taking me on the confession round.

Before leaving I called a meeting of the 'Angels of resistance' to advise them to stop all activity during my absence. I said to them that the most important thing was to remain united for their mutual support, to flee unsuitable stories and to keep me up to date with what happened at the presbytery. Thus, even away from the presbytery, I was conversant with all that took place. I know that after the departure of the parish priest and the leader of the 'Angels of resistance', the old catechist made my little comrades go to his bedroom to be severely scolded. Then, appropriating all the power in the house to himself, he forced them to give back the door keys with the command to avoid any murmur of protest. I also know that to facilitate relations with his little girl friend and divert people's attention, he had put up a notice announcing a project for the husking of rice 'for the presbytery during the night'. He allowed the young Crusaders free access if they wished   (497) to be good enough to render assistance.

Evidently, only young girls would turn up. Young men would never have accepted such a duty, to husk rice ... Most of the young girls were generous, and if a certain number were really good, there were others who were good only for the gentlemen catechists! These latter only liked to come to eat rice pudding, and to taste the sweet words that the catechists spilled into their ears. It was a real pity for those who were sincere. Their only intention was to work for God, for the parish priest and the catechists, so as to give help in the presbytery. They were not thinking of chicken soup or rice pudding. But after a few days, seeing the catechists taking advantage of the rice pudding and the chicken soup, using obscene words and even committing scandalous acts, they were deeply disgusted, and said they would return no more. To go into a holy house and live like devils! Who could tolerate such an abuse?

There remained, therefore, only the young girls of 'beautiful appearance' who had friends in the presbytery, who took the trouble to come (498)   and who, in spite of all their efforts, had succeeded, after a whole week, in husking barely enough to fill a mortar of rice. The old cook was angry and did not allow them to do any more husking. He even deprived them of rice pudding. Yet they continued to come each evening to husk the rice ... In reality, they did no husking at all. It was simply a pretext to visit the catechists.

The most assiduous was Miss Ngoạn, the pretty daughter of the first official of the village and the dearest friend of the old catechist. She even took the trouble to come and visit her friend every day at midday to see if any rice needed husking. My companions then told me in detail all that followed. Miss Ngoạn was in such a hurry that many times, at midday, with her meal hardly finished and not having taken the time to wipe her lips and rinse her mouth, she ran to visit her friend with grains of rice still stuck to her lips and her gasping mouth giving off an odour of fish cooked in brine. On one occasion the young miss came running to announce herself at the parlour door, when her big brother arrived like a gust of wind and with a big stick in his hand; he grabbed her round the neck and led her back to her home to do the dishes. So her (499)   friend, seeing her in such a hurry, did not dare to reproach her and if, after the meal, she did not rinse her mouth and had grains of rice stuck to her lips, that would give him something to lick!

Each day at midday, in order not to be noticed by the young ones, the old catechist, wearing a short-sleeved shirt and swimming trunks, went to the door for some fresh air. In reality, every one well knew that a current of air never touched that door which was blocked on all sides. But Sir loved to breathe the air in this place. Who would have dared touch him? My companions of the 'Angels of resistance' could only stick to orders I had given them.

New tactics

I had some free time away from the house to re-evaluate the plan of action used up till now. I admitted that it had been bold. It is a fact, however, that if I had not acted in this manner no one would ever have paid any attention to the rules. So, although my foolhardy action had not been very successful, it had been nevertheless, a bitter example given to the devil. I realised, on reflection, that the tactic of an imme- (500) diate riposte was never very profitable. I realised that the company of the 'Angels of resistance' had been seriously wounded, and that some of my companions were tempted to turn the clock back, that is to say, to live without any kind of dissent, leaving the gang of catechists the freedom to order and drag them into occasions of sin. I therefore went to explain everything to our Mother Mary, and asked her to teach me a new approach so that my comrades would be no longer oppressed and beaten by the catechists. When the parish priest had finished his confessional tour, I came back to the presbytery where the situation remained the same. The young Crusaders who had friends at the pres- bytery visited them less frequently. The two parties were happy to express their feelings by correspondence. The group of catechists and the 'Angels of resistance' were still cautiously opposed to each other without showing it openly. It was then that I decided to adopt the new tactics concerning the young ladies that the Blessed Virgin had just taught me. I understood that the devil had drawn the handmaids into (501) his trap step by step.

Everybody was aware that it was from the time of the founding of the Crusaders that the public meetings and friendly banquets had begun to increase. The Crusaders of one parish would attend the ceremony of the presentation of medals to the Crusaders of another parish. Among the spectators were necessarily many catechists, who helped with the arrangements. Some were there, also, to ensure that the meals were happy occasions ... and this happiness included some amorous glances from the catechists in the direction of the young girls. The next time it was a case of affectionate words disguised as compliments and, finally, the catechist would open his satchel and offer to the handmaid, as a souvenir, a beautiful picture with some words on the back ... The young lady, in response to the catechist's kindness, did not hesitate to sacrifice a few hens to purchase some lengths of cloth to make embroi- dered handkerchiefs to offer them as keepsakes. These reciprocal exchanges reminded them of the need to attend a banquet on a certain day ... Oh, what deep attachment!

This love expressed in lawful situations is a very good thing. But here (502) it could not be lawful since in everybody's eyes the boys in question had given themselves to God, and it is for this reason that they were particularly respected. Having voluntarily chosen the vocation of catechist they were regarded as religious.*

They loved each other, therefore, in an unlawful manner, and from that moment they searched for means to be near each other or, at least, to express their love by correspondence. The devil's work was done. He handed over to their mutual love the responsibility of dragging them into dangerous waters ...

Don't you find that cunning, Father? We must recognise that the fallen angels still have the power to use the special gifts that God had given when he created them. The devil is a very good psychologist, and much more cunning than man since he is the father of lies.

(503)   But it is now the time for the company of the 'Angels of resistance' to go on the offensive to pull these young girls from the trap of these unhealthy friendships. I mean that it was my intention to use Satan's tactics directly for our counter-attack. The first thing was to find a means of communicating with both groups, that is, the catechists and the handmaids. It was first of all necessary to neutralise Đoán, who served as the liaison agent between both parties. It was a fairly complicated manoeuvre. I got the company together one evening and outlined the change of tactics that I had drawn up earlier. All gave their commitment and promised to stick to the plan I had outlined. First of all I asked them to seize the love letters that the catechists gave every day to Đoán, and even those that the handmaids sent to their friends. We would then publicise the contents, so that people once and for all would make fun of the catechists. Then Đoán would without doubt be suspected. Afterwards we would see ...

In fact, we were able to get our hands on nearly all of the letters exchanged. We divulged one or two of them for a joke and, also, to alert the catechists. We also gave some of them to the parish priest, but only those which the catechists wrote to the young ladies. As for those from the young girls, I destroyed them completely. During this time Đoán was really walking on thin ice. On the one hand he was reproached by the parish priest for being the messenger-boy of a gang of debauched people, and on the other he was accused by the catechists of not

(504)

---

* This explanation on the subject of catechists is from Father Trần Hữu Thanh, CSsR. 'At Ton kin people had a very bad opinion of anyone who had not persevered in his vocation. Once they had entered a junior seminary or a religious juniorate they had to persevere. If one left after three or four years, especially after the years of the major seminary or after the novitiate one was held in contempt by everybody. Young men could not find wives from fervent families nor young ladies good husbands.' This is why most of them remained in the presbyteries as catechists and they were often bitter.

keeping their secrets. In the final analysis he was ousted by them in a shameful manner. While all this was happening I went to ask forgiveness of the old catechist. 'Ah, it's Van, is it? Why this sudden politeness towards me? Would it be because you are afraid of being beaten or is it because your company has disintegrated?'

It was none of those, and no one among the catechists knew my ulterior motive. I was very clever ... Thanks to this ruse, I was much acclaimed by the catechists. They called me 'little brother' and the handmaids who had friends in the presbytery were very happy because 'Van the dog' was now a 'gentle lamb'. There remained only one problem: nobody among them was allowed to touch him. He was often very friendly but nobody dared to lift a hand to tap him affectionately (505) on the head or stroke his cheek. If they had done so his bark would have reappeared. The young girls complained about my attitude, but they found me, nevertheless, quite friendly.

As for Đoán, it was truly pitiful. On the one hand, he was abandoned by the catechists, and on the other, he dared not rejoin the company because of his treachery. I went straight away to find him and, after a discussion with him, Đoán repented and leaning his head on my shoulder and while sobbing, he asked my forgiveness for the past and begged me to readmit him into the company of the 'Angels of resistance'. I immediately agreed as that was my only wish. Henceforth Đoán was more faithful to the company than any of the others. I had therefore succeeded in my plan: the old catechist and his group had confidence in me and without having any need to ask for it they accepted me as their liaison officer instead of Đoán. Thus I had no longer to fear having to be subjected to the cane for my little companions of the company and they were no longer afraid of being the target of the petty (506) criticism of the old catechist and his band. Whatever might happen I will take it all on my shoulders, so that no one will be beaten again. Am I not the 'little brother' of the catechists? Naturally I felt a little uncomfortable in accepting the role of liaison officer between the boys and the girls, but I had to resign myself to living in this way so as to have the chance to free these young girls from the bonds of their insane love.

My work in liaising with the young girls was rather ironical because, since my arrival at Hữu-Bằng, I had never been into the village because the rule forbade it. By that I mean that I did go there many times, but only on business and to specific places. I was disturbed at going from one house to the next. So that, after a stay of more than seven years at Hữu-Bằng I knew only the path which led from the presbytery to the village gate, and the road which crossed the length of the village. I remember that there were five doors on this road which opened up to (507) private properties and where I went ordinarily for specified business. I was entirely ignorant of the other roads and did not know where to find them. However, there was no problem, as I had my companions of the company to look after these things in my place. And all I had to do was to go and tell the catechists that all was in hand.

It was now time for the frontal attack against the young girls. But it was all done as gently as words of friendship whispered into the ear which forced them to listen even if they felt uneasy. One night, torch in hand, I had to escort the girlfriend of the old catechist to the garden door. These watches normally tired me out and made me lose sleep. It was my own fault if I lost sleep because there was a bed for me in the old catechist's room, but I had never agreed to lie down on it when I saw that he was still chatting with his girlfriend. I had, consequently, to

(508)   carry my blanket to the front of the house and wait there until it was time to escort the young lady. I did not complain about this as I appreciated that sacrifices were necessary for success.

I tested the water for the first time that evening, saying quietly to Miss Ngoạn:

'I have an idea that I would like to share with you, but I don't know whether or not you will like it.'

She came close to me, took me by the shoulder and, her face close to mine, she replied:

'What is it, little brother? Say what you want, I am listening to you.'

I blushed and stepped backwards, and said to her by way of excuse:

'Ow! I've got a bad shoulder.' I then continued:

'But I'm afraid that the catechist might get to hear what I'm going to say to you. Then it's hard lines for me.'

We were standing near the latch of the door. I had hardly finished speaking when, immediately, she made as if to say something but she remained silent but, a moment later she answered me carefully:

'No, I swear I'll say nothing to the catechist. Anybody who lies is nothing but a scoundrel ... Now, little brother, what is the secret? ...'

(509)   'No, it's nothing at all; he still loves you as usual, but there is something which I find difficult to say.'

'Then say it, little brother. You need not fear any consequences because I've sworn to keep silent.'

'That's true, you've sworn to reveal nothing of what I'm going to say to you. That is so, isn't it?'

'Yes. Quickly! Anyone who doesn't keep their word is a scoundrel.'

'In my opinion, it isn't right that you should love the catechist as you do now, because he has given himself to God.'

She became very angry immediately, no longer calling me her little brother, but treating me now as 'that little dog Van' and threatening not to keep her word. I hurried to open the door and shove her outside, saying:

'Good. I've told you the truth. If you won't listen to me, too bad. Go home and wait for the shame which God will cover you with for the sins you have made others commit.'

Whilst leaving she replied in a voice full of pique:

'I couldn't care less. I'm the one who will suffer the consequences, not you. Tomorrow I'm going to tell the catechist everything!'   (510)

I closed the door and returned to the house. My mind was perplexed and I was slightly worried, fearing that she would go the following day and repeat my words to the catechist. My final words to her were not meant to be prophetic but God has allowed that they were fulfilled. Just over a year later, this girl brought a child into the world whose father was unknown. It was really ironic. Had she known to listen to the voice of the little dog of the Blessed Virgin who barked to let her know the danger, she would never have had to carry such an ignominious stain.

The young lady came back again at midday the following day. I pretended to sulk and did not present her at the catechist's room. I even threatened to let the dog loose on her. Seeing this, she immediately became friendly and promised to say nothing to the catechist. I was no longer afraid, since I knew that she spoke much but thought little. Then I made a further threat:

'I'm not interested in whether you speak or not, but, bear in mind, if you do speak of me I also will speak of you.' I then recalled for her an   (511)
old tale concerning the time when I had seen her wrap her arm round the shoulders of a young catechist under a banana tree near the parlour. 'If the old catechist heard about that it would not do you any good,' I said. She, therefore, said to me gently and in a pleading manner:

'Enough of that. Why do your recall this meaningless thing? You know I've sworn to say nothing.'

'Very well, but remember, if the catechist questions me concerning what I said yesterday, whatever happens I will never forgive you.'

I led her to the old catechist's room and slipped away.

I had failed in regard to this girl who was the leader of the handmaids. But let me leave these matters for a moment and consider the other young girls who were four in number. I employed this stratagem with them. I soaked in a special liquid contained in an earthenware jar* at the end of the house all the loveletters that the catechists had sent to them and those which they had sent. Not even the devil would have dared to pull out any letter or other paper that the admiral plunged

---

* The jar acted as a urinal.

(512)   into this jar. However, before this operation, I had taken care to have these letters clearly copied, even including the dates. Once these copies were made I no longer allowed the secretary to have anything more to do with them. I carried them all to Our Lady's altar and there I censored them carefully; weighing every word, studying each correspondent's manner of speaking and then I began to ... forge the letter.

I must admit that I had to write these counterfeit letters secretly in a corner of the toilets. It was only during the hours of silence, as during the night, that I could find the peace to do this work. One thing is certain, the Blessed Virgin and my guardian angel must have especially helped me in this work. It would have been impossible for me, without their help, to find the sweet and affectionate words appropriate to lovers. Being still young I understood absolutely nothing about the exchange of feelings between lovers, nevertheless, the counterfeit

(513)   letters were very acceptable to all parties and no one could have noticed that they were forged. I was not afraid that anyone would recognise my writing since I had been able to practise writing in two styles. For the catechists' letters to the young girls I used a more vertical and firmer form of writing, whereas for that of the young girls I used a sloping, more delicate style. To do this I had only to hold the pen quite close to the nib or hold it between the third and little fingers. I noticed, however, that neither party paid any attention to the style of handwriting. On receiving a letter it was read and then it was necessary to make it disappear since, without doing so, anyone could have read it secretly and that would have been dangerous. Love letters!

The most comical thing was to watch the young girls who could not read at all. When a letter was brought to them it was also necessary to read it for them. For these girls I agreed, on each occasion, to reply on their behalf. I read to them some ideas which I sketched out and then

(514)   I continued to write as I wished. In the early letters I used elegant terms firmly to tie the bonds of friendship of both concerned. In the subsequent letters I untied these bonds little by little, sprinkling some reciprocal reproaches, more or less serious. Sometimes I made up bits of stories without foundation. These I slipped into the letters from the catechists to the young ladies reproaching them for some infidelity here or there ... I had to try hard not to laugh when I read these things to the young girls and heard their outrage in saying that the catechists were calumniating them or had had a change of heart and wished to break off their friendship. They found this too unfair, and so it was necessary to reply immediately to the catechists. It fell to me to write the reproaches on behalf of the young girls. And don't believe that I wrote what they wanted! I followed my own ideas exclusively in giving a severe telling off to the band of catechists.

When the latter received their letters and saw the rage of their little friends, they took pains to write conciliatory letters. But 'Miss Van' was the only one to read these letters of comfort. Afterwards she would (515) reply directly, thus doing a good turn for the catechists.

After that they would sometimes meet in some corner, be it the entrance to the parlour, at the sacristy door or behind the church. These pairs of illegitimate lovers sensed a certain mutual lack of understanding ... They spoke with difficulty, or, again, a word which had formerly expressed love could now indicate harshness, dissimulation or irony. Their glances, formerly ardent and passionate, could now be taken as looks of scorn or mockery. The catechists could no longer understand the handmaids and this lack of understanding was reciprocated. While the two sides were in this state of confusion, I hurried to cut the ties. I made up wounding words and went to tell the young ladies: the boy said this about you (I was the boy!). I then went to the catechist to tell him of the attitude (incorrect!) of his little friend in his regard. Having reached this point anything further was unnecessary. From both sides the lovers, imperceptibly, looked for means of avoiding each other and of breaking up completely. I feared only one thing, that they might get together again. However, I believed rather that that would never happen since, (516) when two lovers love each other tenderly and for whatever reason come to hate each other, a reconciliation is very difficult.

This state of affairs was more painful for the girls. I went immediately to them and did not cease to write comforting letters to them, trying to make them understand the meaning of lawful love. I even dared to disclose the method I had employed to pull them from these friendships. What was surprising was, instead of being angry at my conduct, they expressed their gratitude. Those who previously often called me 'Van the dog' would now call me 'little angel' or again, 'Miss Mary'. They called me these names because, afterwards in writing to them I always signed my letters with he words, 'an angel' or 'the little secretary of Mary my Mother'. I know that later these young girls left the Crusaders' group, and that they had broken completely from the group which assiduously visited the presbytery. Today, all four of them are (517) married to good men who are worthy of a sincere and constant love. I still remember all their names: Nhiệm, Tự, Vân and Thận.

After having taken on 'hell' for a good length of time, the leader of the company of 'Angels of the resistance' stood with victory within his grasp. I felt a great joy and an infantile pride. I knew well, however, that all the honour was God's without whom I was entirely powerless, but I could not help myself from being moved on seeing that the efforts and prayers of the company of 'Angels' had been of some avail for the souls that we wanted to help. God is always infinitely more powerful, but he is still infinitely worthy of praise when he uses a little creature coming from his creative hands to achieve works which conform to his will. What a mystery!

(518)   At this moment the struggle is not yet over. The company of the 'Angels' has to struggle all the time against many bad practices introduced in to the presbytery. This struggle, however, has become much easier since the day when the young girls stopped visiting the place. The question of the old catechist's mistress is all that remains, and I wished greatly that this would finish once and for all. This is what I decided; either Miss Ngoạn must stop visiting the old catechist as she pleased, or I would leave the presbytery. One of these possibilities must occur. I had decided, also, after the feast of Christmas of that year, to bring this affair directly to the parish priest, in accusing the old catechist of having ignored the rules of this religious house. If this step was unsuccessful, and if the parish priest sided with the old catechist, I would ask to return home immediately. If, on the contrary, my action succeeded, I would stay. In any event it was necessary to show that I was obliged to protect the chastity of this house of religion where God alone and pure souls live together, since at that particular time I was still among those called with the duty to be on guard to protect the most important feature of the house of God.

(519)   But my beloved had decided otherwise for me.

The little seminary of Saint Thérèse of the Child Jesus

It is probable that the good God, seeing me concentrate all my energies on this work of restoring morals, but still not strong enough in virtue, had decided that it would be good to send me to another place where he could strengthen my soul, and show me my special mission which consists in being an apostle more by love than by work on a great external activity – an apostle by 'Absolute Love', that is to say, by a hidden life of prayer and sacrifice. There, God will send me a master of holiness to guide me and make a model of me. Therefore, my Father, allow (520)   me to continue to tell honestly what God has wished of me.

So, straight after Christmas 1941, I received a letter from my friend Tân telling me that the Father Director of the junior seminary of Lạng-Sơn wished to admit some new candidates at Christmastime, and Tân asked me to go and join him. He had been admitted himself three months ago. At the time of his departure from Hữu-Bằng he wanted me to go with him so that he would have a companion, but my studies were not advanced enough, and also the parish priest was opposed to it because I came from the Vicariate of Bắc-Ninh. I missed Tân a lot after his departure because, outside my family, he was my closest and dearest friend. If he liked me it was only because he appreciated my sincerity and my spirit. He would usually praise me in these terms: 'Van's way is the direct way'. So, after having received his letter, I went to acquaint the parish priest and ask permission to enter the junior seminary of Saint Thérèse at Lạng-Sơn. He deliberated a moment with the old catechist and then gave permission immediately without giving me clothes, sandals or absolutely anything. It was the beginning of the year 1942.

On seeing me arrive, Tân was a little disturbed to see his little friend entering the seminary with faded black clothes and dirty sandals with a (521) broken strap. In the morning, when I went to meet Father Director in the yard, my companions assembled around me to see the new pupil. They cried out: 'Ah, Tâns little brother has arrived! Tân's little brother has arrived!' Tân blushed a lot and protested, saying: 'He's not my little brother at all. I haven't got a little brother in such a pathetic state.' I felt myself blushing a little along with him since I saw that my poverty was making him uncomfortable. I had a strong desire to cry when I heard my little comrades behind me say among themselves: 'It's really shameful. Which parish priest would send this boy here in such rags like a beggar.' The following day Tân threw my old sandals on the scrap heap and bought me new ones. Some days later a parcel arrived from the Carmel in Saigon. It was a present for the poor seminarists. In it there were pens, paper and clothing. Being of the number of the poor, I had my share of the presents.

It was also thanks to these presents that I heard of the Carmel. I (522) heard my companions say: 'The Saigon Carmel has special links with the junior seminary at Lạng-Sơn because it was the first seminary in Asia to choose Saint Thérèse of the Child Jesus as patron saint.' I did not give this much attention at the time. It was only during my stay in Saigon in 1950 that, when visiting the chapel, I remembered the present of 1942. There, I prayed again to express my gratitude to the Carmelites, asking Jesus to reward them for me because I was one with him.

At the beginning of my life as a seminarist I had a strange feeling. At home I was dependent on my mother, but having entered the seminary and being weak at my studies I regarded myself as being a completely useless boy, not even being capable of being mischievous. At the presbytery of Hữu-Bằng I was placed among those who enjoyed the greatest authority, whereas since my arrival here I had to submit to the teasing of my companions who called me 'tatters', and that made my tears flow freely. The greatest difficulty for me, however, was to live among the European priests. Ah, the European fathers! At that time I (523) could not stop myself being startled at the thought of them, because I had already tasted a good caning from a European priest at Thái-Nguyên. For that reason I imagined all European priests were as cruel as he was. Naturally, I did not hate them, but I feared them beyond words. So when I saw a European father I went to hide. There was one exception. On the first day I made an effort to make a good impression in the presence of the Father Director. That apart, I would never dare to speak or joke with them as my comrades did. In addition, certain of my mischievous companions, on noticing my fear, intimidated me even more by saying: 'Ah, yes, the European fathers are really cruel. They laugh readily, but if anyone does anything wrong he is beaten severely ...' I shivered and feared them even more.

(524)   My greatest trial in the refectory was to be seated at the end of the table right next to that of the European fathers. So, on arriving at the table, instead of sitting up straight I sat a little to the side with my head down and my back facing the fathers' table. On first adopting this posture no one made any remarks, but later a Vietnamese teacher, Father Ngữ, came to tell me to sit properly. I obeyed, but I glanced furtively from time to time to see if any of the European fathers was watching me. On one occasion I met the light brown eyes of Father Dreyer Dufer staring at me. I felt the blood flow through my body and I felt as if I was no longer at the table. But I suddenly saw his lips break into a gentle smile, and I felt happy straight away and began eating as normally.

It is probable that the Father Director also understood my attitude, because he called me one Sunday to his office and grabbed me by both arms and placed me in a chair while singing 'Oo-ee' in a funny manner. He tapped me gently on the cheeks and then, turning his back, he continued to hum the song. He went to the table and lifted the needle

(525)   of the gramophone so that I could listen to a record. Then he asked me 'Do you understand it, p'tit Van*?' I smiled timidly, then, shaking my head, I replied: 'It's very beautiful, but I don't understand it.' Without heeding my reply, he began to move his arms in time to the rhythm of the music. He then lit a cigarette, took a game of draughts from a drawer and asked me to draw up my chair to play with him. I was afraid, understanding nothing, but I did what he wished. After having set out the pieces he stopped the gramophone and played draughts with me. I felt uneasy and played in a silly manner in spite of myself and only wanted to cry. From time to time I looked at Father with the intention of asking him if I could withdraw but, afraid of being impolite, I continued to play until the end of the game. And don't forget, Father, I won the game. Father Director took his defeat very cheerfully. He

---

*   'Little Van' is written in French in Van's original text.

slapped his two hands on the edge of the table and laughed happily while nodding his head. He congratulated me on my skill at draughts and then, as a reward, gave me some sweets from a drawer. He took the sweets one by one, took off their wrappers and made me eat them there and then. I felt a glow in my face and could not stop laughing, while   (526) noisily crunching the sweets which would not melt in my mouth. In the meantime Father Director opened his tobacco pouch, filled his pipe to smoke it and then, getting up, he turned the gramophone on again, and turning towards me he asked:

'Is the toffee sweet enough?' I burst out laughing, put my hand to my mouth and answered very quickly:

'Yes, Father.'

'Do you like playing at marbles?'

'I like playing, Father, but I'm not very good.'

'Good: you can play with me then.'

We moved the chairs and began to play. At the beginning I still threw a sly glance at the Father Director so as to be on my guard, but shortly afterwards, I had forgotten these glances and played with great spirit, sending shots towards Father's marbles which sent them right into the corner of the room. But I was eventually beaten as I was not able to play as well as Father Director. As for him, he did not stop nodding his head to congratulate me on playing quite well. I then asked permission to withdraw. But, before giving me leave, he called me close to him, smiled, nodded his head and asked me: (527)

'Are you afraid of me?'

I began to smile and I replied frankly: 'I'm no longer afraid, Father.'

'Good. There's no need to be afraid.'

Then he dismissed me. On leaving his room I felt as if my heart had been relieved of a heavy burden; my soul felt light and from that time I was afraid no longer of the European fathers.

After that I found it easy to open up to the Father Director, who called me to his office from time to time to teach me French. I spoke French fairly well at that period, thanks to this extra tuition, and Father congratulated me, telling me that I spoke with the tone and clarity of a Parisian. I realise that today I am far from speaking as well as I did when I was fourteen years of age. I was always happy when I left the Director's room.

The bursar of the seminary, Father Dreyer Dufer, made it obvious that he understood me better than anyone else did. He was a good man with the gentle appearance of a mother. His face, which was framed by a sparse beard, was always blooming with a kindly smile. This smile   (528) clearly showed that he was always ready to forgive and protect. He was particularly attentive to the younger ones and, thanks to his responsibilities as bursar, titbits fell freely from his hands into those of the youngest who might be feeling tearful ... I must admit that I could do my share of sniffling, but usually I did it in private. Besides, Father Dreyer Dufer did not need to see me crying to give me delicacies. Each time that he saw me with slightly red eyes he took me to his room to give me some. I noticed that I was indulged as in my family, so much so that my love for the father was strong and deep like that I had for my family. From the time of my first entry into the presbytery as a candidate for the priesthood until then, that was the first that I saw the fathers act in a truly paternal way. I called them Father and I never had need to ask myself why they were my fathers since their attitude could not have been more paternal. Father Dreyer Dufer observed me very closely. I noticed that he was prone to follow me, searching for occasions to know my intimate feelings. He understood also that if he did not question me I would never speak spontaneously. Frankly, I was still timid on that score; there are plenty of things I would have wished to explain clearly, but I did not know how to express myself and I was afraid, above all, that I would not be understood. I remember the following episode which illustrates Father's skill in observing me.

(529)

I went into the garden one morning to look for flowers. My favourite flower was the little chrysanthemum, the only flower which fitted the very small vase that I kept on my desk before a picture of the Blessed Virgin. So, before going to the playground, I went to the garden to look for flowers. Suddenly I met Father Dreyer Dufer who was out walking and who asked me:

'Where are you going? Why aren't you playing with your companions?'

'I am going to, Father, but I came this way to collect some flowers.'

He put his head to one side and said to me, smiling:

'You like flowers a lot, don't you?'

'Father ... it isn't for me but for the Blessed Virgin who loves them a great deal, so I'm going to collect some for her.'

(530)

Then, still with a serene face, he added:

'Yes, I know. It's not surprising that a soul like yours loves flowers ... That is good. Go and look for flowers. I'll come with you.'

'Thank you, Father.'

Then both of us, lifting up our clothes, entered the garden, which was still covered with the morning dew. I chose two or three flowers which I found attractive and then I stopped collecting. Father Dreyer Dufer had not yet any flowers but he continued looking very carefully. A moment later I saw him bend down and pick, very delicately, a very small white chrysanthemum. He called me, smiling, and made me look at a drop of very limpid dew which was still resting in the calyx of the flower. He said to me:

'Do you see?'

'Yes, I see, Father.'

'What do you see?'

'I see that it is a white chrysanthemum.'

'No, you don't see.'

I looked at him astonished, letting him see that I did not understand his question. He explained immediately, pointing out the drop of dew in the calyx and saying to me, cheerfully:

'This drop of dew is like the tear of the little flower ... and the little (531) flower ... it's you.'

I burst out laughing, but to tell the truth, I did not yet understand much about the meaning of his word. It was only later when my boat reached the port of the Congregation of the Most Holy Redeemer that, looking backwards, I understood clearly the meaning of these words. Father Dreyer Dufer gave me the flower and told me to go and offer it to the Blessed Virgin. I thanked him and went to place it in a little vase, taking great care not to allow the precious dew drop to fall.

A month after my entrance, Father Dreyer Dufer admitted me to the troop of 'the Cadets of Our Lady' of which he was the person in charge. The aim of the association was to form holy and zealous preachers under the direction of Mary. Children were led to follow a simple and responsible life so that, later, no obstacle would stop them on their (532) apostolic path in preaching the gospel. The programme of training resembled that of the scout movement. It could be said that it was a scout troop of the Blessed Virgin, dedicated to her service. On joining the troop I had, first of all, to do my training as a cub scout, but at Pentecost of that year I was admitted to make my promise and joined the troop of scouts, seconde classe. I received the name of 'Ecureuil of the *Cerf* Patrol'.*

This happy life had transformed me within a short while into a new man. In my opinion this change was due partly to the spirit of charity which animated our teachers, but it was due mainly to divine grace itself which was active in me. I noticed that I had always found it easy to live in intimacy with God, and I had the fairly clear feeling that God was everywhere for me like a palpable reality. In the past my soul had become ill with the anxiety which imprisoned my life in a narrow, parched setting and although it had been set free by God on Christmas (533) night 1940, it still remained more or less sickly as if it had not yet recovered entirely the serenity of early infancy. But at the seminary God caused all the after-effects of the sickness my soul was still suffering to disappear. He used this 'joyful life' to give back to me my former smile.

---

* 'Second class', 'Squirrel', 'Stag': all written in French in Van's original text.

He had opened my soul fully to the wonders of nature, he had tightened the bonds of my love for him during these nights of intimacy and silence under the light of the moon, at the side of a spring or, again, in the peace that one tastes in the shade of a pine at the side of a mountain.

At this point the memory of the days when we went camping comes back to me. Ah, to go camping! This fills me with happiness and brings back to my memory all the joys of those unforgettable days. To go camping was, for me, the sweetest of retreats. There, alone with God with Jesus my leader, the only view the trees, the mountains and all the marvels of nature were for me a stimulus to unite me more intimately (534) to him. The more beautiful the flower, the more gentle the breeze, the more green the tree, the more roaring the waterfall, the more verdant the meadow: the more, also, was my heart uplifted as if by so many steps right up to the highest heavens, and there I loved God and he wrapped me in his tenderness. What intimacy there was between us during those moments of calm and close union! There, I went over in my mind my past life, and I did not see there an instant, not the smallest movement nor the least action, which did not have its origin in divine grace.

Then, once more, I solemnly made this promise to God: 'My God, I consecrate my body entirely to you and all my life, long or short, so that your name may be glorified.' My desire for the priesthood had never been so passionate as it was then. I wanted to become a priest, and a holy priest, and the more ardent was this desire, the more were my efforts stimulated. I had taken this decision: 'Never despise little things'. Each point of the rule is a diamond of honour for the 'Cadet of (535) Our Lady'. I am therefore taking this resolution for life, never to break a single one. On the day of my admission to the troop and facing its three flags, the holy Church and my country, and beside Father Chaplain and our leader, and with my hand raised I solemnly made this promise: 'I promise on my honour and with the grace of God to be always faithful to God, to love the Holy Church and to defend my country. I further promise to consider all men, to help them at all times, and to keep faithfully the rules of the Cadets of Our Lady.' I can say, in all conscience, that up to this day I have never had to blush for having failed to keep my promise. Certainly there were failings but there was nothing to blush about because they were corrected once they were known. To correct oneself is the most valuable point of honour for those who wish to become perfect.

You can also understand, Father, that perfection in man is never the result of chance. He must make an effort. Yes, a lot of effort, and for this effort to become effective it must rely on divine grace. On my (536) admission into the Stag Patrol, symbol of agility and rapid progress, I heard the leader each day at our meeting give us a recommendation full of sense, such as: 'We must make rapid progress in everything and never remain where we are to watch the sun rising or the melancholy evening. Our duty is to go forward, to advance with great strides to the end towards which we are striving.' But this end, what is it? Is it not God himself? Yes, this is the loving end which alone is capable of accelerating my race forward.

I bore the name 'Squirrel' which signified 'joy and speed' to me. At the time of our meetings I spent a time of the prayer in applying this motto to my joyful and eager life by using this formula: 'When I have done all my work, I shall ask for reward only "joy and eagerness" in accepting God's holy will. The only reward I will accept is the will of God. Each time that I have done a favour for a companion, I will know only how to accept with joy and eagerness everything offered to me in return, be it a word of gratitude or an indifferent attitude, and even if (537) it's a question of an ungrateful person addressing me critically, I will accept all with joy and eagerness since this is the reward sent to us from the will of God.'

At the Quảng-Uyên presbytery
Saint Thérèse of the Child Jesus

The holidays came after six months at the junior seminary. That year, because of unusual circumstances, the seminary had to close its doors earlier than usual. I noticed that during the time I had developed and got stronger, as much physically as spiritually. I must admit that during these six months I had received and learned many more good things than during all the time spent at the presbytery at Hữu-Bằng. (All I was able to learn at that presbytery was that children there were compared to dogs, and that the young candidates for the priesthood were only 'boys' useful to the parish.)

During the holidays that year I had to return once again to Hữu-Bằng. I would have very much liked to have spent my holidays with my family but they would never have consented, fearing that the young seminarian, used to being indulged at home might weaken in his vocation and (538) not wish to return. It was a heavy cross for me to have to spend my holidays at Hữu-Bằng. Nevertheless, Our Lady's cadet must accept it cheerfully as it was God's will. Hữu-Bằng had taken on its former aspect during my six months' absence. The company of the 'Angels of the resistance' had been suppressed and Miss Ngoạn had confessed that she had been made pregnant by the old catechist. Nearly all the young seminarists had been dispersed and were working in adjacent parishes. The older ones had entered the school for the formation of catechists at Bắc-Ninh. Although no longer existing as such, the company of the 'Angels of the resistance' still exercised a certain influence by its spirit which had remained at the presbytery since, after my departure, some of my friends, disgusted by the state of decadence which ruled in this place, returned spontaneously to their families. Those who remained, seeing me arrive for the holidays, manifested a wish to re-form the troop.

(539)   But just at that moment sad news arrived. The junior seminary of St Thérèse was forced to close because of lack of funds, and also because the Japanese army was still threatening to requisition it. The students had to disperse. At this news I was like a bird which had lost its nest, like an infant who had lost its father ... and my daily life was no longer able to blossom with a smile. My holidays were without meaning. Only suffering and tears came to visit me every day in lonely corners. Towards the end of the holiday I learned that Father Nhã wanted to send me to the school of the sub-prefecture to continue the study of French, but the big problem was that the school was not Catholic. For more than one hundred pupils there was only one Catholic professor for the normal course and the parish priest intended me to stay with this teacher's family. But it seemed imprudent to me to go to school where I would be the only Catholic. So, I wrote to Father Dreyer Dufer to explain the situation to him in detail, and to ask him to find a happier solution if possible.

(540)   While waiting for a reply my friend Tân suggested a ride to Hanoi. We would use the opportunity to visit the former Director, Father Tailleur, at the Dominican monastery. We arrived just at the moment when he was waiting for us. He received us in a very affectionate and friendly manner. He told me that Father Dreyer Dufer had written to him concerning me and he assured me that he would so arrange things that I did not have to attend a pagan school. When it was time to leave, I left him regretfully and with a very anxious heart, and childlike tears in my eyes. He embraced me and spoke these words of comfort: 'No matter what happens, the day will come when we will meet again.' 'The day will come', yes, but this day will not be on earth! ... I cried, and with good reason. In fact I never again saw this father who was so dear to me. I do not even know if he is still on earth, or if he has left for heaven. In saying 'the day will come' he probably meant the day when we would meet in paradise. Once again I was right to cry.

(541)   I returned to Hữu-Bằng to await Father Dreyer Dufer's reply; but the reply took a long time in coming. Each morning I was certain that it would come that day. I said to myself: 'It's impossible that Father Dreyer Dufer has forgotten me.' But, come evening, I realised that I had been too credulous. My only consolation was to go to the church and bend my head before Our Lady's altar to hide my tears. My state of

soul always remained the same. I went to communion every day, living constantly close to my Lord Jesus. It was as if I had lost the innate character of the 'squirrel', namely, joy and eagerness. I fled from everyone, wishing to remain alone in a corner. My adoptive mother was afraid that I would lose my mind.

Happily the day came suddenly when the Squirrel regained his former character. He learned that he was going to return to his land of forests and mountains. Father Dreyer Dufer's reply came two days before the feast of the Assumption. He told me that I had been chosen (542) with two other friends from the same class to continue my studies at the presbytery of Saint Thérèse at Quảng-Uyên and he urged me to go straight away to Lạng-Sơn so as to arrive in time to leave for Quảng-Uyên with my two companions. This letter drew tears of joy. I got ready without delay, called at my house to greet my parents and, on the very day of the Assumption, I was en-route for Lạng-Sơn. My soul was overflowing with happiness. I arrived at the seminary at nine o'clock in the evening and met Father Dreyer Dufer but, after a few minutes, he made me go and lie down as it was necessary to leave early the next day.

On 16 August 1942 we set off for Cao-Bằng. Hiển and Tám, being younger than me, chose me as their leader. Hiển was the 'nightingale'. He sang very well and had the shy bearing of a little girl, but his timidity was less obvious when he was in the company of the squirrel. Tám was the 'panther'. He was as round as a spinning top. His party piece was to play the guitar without strings, that is to say, he went through the motions of playing the guitar while making the sounds with his mouth. (543) The seminarist Lãng (who afterwards became a priest and a bishop) after having seen us on the train as was necessary, gave the squirrel responsibility for the group and then returned to the seminary. No sooner honoured by the older boy with the title of leader, the squirrel proudly curled up his moustache and called his friends to a meeting right there and then, mainly to elect a deputy leader and secretary. Hiển – sorry – the nightingale, was elected secretary and the panther deputy leader. The latter, stubborn as a mule and inclined to sniffle, accepted his duty as deputy leader and demonstrated an exemplary obedience.

We immediately began a 'camp fire' after the elections as the rays of the sun filtered through the doors and illuminated the carriage. We held each other by the hand, and we danced round a square of light, formed on the floor by the rays of the sun, which served as a camp fire. This carriage was deserted before we lit our camp fire but after our first songs and the first steps of our dancing and the sound of our voices and the noise of our steps rhythmically beating the floor, other passengers, even from carriages some distance away, were attracted to us. There were

(544)   even some Chinese among them who had come to see what these nice young lads were up to. After having cheered up these passengers with their fill of entertainment, we asked for an interval at each station so that we could assist those with a lot of luggage to get on or off. This gesture aroused the admiration of the people even more than the best acts in our repertoire. We had to laugh at the good women from the country every time we helped passengers in this manner. Seeing us offer our assistance, they kept a watchful eye on their luggage, not ceasing to thank us a little bit like this: 'No, no, little one, I've only got this. I wouldn't dream of troubling you.' Others accepted our help whilst telling another member of their entourage to keep an eye on us. 'Heh, keep a good eye on them. You can't trust anybody these days, especially today. There are robbers everywhere.' Others were as white as sheets, fearing that we were from

(545)   the secret police. There were, on the other hand, those who understood what we were and who reassured these good ladies, saying to them: 'Don't be afraid. They are members of a voluntary association. Look at the stripes on their chests.' We continued our duty as scouts, regardless of either confidence or misplaced trust.

The train arrived at Na-Chàm, the terminus of the line, and from there we had to continue our journey by coach to Cao-Bằng. On arriving at this town, all three of us were exhausted with fatigue, especially the squirrel, because of being enclosed in a coach where all sorts of offensive smells were inhaled: the smell of *coula**, of tobacco, of betel chewed by the women, and added to this the smell of oils used to perfume the head which young men and girls of rich families use, and finally, the smell of petrol. They were all there. It was more than enough to give me a huge headache. Heavens, it was terrible! ... And a miracle that I could survive to Cao-Bằng. The nightingale and the panther, seeing their leader in such a sorry state, were also at the end of their tether, and no longer strong enough to force a smile. The cold nature of our greeting at the presbytery completed our unhappiness. Dead tired, we asked for a drink and we were told to drink at the tap.

(546)   For supper that evening we were served red rice with salted fish; at each mouthful we felt that we were swallowing stones, and we looked at each other with tearful eyes. I made an effort through politeness to eat half of my bowl and I then went to lie down. The nightingale and the panther went to the town to get some Chinese soup.

When one thinks of it, it was quite sad, far removed from having 'Mother Dreyer Dufer' pampering us, as at the seminary, who even went so far as to give us his own steak but here there was only a tap of spring water. The old catechist of this presbytery, knowing that we were

---

*   A Chinese sedative.

not pleased at our reception and that we had left the table to eat in town, was annoyed and said words that I would rather have not heard. 'These lads, used to being spoiled at the seminary, are becoming good-for-nothings.' It was fortunate for this catechist that I ignored his words, because otherwise the missionaries at the seminary would have (547) been very displeased with him. I tried to put up with it without showing my feelings, and I comforted myself with these words: 'It is not always possible on earth to have what pleases us. Anyway, a cadet of Our Lady must put up with all trials whilst maintaining his habitual calm.' I don't know when I went to sleep, once in bed, but throughout the night I dreamt of the mountains, only the mountains, and I managed to climb them all without exception. I was proud of my achievement, which was in keeping with the squirrel's talent as a very skilful climber.

We had to travel no more than thirty-seven kilometres to reach the presbytery which was welcoming us. The seminary had chosen these adjacent presbyteries for us to study in, with the idea that we would return when the seminary could reopen its doors. But when would we see this reopening? ... The more I thought of it, the sadder I became. If God wishes it, when I am in heaven I shall accomplish the project of reopening this seminary on the very spot which is still so dear to me, and of which I think day and night just as if I was, still, the very small seminarist of these dear missionaries. I shall always think of the reopen- (548) ing of their seminary.

It was 17 August when we began our journey to **Quảng-Uyên**. At ten o'clock in the morning the bus stopped at the terminus where we waited for Father Maillet OP (Bình).* He took us to the presbytery which was situated about half a kilometre from the centre of the small town. On our arrival and without giving us anything to drink, he took us to greet old Father Brébion (Uy) who was under a lean-to, moulding, by himself, some cement bricks. He shook our hands and showed us his work and the church being built, and said to us: 'I am making the bricks to build a church so that, later, you will have somewhere to celebrate Mass.' Then he began to laugh in a very friendly manner. Father Maillet continued to show us the domain of the presbytery and the work of the missionaries, and how tiring some of it was, and he concluded: 'But all of this is for you. You are the ones who will benefit from the sweat and tears of the missionaries.' I could not hold back my (549) tears at these words. Although I felt worn out, and was feeling as if I was still being shaken in the bus, I dared not ask to go and lie down on hearing these lessons in charity. At midday I refused any food and I

---

* Missionaries had the habit of taking Vietnamese names; Van gives these in brackets.

went to bed, to sleep until the following morning.

On 18 August Father Maillet was ready to send us straight away to class. We went to class happily, although still tired, as we were aware of all the sacrifices Father had made for us. Apart from us there was a pupil of the Meos tribe called Joseph Blau. We were four in number, divided into two classes. Hiển and I were the fifth class, and Blau and Tám the seventh. We had Father Maillet himself as our teacher, and each week Father Brébion taught some hours of mathematics to the fifth class. All was taught in French, except in the seventh grade, where there was a little Vietnamese. Father, you will be astonished to see how weak I am now in French. Let me give you a word of explanation! If I had been able to study French for a few more years I would have become perfect in this (550)   language, but in a short time our programme of study was turned completely upside down, so that, from that time until my entry into the congregation, I had no opportunity to complete the study of French.

Trial

We had immersed ourselves into the delights of study for more than a month when the dry season arrived with its searing sun, which completely burnt the grass in the fields. Added to this, the wells were dry that year, and the presbytery's cows were so skinny that they were in danger of dying. Father Maillet, fearful of losing his herd once again, changed our status from students to herdsmen. He gave each of us a dairy cow with her calf for us to lead to pasture here and there on the slopes of the mountains. It was sad for us to see Father Maillet acting counter to the end we had in view. So, we all asked to leave. Father Maillet reassured us saying: 'But no! that's not necessary. I well understand that you are here to study; however, unexpected circumstances make it necessary for me to ask you to help, but only for a short time.' We were sorry, all three of us, on seeing the total sincerity of our (551)   teacher and we made an effort to take up our new duty. It seemed that Hiển found the work harder than the rest of us, because he was not used to this kind of work. That is why he cried from time to time and asked to leave. After three months it began to drizzle and the grass in the fields became green again. To our great joy, Father Maillet resumed our study programme and Hiển no longer asked to leave.

Separation

We did not suspect for one moment that a trial would compel us to leave the presbytery at Quảng-Uyên. It seems that our return to our studies had scarcely been appreciated by the superior of the tertiaries of Quảng-Uyên. The superior? Father, perhaps you don't yet appreciate the nature of the power of a superior in a house of Dominican tertiaries. It is really something. And the superior of the community of Quảng-Uyên enjoyed an authority far beyond that of superiors of other places. She had the power to oppress not only the young girls of (552) her community, but this oppression reached as far as the presbytery. It could not have been more terrifying, and even today my hair stands on end at the memory of the resistance we had to mount against this superior. Allow me to tell you here the whole truth, without passing judgement on the goodness or the malice of the actions. Obviously I have no intention of fabricating anything to embellish this unhappy period of my life, nor to make it arouse more pity. No, I know only how to relate the facts as they happened.

So – at the presbytery at Quảng-Uyên, after Father Maillet, the superior was the only one to enjoy absolute power. By her physical appearance no one could but assert that she was as gentle as a Buddha but, regarding her inner feelings, they could only be understood in the context of the actions I am going to describe here. I still remember her friendly attitude towards me on the day of our arrival at the presbytery. Father Maillet had taken us that day to the tertiaries' house to meet the superior. She spoke to us in a benevolent manner, rubbing her hands (553) and, with a half-sad, half-joyful smile on her lips, she encouraged us to take pains with our studies and to practise virtue, so as later to be the pillars of the church, in place of the old missionaries. She then made us this promise: our house will provide you with everything necessary to reach the goal you are pursuing. If you are lacking anything, tell me frankly and I will attend to it. Then, opening a box of peanut-sugared bonbons, she invited us to eat some. Father Maillet, holding the box, offered them to all of us, and, whilst taking one himself and putting it in his mouth he said to us, smiling: 'You can see how good the superior is, and when you have been here for some time you will see more evidence of her goodness.'

Just at that moment I clearly heard coming from the veranda the clicking of tongues, and the voices of several tertiaries whispering among themselves. The superior went to look through the window and, raising her voice suddenly, she asked:

'What time do you call this that you are already here?'

'We've finished watering.'

'If you've finished watering, look for something else to do. Why come here to amuse yourselves? Really!' (554)

Father Maillet had to intervene:

'All right. Would you sisters like some bonbons? ... Let me give one to each of them. That should please them.'

Then, taking the box of sweets, he went to give them one, but they had all disappeared. I began to doubt the superior's goodness after having heard her speak to the young girls, tertiaries like her, in such a bossy, cruel and proud manner. Concerning us, it was true that her kind words at the beginning were in keeping with her good manners. From time to time when meeting us she asked about our health, and asked if the young tertiaries prepared our food well. Truly, during the first months we were treated like the superior's indulged children.

Time passes ...

(555)   After having herded the cows for three months, and then having taken up again our books, we had time to play at marbles, go bathing, go for walks and climb the hills and mountains etc. Oh, the odour of cows no longer radiated from all over our bodies ... Perhaps also because of this change, the tertiaries' house lost a certain material advantage. The superior looked unhappy. At first she begged us to continue looking after the cows. Then she complained to Father Maillet, but he did not agree to her request. He invariably replied to her in this direct manner: 'My conscience compels me to attend to the studies of these boys, and if I don't, I must explain to God all the time they have spent for the benefit of the presbytery. When it is necessary I will ask them to help, but now we can manage I must give them back their hours of study.' The superior got into a sulk with father and all the time said she was ill and could no longer concern herself with the presbytery's affairs. In other words, she was going on strike. Although she was absent in body she was not so absent as not to always have present a young tertiary who kept her informed of all that was going on.

(556)   We, therefore, continued our studies in peace and were respectful to the superior and loved the tertiaries as our benefactresses ... But we suddenly realised that the amount of food being served to us had been reduced considerably. In the mornings at breakfast, although the pan of soup was always full, it contained only water with hardly any grains of rice or crushed maize. At midday the rice was insufficient, and the small amount served was doughy like a cake of rice pudding, and furthermore it was burnt. There was no salt in the food and the soya sauce, although taken from the same jar, was tasteless and more acidic than usual. We found it very strange, and it was only later that we found that it was the superior herself who was the author of this 'miracle'. She said: 'Anybody who doesn't work doesn't eat. When one does not look after the cows one does not eat.' The tertiaries employed in the kitchen had therefore, on the orders of the superior, to perform hundreds of

miracles. The situation was becoming more and more fraught from day to day. Nobody among us had reached fasting age but we had to fast every day. It was really painful and, some way, we had to find a solution in order to bring it to an end.

We were together in class and my two classmates, Hiển and Tám, both agreed to delegate me to see the superior so as to discuss the (557) subject of the miracles in question. Not only did she not wish to hear anything, but she roundly reprimanded me, representative as I was, and did not cease to repeat: 'Anybody who does not work does not eat'. Delegate Van had to withdraw, not having achieved anything, but also not having lost his temper. Following this we had to ask Father Maillet to intervene, but the more he scolded the tertiaries the more we saw her miracles multiply. Each day Tám and Hiển, tortured by hunger, wanted to cry. We went to the mountains at recreation time to dig up some wild potatoes to replace the rice. But these tubers were quite rare, and when we were lucky enough to find some edible fruits we devoured them completely, even if they were very sour. As a last resort Father Maillet had to force the tertiaries to prepare our food in the Fathers' kitchen and, before each meal, he carefully opened the pan of rice to see if there was sufficient quantity and if it was well prepared. This solicitude on Father's part moved us to tears.

But Father's careful attention had not uncovered the superior's (558) secret and malicious intent. The pan of rice was always full, but the rice was always doughy, and the bottom of the pan was always empty. It was a strange thing that we could not understand. But one day I ended up by discovering the secret. As I sat at the table the server brought me a very hot bowl of rice. I mixed in it a little soya sauce and I began to eat. I sensed immediately that the sauce was giving off a strong smell similar to lime, but I paid no attention and continued to eat with my normal appetite, believing that the smell came from the soya sauce which was already quite old. I noticed in glancing quickly at my companions that they were happily chewing mouthfuls of rice seasoned with the soya sauce. This reassured me, and I concluded that the smell of lime I had noticed was pure imagination. The second bowl arrived and I smelled, as previously, a strong smell coming from it, but I continued eating (559) without paying it much attention. After having swallowed some mouthfuls I suddenly crunched a little stone the size of a grain of maize which had a bitter taste ... like lime. I hurriedly excused myself to my friends and ran out. Having spat the rice from my mouth, I saw clearly that it was a little stone of lime that had been mixed with the rice which I had crushed whilst chewing. I again sensed the bitter taste which permeated my entire mouth. I let out a long sigh and going back once more to the refectory, and seeing Hiển and Tám still eating with an appetite, I suddenly felt tears come to my eyes. I excused myself and went, sobbing, to lie down. Tám, believing I had not got enough rice, was unhappy and got up from the table and went to tell Father Maillet, 'There's not enough rice. Van is hungry. He is crying and has gone to lie down.' Father Mallet went quickly to the tertiaries and shouted so loudly that the superior and the cook both became very pale. Father,

(560)   throwing down the serviette which was hanging from his neck, returned to his table and took the remnants of his food and brought it to my bed. But I did not eat it, and I did not even tell anyone why I was crying. Hiển and Tám, seeing this, began to cry also. Father Maillet shouted angrily at us: 'Throw the rice to the dog'. This made us cry even more. That evening Father closed the class.

He began to doubt us from that moment and he allowed free rein to the superior's nastiness. At this I had to speak to Hiển and Tám in these terms: 'We can't stay here very long, but let's try to continue until the end of the school year.' I saw clearly that the pink and innocent faces of my two friends had become yellow and swollen from having eaten limed rice. In Father Maillet's eyes we were all as fat and healthy as the little calves of his herd, and for this he congratulated the tertiaries on their skill in feeding us well. Once the Vietnamese New Year was over, Hiển felt unable to live under such conditions: he packed his luggage and

(561)   asked to leave. I was very sorry at his departure and I shed bitter tears because Hiển was my close friend on the path to perfection. Shortly afterwards an employee left the presbytery and then it was the turn of the little mountain dweller, Joseph Blau, who found life too hard in this house where justice and charity left so much to be desired. Finally it will be my turn to leave this place, chased away ignominiously like a terrible criminal. I will speak of these things in greater detail later.

The little way of childhood

My dear Father, having arrived at this point in my story, I feel the necessity to interrupt things to make you aware of an unexpected discovery on the way to perfection. It is God himself who is the origin of the discovery and who has guaranteed its success. At Quảng-Uyên just as at Lạng-Sơn, although the conditions were very different, my soul

(562)   had not ceased to live in a similar intimacy with God. But there was this problem. In spite of my great desire to attain holiness, I was certain that I would never succeed, since to be a saint it was necessary to fast, give oneself the discipline, carry a stone round one's neck, wear chains and a hair shirt, put up with the cold, scabies, etc. ....! My God, if that's how it is, I give up! since, as I understand it after having read many lives of the

saints, sanctity can be summarised quite simply in these external practices, with for good measure, prolonged ecstasies, nights spent in prayer ... etc. All of these things being too much for me, I was in despair, faced with these conditions which were so hard to accomplish, and I came to the conclusion that my desire for sanctity was for me pure madness; a serious temptation which I had firmly to rule out. I don't know why, but the more I chased away this temptation the more it plagued me. The more I tried to flee it the more it returned with greater insistence. I had to beg the Blessed Virgin often to free me from this troublesome idea. It was obvious to me that sainthood was impossible.

Compatible with my personal idea, I would have wished that my life (563) of sanctity could conform to the thought of Saint Augustine: 'Love and do what you wish.' Yes, I would have wished that all my actions, all my gestures were devoted to the service of God, so as to reach right up to him who is absolute perfection. But how can I dare to run such a risk, since I have not yet succeeded in finding an officially recognised guide to approve as acceptable my notion of sanctity? I have even scoured the entire series of the lives of the saints without finding a single one who was joyful, who laughed and could be mischievous like me. From their early childhood they showed an aptitude to put up with hunger and to spend long hours in prayer. And as for the saints who had first of all led a sinful life to be converted afterwards, they practised frightening corporal penances. I was looking, therefore, for a saint of my imagination but where then was he hidden, as I could not find him anywhere? I dare not invent a new way myself. So, what was there to do?

The good God undoubtedly must understand me. I loved him, and I (564) wished to prove my love in any way, be it even with a smile or a mouthful of good rice. I hardly liked the discipline, which always frightened me, but when one loves is it necessary to give oneself the discipline? People normally get more pleasure from a simple glance of love than from a thousand presents which may be offered to them. That is why I always remained undecided, not daring of myself to be the last in the world to become a saint, in spite of all the love I had for God. That's how it was. God brought the reply to this thorny question to me.

One evening, at a special visit to the Blessed Sacrament, when I was absorbed in meditating on the Incarnate Word hidden under the appearance of bread, as the books tell us, suddenly my mind was invaded by a strange thought which drove away all the sweetness I was tasting in the presence of God; a thought which urged me to become a saint. Ah! To become a saint! ... How many more times shall I consider this thought as being a temptation to pride? and I chased it away with all my strength, even asking the Blessed Virgin to come to my aid. I was (565) powerless before the thought, as if a supernatural power was obliging me to keep it fixed firmly in my mind. No! I decided to resist ... 'Jesus, Mary and Joseph, come to help me! ...' No! No! It is not possible for me to become a saint. I have a great fear of the discipline, my stomach is too weak to fast, and I am incapable of staying on my knees for a long time in meditation. 'O my God come to my aid, deliver me from this temptation.' I opened once again the book, *Visits to the Blessed Sacrament** and, I don't know why, but it was as if the thought of becoming a saint was totally obsessing my mind and body. The strength of my resistance made me tremble, and I no longer knew to what means to have recourse in order to break entirely with this thought. I was extremely worried. I was afraid that by saying 'Yes' to my conscience, I was committing a sin for having 'dared to want to become a saint'. I still categorically refused, therefore, and I looked for every reason to reject this thought.

(566)   The hour having passed, I had to return to the study room. I went to throw myself at the feet of the statue of Our Lady of Grace before leaving the chapel, and I said this prayer to her, 'O dear Mother, show you are truly my Mother. I beg of you to give me a sign which will allow me to understand if the thoughts which are torturing my heart at this time come from God, or from the devil who wishes to trouble me. I want you to hear my prayer. Tomorrow, permit me to come back close to you in the hope of receiving your counsel and of recovering peace.' I then returned to the study room. It was the time when, ordinarily, I did my homework and learned my lessons, but this time I had already finished both. I wished to use the time therefore to read a life of a saint. I went to the mantelpiece with the idea of taking a volume of the Lives of the Saints.

I saw with a quick glance that all the dust-covers of these books were known already to me. There were also among them some volumes that I had never touched, for the simple reason that they had no pictures, which removed any desire to read them. I said to myself: 'If I don't spend the time reading a life of a saint now, what can I do?' Tám and Hiển, leaning over their books, were applying themselves to their homework. They wished to finish as soon as possible so that they could also devote some time to reading the life of a saint. After reflection I

(567)   decided to choose at random the life of a saint, a life which would fall into my hands. I would read it even if I had already done so. I put this into practice immediately. With my eyes tightly closed I mixed the books together, higgledy-piggledy, and, waving my arms three times, I let my hand fall on the pile of books and, as agreed, I would read the book upon which my index finger landed firmly. While following this

* A work of Saint Alphonsus Liguori.

procedure I recited a kind of magic formula to the Blessed Virgin to guide my hand on to a volume which was, at least, interesting. It's done ... I opened my eyes, not knowing what was happening, and I did not know what to do. I had just put my hand on a book ... that I had not yet read, but had already dismissed as containing nothing unusual. I took hold of it and read the title:

The Story of a Soul

I let the book fall noisily on the pile of books, with the intention of leaving it to one side without even opening it. But I reproached myself: 'Ah! by acting like this you have broken your promise. No! A cadet of Our Lady would never permit himself such reprehensible behaviour.' I took the book again with my head full of muddled questions of this (568) nature: 'What is this *Story of a Soul*? Who is this Saint Thérèse of the Child Jesus? Where does she come from??? What is certain is that she resembles many thousands of other saints.' Then I summarised her life in an amusing manner in these terms: 'Since her birth until her last breath she had many ecstasies and performed a number of miracles; she fasted on bread and water, only taking one meal a day; she spent the night in prayer and gave herself the discipline until she bled. After her death her body exhaled a very pleasant fragrance and many extraordinary things happened on her tomb. Finally, she was canonised by the Holy Church ... etc.' Today I see clearly how rash these thoughts were. Without knowing anything about Saint Thérèse I had dared to sketch out her life in such a summary manner.

O, my dear sister, you must necessarily be a saint of heroic courage to (569) put up with the erroneous judgements that I have held on your life. On that day you doubtless had to exercise much patience in my regard, and perhaps had to make an effort not to smile on seeing me allowing myself such childishness. But you were there, waiting for me in such a way that a few minutes later your unfortunate little brother sees the word of God come true: 'The stone which the builders rejected has become the cornerstone.' The book which with pique he had just rejected pitilessly, was the book which most harmonised with his own soul. One could even maintain that it was the description of his own soul, the story of his own life.

I did not stop looking at the book, but I did not commit myself to open it and read it. I remember clearly that in the Lạng-Sơn seminary my friend Câu, who was in charge of the library, had passed a similar book to me; unfortunately I had only leafed through it from beginning to end, but seeing that it was not illustrated I had returned it to the

(570) library and asked for another one. This was the first time since then that it had again fallen into my hands, and once more I did not feel any sympathy for it. But I had promised to read it ... I must do so. So, taking hold of it, I went to sit down with book in hand and I began reading. Shortly afterwards I moved my chair to a corner near the fireplace so as not to disturb Hiển and Tám, and again I read a little. Oh, what an interesting book! I turned the pages quickly to the last chapter to see how it ended. At that moment I no longer despised the book. I went back to the first pages and began reading once again. On finishing the preface, I felt my soul immediately relieved and overflowing with happiness. I comforted myself in this way: 'So, to become a saint is not only to walk by the path of "saints of bygone days". There are many paths leading to holiness.' I continued to read the first chapter.

(571) I had not read more than two pages when my eyes began to mist over little by little; then two streams of tears flowed down my cheeks, flooding the pages of the book. It was impossible to continue reading. My tears were the witness of my repentance for my attitude of a short while ago, and at the same time a source of indescribable joy. Yes, only the tears springing from my heart under the impulse of a strong emotion were capable of expressing the intensity of my happiness. I had the sensation that my heart had melted into burning tears which were flooding my face. I do not understand how in the grip of such a great joy it was, nevertheless, impossible for me to hold back my tears. What moved me completely was this reasoning of St Thérèse: 'If God only humbled himself towards the most beautiful flowers, symbols of the holy doctors, his love would not be an absolute love, since the characteristic of love is to humble oneself to the extreme limit.' Then, taking the sun as an example, she writes: 'As the sun shines at the same time on the cedar and the little flower, in the same way the divine Star especially lights up all souls, big or small.'[*]

(572) Oh what reasoning, so deep in its simplicity! In reading these words I was able to understand, a little, the immensity of God's heart, which goes beyond all created limits; that is to say, it is infinite. So, without need for any further reasoning, I found in these words the key which opened for me a way which was direct and pleasing, leading right to the summit of perfection. I understood that God is love and that Love adapts itself to all forms of love. Consequently, I can become holy by means of all my little actions: a smile, a word, a look, provided that all are motivated by love. What happiness! Thérèse is a saint who corresponds totally to the idea I had in my mind of holiness. From now onwards, sanctity will no longer frighten me. I have found a way which,

---

[*]   ref. to Saint Thérèse of the Child Jesus, Manuscript A, 2v.–3.

less than a century previously, had been followed by a soul: and this soul has reached the ultimate goal, just like many other saints who led lives of sorrow, and sown with thorns. It is the way of love of Saint Thérèse of the Child Jesus.

My tears were still flowing like an inexhaustible spring. I have prob- (573) ably never felt such strong emotion nor shed such abundant tears in all my life. However, the more I cried, the lighter was my soul. In exchange for these visible tears I experienced such a sweet joy that I had the feeling of no longer having a body, of not feeling anything again outside this unspeakable joy. After a time, whose length I was unaware of, I raised my head and noticed that the daylight had changed. The setting sun was still releasing some rays on the courtyard in front of the house. Tám and Hiển were still seated at the table engrossed in their homework. I quickly wiped my face with my hand-kerchief so as not to attract their attention.

I took up the book again to read the following page, but because I had inadvertently bent my head over the open pages, a whole page had been moistened by my tears so that it was impossible to move to the next (574) one. I had to resign myself, very reluctantly, to closing the book. Then coughing as if to regain my breath, I slipped out of the room so that Hiển and Tám suspected nothing. I ran to the chapel and as soon as my eyes met the statue of Saint Thérèse, tears started to flow once again and they lasted until supper time. I helped my friends to prepare the meal but, seeing that I did not feel hungry as I did on ordinary days, and on the pretext of feeling tired, I went to lie down. Hiển and Tám, noticing that my voice had lost its customary resonance, believed that I was ill and allowed me to leave without any questions. My head was barely on the pillow when, as in the chapel, streams of tears gushed from my eyes. When did these tears cease? and when did I fall asleep? I do not know. What I do know is that the following morning when I awoke my pillow was still quite damp.

I got up cheerfully that day, refreshed and in good form and my (575) heart still exuberant with joy. I had never known until then such a beautiful morning. I went immediately to Our Lady's altar after my morning offering and I said to her: 'Blessed Virgin my Mother, today is truly the first day that I have been given to taste such a sweet happi-ness; the day which introduces me to a new way. I feel that God loves me, and because he loves me, he has called me to follow him on the path to perfection. Oh Mother, his love is truly an infinite love, and in view of such love I do not know what words to use to express my gratitude to him nor what heart to offer him which is capable of a love which responds to his Love. Let me come to you with my poor heart, to place it in your hands so that you can offer it to the Holy Trinity. You know

(576) well that the worthy offering that I give to the Blessed Trinity is none other than the Love of God, but to hold this Love of God I have nothing but my poor heart. From now onwards, my Mother, guide me in my new way, teach me to love God perfectly and to offer myself to him with total confidence. I dare again to express a wish to you: that I may be wrapped in your love as was, formerly, Thérèse, your white-as-snow little flower. I even wish you to give me this saint as my guide in her 'little way'. Oh, what happiness then for me! since I feel that my life cannot free itself from the feelings of childhood that God has engraved in my soul as an innate gift.

I was as full of happiness after having received communion as I was on the previous evening, and I shed many tears, but for a shorter time, however, than on the previous day. I was bold enough to say to Jesus, still as I was under the influence of the happiness which intoxicated me: 'O Jesus! my only and beloved Master, you know that I love you and look only to respond to your wishes. Yesterday evening, despite my

(577) ingratitude towards you, you called me to follow you on the path to holiness. You have aroused in my mind the desire to become a saint. Then you made me find in a very simple manner the little way by which you guided St Thérèse of the Infant Jesus. In short, you have used the hand of this little saint to write for the use of souls the sweet counsels to which you have led her on her little way. Today, I know that you love me, and that in your immense love you behave towards me as with a little child. Oh, how you deserve to be loved in return! From now on I have decided to follow in your footsteps as you wish. And so that each of my steps conforms to your will I wish, o my God, that you grant me this favour: give me Saint Thérèse of the Infant Jesus as my guide, so that she can teach me to love you as I ought, since I am very ignorant. Grant me also the grace to persevere in your love right to the end, so as to love you afterwards eternally in the homeland of love reserved for those who love you.'

(578) ## Spiritual sister

I had received, therefore, that afternoon a source of grace and happiness. The book, *The Story of a Soul*, had become my dearest friend. It followed me everywhere and I did not cease reading or re-reading it without ever getting weary of it. There was nothing in this volume which did not conform to my thoughts, and what enthused me still more in the course of my reading was to see clearly that the spiritual life of Thérèse was identical to mine. Her thoughts, even her 'yes' and her 'no' were in harmony with my own thoughts and the little events of my life. I dearly loved the chapter where she recounts her childhood in the bosom of her family, but I was very moved also on reading the passages where she described the death of her mother and her farewell to the family. It was really upsetting. So, I felt choked when, looking at my past life, I noticed that there was no difference between our two sorrows.

Truly, never in my life have I met a book which was so well adapted (579) to my thinking and feelings as is *The Story of a Soul*. I can confess that the story of Thérèse's soul is the story of my soul, and that Thérèse's soul is my very own. It is also from this time that I felt the need to be familiar with her as a little brother with a big sister. I greatly loved educating myself by being close to her and giving her the name of 'sister'. Nevertheless, concerning the name of 'sister', until then I had never dared use it, sticking always to the name of 'saint' which I considered suitably formal. One day, however, God will answer my wish to give her the name I preferred.

Here is a fairly amusing story and one which could not be more child-like. I remember that it was on a Thursday evening and, if I am not mistaken, the facts referred to happened on a Monday evening during the month of October. According to the programme fixed by Father Maillet there was no class on Thursdays. It was the day when we had to wash our clothes. Apart from working in the kitchen, Father Maillet did not wish us to disturb the tertiaries with any other work, not even for (580) darning our clothes. We were obliged to do our own mending. We found washing our clothes easy enough, but darning was a real torture. Each hole necessitated a month's work, and very often it was not a pretty sight. What is more, when we wore any clothes which we had repaired, the tertiaries made fun of us. That was the most hurtful aspect. Faced with this state of affairs we became lazy. Consequently, when we had a torn article of clothing, after having washed it, we put it to one side and put on something else, in the hope that, once the holidays had arrived, we would have it repaired by our mammys at home. If it happened that in the winter we were short of an article of clothing, we put on two or three garments, one above the other, and everything was all right. The thought of always having to act in this manner was difficult, but it was much more painful to have to go without a game of marbles or a climb in the mountains, especially from the time when the superior condemned us to fast, since Thursday was precisely the day when we went to look for refuelling on the mountain. What time remained, therefore, to mend our clothes?

Therefore on the particular Thursday, all three of us were deliberat- (581) ing together in the study room on how to find a means of repairing our clothes while reserving time for our games of marbles, our walks in the mountains and our gathering of wild potatoes. Our first plan was that each one of us in turn would stay one week in the house to do the darning, regardless of method, provided the holes were filled. This solution was totally inconvenient because it required three to gather the wild potatoes quickly and easily. After a long examination and discussion of the problem, the three forest animals could not find a satisfactory solution. Then the squirrel solved the problem: 'Come on, is it necessary to tire ourselves out deliberating? Let's think! Which tertiary is fairly well disposed towards us? Let us write her a letter to let her know that we are choosing her as our big sister, that we are confiding to her the responsibility of repairing our torn clothes ... and the problem is solved. Of course we will promise to recite the rosary for her

(582)   intentions. She could not be happier. What can one say more? Tertiaries love to do good works. Things will work out, you'll see ...'

Tám and Hiển – oh, forgive me, the panther and the nightingale – agreed immediately and in their enthusiasm moved rhythmically from side to side as if they were sitting on a chair with springs. Together they asked me:

'In that case, who are you going to choose?'

'Miss Tin. She still seems to have some sympathy for us. I mean, doesn't she give us the remains from the parish priest's table every evening?'

The nightingale, rolling his eyes, said:

'Hold on. She's the superior's niece.'

'Niece as much as you like,' said the panther. 'She treats us well. That's good enough.'

'I am afraid she might use her diplomatic skills to spy on us, and then report back to the superior and ...'

The panther, irritated, said:

'You are really pessimistic!'

(583)   Then, turning towards the squirrel:

'OK Van, let's agree on Miss Tin. She's a good choice.'

'But what about Hiển? Come on, Hiển, what's your opinion?'

Hiển, to whom tears came easily, let two drops fall on the table, then, wiping his eyes with his hand he replied in a sullen manner:

'Do what you want. I agree with you to accept Miss Tin.'

'Very good. Let us choose her for the time being as our big sister and if circumstances change we'll sort that out later.'

'And how do you intend to do that?' asked the panther.

'By choosing the superior herself.'

They burst out laughing and, thanks to this wisecrack, Hiển succeeded in getting rid of the sadness from his face.

'But we'll have to be discreet, won't we? Because if Father Maillet gets to know about it, not only will we lose our big sister, but also all the clothes given to be repaired will be seized.'

So we agreed among ourselves to write a letter full of pretty compliments, and to send it to the tertiary-cook at the presbytery. The dominant theme of the letter was gratitude for all the work she had undertaken for us until then. It was only then that we introduced the (584) business of the torn clothes, and our intention to choose her as our spiritual sister. This was all drawn up by the squirrel in a very clever manner. At ten o'clock, profiting from Father Maillet's absence at the post, we parachuted three parcels of torn linen together with the letter we had just written, to Miss Tin in the kitchen. After this operation we returned to the study room, crying: 'Yippee! Our sister Tin will repair our beautiful clothes for the feast days, won't she? ... Hurrah!'

After this happy parachuting we applied ourselves to finishing our homework as quickly as possible so as to go and play marbles. As for the squirrel, his only wish was to have in his hands the book *The Story of a Soul*. I had already read it once; I was now reading it for the second time, and I had reached the place where Thérèse describes the death of her mother. Just at that moment a shadow passed quickly before the window of our study room and threw in a little paper, on which was badly-formed writing whose ink was scarcely dry. I recognised immedi- (585) ately Miss Tin's handwriting. Seizing the note quickly, I took it without delay to Tám, while smiling. The latter began to read, haltingly, in a loud voice: 'Who has put it into your head to make such a suggestion?' We burst out laughing. Then Tam continued to read the following quickly: 'Personally, I am very hesitant ... However, I will look after Tám and Hiển readily; as for Van, I think he is able to look after himself ... Sister Tin.' How unfortunate?!

Hiển and Tám burst out laughing, teasing the squirrel in these words: 'You've had it, Van. You suggested choosing Miss Tin as our spiritual sister, and there you are: to annoy you, she does not want you.' They then continued teasing. But the squirrel, absorbed in his book *The Story of a Soul*, did not pay any attention, and was in no way saddened. He suddenly let out a cry of satisfaction since the disappointment he had just experienced had brought to him an incredible opportunity. I (586) had just reached in my reading the passage in which Thérèse wrote: 'Always accustomed to follow Céline, I should have done well to imitate her in such a good action, but I thought that Pauline might, perhaps, be unhappy and feel neglected at not having a little girl; and then, looking at you tenderly and leaning my little head on your breast I said in my turn, "For me, my mother's going to be Pauline."'* At that

---

*   Cf. St Thérèse of the Child Jesus. Manuscript A. 13 r.

moment I clearly understood Thérèse's words, and I did as she did, saying to myself: 'Right now Thérèse is expecting a little brother, but no one has chosen her to be their sister so it is not right to make her suffer in this way.' So I got up, and went to the church and kneeling down at Saint Thérèse's statue, I said to her with a sincere heart, 'For me it is Thérèse who will be my sister.' As soon as I had said these words, my soul was invaded with such a current of happiness that I remained stunned by it and was incapable of thinking for myself. I was dominated entirely by a supernatural force which flooded my soul with unspeakable happiness. And this force propelled me to the foot of the

(587)   mountain. I left the church hurriedly and ran to the study room to replace my book, *The Story of a Soul*. Hiển and Tám were still there, and seeing me they both laughed. Nodding my head I said to them, cheerfully: 'What? You think that the squirrel will be totally deprived of a sister? Wait and see, and you will find that I also have a spiritual sister, and a very fashionable one too.'

Impelled by the spiritual force which guided me, I ran to the foot of the mountain, my soul overflowing with a joy which I could only express with a great variety of songs and a thousand childish skips ... I jumped from rock to rock, from tussock to tussock, crying out my happiness and sending into the air all the songs I knew by heart in Vietnamese, in Thai, in French and in Chinese. How could I express in mere words all the happiness I was then tasting? I can only summarise it all with these words of St Paul: 'That which the heart of man has not

(588)   conceived.'* I gambolled about for several minutes like a madman or rather, like a butterfly that the wind carries here and there up to the clouds in a light and limpid atmosphere. Then, feeling worn out with fatigue, I had to put an end to my capers, but without losing anything of the intensity of my joy. Panting, out of breath, I sank on a rock, both arms stretched out behind me to enable me to expand my chest and breathe more easily, both legs stretched out, and having no more strength to move. In spite of this, I made an effort, from time to time, to sing a few words out loud. Slightly recovered from my tiredness, I went over my behaviour in my mind and I felt a certain shame, asking myself: 'Have I lost my mind? If not, why am I so full of joy?' And from that moment I remained in silence, contemplating the spectacle of nature which was reawakening under the gentle rays of the sun climb-

(589)   ing from the horizon. I returned time and again to the same question: 'Why am I so happy, and why am I like someone who has lost his mind?' Suddenly I gave a jump. I heard a voice which called me by my name: 'Van, Van, my dear little brother!' Is someone calling me? Then I

---

*   1 Corinthians 2. 9.

glanced round to see if there really was someone calling me. I remember that the voice seemed to come from my right. Intrigued, I laughed inwardly, convinced that there was someone there, and I said to myself: 'It's strange! Which tertiary can really call me her little brother in such an intimate fashion?' because I clearly heard that it was a woman's voice.

Still amazed, I heard again the same voice, gentle as the passing breeze, which called, 'Van! My dear little brother!' I was stunned and a little troubled, but I remained calm as usual, and guessed immediately that this voice which called me was a supernatural voice. I then let out a hurried cry of joy: 'O! It's my sister Saint Thérèse! ...' The reply was not long in coming. 'Yes, it is really your sister Saint Thérèse who is here. I hardly heard your voice when I understood, deep down, your guileless and pure heart. I have come here to reply to your words which (590) have echoed in my heart. Little brother! You will be personally and from now on my little brother, just as you have chosen me, personally, to be your big sister. From now onwards our two souls will be separated no longer by any obstacle as they formerly were. They are already united in the sole love of God. From this moment I will let you know all my beautiful thoughts on love, that which has occurred in my life and has transformed me in the infinite Love of God. Do you know why we are meeting today? It is God himself who has arranged this meeting. He wished that the lessons of love which he has taught me in the secret of my soul are perpetuated in this world, and, for that, he has deigned to choose you as a little secretary to carry out the work he wishes to entrust to you. But before this choice he wished for this meeting to let you know, through me, your beautiful mission. Van, my little brother, just as you consider me a saint according to your wishes, in the same way also, you are really, for me, a soul entirely in accordance with my desires. God has allowed me to know you for a long time, that is to say, (591) even before you existed. Your life has appeared in the mysterious glance of the Divinity, and me, I have seen you in the light coming from this mysterious glance. I have seen you, and God has given me the responsibility of looking after you as the guardian angel of your life. I was with you, following you step by step as a mother beside her child. Great was my joy when I saw in your soul points of perfect resemblance with mine, and a conception of Love different in nothing from mine. This is an effect of divine Love which in its wisdom has so ordained it.

'Yesterday you criticised yourself for having disdained me; in reality it was nothing of the sort, since to feel love or scorn for anyone, it is necessary first of all to know them. Not yet knowing Thérèse, how can you say you disdained her? You grumbled again, saying: "I wish I'd known you a bit sooner! And then, from how many illusory fears my

life would have been liberated, how much more would I have tasted the charms of love!" But no, little brother; the dispositions of provi-
(592) dence are realised, necessarily, at a very precise moment which is not brought forward, even for a second, nor does it allow an instant's delay. Who knows? If you had known me an hour sooner, perhaps you would not have found yesterday the source of grace which filled you with happiness. That is a mystery, and we can only believe in the mercy of God our Father who, in his wisdom, rules in the slightest detail the lives of each one of us. You don't have to complain any more, since Thérèse has always been your Thérèse and you, Van, have been equally the little brother of Thérèse since the moment when we existed, both of us, in the thought of God. The ardour of your desires until now has led the good God to lead you to the truth. He experiences a great joy in seeing that you look only to follow him and to learn the means of pleasing him. Try to imagine if there is any happiness for a father comparable to that of seeing his small child follow him everywhere, offering him everything he can collect, and finally to have complete freedom to carry him in his arms, and to
(593) caress him whenever he wishes. Yes, try to imagine with what love this child will be loved by his father. Can he want or ask for anything that his father will not give him, often even more than he asks for? And, although he is only a little guileless child, what wonderful reward has his father not already prepared for him for the future . . . ?

'This infant I have just described is your soul. You have run after Jesus, seeking only to please him. Sanctity consists precisely in that. You have practised this holiness until this day, but without well and truly understanding its real nature. Thanks to the sincerity of your heart, this error was not intentional on your part; it only came from a lack of guidance. Also, far from harming you, it has been an opportunity for you to progress in holiness because you have suffered much. You will certainly have to fear no more this false conception of holiness, since, once transformed by divine Love, you will see clearly that sanctity consists only in being at one with the will of God. But this unity is the work of divine
(594) Love; as for you, all you have to do is to love and to abandon yourself entirely to the action of this Love, and you will be perfect.

'I will have many opportunities later to come back again to this subject, but today I want to make you understand a little the Love of the Father. Let us see, Van; have you ever heard it said that God is your Father?'

'Never, my sister! When I was small I heard my mother teach me many things about God and perfection, but during my stay at Hữu-Bằng a thousand torments were used to divest me of all my beautiful thoughts . . .'

I began to cry.

'Van, my little brother, don't cry too readily. You say that these inhuman creatures have deprived you of your beautiful thoughts by means of a thousand torments. In reality it is nothing of the kind, since the grace of God is indestructible, like God himself. Consequently, even the damned who burn in hell are incapable of destroying the effects of the love that God has placed in their hearts, and in this is their greatest torment. Therefore, little brother, remember well to see if in those days you have ever lost confidence in God. Have you ever dared to think that   (595) God deserved to be hated, and that he deserved to be expelled from your heart? Or, to put it more clearly, have you ever approved as good the actions of these inhuman creatures?'

'No, I have never approved them in such an insane manner. Neither have I ever lost confidence in God, since, if I had abandoned God, who then would I have been able to follow? Nothing was more painful to me than to notice in my relations with God that there was a sort of veil which separated me from him.'

'Your reply proves quite evidently that your heart has always been faithful to God, that you have accomplished perfectly your duty as a child, not ceasing to regard God as your Father and your divine master. Consequently, the cruelty of these inhuman creatures towards you should be considered as nothing more than a veil or layer of dust covering all your beautiful thoughts of which it was absolutely impossible to divest you. And, thanks to your sincerity, this layer of dust has already been completely removed.

'Now, my little brother, I am going to speak to you about the Father's heart. Listen very carefully. God is our Father. What do these words   (596) mean to you? Naturally they give birth in your soul to profound feelings of affection. Is that not so?'

'Yes, my sister. I prefer to call God Father rather than Lord.'

'Although he is always Lord, he behaves towards us only as a father towards his child. As for his divine majesty, he only shows it to the proud who oppose his commandments. I mean that God is forced to show his majesty only to those who do not like his feelings as a father.

'Listen, little brother, while I continue. Therefore, God is Father and this Father is Love. His beauty and his kindness are infinite. There is only the infinite which is capable of giving meaning to the name of Father given to God the Trinity. Only by contemplating the physical creatures of this world, only by looking around you and in you can you recognise how good God is, and how he loves us. Since the day when   (597) our first parents sinned, God has had to make his anger felt and impose a punishment on humanity. And since then, the fear which has invaded the human heart has made it tremble and has even taken away the thought of God, who is an infinitely good Father. Even then, God acted towards ungrateful humanity with a father's feelings, since, if at that moment he had made his divine majesty felt, how would humanity have been able to survive until today? Do you see, little brother?

'God had hardly declared the punishment to our first parents when he immediately gave them a source of hope: he will send his Son to become man on earth, to give to humanity the grace lost by our first parents. After such a token of love, what more can he do? And even from that day nobody dared yet to give God the name of Father. It is only after the incarnation of the Word that Jesus, the saviour of the world, has given to God the name of Father and has taught the world to use this name to pray to God the Most High.

(598)   'Van, my dear little brother, you see God is our Father. But because man, poor sinner, dominated by fear, dared no longer to give to God the name of Father, God himself lowered himself in becoming man, to remind his human brothers of the existence of a source of grace that the love of God had made to gush forth, and which would continue to flow unendingly. So from his own mouth he has taught us to give him the name of Father.

'Yes, God is our Father, our true Father, a very real Father and not an adoptive father as many celebrated orators describe him, stating: "There is only one Jesus who is the true Son of God. As for us, we are only adopted sons." Little brother, never give credence to the comparisons they advance to prove their assertion since, although their words are reasonable, they lean only on human reason without going back to the ultimate, which is the Love of God. To be God's children is for us an incomparable happiness. We are right to be proud of it and never to give way to an excessive fear.*

(599)   'God is our beloved Father! O dear little brother! I wish to remind you unceasingly of this so-sweet name. I am asking you to make sure from now onwards always to keep the memory of this name of Love, and never to adopt a worried air or a fearful attitude in the presence of this Love which is infinitely paternal! Yes, remember always that God is

---

*   It is necessary to distinguish: 1. Filiation by nature, that of the only Son of God and God himself. 2. Filiation by participation ('participants of the divine nature.' 2 Pet. 1. 4) where one receives the life of God. This filiation St Paul calls adoptive in comparison with the filiation by nature of the Only Son (Rom. 8. 15, 9. 4; Gal. 4. 4–5; Eph. 1. 5). 3. Adoptive filiation, simply human, juridical, natural, legal, which is not an ontological reality.

In the text Thérèse explains to Van that God is not an adoptive father in the human sense without any ontological consequences. He is truly our Father since, through his will, we participate in his divine nature, we are of God's race (Acts 17. 29); he is therefore, for us, 'our Father, our true Father, a real Father'. (Editor's Note)

Father, that he has filled you with graces, that he has never refused to answer your smallest wishes, and that very often he has granted more than you wished for. Truly, everything proclaims the goodness and the power of God, and he only uses this power to show the kindness of his heart towards his creatures.

'Never fear God. He is the all-loving Father. He knows only how to love, and he wishes to be loved in return. He thirsts for our poor little hearts which come from his creative hands, and where he has placed a spark of love which comes from the very hearth of his Love. His only wish is to gather these sparks of love and unite them to his infinite love, so that our love lives on for ever in his. Finally, it is still the force of the attraction of Love which will draw us into the eternal fatherland of Love. Offer all of your little heart to God. Be sincere with him in all   (600) circumstances and in all your points of view. When you feel joy, offer him this joy which swells your heart and, by so doing, you will transmit your joy to him. Can there be a greater happiness than a couple loving one another and exchanging all they possess? To act in this way with God is to say thank you to him, which pleases him more than thousands of touching canticles. If, on the other hand, you are invaded by sadness, say to him again with an honest heart: 'O my God, I am really unhappy!' And ask him to help you to accept this sadness with patience. Really believe this: nothing gives as much pleasure to the good God than to see on this earth a heart which loves him, who is sincere with him with each step, with each smile, as well with tears as with little momentary pleasures.

'Now, little brother, is there perhaps still one more thing that you are afraid of? Have the patience to listen to me so as to practise it and then you will get the habit. So, when you speak to the good God, do so quite naturally as if you were talking to those around you. You can speak to him of anything you wish: of your game of marbles, of climbing the   (601) mountain, the teasing of your friends, and if you become angry with anyone, tell it also to the good God in all honesty. God takes pleasure in listening to you; in fact he thirsts to hear these little stories which people are too sparing with him. They can spend hours telling these amusing stories to their friends but when it's a question of the good God who longs to hear such stories to the point of being able to shed tears, there is no one to tell him about them. From now on, little brother, don't be miserly with your stories to the good God. All right?' Thérèse laughed.

'But, holy sister, God already knows absolutely all of these things. Is it still necessary to tell them to him?'

'It is true, little brother, that God knows everything completely. All is present to him from all eternity. From all eternity, also, God knows, absolutely, all of that so nobody has any need to speak of it to him.

(602) However, to "give" and to "receive" love he must lower himself to the level of a man like you, and he does it as if he's completely forgotten that he is God who knows everything, in the hope of hearing an intimate word springing from your heart. God acts in this way because he loves you; he wishes by that to fill you with precious graces, to let you know of all the good desires and all the delights that one tastes in his love.

'I want to make use of an example here. When a daddy wishes to give his little child a kiss, of course he cannot remain standing up straight and lazily demand that his child heaves himself up to his lips to receive this kiss on his cheek. Could such a kiss be called an affectionate kiss? Evidently not! To give a kiss to his little one, it is understood that the daddy must bend down a lot, right to within reach of his face, or again, take the child in his arms. In both cases he must bend down.

'Have you understood, little brother? God is our loving Father. In order to show us his love, and to receive the love which we offer to him, he has really wished to lower himself to our level. For love, there is no difficulty in lowering oneself in this manner. The only problem, before which God appears to be powerless, is to notice our lack of love and confidence in him. He sees himself rejected in a totally unfair manner, yet he never rejects us.

(603) 'Little brother, to comfort the good God, follow this piece of advice: never be miserly in the things I am going to speak to you about. Be always ready to offer him your heart, your thoughts and all your actions. In welcoming them it will be for him like welcoming a new paradise where all the Trinity finds its delights. Remember this: although he is God, our heavenly Father never scorns little things. He takes as much pleasure in things which are apparently insignificant, as in the most wonderful spectacle because all of it is the marvellous work of his love. Besides, in order to maintain that there is love, it is necessary that there is unity. Now unity between two loves demands from one side and the other personal knowledge and mutual understanding. On his part, God our beloved Father knows himself personally, and understands us thoroughly. As for us, we need him to get to know ourselves and to understand him. Consequently, if you did not wish to collaborate with him in the work which leads to unity, telling him all your intentions, your words, your actions and all your efforts, you (604) would never attain unity. Little brother, try to think about it in order to see clearly. There is no exaggeration in my words. I love you because you are a soul which is a member of my phalanx of Love. As for you, my little brother, my only wish is to see you accomplish the works that the divine love desires so ardently for you. So, little brother, listen to me. From now on, in your relations with your heavenly Father, do not fail to follow my advice.

'Now it is late. Allow me to interrupt our conversation here. Since it is already meal-time, Tám and Hiển are waiting for you and Tám is getting impatient ... I am giving you a kiss ... We will have plenty of opportunities to chat together again, and we can do it no matter where, without fear that anyone might know.'

....

Thérèse stopped talking. I was like someone coming out of a dream, half anxious, half happy. When Thérèse said to me: 'I am giving you a kiss', I immediately felt as if a gentle breeze was lightly touching my face and I was overcome by such a joy that I momentarily lost consciousness. Some of this sweet joy stays with me today but I do not know what to (605) compare it with exactly.

Still in the grip of this joy, I looked at the countryside around me. There was silence everywhere. The sun, already fairly high, made me feel the warmth of its rays which fell directly on to my head. I heard Hiển and Tám's voices calling me from the house. The latter was grumbling: 'It's strange! Where has Van gone to play, to disappear like this and to make us wait until now for lunch? ... What a blockhead!' I hurried to leave my rock and run straight to the house. My heart was still beating with joy. As soon as he saw me, Tám bombarded me with questions: 'Where were you? Didn't you feel hungry, to make us wait indefinitely? Do you think you are a saint already?'

I began to laugh to hide my shame and asked: 'What! It's lunchtime already? Please forgive me, I'm a bit of a daydreamer.'

Tám probably suspected that I was sulking and refusing to eat because Miss Tin had not adopted me as her little brother. He showed his suspicion by speaking to me in a reproachful manner: 'You are big enough, and yet you still sulk like a child at the slightest thing.'

I did not answer this criticism, which in no way saddened me, since in fact at that particular moment even the bitterest things were incapable of (606) casting a shadow over the joy which filled my soul. Hiển, interjecting, cut Tám short and I saw that they were whispering to each other discreetly and with a surprised air. They then stared at me, and Hiển asked me:

'What were you doing on the mountain that you are so happy?'

'Ah Hiển ... it's a big secret ... This is what I was doing ... But it's a secret ... Anyway, I've already told you. I have also got a big sister and she's far more chic than yours.'

Hiển came close to me and asked me, smiling:

'Who is it? ... Whisper!'

'No! ... Never! ...'

'You'll tell me later, won't you?'

'No, I'll never tell you my sister's name. It's a big secret.'

Tam, vexed at me, said:

'You are boasting.'

'Yes, that's true, but really, you can fuss as much as you like, but my lips are sealed.'

Hiển, tapping me on the shoulder, said to me in a friendly manner: 'Later, OK?'

(607)   We were at table. Tám spoke to me in an ironical manner, whilst Hiển continued to be more friendly. I only went through the motions of eating during the meal. Everything appeared insipid. I went over in my mind everything she had told me, concentrating all the time only on Thérèse. At certain times I was restless, and wanted to cry out in a loud voice: 'My holy sister loves me a lot! ... Thérèse loves me a lot! ... She has a very sweet voice and speaks the Vietnamese language very well!' ... My behaviour astonished my two companions even further and they looked to discover my secret. From that moment they did not cease spying on me especially when they saw me go alone to the foot of the mountain.

Thérèse's conversation with me had lasted for two hours. She expressed herself very well, but there were many words that I did not yet understand. So at my request she had to break off often to explain (608)   clearly to me the meaning of each sentence. Furthermore, my Father, you have been able to observe that I am quite analytical. I thought that on many points Thérèse would have been justified in getting angry, since I did not cease from reasoning forcibly. But how could she be annoyed with her unruly little brother? knowing full well that his stubbornness was restricted only to the time of discussion, but once he had understood, it was over, and he would have been ready to defend the contentious point even at the cost of his life. Thérèse spoke for a long time, but I can only summarise, as I have done, all that she said to me. And although this draft does not perhaps agree with the preceding one, it remains that the thoughts expressed are the same. If you notice any difference it is because each time that I write I sometimes remember such a sentence and sometimes another, and it happens that in remembering one sentence I forget another. I hope, therefore, that you will pay more attention to the ideas than to the words.

(609)   I returned secretly that afternoon to the foot of the mountain, and Thérèse spoke to me once again of the love of God, teaching me the way to show him our love. These lessons about love enthralled me so much that I forgot everything else, and each time that she spoke to me, if my holy sister had not been careful to remind me of the time, I would not have known if it was day or night. I was so absorbed by her words on certain days that I would have wished even to have given up my studies, meals and siestas in order to listen in silence, be it in the chapel or under a tree, to the explanations that she gave to me on Love. But

Thérèse never agreed to this concession. She wanted me to follow the programme like the others. She again said to me:

'From now on, where you are, I will be there also, and we can talk together everywhere.'

'But, my sister, if someone heard us speaking by mistake, what will happen? They will make fun of me.'

'How could anyone hear me? To hear my voice is a privilege reserved only for you.'

'Can't the devil hear you?'   (610)

'Even if he could hear me, he could do nothing.'

'But suppose he imitated your voice in order to deceive me?'

'The Father who is Love will not allow his dear children to be tricked by the enemy. It is also true that at certain moments the devil will spot opportunities to bring trouble to your soul, but it will be easy for you to unmask the error contained in his advice. Remind yourself again, the devil will imitate the tone of my voice, but he will never urge you to love Jesus as I will. He will, hypocritically, suggest things contrary to the will of God; consequently, if you hear Thérèse's voice at meal times telling you to leave your meal to go and visit the Blessed Sacrament, or if again at the time of visiting the Blessed Sacrament, this voice tells you rather to go and study your lesson, and to do this as an act of mortification and to please God, don't listen to it. You are dealing with a false Thérèse who is no other than the devil. In fact, it is only with God's permission that the devil may talk to you and to hear his voice a special privilege is still necessary which God reserves for only a small number of souls.'

'My sister, ask the good God not to give me this privilege, all right?'

'Relax, little brother. But you must understand this: when the good (611)
God gives an extraordinary grace to a soul, he gives it at the same time everything which is necessary for this grace to bear fruit. For example, when God created the flower, he gave it at the same time the warmth of the sun and the coolness of the nightly dew to preserve it and allow it to bloom in the manner he has arranged for it. Therefore, don't worry yourself. Abandon yourself to the will of God, rather than allowing yourself to indulge in ludicrous and useless worries which would wear you out and even hurt the good God.'

'If that's the case, my sister, drop the request I made to you earlier. My God, I give myself entirely to your Love! I believe that you love me and only look for my happiness. I love you with all my heart.'

Each time that I repeated these words Thérèse gave me a very friendly kiss. In many other situations she taught me how to talk simply with God as two friends would do. At the beginning I was afraid to do so, but later I became accustomed to it. It is not possible to describe in detail all the circumstances, since they were many and followed each

(612)   other like intakes of breath. I still put into practice today the lessons given to me then by my saintly sister. Thérèse spoke to me a lot during my first novitiate, but everything she told me resembled the first lessons that she gave me at the foot of the hill at **Quảng-Uyên**.

After having taught me to converse naturally with God, she often reminded me to pray that children, still pure, are not contaminated by bad examples. She reminded me again to pray for sinners and for priests.

She spoke to me once of the Holy Father, and asked me to pray for him. I replied to this:

'Why? Has the Holy Father got need of my prayers?'

'Why not? He suffers a great deal, little brother. The holy Church is the Mystical Body of the Divine Redeemer. The Holy Father takes the place of Jesus to be in charge of the whole Church on earth, or, to speak more precisely, he is the presence of Jesus, he is Jesus present. How the Church suffers today! It can be compared to the agony that formerly our Divine Saviour had to suffer on the cross. Yes, the holy Church suffers, and these sufferings cruelly torment the heart of our common

(613)   father. And since he remains a man like you, he has need of a super-natural power to sustain him in these ordeals. Pray a lot for him so that he has the courage to put up with trials that, in their cruelty, Satan's supporters inflict on him. The mystical body of Christ is cruelly torn. Alas, in the whole of humanity, it is the Holy Father who actually suffers the most because he is the father. Yes, the Holy Father has need of sacrifices and prayers.

'Little brother! My dear little brother! Whoever says that he loves God but does not think at the same time of the Holy Father has only got a frivolous love, which is still lacking substance. To perfectly fulfil your duty as a child loved by God, you must offer every day, in union with the Holy Father, all the sufferings of the holy Church to the divine Redeemer. When you say, "The Holy Father is victorious", it is as if you are saying, "Christ is victorious".

'Little brother Van, do you wish to be the comforting angel of the Holy Father?'

'Certainly, my sister, I wish it with all my heart.'

'In that case, have the courage to pray a lot each day for the Holy Father and make numerous sacrifices for him.'

(614)   On another occasion, Thérèse asked me to pray for France and for Vietnam. I immediately felt a strong reaction, and I said to her: 'Pray for Vietnam, yes but to pray for those devils the French colonialists is a waste of time. Forgive me, sister, if I'm lacking in politeness towards you, but I think it is never necessary to pray for this gang of white devils, and all I wish is to ask God for the earth to open up and swallow

all their race in hell, as happened formerly to the Israelites who revolted against Moses. I would ask, however, that the missionary fathers and sisters are exempted since I consider them and love them as the fathers and mothers of the Vietnamese people. As for the others, the French colonialists, may they be thrown into hell to teach them what they are. Their cruelty is diabolical and they consider the Vietnamese as a contemptible race only deserving to be crushed under their heels. How much cruelty have they committed in their arrogance! They are all born from the devil of impurity ...' I was so annoyed when I said these words that I began to cry. It was only afterwards that I added: (615) 'Curse you, French colonialists! God, in his justice, will punish you severely for your sins ... Thérèse, my saintly and much-loved sister, you know that I am of the Vietnamese race! ... I am very much annoyed ... If I had in my hands only one revolver I would, nevertheless, dare to raise the standard of rebellion to fight against the French, and even if I only killed one of them, that would suffice to make me happy. I thirst for French blood in a spirit of patriotism, as the stag thirsts for water. I have never had the idea of praying for any French person since the day when I realised the true situation of my country, buried in darkness through the fault of French colonialists; neither would I have agreed to pray for this gang of colonialist devils of such shameful greed.'

During this outburst of anger when I allowed myself these violent words and gestures, Thérèse kept silent and patiently put up with it all. Her example led me afterwards to repent and to ask her forgiveness. I even shed tears on seeing in her such patience and generous condescension. I felt ashamed as soon as I had finished speaking, and I (616) blushed and no longer heard the voice of my sister Saint Thérèse. It was only a short time later, when I had recovered my composure, that she said to me, gently, 'A revolver, what good is that? I have here a still better tactic, capable of killing thousands and thousands of French without having to raise the standard of revolution at the cost of numerous soldiers and a huge quantity of ammunition.'

I replied, laughing:

'My sister, tell me this tactic so I can protect myself.'

'Little brother, do you promise to use it?'

'Yes, my sister, I promise.'

'Little brother, I am talking of the tactic of "prayer". I don't approve of the French at all in their reprehensible behaviour towards the Vietnamese people. I also know that they would deserve to be put to death because they are the enemies of the people. But what good would it do to accumulate a heap of dead bodies, if the cupidity and sensual pleasures and all the other kinds of selfishness were to continue to survive amongst the survivors? So, in my opinion, the tactic of prayer is (617) the one which can kill the greatest number of French. And for that to happen it suffices to say a short formula, something like this: "O Jesus, drive out the sinful man from the hearts of the French. I beg of you to come to the aid of Vietnam, my dear country, which bows under the yoke of domination of these sinful men." Know this well, that once sinful men (the French colonialists) have been expelled by divine grace from the French hearts, they will no longer be full of cunning as they are now, but they will learn to love the Vietnamese people as themselves. To reach this stage, little brother, many prayers and sacrifices will be necessary.'

From that day, each time that my holy sister asked me to pray for sinners, she also reminded me of the sins of the French people and said to me:

'Little brother, avenge yourself on the French according to the spirit of the Divine Redeemer; in other words, leave all resentment to one side and offer your prayers before the throne of God to obtain for them the graces of pardon and holiness.'

(618)   My sister spoke to me once of the war to come between the French and the Vietnamese. She then concluded in this manner:

'No power will succeed in driving the French colonialists from Vietnamese soil if it is not prayer. Yes, prayer. Pray therefore, my dear little brother, pray a lot for the French people. Later they will be no longer the enemy of your country Vietnam. Thanks to prayer and sacrifice France will become your close friend and, furthermore, she will regard Vietnam as her little and most dear brother. But before this friendly agreement is reached, the devil will incite numerous obstacles so as to sow division between the two countries, since he well knows that when the two are closely united, he himself will suffer heavy losses in his march forward ... It is necessary that a soul offers itself to sacrifice and prayer in the shadows, in order to stop the momentum of these infernal forces.'

'My beloved sister, if I had the honour to be this soul, how happy I
(619)   would be! But I do not know if the good God will agree.'

'Why would he not agree? That is exactly what he wishes. From now on, little brother, leave to one side all rancour concerning these French; prepare yourself to suffer and to pray for them, so that the friendly confluence that Love wishes may come true. Pray that the two sides may have understanding and mutual confidence, so that together they find a friendly peace. Peace is the sign of love. When the two countries enjoy peace, carrying together joyfully between them the yoke of love, then the reign of Jesus, the king of Love, will spread itself quickly and you, little brother, will bear the name of apostle of love.'

How I came to detest the French

Dear Father, so that you are spared too much anxiety concerning certain events in my life, allow me to give you, honestly, some explanation on the subject of my feelings of 'hatred for the French' which I mentioned earlier. To tell the truth, never in my life have I been politically-minded. I did not even clearly understand the meaning of the word 'revolution'. All I do remember is that before the age of twelve I had never concerned myself with this question of hatred for the French. (620) On the contrary, I liked them very much. At the time when I was still at my parents' home I saw the family of the chief of the military post who used to come to attend the parish Mass. They were courteous, distinguished and kind French people. Their children, boys and girls, had kind manners, and they were clean, unaffected, and possessed still other qualities which made me want to live like them. As proof of what I am saying, I recall a little incident which was related by my father himself: 'The first time that little Van saw the son of the military chief at Mass, dressed in an elegant and well-fitting suit, he could not stop looking at him and seemed to want to have one like it. In fact, on his return to the house, he did not stop pestering me to make him a suit of the same kind. At that moment, clothes of flowered linen and white silk trousers no longer had any attraction; he wished to get rid of all that in exchange for a French suit.'

Naturally, my father did not agree that I should wear a French suit. Without doubt I shed tears at this refusal, a thing I did often when I (621) was small. But when I reached twelve years the external qualities of which I spoke earlier were no longer able to gain my respect. I must confess, frankly, that I began to detest the French when I saw the film, whose title I cannot remember, when I was at Thái-Nguyên and to which I have referred earlier. From that day, I considered the French as 'enemy number one' of the people. I hated them and wished only to destroy their cinemas ... Later, at the time of the Japanese invasion, making use of the opportunity, a quantity of revolutionary pamphlets was launched which were found everywhere. As well as these pamphlets, there were also revolutionary lectures lasting about ten minutes, given by members of the revolutionary party who were sent into the countryside to awaken the souls of the people. These members were teachers in large measure.

To tell the truth, I did not at all like them in those days, and I did not wish to attend their meetings! Nevertheless, their words reached my ears and entered my soul. I remember one day being in class with my (622) companions to prepare for an examination when we noticed, coming from I know not where, a refined young man who was looking furtively through the school door. About fifteen minutes later he entered hurriedly and politely saluted the teacher and the pupils. He was acting like a young intellectual, but to judge by his appearance there was absolutely nothing of the educated man about him: his hair was standing on end, his face was bony, his clothes were untidy from his shoulders to the legs of his trousers. He placed his old leather satchel on the teacher's desk, rubbed his hands and asked permission to say a few words on the current situation to the pupils. All of us, teacher and pupils, were amazed at his completely unexpected behaviour. He spoke up, and held forth, gesticulating, on French colonialism and the slavery of the Vietnamese people. There was an eloquence and a decisiveness which affected us all, and at the end we were moved to follow him. He concluded abruptly with these words: 'A pupil who does not love his country, who is not interested in his compatriots and does not concern himself about freeing his country from slavery, deserves to be buried alive.' Then, saluting everyone, he took his satchel and withdrew.

(623)

After this meeting and subsequent ones my comrades pressed me to go to listen to these 'ten-minute meetings' which were delivered at the entrance to a street or in a corner of the market, and to which people were invited. The speakers were young people with dishevelled hair, who expressed themselves eloquently. These speakers meant absolutely nothing to me. I sometimes whispered to my friends who were listening to me: 'This gentleman has almost certainly already been imprisoned by the French, to be so furious with them; but the French have never had towards the Vietnamese the bad intentions that he attributes to them.' Most of the young listeners thought as I did. Later on, having sometimes been to the countryside, I reproached myself for having judged the revolutionaries so harshly. I have seen with my own eyes the cruelty of the French towards the Vietnamese. The speeches I had heard were from that time printed deeply in my mind. I found that the speakers had spoken the truth. It is also from this time that my deep resentment towards the French dated.

(624)

But the more I hated the French, the more sympathetic I felt towards the Japanese. When I went anywhere, I liked only the company of the Japanese, and whenever I met a disorderly Frenchman wishing to oppress the Vietnamese, I went immediately and asked a Japanese soldier to intervene. Then the Frenchman, faced with Mr Japanese, was like a mouse before a cat, and, in spite of all his pomposity, he had to withdraw, since, if he had not, the Japanese would have been capable of splitting open his stomach! During our war games I would never accept the role of a Frenchman; I always used to choose that of the Japanese so as to have the opportunity to revenge myself against the French, at least in my own eyes. Ordinarily, people scolded me, saying: 'These folk from Bắc-Ninh are the seeds of revolutionaries. Be careful, or you will lose your head . . .'

I did recognise that my feelings of hatred against the French did not (625) come from a bad motive, nor from bad treatment that I may have been the victim of, since I was still young. I sincerely hated them as I hated anything unjust. As I was a very sensitive child I had a great compassion for those who suffered; therefore how could I not have felt thus against those who abused their power to oppress any of my people. One of my great trials was my inability to avenge my compatriots as Moses had done in former times. In my anger against the French I asked God to send the archangel Michael to drive this diabolical gang from Vietnam. I considered death then as nothing, and if I had been given the chance to die in overthrowing the French, I would have regarded this death as a joy akin to that of martyrdom.

It was at that moment that God sent me a saint to teach me the revolutionary method of the gospel. However, I don't know why, but each time that I have to pray for France, I feel a malaise and I suffer as if I've placed a kiss on a branch covered with thorns. Today, praying for (626) France has become part of my daily routine, but this unease persists; therefore each time I have to force myself to pray. Even so, my heart is sincere, as God well knows. But, whilst detesting the French, I did love the French missionaries. This is because I have noticed that the missionaries, while belonging to a colonial nation, are not themselves colonialists. They are French, but dedicated totally to Vietnam; so much so that they could be called the fathers and teachers of the Vietnamese people. Their sacrifice is truly great and only the eternal life of an infinite prize would give them just reward.

During my stay at Quảng-Uyên I was able to experience at first hand the kindness of the French missionaries towards the local people. They have invoked respect for the rights of man in confronting the French colonialists, and preventing them from using force to subject the people. I remember one incident very well which happened during the 1942 harvest. That year the head of the military post, (a Frenchman nicknamed Mr Three Marriages by the folk of the country because he (627) lived with three women: one French, one Vietnamese and one Nung), had the reputation of being very wicked and of appropriating public funds as easily as drinking lemonade in summer. The inhabitants of the region were afraid of him as one fears a tiger, and when there was a brush with him one could only have recourse to the Father to seek his intervention. This fellow had decreed that at each harvest every owner of a paddy field must bring to the military post a predetermined quantity of straw which would serve as litter for the cows and goats. Some obeyed this order, but there were others who did nothing, or reduced their contribution so as to keep sufficient for their own animals. So each year the military post was short of straw. Consequently, this particular year, the head of the post ordered the Vietnamese soldiers (naturally it was only the Vietnamese soldiers since these were the 'boys' of the French soldiers) to go and seize all the straw of the people to take it to the military post.

Father Maillet, when the people came to complain, jumped on his bicycle and went to the post to seek an explanation from Captain Three Marriages who was persecuting the people. Learning that Father

(628)   Maillet was coming about the business of the straw, Mr Three Marriages commanded the soldier on duty to inform Father that Sir, the Captain, was absent. In fact he had just returned from a ride around the town and he was arriving at the post on his horse when he saw Father arriving on his cycle. Eventually he had to send his adjutant to see Father. The latter, of fiery temperament and feeling that right was on his side, treated all the people at the camp, from the captain to the lowest soldier, as a band of snotty-nosed children. The adjutant, roundly told off by Father, was dumbfounded and shook like a reed. He lowered his head without knowing what to say. It was even reported that he shed tears when he heard Father say: 'You are a gang of colonialists, which means that you devour the people of the colony.'

Was he crying with emotion or anger? I don't know. After this hand-to-hand skirmish with the authorities at the camp, Father got back on his bike and returned home. His action prompted the captain of the

(629)   post to send a greater number of soldiers that very evening to take possession of the people's straw. These, going once again to complain to Father, received this reply: 'You have the right to defend yourselves in opposing those who come to steal your goods.' Then Father, holding in his hand a staff sharpened at both ends, went as the head of a troop, in blue clothes and bare-footed, to send the soldiers back to the camp. And can you believe it? Mr Three Marriages' soldiers had to capitulate! From that date the captain of the camp dared no more to send anyone to steal the peoples' straw.

At the same time, after this incident the commander ordered that the two fathers be deprived of their wheat bread which was sent to them every week. This bread was a present sent each Sunday from the camp to the fathers, but from the day when Mr Three Marriages' soldiers had to capitulate before the law, the latter, in his anger, deprived them of the bread. A month later Father denounced this commander to his superiors and this resulted in his being sent to another post. His successor, hearing how the priests had been deprived of their bread, ordered the service to be resumed the following Sunday, but Father Maillet

(630)   refused to accept it saying: 'We were deprived of this bread for having

spoken the truth; henceforth we will eat this bread no longer, so that our tongues are always free to defend what is just.' This story proves fairly conclusively that the missionaries are not colonialists and without their presence countries dominated by colonialism would be subjected to situations even more humiliating.

Concerning the story of the big sister and the little brother

From the day when my two friends Tám and Hiển noticed the reflection of an extraordinary joy on my face (at least that's what I heard them say in a low voice when they were chatting to each other, since for myself I was unaware that there was anything unusual about my face), I felt clearly at the bottom of my heart a spring of inexhaustible happiness. So from that day my companions did not stop talking about this matter and used all kinds of ruses to drag my secret out of me. But all (631) of their attempts failed. Once only, out of consideration for Hien, I told him vaguely: 'The name of my sister also begins with a letter "T".' As for Tám, he tried to annoy me by teasing me a thousand times, hoping thus that my spiritual sister's name would finally slip out. He would come back on the attack from time to time hoping to provoke a reaction: 'Van's sister has sticky eyes' (*Toét mắt*) or, maybe, 'club feet' (*Thọ chân*) since these are the only two handicaps which begin with the letter 'T'. I allowed him to ridicule as he wished the name of my secret sister. I did not take offence, nor did his annoying behaviour succeed in making me speak. One time or another in conversing with Saint Thérèse, I have referred to Tám's words ridiculing her but she was content to say with a smile: 'Truthfully, Tám is a psychologist but he lacks prudence.' As his teasing was unsuccessful, Tám could find nothing better to do than to go and tell everything to the cook, to find out through her intervention if there was a tertiary whose name began with the letter 'T'.

At this juncture the business becomes complicated. As soon as Miss (632) Tin heard: 'Van also has a spiritual sister whose name begins with T', she was seized with jealousy and made this bet: 'I shall point her out to you so you can physically see Van's sister.' Then she set to work. She began observing me with the greatest care. Hiển and Tám also followed me everywhere like two spies. If I went to the mountain they secretly followed me; if I went to the church, they did likewise. They wanted to know what I did in those places where I liked to be alone. They knew well that it was a waste of time to question me any more, because I always replied in a 'mysterious' manner.

One day I heard my spies spread this amusing news among the tertiaries: 'Van sees apparitions of the Blessed Virgin'. The young tertiaries, given to dreaming for the most part, on hearing this news believed it immediately without the slightest difficulty. They rushed round to ask me to ask the Blessed Virgin to obtain such-and-such a favour for them, just as if great miracles had happened at the foot of the mountain. Their thoughtlessness appeared very puerile to me and I forced myself to contradict this rumour, but Hiển and Tám continued to insist it was true. They relied for evidence on the fact that they had surprised me sometimes on my knees reciting the rosary in the crevice of a rock, and they added: 'It was really extraordinary; one would have said that the Blessed Virgin was really present.' My friends believed that it was through humility that I denied these alleged miracles. But when in an irritated tone I posed them this question: 'Dare you state this fact with certitude and accept all responsibility?' they both giggled and ran away. This did not make them more hesitant and they continued to insist that I tell them the truth. I answered them: 'The truth is I have seen no apparition of Our Lady.' I had to put up above all with the young tertiaries who, seeing me somewhere, asked me by roundabout means: 'Van, is it true?' As for the older tertiaries, they did not deny the rumour but simply voiced this doubt: 'It may be true! ... It would not be surprising that the Blessed Virgin appears to him; he still has a guileless demeanour' ... I felt troubled by these muddled discussions, but I could only cry secretly and ask the Blessed Virgin to see to it that people no longer gave credence to such daydreams.

(633)

(634)

Two or three weeks later the story of the apparition had been forgotten. Be that as it may, I must also admit that the Blessed Virgin was being kind to me in a very obvious manner: many requested favours that people brought to me to present to our Blessed Lady were granted as if by a striking miracle. Once again I was even more suspected of having seen apparitions of the Blessed Virgin. In fact she has never appeared to me, but I was privileged to hear her voice in the same way as that of my sister Thérèse. She does not normally speak to me directly, but she would turn to my holy sister to warn me to do such or such a thing. For example, I heard her say one day to my sister Thérèse: 'Tell your little brother Van to take pains to recite the rosary every day, and to love me with all his heart with Jesus my son.' Each time that I heard in this way the words of the Blessed Virgin, my sister Thérèse had no need to repeat them since I had already heard them.

(635)

After a certain time the affair was no longer spoken of, and the spies were no longer on my trail. Hiển seemed to be in a reflective mood, and I had the feeling that a big change was taking place in his soul. A week later he dragged me to the foot of the mountain. This time, unlike the preceding time, his intention was not to get round me, nor to drag out of me by trickery the name of my mysterious sister. He wished, quite simply, to open his heart to me. He admitted to me quite frankly all his thoughts in my regard from the day that he had guessed with certainty that an extraordinary favour had been granted to me at the foot of the mountain. He reminded me of it once more in these words: 'The day when you came back from the foot of the mountain, I saw clearly on your face the imprint of a quite extraordinary joy which astonished both of us, Tám and me, and without the slightest doubt we assumed (636) that you had received an extraordinary favour there. I have also noticed that from that day your daily timetable has changed completely. Outside the hours of work you give the impression of being no longer of this world. This made me think ... And, my dear Van, I want to change also and follow the same programme as you. Furthermore, I want to have the same guide as you so that, with you, I can understand much better the path to perfection.'

Hiển's voice was stamped with confidence and sincerity. I discovered in him, just as before, a simple, sensitive, soul full of a sincere love. That is why after these confidences I did not hesitate to clasp him to my heart, and to reply to him with an equal sincerity, while using the very words that Saint Thérèse then dictated to me, and which she allowed me to repeat. I mean, she allowed me to repeat only the things which had no relation to the mysterious communication established between her and me. Hiển listened attentively when from time to time I depicted my spiritual sister to him. From time to time he allowed (637) burning tears to fall on my shoulders. My words moved him a great deal, and brought him a great joy. Leaning his head on my shoulder like a fragile branch, he said to me with a voice choking with emotion: 'Van, you are truly very fortunate! Frankly, until now I had never heard it said that there are such intimate relations between earth and heaven. O Van, I wish to have no other spiritual sister than your beloved sister! I want to break with Miss Tin and ask Saint Thérèse to be my sister in her place. I will then be happier and it will also be more discreet. Also, Van, from today I am choosing you as my spiritual brother so that you may be my guide on the way of perfection, since I am still very imperfect.' From that moment Hiển and I, like two flowers from the same stem, lived closely together, helping one another in our ascent towards God. I passed on to Hiển all the advice that my sister Thérèse gave to me, and he put it into practice exactly.

I noticed shortly afterwards that the divine grace acting in his soul (638) enabled him to make rapid progress. It could be said that we had both arrived at a level of the spiritual life which could be described as reckless since we allowed ourselves to be guided by this doctrine of Thérèse:

one responds to love by love and a perfect confidence. Love was the sole motive for our actions in our relations with God, yet most would consider this way of acting as being disrespectful and foolhardy. This has never troubled me, however, since the path I followed was at the same time straight and smooth. Hiển, unaware of the secret messages I received from Saint Thérèse, often showed his astonishment on hearing me give instructions such as a saint might have done after long years of experience. Furthermore, God has given me the grace to read Hiển's soul and to understand it. I know his wishes and his sufferings, and I give him appropriate advice. He made this revelation to me one day: 'Van, I think that if I had never met anyone in my life like you to understand me, I would have probably died of sadness.' Hiển has been my first little brother, the first flower of the season. It is Saint Thérèse who has enabled me to find him, pick him and offer him to God.

(639)   But what will become of Tám? With time the bond of friendship between Hiển and Miss Tin loosened, which resulted in disturbing Tám and gave rise to suspicion in Miss Tin's heart. Tám, seeing that Hiển was more than ever on good terms with me, and that without wishing to ignore him we normally went together, speaking of private things, he was hurt, and concluded that Hiển had joined me and chosen another tertiary as spiritual sister, through contempt for him and Miss Tin. He went quickly to the latter to bring her up to date, saying to her: 'Hiển is now in alliance with Van and he has chosen another spiritual sister whose name also begins with T.' Miss Tin turned quite pale on hearing this news, and in her anger made this threat: 'Very well, don't worry. I know very well how to uncover this sister of this fellow Van. You will see.' She first wrote a letter of reproach to Hiển before breaking completely with him. We both understood that Miss Tin's behaviour was prompted by a jealousy based on a mistake. Her jealousy further

(640)   complicated the situation. Faced with her indignation we had to explain to her that, far from looking down on her, we still respected her and were prepared to obey her as appropriate. She was also annoyed because we had refused to accept the special dish she had prepared for us. How could we eat these special dishes when we wished to practise mortification? Having heard from Tám, falsely, that we had chosen another sister to show that we despised her simply added to her anger. How could we despise her since we did not stop praying that she would remain in the kitchen? She did not stop watching us, as she wished to discover the identity of our spiritual sister.

I was disturbed at that time because there were two camps in the tertiary community: the superior's group and the opposition. Each group spied on the other and denigrated it disrespectfully. The group opposed to the superior consisted mainly of young, intelligent and lively tertiaries, but they had no authority. They were opposed to the superior simply because she was cantankerous. As for the superior's   (641) group, although they were very critical, they maintained a semblance of togetherness because they enjoyed the authority. Miss Tin, the superior's niece, was necessarily in her aunt's faction. This is precisely why she was given charge of the priest's kitchen near the presbytery. It goes without saying that the opposition opposed and corrected her very often.

To tell the truth, she did act the 'dictator', objecting to any tertiary but herself having any amicable dealings with us or calling any of us 'little brother'. That was her exclusive prerogative. Nevertheless, she had to hide her pretentiousness from Father, just as a tortoise hides its eggs. Not to do so was to run the risk of being told off. Both groups sought influence in the presbytery as both wished to be strong, and normally the stronger one was the one which had most members active in that sector. It was necessary, above all, to count with the young boys who, day and night, lived close to Father. He was fond of them and they had his ear. The tertiaries also spoke to us a lot and brooded over us as   (642) one protecting a fragile egg.

When we chose Miss Tin to be our sister, she adopted a rather cold front and behaved in a slightly authoritarian way, but in reality she could not have been happier and her only fear was of being sidelined. In her immediate response, her rejection of Van was simply a joke: she liked him a lot, as he was better-behaved and more mature. She pretended to refuse him simply to see his reaction, never suspecting that he would put her to one side and look for another spiritual sister.

And lo and behold! she learned a few weeks later that Hiển had followed Van in choosing the same spiritual sister, and she was left only with Tám. She became jealous, and her great fear was that Van and Hiển's sister might belong to the opposition, and that would have been dangerous. She feared nothing more than to lose her supporters close to the presbytery, since in that eventuality she would have found it difficult to work peacefully in that area. In fact the young lads, although not having any authority, could very easily manipulate things to effect   (643) changes among the tertiaries working in the service of the presbytery. Furthermore, Miss Tin wished to discover the real name of our sister, so as to see clearly which side of the fence she was on. If she was a member of her own group she would leave things as they were, but hard luck to the tertiary of the opposing group who had dared to accept these boys as little spiritual brothers! She was determined to make trouble. Since apart from Miss Tin herself, no tertiary had a surname beginning with the letter T, she supposed it was, perhaps, a question of a baptismal name. So one day she made the following announcement in the middle of the tertiaries in a natural but carefully prepared manner, and in a loud voice: 'If there's anyone here who has the saint's name of Thérèse, will she step forward to receive a letter from a "little brother".' Normally young tertiaries love getting letters, so in this way Miss Tin thought she would succeed in trapping Van's sister, as she had promised herself. But she was frustrated once again, as no one bore the name of Thérèse.

(644)   She would not admit defeat. She wrote a letter to me couched in very friendly terms and which finished with these words: 'The other day Saint Thérèse of the Child Jesus spoke to me in these words, "Van must tell you the name of his spiritual sister."' This time Miss Tin spoke to me like a big sister speaking to her little brother. She thought she would frighten me with this threat but this is how I answered her: 'It's a great pity! Saint Thérèse spoke to you and you did not ask her directly to tell you the name of my sister, so you are still obliged to have recourse to threats. Believe me, the saint who spoke to you like this is a silly saint!' Certainly, on receiving such a reply, she would not have been able to stop herself from blushing with shame. Eventually she stopped suspecting that I had chosen a tertiary as my spiritual sister, and she supposed, correctly, that perhaps Van's spiritual sister was none other than Saint Thérèse of the Child Jesus. To assure herself of the truth she looked for occasions to spy on me, to see if I lived intimately with this saint and visited her often. She may have been perspicacious but I never allowed anyone to see my affection for Saint Thérèse.

(645)   Once, however, not being sufficiently on my guard, Miss Tin was able to recognise the face of my mysterious sister. From that day, her jealousy became a little less caustic. Thanks to Tám she learned in detail my daily programme: when I went to the chapel, what route I took, which door I entered, at what time I walked alone to the foot of the mountain, etc. She looked closely and inquisitively at each detail of the programme, and tried to follow and surprise me. One day at the nine-thirty recreation I made my way to the church. There was normally no one there at that time, and I was sure that the cook would not then have time free to spy on me. I, therefore, entered God's house in a relaxed manner as if I was entering my own house, as if I was climbing on my mother's knee or throwing myself into my father's arms. After a visit to Jesus in the Blessed Sacrament I lovingly approached Saint Thérèse, a little like a child who wishes to be cajoled, and there I laughed, I spoke to her, showing my love very naturally. Suddenly I heard someone laughing behind me. On turning round I saw Miss Tin who, with a hearty laugh, was climbing painfully from below a bench. Her face was as red as a tomato. Pointing her index finger while leaving the church,

(646)   she said softly: 'Now I know!' I was a little annoyed and felt the blood

rushing to my face. It is not surprising that Saint Thérèse did not respond to me that day.

I intended to run after Miss Tin to beg her not to say anything but just at that moment my sister Saint Thérèse spoke out to prevent me:

'Don't do anything, little brother,' she said to me. 'If you run after this young lady and talk to her, she will only be more curious. Relax. There is nothing in this to make you blush. These are ordinary things for a soul like yours.'

'Yes, my sister, but suppose Miss Tin tells this to everyone; I will be upset and made fun of.'

'So much the better, little brother. The lot of the just in this world is to be exposed to scorn. Your discomfort does not matter, so long as you offer it to Jesus, and then it is already good.'

Fortunately Miss Tin did not mention it to anyone. Perhaps she was afraid of having to describe the scene when she had to climb out of the bench ... Some days later she wrote a short letter to me whose first words were: 'Very kind little brother of Saint Thérèse of the Child Jesus (647) ...' and from that day Miss Tin's jealousy concerning my spiritual sister no longer contained anything irritating as formerly, but disappeared completely. It even seems that Miss Tin ended up by being sympathetic towards my much-loved sister, whom she visited very often.[*]

Entering into religion with the apostolate of prayer as a mission

People said of me: 'In any event he will become a holy priest.' As for me, I was resolutely determined to become a perfect priest, an apostle who knows how to sacrifice himself. In order to remain steadfast in this resolution, I had to impose on myself a lot of effort, as much from the spiritual as from the corporal point of view. I still followed the same lifestyle as at Lạng-Sơn, and the more progress I made the more I understood the size of my task as a future priest. I did not shrink before any difficulty in order to forge an upright, adaptable and steadfast character. I lived only for God, and it is towards him that I wish to make (648)

---

[*] Around Christmas 1942, Van had written to his family, telling the story of the 'spiritual sister' and Miss Tin, which made Lê laugh a great deal. Then he spoke a lot of Saint Thérèse of the Child Jesus without saying why, encouraging them to love her and to pray to her, and to place themselves under her protection. His family was quite astonished about her whom he called Sister Thérèse of the Child Jesus.

During 1943 Miss Tin went to Ngăm-Giáo, and was a little uneasy with Van's two sisters, thus proving the authenticity of Van's words. [Tế.]

all things converge. To attain this ardently-longed-for goal I had only one wish, to become a priest dedicated entirely to the love of God. Alas, in spite of this beautiful and so sincere dream, God really wished to guide my steps in another direction! ...

One day my sister Saint Thérèse took me for a walk to the foot of the mountain. She spoke whilst laughing happily, and I hoped to hear from her some very pleasant things. But after some words on the beauty of the grass and the clouds, this is what she suddenly said to me: 'Van, my little brother, I have something to say to you, only I'm afraid that it will make you sad.'

'But, my holy and beloved sister, how could I be sad with you? Up till now have you ever seen me sad because of anything you have said to me?'

'That is true, but today I know that anyway you will be sad, really sad ... This is why I am, first of all, pausing to ask your consent before speaking to you about it. And now, promise me "not to be sad". It is on this condition that I will dare to speak.'

(649)   'I promise, my sister.'

'In that case I will tell you. Van, my dear little brother, God has made known to me that you will not be a priest.'

'Dear Lord, is this really true, sister?'

I began to cry. But why that? How is it that I may not become a priest? ... Oh no! No! I will never resign myself to life if I can never become a priest. I want to become a priest to say Mass, to go and preach our religion, to save souls and to procure the glory of God ... Yes, it's already decided. I must become a priest.

'Van, wait a bit before crying. I have not told you everything, little brother. Yes, to become a priest is not difficult. I have not said to you that you cannot become a priest. On the other hand, who would dare to boast to be worthy of the priestly vocation? So, if God wishes that your apostolate is practised in another kind of life, what do you think? Had I not myself originally wished to become a priest to go and preach the gospel? But God did not wish it.'

'It's different for you since you are a girl, but me, I'm a boy.'

(650)   'That's true,' (Thérèse is laughing), 'to be a boy is a precondition to be ordained to the priesthood. But when God wishes it he can easily change a girl into a boy to make a priest of him. That is an example I am giving you, so that you may more easily understand. God could, if he wished, make stones become the children of Israel. The priestly state is a sublime state, but it is impossible to embrace it if God does not wish it. Before all and above all, the state which is above all others is to conform oneself entirely to the will of our heavenly Father.'

I again asked the question:

'But why is God not choosing me to become a priest?'

Without giving any explanation, Thérèse replied to me:

'Come on, little brother, whilst not being a priest, you have nevertheless the soul of a priest, you lead the life of a priest: and your apostolic desires which you intend to achieve in the sacerdotal state, you will accomplish just as if you were really a priest. Truthfully, that presents no problem for the almighty power of God. Really believe that God, infinitely powerful and just, can never refuse to welcome (651) the wish of an upright soul who, through love for him, wishes to accomplish great things. Yes, firmly believe that your desire for the priesthood is very pleasing to God, and if he wishes you not to be a priest, it is to introduce you to a hidden life where you will be an apostle by sacrifice and prayer, as I used to be. Indeed, there is no cruelty in the will of God. God knows you better than you know yourself, and it is he who has fixed in advance the length of your life of which he knows all that happens. It is why, in his wisdom, he has had to arrange things in such a way that you can practise your apostolate in this world without delay. Little brother, rejoice and be happy at having been placed among the number of "Apostles of the love of God" who are privileged to be hidden in the heart of God in order to be the vital force of the missionary apostles. Little brother, is it possible to have a greater happiness than that? If at this moment you let your tears flow it is without doubt because you have not yet understood. But when you have understood your vocation and the exceptional favour that God has given you, you will be so happy that (652) you will not know what words to use to let him know of your gratitude.'

'Yes, my sister, but I would wish to ask another question. Although Jesus does not want me to become a priest, is it even possible for me to ask him to pass on, to a soul of his choosing, all the desires and plans that I had set myself to carry out in my priestly life so that, thanks to this soul, my desires for a missionary apostolate may become reality?'

'How kind you are, little brother! Cannot all priests replace you or do you need to delegate your projects to one of them in particular? Nevertheless, in conformity with your wish, Jesus will see to choose a soul who will take your place as you desire. As for you, little brother, your function will be to be always the "hidden apostle of love".'

'My sister, in what will this hidden vocation consist? If I am not to become a priest, what can I do then?'

'You will enter religion.'

'What! How? ... enter religion! What happiness, my sister. Yes, I (653) shall ask to enter Carmel, like you, nothing else.'

'A boy, enter Carmel?' said Thérèse, laughing.

'You have just said that my vocation would be a hidden vocation ...
It is only in Carmel that one can lead a hidden life ...'

'You don't yet understand, little brother ... but you will eventually.'

'What do you mean, my sister? I can certainly become a Carmelite ...
I can conclude from what you have told me that God, infinitely powerful, can easily change me into a girl if he wishes.'

After having laughed for a moment, Thérèse answered me cheerfully:

'Very good! This evening, during your visit to the Blessed Sacrament,
let Jesus know of your wish to enter Carmel, and ask him to change you
into a girl in order to be admitted. Yes, it's interesting! Speak to Jesus
as well as you do to me without hiding anything from him. Do you
understand?'

(654)   'Very well, but I am also asking for your support in my request, all
right?'

In the afternoon during the visit to the Blessed Sacrament I spoke
to Jesus as Saint Thérèse had recommended but for some reason I felt
uneasy. Evening arrived. I was still hoping that, in some way, by the
next morning I would have become a girl. God has not judged it
fitting to grant my request. Van has remained Van, and this Van
continues to be a boy! I was ashamed afterwards at having made this
request, and never again would I dare ask God to perform a miracle
to change me into a girl. In fact, my only reason for wanting to enter
Carmel was because I had read the life of Thérèse, and I did not
know of any order other than Carmel, so there was only Carmel I
could wish to enter.

One morning after communion I began to sob, and I complained to
Jesus: 'How can I enter Carmel which only admits women, since I am a
boy?' Thérèse, not wishing that I waste my time in such an insane
manner, said to me cheerfully:

(655)   'Little brother, have you made your request yet to Jesus?'

'Yes,' I said to her, giggling, 'but Jesus has not granted it.'

'Van, you are so naïve. It is easy to find little souls, sincere souls like
yours. I love you, little brother.' Then she added: 'It is true that the
infinitely powerful God can do anything he likes. He would be able,
therefore, to change you from a boy to a girl in the wink of an eye.
But you must also understand that the good God never performs a
miracle of this kind. Although such a miracle is possible, he does
not do it because of the fact that it is not necessary. Furthermore,
God, being infinitely wise, never does anything which would be
useless.'

'From now on, my sister, I will mend my ways and never again will I
dare to ask for such a ridiculous favour. There is only one thing that I

am not happy about: you yourself knew that my action would not succeed, but you did not let me know, thus occasioning me a disgrace which has been very painful.'

'Yes, I knew well that your wish would not be granted, but since you were so sincere I asked you to speak to God about it to please him. You must believe this: because you are so sincere with God you have won his (656) heart even in fanciful things of this nature, and he gives you a great number of very precious graces. Remember, God loves little amusing stories like the one you have just told.'

'Sister, if I cannot enter Carmel because I am a boy, which congregation will I be able to enter?'

'Which congregation? You will have to have recourse to the Blessed Virgin on that subject.'

'But I'm thinking that you, also, know it very well.'

'Yes, I do know it very well: but it must be our Mother Mary who will make it known to you. That is her territory. Does this appear complicated? Don't worry about it. Mention it to our Lady, and she will answer you without delay.'

'But, my sister, how do I make this request to her?'

'I have already told you many times. Tell her frankly what you think, without worrying. It is very easy. Say to her, simply:

"O mother, please let me know the congregation in which God wishes me to dedicate my life to him." Each day when you pray to Mary, make (657) this request and be assured that she will answer you. It is not necessary for this that she speaks and you hear her voice. Be patient, little brother, and pray a lot. Will you?'

A dream: 'My child, do you wish?'

From the day that my sister Thérèse recommended that I have recourse to the Blessed Virgin to find out the congregation that God wished for me, I have followed her advice and, at the same time, I made enquiries about the Dominican order that I had just got to know, but I did not feel drawn to their way of life. On looking further I discovered the Cistercian order, but this order did not please me either, since I feared walking barefoot and having my head shaved. I feared especially having to eat only rice with water. I went many times every day to (658) Mary's altar to ask her advice, but apparently without success. I received no reply from her. This silence puzzled me. Of the two orders I had known for a short period, I did not know which one to choose. Besides, how could I make a choice, since I felt attracted to neither? I was at that time unaware of the existence of other congregations, and I asked myself why my Mother Mary was not answering me. I was anxious and disturbed. It was at this juncture that the Blessed Virgin sent me a very sweet dream.

One winter's night, two weeks after Saint Thérèse had asked me to pray for the intention mentioned above, I was feeling the cold more than usual. I had just fallen asleep, when suddenly a current of freezing air passed up to my bed through the slats in the window and made me open my eyes suddenly, as if someone had come to wake me up. Afterwards I could not go back to sleep. From time to time a gust of impetuous wind coming from the mountain like a waterfall gave me the impression that it was drizzling. The further the night advanced, the (659)   more intense became the cold. Alone, rolled up in my two thin blankets. I still felt the biting cold as if I was stretched out on a rock. It was very difficult to sleep, not because I was tired, but because of the biting cold.

Winter at **Quảng-Uyên** was pure torture for me. During the day I had to remain in class, and to warm myself a little I burnt some little pieces of wood in a tin, but during the night the cold wind could not be more unpleasant. I had difficult in sleeping, and I looked forward to daybreak to warm myself up with the rays of the sun. Throughout the winter my hands and feet were habitually frozen and covered with chapped skin from which the blood oozed. Father Maillet knew nothing about this, and myself, I considered it as a special favour which I must keep secret, all the more so since I was a poor pupil.

Therefore, during these sleepless nights I spent my time saying the rosary, on watch with the Blessed Virgin and conversing with her. This particular night followed the same routine but, after having meditated on the joyful mysteries and begun the sorrowful mysteries, I suddenly fell asleep and it was then that I had this happy dream. I dreamt that, lying on my side, my face turned towards the wall, I continued to say (660)   the rosary carefully just as when awake. Suddenly I noticed someone coming from the side of the study room and walking towards the head of my bed. The study room and dormitory were two adjoining rooms separated by a simple partition, and the head of the bed stood against this partition which, in my dream, was not there.

The person coming towards me was fairly tall, dressed all in black and his face revealed a great goodness. I noticed that he wore a black soutane tied by a cincture which reached to his heels. He was wrapped in an ample cloak of the same length and he wore a black skullcap on his head. Something white showed on the collar of his soutane. His two arms, half hidden under his cloak, were visible only from the elbow. He was holding a rosary with big beads which almost reached to his knees but of which I could see neither the crucifix nor the end. I thought at first that I was dealing with a ghost, and I thought of taking flight but, regaining my composure immediately, I said to myself: 'Does a ghost carry a rosary in his hand? Perhaps it's the Blessed Virgin? But why is she dressed all in black? Unless it's Our Lady of Sorrows? Yes, it is (661) certainly she, who comes to me dressed in black because I was about to meditate on the sorrowful mysteries.'

While I was thus confused by my own questions the person came forward right to the head of my bed. I distinctly noticed a radiant and smiling face. It looked at me affectionately. The beauty of the person was such that it had the appearance of a very gentle ray of light. At the sight of such beauty I turned hurriedly to lie on my back so as to contemplate it more comfortably and I cried out with joy: 'O, Blessed Virgin, how beautiful you are! Yes, extremely beautiful!'

Nevertheless, I was afraid to ask the person's name because, in my opinion, there was no doubt: only Our Lady of Sorrows could have dressed herself all in black. However, there was still some doubt (662) because of the little skullcap whose shape was a little strange. It would not be exact to say that the Blessed Virgin's head was covered with a veil, but it is certain that she wore a black skullcap. The person, there-fore allowed me to look and to think what I wished and, without revealing any identity, was happy to smile and caress me in a manner which could not have been more affectionate. Then I saw the face light up again and all the body shone with a ravishing beauty. I very much regret having to limit myself to saying that it was beautiful without being able to describe the nature of this beauty. Then, gently, the person asked me this question: 'My child, do you wish?' Surprised, I did not clearly understand what was being asked of me but I spontaneously replied: 'O Mother, yes, I wish.' After this reply I waited to see if the person would say something else to me. I thought in fact that after this preliminary question I would be given an order, but nothing happened. I had hardly made my reply when the person saluted me with a bow and withdrew slowly, moving back towards the study room, still looking and smiling at me affectionately ... In spite of my aston- (663) ishment, I felt myself immersed in an immense joy which served to draw me towards this person. I wanted to get up quickly in pursuit ... But, disappointment! the pleasant dream had vanished! ...

On opening my eyes I saw myself seated on my bed in the position of someone getting ready to run, and I realised I had been dreaming. In spite of this I felt an indescribable joy in my soul. I remembered in its most minute details the dream which had just ended, and I did not stop repeating: 'O Mother, how beautiful you are and how you love me!' I touched my hair on the spot where the Blessed Virgin had placed her hand to caress me. I even touched the place where she had stood at the head of my bed, and I did this very regretfully ... I found sleep impossible throughout the night, no longer because of the cold but because of a consuming joy. I repeated over and over again the question that the Blessed Virgin had posed but I did not understand what she meant when she said: 'My child, do you wish?' I was impatient for morning to come so that I could share my dream with Hiển and Tám, and ask them

(664) if they believed, like me, that the person in question was Our Lady of the Seven Sorrows.

The next day, on coming out of Mass, and even before breakfast, I called my two friends to the study room to tell them my dream of the previous night; describing to them in great detail all the positions of the apparition. They both believed without doubt after having listened to me that it was Our Lady of the Seven Sorrows. I then asked them: 'Then why was there a touch of white showing on the collar of the habit?' Hiển replied: 'It was, certainly, the collar of an inner garment which was showing a little.'

'Perhaps ...'

From the beginning I thought as Hien did, but the question, 'My child, do you wish?' remained, and no one could explain it. It happened that later this story in all its simplicity came to Saint Thérèse's ears. Instead of explaining the dream she was happy to say, laughing: 'Ask Our Lady to explain it to you.' Then, in agreement with my way of thinking, she also called the apparition Our Lady of Sorrows.

(665) In fact, my Father, was this person really Our Lady of Sorrows as I believed? No: and it is only after my entry into the Congregation that I clearly recognised that the person seen in the dream was not Our Lady of Sorrows. So who was it then? Here I must try very hard not to laugh at my mistake. However, my mistake was so sincere that I could not imagine anyone other than the Blessed Virgin. But it was not her: it was none other than Saint Alphonsus, the founder of the Congregation of the Most Holy Redeemer.* Although it was only a dream, all the shapes and movements noticed then are imprinted deeply in my mind as if they had actually happened. Time, even, has not been able to diminish their memory. On this subject: later, during the winter of 1944, seeing that the Redemptorist fathers of Hanoi, (Thái-Hà-Ấp), were wearing a kind of cloak similar to that of the apparition seen formerly in my dream, I began to doubt, and I asked myself: 'Why are the Fathers

(666) wearing a cloak similar to that of the Blessed Virgin of the apparition?' And I wondered ... I went to the chapel a few days later, after the morning's work, to make a short visit to the Blessed Sacrament. I lifted my eyes to the wall while climbing the stairs, and I noticed, quite unex-

---

* Saint Alphonsus Liguori (1696–1787). He founded the Congregation of the Most Holy Redeemer (the Redemptorists) in 1732.

pectedly, a statue of Saint Alphonsus standing on a pedestal. The right hand was raised in blessing, his left hand was holding a biretta, his head was inclined forward and his demeanour was almost the same as that of the Blessed Virgin standing, formerly, at the head of my bed. I stopped to look carefully at the statue for a while, and I asked myself: 'Am I mistaken? Am I really sure that the person I saw that night was Our Lady of Sorrows? Was it not, rather, my father, Saint Alphonsus?' Suddenly I heard my sister Thérèse's laughing voice who replied in a friendly way to me:

'You need doubt no longer, little brother. Rest assured that the person who appeared to you on that night was none other than your Father, Saint Alphonsus ... Today I have nothing more to hide from you. I will tell you frankly so that you can recognise your mistake. Yes, (667) the person you took for Our Lady of Sorrows was your benevolent Father, Saint Alphonsus himself.'

'Now I understand why I found him so similar. But, my sister, why, knowing that it was my father Saint Alphonsus, did you not tell me immediately, leaving me mistaken and risking making me cry?'

(Thérèse, laughing): 'It's a great pity, but since on that day you did not yet know your father Saint Alphonsus, how could you tell it was he? If I had told you, you would have understood absolutely nothing and then you would have been confused, because you did not know who Saint Alphonsus was, and that would have been much more painful for you. This is the reason why I have happily allowed you to believe that it was Our Lady of Sorrows. Nevertheless, on learning the truth today, you may think it is still too soon, since, in reality, your father Saint Alphonsus still remains your father Saint Alphonsus and as long as you are faithful to his rule, scrupulously observing even the smallest points, you will remain his dear child. Little brother, what were your feelings in seeing him take such a special interest in you? It was Our Lady, herself, who sent him to accept you into his congregation. Truthfully, that night in saying to you: "Do you wish?" he intended to ask you if you (668) wished to see again, while passing by that staircase, one or other traits of Our Lady of the Seven Sorrows; in other words, if you wished to enter the Congregation of the Most Holy Redeemer? (Thérèse laughed.) And when you replied: "O Mother, I wish it," your "Sorrowful Virgin" accepted the wish of your heart and, from that day, she has considered you as her dear child and has never ceased to wait for you until now on this staircase.'

I shed tears of emotion. Thérèse continued: 'Are there souls in the world who are treated so tenderly as you? You owe this privilege to your sincerity and your childlike simplicity ...'

'Thérèse, my sister, I recognise now that my happiness is truly great and I blush at not being worthy of it. Nevertheless, I now feel more ashamed for having been until now almost indifferent towards my father Saint Alphonsus, whereas during all this time he never ceased to be interested in me with so much affection. I have been really ungrateful! So, in following your advice, I intend to honour him more and to please him by keeping perfectly the instructions he has given me in his rule.'

(669)

I wish to enter the Congregation of the Most Holy Redeemer

Some days after this blessed dream, I was charged with making sure that part of the house was clean, and whilst doing so I was able to pull out from the bottom of a cupboard drawer a stack of the magazine, *Our Lady of Perpetual Help* (*Đức Bà Hằng Cứu Giúp*) published by the Redemptorist Fathers. This was, I don't doubt, a favour from Our Lady. I put these magazines in order, and then ran through them to see if they contained any articles on the Blessed Virgin. I quickly noticed that these annuals had helped me to intensify my devotion towards my heavenly Mother, and further helped me to get close to the goal towards which I was aiming. I began to know and love the congregation for the simple reason that the Redemptorists had a very special devotion to the Blessed Virgin. This is the reason why the congregation pleased me and my only wish was to be admitted to it.

I explained these matters to my sister Saint Thérèse, who joyfully assured me:

(670)?

'You wish to join the Redemptorists? Very good, little brother. This is precisely the congregation the Blessed Virgin wishes to take you to. Now that you have agreed, her will is accomplished. Yes, later, you will enter the Redemptorists.'

Then Thérèse, changing her tone, continued:

'However, my dear little brother, my very little soul, you will encounter some thorns on the way and the sky, serene at the moment, will be covered with sombre clouds. I have to advise you beforehand so you will be ready to accept the trial which will precede your break with the world to enter religion, as is your wish. Adversity awaits you ... You will shed tears, you will become unhappy and you will have the feeling of being a man reduced to despair. Here even at Quảng-Uyên, you will be abandoned, you will be made fun of like someone who has lost his mind; you will be driven away and covered with shame. But remember, that's how the world treated Jesus, and if you wish to become a Redemptorist you must accept to be badly treated like Jesus our

Saviour ... And after having been trampled on in this way, your family will again be a cause of bitterness for you, which will make your sepa-   (671) ration from the world complete. But, Van, don't be afraid! Whilst you will be subjected to this storm in your heart, Jesus will continue to live in the bark of your soul and there, although sleeping, he will not stop loving you and will help you to fight against the storm. Don't worry when you see a drought take a firm hold of your heart. Remain convinced that this is evidence of your deep love for Jesus, since it is by love that you put up with this suffering whilst ardently longing for his coming. In addition, you will no longer hear me chat familiarly with you as at present. Don't believe too readily that I have abandoned you. On the contrary, I am beside you all the time, little brother, as my duty as a big sister demands. Really believe this: to accept scorn through love, that's the glory of love; to suffer through love is to give love greater consistency, greater intimacy. It is suffering in this world which is the proof of your love; it is suffering which gives greater meaning to your love and gives it all its value.

'Remain peaceful, little brother. Chase away all worries. You will soon hear me once again talking with you, and then the world will be amazed   (672) to see that the flower it formerly wanted to crush now has buds which will bloom with all their beauty in Jesus' hands. Never give way to discouragement; don't stand back from difficulty; don't be afraid of suffering. One day you will attain glory, and the most magnificent glory will be to attain that which is the object of your desires. Van, my dear little brother, I kiss you and wish you a happy journey.'

Thérèse spoke to me no more from that moment, and for me it was the beginning of a sombre and sad life.

Confusion

Saint Thérèse speaking to me no more, I was like a compass which has lost its magnetic needle. Confusion immediately took hold of my soul and I welcomed it with the shedding of tears ... My wish to enter the Redemptorists was, at that time, very difficult to realise, since, having told Father Maillet of my wish to enter religion, he had written to the   (673) Director of the Dominican Juniorate at Hải-Dương to ask for me to be admitted. I had, nevertheless, made him privy to my intention, telling him that I had not yet decided to ask permission to enter the Dominicans. Father replied: 'I will leave the choice to you ... However, you could perhaps try it for a while and then, with the grace of God, make your choice.' He continued to write to the Father Director of the Dominican Juniorate at Hải-Dương.

I had meanwhile discovered the Redemptorist congregation. How to let him know? That was the question. He was very hot-headed. Often, when I went to confession to him, and I heard him sigh a little heavily, my heart would beat as if it was breaking, and I forgot all my sins. How would he react if I asked permission to change my mind? Where would I find the courage to take on his piercing gaze or his shrug of the shoulders which was capable of overturning a chair ... or, above all, the blow of his fists on the table and his frightening outbursts ... O my God! Your will be done; but if it is necessary to go this minute to tell Father (674) Maillet that I want to enter the Redemptorists, I give up. I prefer to put up with this difficulty until the moment when it's time to leave the presbytery at Quảng-Uyên ... I shall see to it then. To go and talk about it now would simply aggravate the problem. So I shall keep quiet and wait until my departure before asking permission to join the Redemptorists.

Being badly treated

During this time big changes had taken place in the presbytery. Hiển had asked to leave, because he was not getting enough food. A certain number of familiar faces had also left for the same reason. The tertiary superior's group was blowing hot and cold, hoping thereby that not a single man would remain at the presbytery. As for those who remained, if they wanted to survive, the hope was to force them to live elsewhere, otherwise, they could die of hunger, as I have already indicated. Among those residing at the presbytery was an old catechist who used to enjoy a certain prestige but who, at this particular time, was subjected to the same form of oppression. As for me, I had openly expressed my discontent, not only for myself, but more so in consideration of my companions.

(675) I decided to go and find Father Maillet and ask him to intervene with the superior, and to make her admit that her conduct was not only contrary to charity but totally inhuman. Father Maillet accepted my reasons and demonstrated an unusual confidence in me. But it was because of this special confidence in me that the superior hated me more than the others. I dare say that she had falsely accused me of many things to Father Maillet so that he would lose confidence in me. But, aware of my sincerity, Father treated her accusations as the words of a gossip, and paid scant attention to them, or if he paid attention, it only made him think the better of me. Truthfully, I have no need to boast but, with the help of God, I did my work with a lot of application so that Father Maillet was very pleased with me, and perhaps he may have admired me. He also dealt with me as his bursar, and practically everything in the house was my concern.

So you see, Father, it was not without reason that the superior, on her part, was jealous of a boy like me. It remained that we were always short (676) of food, and it was as if I was the only one capable of saying anything. I know well that to speak of food is considered a trivial matter, but on the contrary, it is rather important, because one cannot live without eating. In the study room one day Father Maillet complained about us: 'Why is it that nowadays all you do is complain about the food? I must tell you that this is something very bad! ... Very bad! ...' Then he grimaced and lifted up his nose a few centimetres. My friends kept silent but I, after a moment of interior prayer to seek enlightenment, got up and asked to speak: 'Father, we complain because we are suffering from hunger. You say that you consider it as something very bad. To tell the truth, it is only bad for those who, having a full stomach, are only hungry with their eyes ... But it can't be bad for an empty stomach. To want to be satisfied when one is hungry depends on the action of eating, and if one does not eat one can only die of hunger. The action of eating and the wish to eat when one is hungry are the work of God who wished that man should be thus and act accordingly. Allow me to make a compari- son; let us suppose that at this moment someone forces you to fast for (677) two successive days: I dare say that at the beginning of the third day all you will think about is eating. And if you are a "living saint" who can accept suffering without complaining, you will think only of God and you will only think of him to ask for food ... and only enough to satisfy your hunger ...' Father Maillet shrugged his shoulders and pulled a face for a long time.

After this discussion, and especially after another I had with him, he called me particularly into his room, to question me on my intention to enter religion. It was the first time I saw him so closely interested in my vocation ... I also guessed that change would soon take place for me. My first wish was to be able to leave Quảng-Uyên quickly. Father Maillet, after having questioned me cheerfully on mundane things, changed his tone and questioned me harshly about the food.

'Why are you the only one among your companions who comes and complains about the food?'

'For the food, as with anything else, I am the only one among them (678) who takes the initiative. You know well that I don't run away from any responsibility, and regarding the business of the food, I don't complain for myself only, but also for my companions.'

'I am sure,' Father said, 'that you are the only one who is so difficult. As for the others, they are usually satisfied.'

'Father, you say that only because you are lacking in observation: in fact, they want to eat all day because they are hungry. I think you may remember the day in class when, to make fun of me, you asked my friends this question: "And you, do you also feel hungry like Van?" Did you see a single one reply at that moment? On the contrary, they all lowered their heads and shed copious tears as at the death of a father.'

'You are impolite!'

'That is true. Please excuse me. However, I have spoken the truth.'

Father went through the motions of reflecting for a moment then, once again, he said quietly:

(679)   'Quite frankly, I have given this question of the food a lot of attention, to make sure that you were given enough, but there is one thing I must complain about: you lack frankness with me.'

'Father, I think we could not be more frank. Let's examine the situation. I have had the frankness to come and tell you everything, and yet you still blamed me for this or that. Consequently, who would dare to be so mad as to be frank with you? I dare assure you that ten out of ten of my companions have not the courage to come and tell you anything, simply because they are afraid of you.'

'Why do you say that? I am not a tiger so that people have so much fear of me.'

'Of course we dare not say that you are a tiger but, as you will have noticed, is there one among us who dares to come near you and speak to you in a friendly manner?'

'So you find me very nasty, do you? ... Perhaps it's true! ... But let's move on. I will pay attention to what you say to correct myself ...'

A moment later he continued:

'But as far as you are concerned, I am telling you this in advance; being on the point of entering religion, you must understand that once you've been admitted into the community you will have more still to (680)   suffer because of the food. You will eat only food which is prepared for you. If something is lacking, you will not be able to make demands. If it is too salty or too bland you will not be able to complain either. I think that the food regime here leaves nothing to be desired, and yet I see you unhappy. You must alter your ways so that later in religion you will be able to discipline yourself more easily. I forgive you all your complaints up till now concerning the food but, from now on, remind yourself, you must be careful to behave better.'

'Father, I thank you very sincerely.'

Then I was silent. During this moment of silence I asked Saint Thérèse to let me know what I ought to say to Father Maillet. But she did not reply. I began to cry and then to sob. Father, astonished, asked me:

'Why are you crying? Do you find unjust what I have just said to you? In that case you are still very proud.'

I replied, stammering:

'Father, I find your words in my regard accurate. I am both greedy and proud: but there are still my companions.'

'Don't bother about them. If they are hungry, they can come and tell me.' (681)

'And if they are afraid to speak?'

'Then too bad for them.'

'In this case you are practising a charity based simply on reason. He who speaks is satisfied, but he who does not speak is allowed to go hungry. In that case I ask you to give only me a pan of rice from now on so that I, alone, eat sufficient because I have spoken.'

'No, no, I don't place limits on charity but I am sure that they are not hungry as you maintain.'

'Father, why has Hiển asked to leave? Why did Blau leave? And the three employees of the presbytery, why have they stopped working? Do you know, Father? And before their departure, did they not tell you that it was hunger which forced them to leave?'

'Oh, that lot! They don't count!'

'They don't count to you, but you must admit they prove the truth of my words.'

'Those who asked to leave were unsavoury types. I know them very well, and if you wish to use them to verify the truth of your words I consider you as being still more depraved than they were.' (682)

'You are right concerning me, but concerning those who have left, I found them, on the contrary, very good, simple and straightforward: they have, however, been oppressed and persecuted by the people of your entourage [I was referring to the superior of the tertiaries] and that is why they have been forced to leave.'

'And who do you mean by the people of my entourage?'

'My Father, I think you know. It's certainly not me, since I maintain that they were very good. It is neither the old catechist nor Tám since they are both in the same unhappy situation. You don't have to think deeply to know who it is.'

'I know you are referring to the tertiaries.'

'That's it precisely, Father. You would consider those who left as vicious, because you have only heard the superior and the tertiaries of her group who despised them. On the other hand, you have not noticed the many good qualities they possess and of which they have given you proof. That is why you judge them as being nasty people. The good God will judge you on this injustice. You are too gullible with the tertiaries: what they say as bad, you immediately judge it as bad, (683) what they say as being good, you judge it also as such. How can a holy man like you still have such superficial feelings? ...'

'Perhaps it would be more correct to say that it is your judgement which is a little superficial since, in fact, I am not at all credulous concerning the tertiaries.'

'God knows. As for me, I can only speak according to the evidence of your actions.'

When I decided to speak again about the superior and the groups among the tertiaries, and even to mention the mortification that I imposed upon myself at the table, to prove to him that I was not so greedy as he thought, I saw him suddenly sigh deeply and adopt an unhappy air. Feeling tired, I asked to withdraw. But Father made me sit down again, and continued by giving me a long sermon on the virtue of mortification. I don't know why he returned to this subject. He even ridiculed me by reciting the Holy Scripture. He read to me the story of the Hebrews wandering in the desert for forty days, telling me of their desire to eat meat, and their nostalgia for the onions of Egypt. He concluded: 'The saints consider the act of eating as being bad beyond all imagination, but you consider it as being important.'

(684)

'Yes, Father,' I said to him, rising immediately to explain myself more clearly. 'The reason that the Hebrews coveted meat, is because they had no meat; and if they missed the onions of Egypt it is because, previously, they had tasted the excellent flavour of these onions, and then they had no more of them to eat. So, that they missed them and desired them was quite natural. Just like the other day when, speaking to us in class about yourself, you said that although having given up tobacco for more than twenty years, even now when you smelt tobacco, you still felt the desire to smoke it. Why have you this desire to smoke? Secondly, you said that the saints would consider eating as a bad act; I dare to say to you that the saint who spoke thus was a "boastful saint". If the act of eating was bad, why did he continue to eat? If such a saint exists who considers the act of eating an imperfection, he does not understand the importance of this action; moreover, he does not know how to eat. Personally, I consider the act of eating as a necessary condition to become a saint, on the same footing as all the other acts performed according to God's will and through love for him. My Father, one can become holy by putting up with hunger. It is an extraordinary favour which I have not experienced. So, not having received such a favour, I must satisfy my hunger in order to become a saint. I cannot lack faith to such an extent that I allow myself to die of hunger in the presence of this infinite power who is God, my true Father. When I am hungry, I ask him for food. When I am thirsty, I ask him for drink. That is what God wishes me to do. If I did not act in this way it would seem that I was behaving towards him as towards a stranger.'

(685)

'I am not forbidding you to eat, but why do you wish to eat only what is good?'

'I don't think that the good God forbids this taste for good things, and I am certain that you, like me and like everyone else who lives on earth, like good things.'

'That's very true, but it is also necessary to know how to practise self-denial.'

'To fast is one thing, but you cannot say that if you wish to deprive yourself of some food, you must oblige everyone else at the same time to do likewise, and if you wish to eat a particular dish as an act of self-denial all must do likewise. Of course not! That would be the behaviour (686) of a dictator. Now, who can become a saint by acting as a dictator?'

'Your words are very hurtful to listen to. I have never, since I became a priest, heard any of my charges speak to me so stubbornly. I repeat: you are full of pride.'

'Yes, I admit it, and for this reason I will certainly not be able to join the Dominicans.'

'As you wish. Anyway, it is possible.'

'I can't wish it when I notice that in your order there are only saints who do not eat, who wear thick beards and shave their heads like you. I recognise that I cannot become holy in that way. For me, I can only reach holiness by conforming to the human condition fixed in advance by God. I have need to eat sufficiently, to wash, to shave, to be clean and pay sufficient attention to the care of my body. If, after having followed this line of conduct I fall ill, I will recognise that this is a special favour from God, a cross coming from his hand, and I will accept it willingly through love for him. A saint who would live in squalor to become ill, and once ill, would moan on his bed saying that he puts up with his (687) illness with joy because it is the will of God: I would consider him as a strange saint and I would ask myself if he is really sure that God can rejoice to hear him attribute this sickness to his holy will.'

At that I got up and asked to withdraw but I added:

'As for myself, I also know that I will not be able to stay here for a long time; in fact, I wish to leave as my companions have done: and anyway, I hope that you will authorise me to go.'

Father Maillet shook his head and said:

'I now see clearly that you are a proud person who has skilfully disguised this under a veneer of virtue in order to deceive me. I've had enough! . . .' Then, making a gesture of repulsion: 'From now on, I no longer have confidence in you for anything.'

He thought for a moment and then continued:

'Do you understand? Go wherever you like. I will not tolerate a hypocrite in my house.'

Crying, I left Father Maillet's room without saying a word. I was totally exhausted after a discussion of over an hour with him. I was surprised at the same time, unable to explain to myself how I had been able to speak with such audacity. On the other hand, I entertained a

(688)   certain hope of leaving Quảng-Uyên soon, since Father Maillet's last words made very clear his intention of no longer tolerating my presence at the presbytery. But the business was not settled as easily as I thought: the tragedy was only at the opening curtain. Thérèse had predicted this exactly to me: 'When you will ask to leave you will not be allowed to go, and when you will be allowed to leave you will be chased away like a criminal.'

From that day Father Maillet distanced himself further and further from me. He heard the superior denigrating me excessively, and so skilfully that Father could no longer hide his bad opinion of me. Therefore when something concerning me displeased him, he stamped his foot, waved his arms and shouted: 'He's a hypocrite! A miserable so-and-so! You could not find anyone more hypocritical or naughty.' After each scene of this kind I had to go to his room and make known to him, clearly and by all means possible, that I remained loyal to him and that I had total confidence in him. It still remained that I was determined not to enter the Dominicans, but I had not made known to him my intention of joining the Redemptorists because Saint Thérèse had asked

(689)   me not to speak to him about it. Father Maillet said that I had become an irremediably lost boy. He no longer believed in the least of my words; he took away all the responsibilities he had given to me, treating me as a total stranger, and if sometimes he had to speak to me again, he knew only how to gesticulate and complain:

'Unfortunately he's a wretch! A hypocrite! A glutton!'

Father, there's no need for me to tell you how this situation broke my heart. My only recourse was to go before the tabernacle each day and open my heart to Jesus in the Eucharist, and to take refuge near the Blessed Virgin, and there hide my tears. The most painful thing was that in those difficult hours when I had need of Thérèse's counsel, she kept silent as if she had lost all interest in me, allowing me to be immersed in a thousand worries with no one to open my heart to. I believed that the chalice of bitterness which God had given me to drink would empty bit by bit each day but, on the contrary, just when I thought it was empty, it became fuller than ever.

I was grappling with hell during those three long months, swallowing

(690)   my tears in silence. I thought it was not necessary for me to remain any longer in the presbytery. I dared, therefore, to ask Father Maillet to allow me to leave. But he answered me with an exaggerated shrugging of his shoulders; that is to say, he could not have been more scornful. A week passed from this moment until the day when Father Maillet granted me leave to go. God again allowed the storm to rise in a most

violent manner. I can state that without divine intervention I would have given way to discouragement a long time ago.

It was on the first Tuesday of the month of June that I left Quảng-Uyên although I was not at all expecting to go on that day. At nine o'clock in the morning I asked Father Maillet's permission to go to the market for a haircut, because for two months my head had been like a forest of reeds because I was not able to go to the hairdresser. It was Father Maillet who reserved to himself the privilege of cutting our hair, following his own special style which consisted in shaving the head completely like a coconut. He was afraid that in sporting a well-combed head of hair we would be a source of temptation for the tertiaries. He obliged us to keep our heads shaved like a bonze, and he regarded this style as being of the highest level of modesty and dignity. For us, on the contrary, the style was unbearable, as much from a moral as from a (691) hygienic point of view because every time our hair was cut in Father Maillet's style we caught a heavy cold which lasted a fortnight. We had pointed this out to Father but he questioned our motives, thinking that we wished to make ourselves handsome in order to attract the attention of the tertiaries, and that we raised this argument to deceive him. This time I had decided not to concede. I went to tell Father Maillet that I could not agree that it was necessary to shave one's head to enter religion, and if he did not give me the necessary money to have my hair cut satisfactorily by a hairdresser I would remain as I was, with my head in its dishevelled state, until the day he allowed me to return to my parents.

Father Maillet, confronted with my determined attitude, approached me aggressively and shouted: 'Wretch! Proud wretch! Are you trying to force me to kill you?' Then he went to look for a twenty-five sou note which he threw at my feet while gesticulating the same abuse. His face (692) was quite red and his eyes were popping out. As for me, accepting everything, I picked up the note and went to the market to look for a hairdresser. Unfortunately the hairdresser was not there. I returned with the twenty-five sou note which I gave back to Father, intending to ask him for it the following day. But on seeing me returning, Father Maillet immediately gave me the order to pack my bags and go that very morning. He continued to shout as before, and while following me he added: 'I am sending you packing. Do you understand? Yes wretch, I am sending you away to be finished with you.' These words, 'I am sending you away', had the same effect as an unexpected blow from a bludgeon. I collapsed on my bed and began to sob bitterly as if I had learned of the death of my mother. Nothing could have hurt my heart more than to hear the words 'I am sending you away'. I knew that with these words 'I am sending you away', my reputation was lost. I knew

(693) also that if I appeared before my mother after having been expelled, it would be capable of making her faint for hours. Indeed, the good name of the family had always been like a precious stone with which my mother had adorned me with care since infancy, in the hope that this good name would be perpetuated by her children. I had formerly been accused of dishonourable deeds, and my mother had been deeply affected for months. She had been led to doubt me and to consider me as a degenerate son. Now that my sentence had been delivered by a priest habitually regarded as being the most virtuous of men, what words could sufficiently defend me before my mother, and prevent her from having her heart broken? O my God, I want to die, and die even now, so as not to have to bring this shame into the presence of my family.

Suddenly I heard my sister Saint Thérèse's voice calling me: 'Ah, my dear Van, you sulk very easily. Come on, stop crying and get up. You doubtless remember what I said to you the other day, "You will be covered with shame". Yes, following the example of Jesus you must accept to be torn and oppressed. Don't give in too easily to discouragement as if you were alone in this world. Get a grip on yourself, put up with it all and offer it all to Jesus who waits for you. Come on, try to

(694) smile and sing joyfully to chase sadness away.

> Sing sing, little brother!
> Get up and dance with me on the long road.
> Why do you worry?
> Jesus is there who waits for you. Be happy and sing!

On hearing Thérèse's voice, which had been silent for a long time, my sadness was calmed a little but it was impossible to respond to her with a single word. I was happy to put her advice into practice. I got up and set about organising things. At that moment, in spite of all the effort I made to calm myself, a deep sob escaped from me from time to time and my tears did not cease to spring from my eyes as from a little spring. At the presbytery everyone, even the tertiaries, knew that I had been expelled by Father Maillet. Not one of those who were friendly towards me dared come near me to comfort me or say farewell, since Father Maillet kept a very sharp eye out. It was 1 pm when I left. Before leaving I went to say goodbye to old Father Brébion. He was very unhappy since the morning when he heard Father Maillet's attitude towards me,

(695) and he advised Father Maillet not to act in that way. But the latter, still determined to send me away, shouted into Father Brébion's ear: 'He's a hypocrite! A wretch! An out-and-out hypocrite!' Father Brébion continued to disapprove of his action right until my departure. When I went

to say farewell, he clasped my head between his hands and comforted me gently: 'Don't be sad. I've always noticed you to be a fervent child and truly virtuous. Perhaps Father Maillet has made a mistake in treating you like this. However, don't be unduly sad since, God apart, no one can understand you. Now, until the moment when God testifies in your favour, don't worry! He will come to your aid. Remain, therefore, in peace; abandon yourself to him with joy and with complete confidence. Safe journey! And may you soon find happiness!'

Father Brébion's words comforted me greatly, but my sobbing only increased. Not knowing how to thank him, I was happy to follow him to the door. Before leaving, I went to Father Maillet to show him my (696) loyalty and my eternal gratitude and to ask his pardon for all the pain I had caused him. But he stubbornly persisted in cursing me: 'May God scowl on you, wretch, should you find peace in life! Wretch!' These curses rang in my ears like a thunderbolt, and I could not control a feeling of deep emotion. I intended to reply to him in a few quite short words, but just when I was about to open my mouth, Thérèse intervened: 'Enough, enough, little brother. It's over. Go in peace! The lot of the just, always and everywhere, is to be regarded as pitiful and deserving of being cursed. Dry your tears! Offer it all to Jesus, your beloved who is looking at you now, who is delighted by your sorrowful tears which he appreciates as many valuable pearls.'

I left immediately on these words of Thérèse, and passing before the chapel I meant to enter to greet Jesus in the Blessed Sacrament, to greet him for the last time residing in this dear place, but just when I stretched out my hand to grasp the door handle Father Maillet ran (697) from the house towards me and cried out at the top of his voice: 'That's enough! Go away, wretch! Hypocrite! You are wasting your time pretending. No one believes any more in your virtue.' Old Father Brébion ran behind him to restrain him. On hearing Father Maillet's words my hand became as heavy as a big hammer, and having no more strength to grab the door handle, my arm fell through exhaustion. Stunned with amazement, I was seeing stars, my head was spinning and I was on the point of falling. Having reached the Mandarin Road a few metres from the presbytery, I sat on the grass beside the road and there, sure that Father Maillet could no longer see me, I wiped my eyes and sighed with Jesus: 'O Jesus my love! This morning I had the happiness to receive you into my heart; I believe that you remain with me still, and that there you see my broken heart and understand me perfectly ... O my beloved Jesus, I offer everything to you. Yes, absolutely everything! ...' I burst out sobbing on these words. Then, (698) making an effort to get up to regain the road, I staggered as if I was suffering from sea-sickness. Having reached the end of the road, I heard a voice behind me calling me, and I saw Tám who had followed me to accompany me to the coach park.

In the evening, towards 6 pm, I reached the presbytery of Cao-Bằng where I spent the night, and the following day I had to take the road for Lạng-Sơn. I was assailed many times during the journey from Quảng-Uyên to Cao-Bằng by a host of troublesome thoughts which were leading me to despair. A spirit of pride, under an appearance of good, brought trouble to my soul, making me imagine the wonderful fruits of a priestly, missionary life. Then discreetly, under the form of a reproach, it said to me: 'Little brother, why commit such madness? In wishing to follow this idea of entering religion, are you sure that it is in accordance with the truth? and the words that you claim come from Thérèse, without any basis, how certain can you be that they are true?

(699)   Was it really a saint who spoke to you then? Could it not rather be your pride searching for some novelty? Ah! You will see! ... You will see! ... It will become impossible for you to see the light. The route that you are now forcing yourself to follow can only lead you into a dense forest, into a bottomless gulf and into a night of dense darkness ... You will see ... You will see, instead of the path leading to the religious life, nothing but emptiness, loneliness and sadness. You have deceived yourself' ... These sombre words, with their semblance of truth, made me suffer a lot but I did not know on whom to lean, having no one to open my heart to. I had only tears to express the sadness which engulfed my soul.

I don't know if anyone paid any attention to me in the coach in which I was travelling but from the moment when I stepped aboard all I could do was brood over my unhappiness and my shame. I went over in my mind Father Maillet's words before my departure, and I was a prisoner of anxiety. The extent of my humiliation was encapsulated in these words: 'I am sending you away, hypocrite and proud brat.' At that moment the devil was exploiting all these words and curses of Father

(700)   Maillet to drive me to despair. Nevertheless, in spite of my anxiety and sadness I was able to say this prayer to God: 'O Jesus my love, if I have really deceived myself in having such an exaggerated self-confidence, I ask you to lead me back to the route which you were guiding me on. If, on the contrary, I have acted in accordance with your will, deliver me from this temptation.' I regained peace at that very moment and then, instead of shedding tears of sadness, I cried tears of gratitude, love and happiness. The devil, however, did not agree to withdraw entirely. From time to time he returned to the charge on other matters, hoping thereby to make me lose peace; but knowing well that that was a trick of the devil, I did not pay any attention, so that he had to stop bothering me: but the fact remains, he made me shed many tears.

On arriving at Cao-Bằng I felt tired and exhausted, as if I was suffering from a bout of fever. It was already dark and the districts in the
town lit up by electricity were scarcely visible. The birds were warbling
in the trees inviting each other to return to the warm nest. Night was
about to fall on this lively town but in my heart it was as silent as the
grave or in a battlefield after the armistice. There, after fierce resis-   (701)
tance, the defeated have fled, while the victors have bandaged their
wounds and buried their dead. A shivering silence reigns everywhere
... just as in my heart at that moment. I have never felt such sombre
and cold feelings as I did that evening. My tears did not stop flowing. I
went first of all, to the church and I quietly sang this canticle: 'Darkness
spreads over the earth', to unload all my sadness into my Mother's
heart. I felt comforted as soon as I began to speak, quietly, to her: 'O
dear Mother, I have had to go through a terrible battle. I have taken a
first, definite step on the road where Jesus calls me. But, O Mother, this
evening I felt how weak my soul was, and almost at the end of its tether.
Faced with the long path I have to tread, I am extremely sad and feel
only fear and disgust. I do not know if I shall have the courage to go
right to the end, or if I shall manage to gain again at least one victory
... O Mother, how my heart suffers! ... Nevertheless dear Mother, I   (702)
abandon myself entirely to you. With you, I dare to say I will go right
to the end, and I am very determined to gain the victory ... Today,
under the sad rays of dusk, with my eyes full of tears, I do not know
what to say to thank you for your solicitude in looking after me. Small
and puny as I am, I have only my wounds and tears to offer you as a
testament of love and gratitude in return for the protection you have
afforded me in this fearful battle! O Mary, receive my heart: and from
now onwards, I beg you never to distance yourself from me, because in
your glance is the strength which will lead me to victory. You are still,
O Mother, my protective rampart, the remedy for my injuries, and the
nurse whose hands are always busy bandaging the wounds of my heart
and wiping away its tears. O Mary, all I can do is keep my eyes fixed
always on you, and confide myself to your protection.'

After this prayer I entered the presbytery happily. There was general
astonishment when they saw my dirty hair standing on end. Everybody   (703)
laughed ironically and called me 'the savage'. I cried, but managed to
excuse myself cleverly by saying: 'It's thanks to my hair that no tiger
dared to come near me during my travels ...' Nevertheless, no one
understood much, and all were unanimous in saying: 'It's always the
same with Father Maillet's children: either a shaven head or a bushy
one! It's really strange, if not to say despicable! If anyone can put up
with Father Maillet, he will later deserve to be canonized twice.' I was
not the only one to know of Father Maillet's holiness; others knew of it

also. Afterwards, people who came to see me criticised Father Maillet a lot in my presence. But for me, I kept silent or, if the pressure was too much, I cried or tried to change the subject.

(704)   That evening the curate, a Vietnamese priest, called a hairdresser to cut my hair, and once this was done, I was no longer regarded as a strange creature. I went by bus the next morning to Na-Chàm. There I met Father Tân (Dreyer Dufer) but I could do nothing but cry. He probably already knew that I had been expelled by Father Maillet, but he did not make any gesture of discontent in my direction and did not quiz me on the subject. On the contrary, he was busily fussing about me until the time of my departure. I am certain that he understood completely the reasons for my tears at the time of our last farewell. This is why, on taking me to the train, he said these consoling words to me: 'Since the good God has allowed it to happen, it's a waste of time crying. In his eyes there is a reason for this trial, because what he does always has a meaning.' Nevertheless, I could not hold back my tears on seeing Father Dreyer Dufer wave his white handkerchief to me until the departure of the train. This was my last meeting with him, and from that time I no longer expected to meet him again or to correspond with

(705)   him. His memory only remains, with the hope of meeting him again in the eternal homeland. It was on that day that Father Dreyer Dufer gave me the rucksack that I had formerly used when I went camping. He asked me to keep it as a souvenir. This present gave me great pleasure, and I believe that if Father had not given it to me I would have insisted on keeping it as a little souvenir of happy days spent in the troop of cadets of Our Lady and of many graces received in my heart when we pitched our tent.

I arrived at Lạng-Sơn that evening, where I was treated as I had been at Quảng-Uyên, but I had to suffer more from irony than from bitter accusations levelled against me. I had to try hard not to cry, because in his letter to Father Joseph Toàn, Father Maillet blamed me for many abominable offences, which in his mind meant, ordinarily, pride, hypocrisy and greed. Father Toàn then preached me a long sermon, and finally considered me as a twist of straw that one throws into the dustpan. He declared: 'If I see him somewhere, the blood rushes to my

(706)   head and I am tempted to kick him to make him disappear completely so as never to have to see him again.' I had, therefore, to keep my distance, hidden in the shadows of the church as near as possible to the tabernacle, and in my hiding place I cried with Jesus, and it is there, also, that I drew upon a new courage to pass through this time of trial.

The following evening I took the six o'clock train for Bắc-Ninh where I arrived only at seven o'clock the following morning, which was a Friday. I wanted to make a detour to visit my family, but I had not been authorised to do so. Father Toàn did not want me to go home before delivering his letter to the parish priest of Hữu-Bằng, Father Joseph Nhã. Consequently, in spite of the wonderful opportunity which had arisen, I dared not disobey Father Toàn. The letter which I was carrying with me since Lạng-Sơn was no ordinary letter. It was my condemnation. Condemned at Quảng-Uyên, I had been sent to Lạng-Sơn to be sentenced, but at Lạng-Sơn they, horrified at the presence of this criminal, did not deign to inflict the punishment nor even to question him. Hoping to humiliate him further, after having made a copy of (707) the act of judgement, they obliged him to carry it with him to the place where he had formerly lived, so that the punishment could be carried out there.

In truth, all I can say of those humiliating days is that they were known to God alone. I had hoped that, in spite of the injustice of the punishment, to be subjected to it at the very place where I had been sentenced would have spared me much of my pain. But there it was. I was forced to endure the worst of punishments, that of being chastised in the presence of people who knew me very well. By that I risked losing my reputation and people's confidence in me, whilst the enemies of my vision would profit from the opportunity to insult me even further. At Hữu-Bằng, although I was a little lad leading a hidden life in the presbytery, I was well known among the people. It was known that I never drank alcohol and that, on occasions, I would sell my clothes and use the money to help my companions ... Yes, even if I did not know the people outside very well, they knew me to a certain extent. The group opposed to me also knew me and discussed me a lot. In any event they would hope to have the chance to get their own back. (708) In spite of all this I had cheerfully to accomplish God's will. Deprived of a visit to my family, (perhaps they were afraid I would escape punishment) I therefore cheerfully offered to God to continue my journey by train to Yên-Viên to face all the ordeals.

It was seven o'clock in the evening that same Friday when I arrived at Hữu-Bằng. I found Father Joseph Nhã there, stretched out on a chaise-longue and surrounded by some young girls who were giving him a massage. He guessed there was something wrong as soon as he heard of my arrival, since the school year had not yet finished. I knew, however, how to restrain his anger, by offering him a dozen mangos that I had bought at Yên-Viên but in my embarrassment I told him, while scratching my ear, that they were from Lạng-Sơn. Having read the letter that I had brought, he sighed deeply and told me to go to supper. When the meal was over I heard the folk from the presbytery saying among themselves: 'Van has been expelled! I don't know why!' In spite of that no one dared to criticise me; they looked, quite simply,

(709) to question me amicably so as to get the facts without any fuss. That being the case, I spoke of Father Maillet as cheerfully as possible, and only to say good things, and I finally concluded with these words: 'I don't know why Father Maillet sent me on holiday earlier than usual, intending that I should not return; that is to say, he has expelled me but I do not know the reason for his action.'

Two weeks later Thận arrived from Lạng-Sơn to spend his holidays there. Naturally he could only speak in the same way as those who had condemned me. Thus the people of the presbytery were sure that a 'saint' had shown me the door, but they could not find in me the slightest lack of loyalty capable of promoting my dismissal. Father Nhã informed himself of the facts very scrupulously so as to punish me, if it was warranted, from an informed position. His enquiry was inconclusive. He judged it absolutely impossible that I was a hypocrite to the extent of being able to hide it from a hundred eyes always focused on me to spy on me everywhere. After a month of scrutiny only a unanimous verdict could be given: 'Van is innocent!' Therefore I was not

(710) punished, and as a result many understood me better than before. One thing is certain, I had never hoped for such a happy outcome. The Lord, seeing me willing to accept humiliation for love of him, had really wished to change to sweetness all the bitterness of the chalice. There it was, his mysterious will: but who can know it in advance?

One month later Father Nhã received a letter from my parents requesting that he allow me to spend my holidays at home. At that particular time, my parents did not yet know that I was at Hữu-Bằng. They thought I was still at Quảng-Uyên. In this letter my mother expressed in distressing terms her wish to see me again, and judging by her words, she believed that I had gone missing. After receiving this letter Father Nhã sent me immediately to visit my family, informing my parents that Father Maillet had dismissed me but without saying anything further. He simply asked them to keep an eye on me to see if the judgement passed on me was true or not, and to correct me accordingly.

(711) # Not guilty!

My arrival home with such a letter made my family lose a bit of their joy. Nevertheless, my parents surrounded me with affection and spoiled me in a thousand ways. Because of the letter they had received from Father Nhã, they looked at me more closely; my mother, however, after having probed my intentions several times and observed my behaviour closely, declared me 'Not Guilty'. I let my mother and my sister Lê know of my wish to enter the Redemptorists. My mother agreed to let me go, on condition that I first of all obtained the approval of Father Joseph Nhã, the parish priest. As for my sister Lê, she did not show much enthusiasm, saying that I was still young and that I was making progress in my studies, and that my vocation to the priesthood was really wonderful and as clear as day. Why do something stupid by entering a monastery where only salted rice and water are consumed? But my greatest fear was that I would not be able to persevere, that I would be forced to return to the world, to the great shame of my family. (712) I explained to my sister the way of the holy will of God and the life of abandonment of a soul totally dedicated to the Lord, telling her that such a soul had nothing to fear whatever might happen to it in the course of its existence. My sister allowed herself to be convinced, and agreed that I give myself to the Lord. I did not breathe a word of this to my father, although normally I would have spoken to him of it ... It was not easy to speak to him about it, and I did not know how to express myself. Besides, my mother did not want me to speak to him about it; she said to me: 'Leave it to me, and if necessary you will speak to him when you are about to leave.'

I returned to Hữu-Bằng after a stay of two weeks with my family. I wrote two long letters to Father Maillet before continuing the approaches necessary regarding my admission to the Redemptorists. In the first I explained to him in a vigorous manner my disagreement concerning the absurd abuses which existed in the tertiary community in Quảng-Uyên. I disapproved equally of his prejudiced behaviour regarding the tertiaries and the personnel of the presbytery, and I (713) concluded: 'Such a form of charity cannot but lead to the ruin and unhappiness of souls who are its victims. If this situation does not change I dare to challenge you to be able to keep this community of tertiaries, and to manage to maintain unity between the people around you, and that, even if you are a saint with two, three, eight or nine halos around your head ...' Right at the end of the letter I asked him to forget all my shortcomings and to pray for me, so that I could remain faithful to grace right to the end.

This letter was not answered. After having waited for a sufficient period of time I wrote a second one to him where I pointed out, in a measured way, the reasons which had forced me to ask to leave Quảng-Uyên. I did not forget to say to him: 'I thank the good God with a light heart, since I did not suspect that it would be given to me to leave with the strength not to have any feelings for anything at Quảng-Uyên. I have forgotten all that happened, and I can only recognise, now that things have calmed down, that I am your separated child. I hope you will forget all my faults and all the pain I have caused you. It is on this (714) condition that I will feel happy and that I will continue to be faithful to grace.' Again I received no reply from Father Mallet. This made me understand that there would be no longer any contact between us. I went to speak to God to ask him to bear witness that my only wish was to be conciliatory and to follow the way of Love right to the end. After that I continued without delay the steps necessary for my admission to the Redemptorists.

Imprudence

(715)

My dear Father, you know that until then I had not been in contact with any Redemptorist Father. You know, also, that if I wanted to enter the congregation it was with the intention of being able to love the Blessed Virgin more. All I knew of the congregation I had learned from the magazine of Our Lady of Perpetual Succour. Now that the time had arrived to seek admission, it was necessary to find a means of getting in touch with the Fathers. Alas, what could I do? At Quảng-Uyên I had said to myself: 'When it is time, Saint Thérèse will certainly speak to me.' But nothing happened, and I did not know where she was: she spoke to me no longer. Even though I waited for her and questioned her she kept silent like an inattentive child. Now, what could I do? Wait for her? But who knows when she would reply to me? I had to look, once again, for a means of entering the Redemptorists. But how was I to communicate with them and how was I to express myself? To put an end to the situation I risked asking the opinion of a catechist whose younger brother (Brother Vitus) was in the congregation. He told me straight away how to let the Fathers know of my wish. I wrote my first letter. (My Father, it was very difficult. No wonder that Thérèse had hidden herself!) Once my letter was finished, and without thinking that I was acting imprudently, I signed myself very quickly, in such a way that the recipient would have to make an effort to guess the name of the

(716)

sender. I must admit frankly to you, Father, that it was my teachers who had taught me this; the quicker and more tortuous the signature, the more value was given to what was written. And at that time they were considered skilful teachers who knew how to hide their name in a tangle of rapid strokes. But because you, Father Boucher, had not the knack of unravelling this type of signature, you had to write to Father Nhã, the parish priest, to ask him the name of the one who wanted to enter religion. This put me in a pickle. I wished, absolutely, to hide my intentions from the parish priest, since I knew that if I told him of it, he would just let things drag on. Further, if he had kept silent during this time of waiting I would not have been troubled, but there was this problem in the presbytery: if anything, even the most secret, came to anyone's ears, all the personnel of the house knew of it. If, once privy (717) to the secret, they knew how to cooperate with the one who was its subject, how easy it would have been; but they wished to know secrets simply to approve or criticise them according to whether or not they conformed to their own ideas. For example, concerning the business of my entering religion I had been very discreet: nevertheless, in less than no time everybody at the presbytery knew my secret. The worst were those women involved with life in the presbytery and who often traded in stories and stretched them beyond belief! Brought up to date on the question of my entry into religion, they chatted a great deal on the subject. They called me 'the saint', but if I was guilty of the slightest lapse they blamed me, saying: 'For somebody who is about to enter religion you are far from perfect' ... I made sure to keep out of the way of the parish priest but I had been so imprudent as to hide my name from the Redemptorist Fathers. That is why Father Boucher CSSR had to write to the parish priest. So, my story was out in the open.

On receiving your letter on the subject of indecipherable letters, the parish priest was extremely astonished and called me immediately to reproach me:

'On whose authority have you dared to write to the Redemptorists to (718) ask permission to join them?'

'Father ... that is to say ...'

'What does this mean? Do you wish to dishonour me?'

'Father, I would never dare to. I simply meant to write to get information and then to speak to you afterwards since, anyway, I must have your permission before deciding anything.'

'Have you spoken to your parents about this?'

'Yes, I have indicated my intention briefly, but my mother said to me that she would allow it on condition that you, yourself, were in agreement.'

'Hm! ... You don't look at all like a religious ... All right, that's enough! Go where you will, but you must manage on your own.'

'Yes, Father.'

The parish priest did not question me further. He had given me his approval, leaving me completely free to sort things out as I wished. I hurried to write a new letter to you, and this time I signed it legibly in capital letters. I was quite certain that the Fathers could not make any more mistakes and that soon I would receive good news. This 'good (719) news' seemed to be nothing more than a dream but on receiving your letter a few days later I felt an indescribable joy. Having read it, however, I realised that my joy was premature. Without refusing my admission, you suggested a choice between two possibilities. The first was that if I was good enough in my studies I could enter the junior novitiate at Hué with a view to study for the priesthood. The second, if I wished, was to enter as a lay brother. This entailed waiting until I was eighteen years of age which meant another three years. It was very difficult for me to make a decision. On the one hand I could not be admitted to the juniorate at Hué, even if I had the required ability, because Thérèse had told me that I will never be a priest. On the other hand, if I chose the life of a lay brother, I would still have to wait three years before being admitted. Three more years! Oh how long it was! And who knows, if after having spent three years in this deplorable presbytery, I would still have enough strength to follow my vocation. O

(720)   my God, what can I do? If the Fathers understood my actual situation, they would probably not have dared risk making me wait so long.

After days and nights spent without eating and sleeping, I was able to lift my gaze to Jesus cruified, and pronounce my *fiat* in obedience. I wrote a third letter to you explaining clearly my situation, but without receiving a reply. Impatient, I sent you a fourth letter which suffered the same fate. After waiting a long time for your reply I was worried and I wrote a fifth time ... It was not until three months later that I received your reply. All I knew during all this time was to pray and accept this trial in silence. My soul was exhausted like a withered branch. I saw myself on the brink of discouragement, and in my trouble I said to myself: Perhaps the good God wishes me to entre another congregation'.

One day, impelled by sadness, I told Saint Thérèse of all the difficul-

(721)   ties which were tormenting me. Would you believe it, against all expectations my sister broke her silence to tell me: 'Dear little brother, why do you torment and tire yourself so needlessly? Follow my advice: chase away all preoccupations and remain in peace. Listen to me. Write another letter to Father Antonio Boucher. If he does not answer, write again. All these letters can't harm you. If you are patient and ask many times the Father will certainly end up by giving you a reply.' Encouraged by these words, I wrote another letter to you, and it was Saint Thérèse herself who suggested content and form. It was the same for those that followed. Thérèse gave me the model during a visit to the Blessed Sacrament; it only remained for me to take up the pen and write. That is why, from that moment, it was easy to write to you and open my heart to you. You replied to the letter but without giving me any reassurance, as I told you frankly in my following letter. I have been able to understand a little the meaning of those days of waiting that God has imposed on me, and I was no longer in such a hurry to enter reli-

(722)   gion as soon as possible. The wish to enter religion soon was, without doubt, my greatest desire, but I had to recognise that in this action I was

thinking more of myself than of the good God. I must also admit that in all that I did at that time, I loved only that which made me resemble Thérèse. As we loved each other, it pleased me to walk in her footsteps in all things. And I said to myself: 'If I could be admitted into religion at the age of fifteen years how happy I would be!' I sometimes had foolish dreams of this nature, namely, that time would slow down its flow to allow me to enter religion at fifteen although it might mean that afterwards it continued its normal rhythm. This wish, like the one of being changed into a girl to enter Carmel, lets you know how naïve I was still. It was therefore necessary that the good God allowed me to live through some experiences in the world so that, later, I would learn to appreciate my vocation and remain faithful to it. I can state proudly, today, that I have had to shed abundant tears to safeguard my vocation, so that nothing in the world could make me abandon it, except the will of God. But God would never be in opposition to himself.

I have accepted willingly, therefore, the delay which has been (723) imposed on me, and I was still ready to endure all the sacrifices and all the inconveniences that God would really wish to send me. Thérèse again gave me this advice: 'During this time of waiting, you must not forget to remain in touch with the Redemptorist Fathers. This is important so that your vocation does not become a muddled business'. My Father, that is the reason why I wrote to you from time to time to let you know the state of my soul. Thanks to your letters I felt some comfort, which helped me to find the time a little less long. Each one of them made my soul grow to a certain degree and drew me more to the congregation, which I learned to love more and more each day. It also seems that the devil became disheartened before the wise directions you gave me in your letters. I found them a great consolation, since at the time when God was obliging me to live with a weak body in the middle of the forest of the world, he had not forgotten to be lavish with his attention in the flower of my heart so as to give it greater beauty. Without doubt, in the forest of the world there was poor soil; but where I lived then, I must say that the soil did not contain more than a (724) centimetre of nutritious material. If, therefore, the flower of my heart had been able to live and keep its freshness, it is thanks to the nutritious substances which came to me from the Congregation of the Most Holy Redeemer.

Meditation was one thing that I never heard anyone speak of. Even Thérèse had never used this word to explain in what this form of prayer consists. She had taught me, only, the way of talking familiarly with God, telling him simply about things just as they are: but concerning lifting up the spirit towards God, reflecting and uniting oneself to him, Thérèse had never spoken to me of it. When I received your letter giving me advice on meditation, I understood absolutely nothing. I questioned Thérèse who replied to me: 'You have Father: question him.' You then gave me some explanation and sent me a sheet explaining the method of meditation of our Father Saint Alphonsus. It was then that I understood that meditation was a method of uniting oneself to God and conversing simply with him. At the beginning I followed the

(725)   method exactly, but I found this very difficult because I did not at all understand how to meditate. I have had to return to my personal feelings, conversing with God as I ordinarily do with people. If I met any difficulty I would speak of it to the good God, and during moments of fatigue and aridity I was happy to repeat, at least, these words: 'O my beloved Jesus, I love you a great deal, a great deal'.

Usually I did not hear Jesus reply as did Saint Thérèse, but I felt comforted many times, and I felt all the depth of God's love. Now and again this love made itself felt with such intensity that my soul felt as if it was being melted into one with him. Now and then I had the feeling of being very close to God who lavished on me marks of tenderness. Confused in the presence of such a love, I had to tell him in the sincerity of my heart: 'O my God, you know that I am a very small creature. In your love for me, don't be too lavish with your intimate kisses ... since I could die because of them! ... And that being so, it would be a great pity, since not yet having entered the religious life, I would not enjoy the happiness of being intimately united to you by vows and, also, I would not yet have done anything in response to your love.'

(726)   ## With the children: the beauty of love

During this time of waiting God has again given to me the happiness of living in the middle of children. Father Nhã, knowing that the Redemptorists were making me wait for a long time before joining them, took me everywhere he went, especially at the time of retreats in the neighbouring parishes. Most of the time he gave me the task of teaching the catechism to the children. If the catechists found this work tiresome, for me there was no happiness comparable to it. To amuse myself I gave the children nicknames such as 'little angels with dirty faces' or 'little saints' or 'snotty-nosed, greedy, troublesome beggars' ... My teaching method consisted in playing with them, and spoiling them with things they liked. Important among things which they liked were silly things, but not wrong things. It was therefore necessary that they were interested in order to educate them, avoiding being too serious or

(727)   too hard, which would cause them to be afraid because, once they are afraid, all they will think about is running away.

I noticed that the children learned their catechism very quickly only when I taught them through play; and what they learned they retained a long time. Although there was an hour fixed for each lesson, I tried to change this hour, traditionally long and serious, into a happy hour which passed in no time. In following this method I realised that the children learned very quickly. For example, during a lesson I might ask a little one:

'How many persons are there in God?'

'There are five.'

'No, you are mistaken. To answer correctly you must say, "There is only one God but three persons in God." Repeat it again.'

A moment later I asked him the same question and he answered as the first time:

'There is only one God but five persons.' So what could I do to help him remember? I organised a game for those who had not good memories; a game of Indian style, one, two, three, and the loser would receive three flicks on the nose. After having played for a short while I questioned him again ... He had still forgotten. 'Come on, how can you forget? There is only one nose which receives three flicks which can be compared to only one God in which there are three persons. That's (728) very easy to remember. Begin playing again, but you must remember that there is only one nose but three flicks.' The children burst out laughing, and subsequently if anyone answered my question incorrectly, I had only to point my finger to my nose for them to remember, immediately; 'Only one God but three persons'. I did find it difficult, nevertheless, to get the children to remember the lessons I taught them. They have not all got the same level of intelligence. For many, if it was a question of learning a game, they were very quick, but as soon as I questioned them on the 'Hail Mary', their minds seemed plunged into darkness. They could only mumble without being able to say anything. Much patience was needed to find a means of understanding them so as to give them a kind of explanation adapted to their intelligence. They must not be discouraged for fear they might dig their heels in. As for me, in such circumstances I had recourse to another method: prayer. I understood that an educator who is not patient can only harm his children. Now, to obtain patience it is necessary to pray at the actual moment. The method of prayer! It has helped me to get good results (729) more than all the other means.

I sometimes came across stubborn or unruly children. These children could also be impolite or ill-disciplined, even towards those who showed them affection. In such cases, it is necessary first of all to remain calm, to give instructions quietly and naturally, in such a way that the children are happy and fond of the teacher. It is necessary, also, to ask immediately for the support of a supernatural power which means that one must pray. This is how I proceeded in a case of this nature. If I met a child as described above, I called him close to me when the others were not paying him any attention. I spoke easily with him without pointing out any of his failings, as follows: 'The good God needs our prayers at this time to give a sinner the grace of conversion. If you like we could go to church to say a little prayer.' They would usually ask me to tell them the sinner's name. But I waited until they had prayed before telling them clearly one or two of their weaknesses, and I always got good results.

(730)

If I was dealing with a child with an easy-going character, I corrected him on the spot, but always without getting annoyed. One thing I noticed which is quite obvious is that all children are full of self-love. So if, in correcting them, one does not know how to act prudently, one can do a lot of harm. Little girls are more attentive than little boys. Furthermore, boys are not so careful as girls in weighing the words they hear. A word to a boy can mean nothing, while the same word addressed to a little girl can appear very serious, and provoke copious tears. The educator must therefore be very alert on this point, and pay a lot of attention to it; without that he will do harm. It is only after experiencing many difficulties that I have succeeded in understanding something on this subject.

(731)

In dealing with children one must know how to use affection rather than threats. Everywhere and always I noticed that children liked only affability and gentleness. One day, as an experiment, I posed the following question to a group of children: 'When you speak to God, which of these two do you prefer? to call him "Father" and be called "children" or to call him "Lord" and be called "servants"?' With one voice they replied, 'We prefer to call him "Father" and to be called "children"' ... This proves that children always prefer that which is friendly. It is never necessary to frustrate them in things which please them. It is necessary, however, to make them understand that their actions are useful or harmful, good or bad. If they suggest something good, the educator must collaborate with them to raise them to perfection. If their behaviour is bad, one must again encourage them to suppress entirely such behaviour. Children's consciences are different from those of adults. Sometimes, without knowing it, they place themselves in inappropriate places; sometimes they do good without being encouraged or guided by anyone. The heart of a child is easily attracted, so if the educator knows

(732)

how to gain their friendship, the work of educating them will become very easy. I have noticed that when children liked me, they listened to all I had to tell them and agreed with all that I wanted. They had become like soft putty in my hands from which I could easily form the shape I wanted.

It remains, nevertheless, that the educator's cross is far from easy to carry ... If I speak in this way it is because at this period when I was teaching the catechism to the children, I knew much bitterness. At that time, I followed the method which Saint Thérèse had taught me for the little children, who understood a little the manner of living completely naturally and familiarly with God, as with people who are close to us. One day during Benediction of the Blessed Sacrament I saw a young boy (Joseph Bái) who from time to time glanced at the tabernacle, and then lowered his head and laughed silently. I guessed that there was certainly something interesting happening between himself and Jesus. After Benediction I was sufficiently curious to call him over to question him. This is what he said to me, very sincerely: 'Because I had not known my lesson this morning, the teacher has punished me by depriving me of my dinner. Towards eleven o'clock, already famished with hunger, I went to (733) the church and, following your advice, I spoke to Jesus to tell him: "Dear Jesus, I am very hungry. Find a means of satisfying my hunger a little." On stepping out of the church I met you. You asked me if I was hungry, and you gave me twenty sous to go and buy some cakes ... There!' Then, full of joy, Bái continued: 'Don't you think it is profitable to be so direct with Jesus? That is why, each time I looked at Jesus during my visit to the Blessed Sacrament, I could not stop myself from chuckling.'

My Father, there you have one of the successes I wanted you to know about. The children were, naturally, simple and open with me. They were attached to me as to a big brother, and they were happy to follow all the directions I gave them. People said: 'Everywhere he goes, children surround him like flies round a rice pudding.' It is quite true. However there are few who understand why I love children, and why they love me. (734) Some believe it is my temperament to love them, but I must add this: if children attract us and are dear to us it is not only a question of temperament but also because of the beauty and limpidity of their souls completely filled with God's love. For me, living among a group of children is like living in paradise. And, in my opinion, if the good God had not called me to lead a hidden life in religion it is probable that I would have become a priest solely dedicated to the service of children ...

But here I am, far from the story of my vocation which I have interrupted because of the children.

Farewells

On 22 June 1944 I received a letter from Father Létourneau* authorising me to enter the community as soon as possible. A list of the things

---

* The new person in charge of the recruitment of Brothers.

(735)   necessary for admission was included in the letter. This sudden news took me completely by surprise, but I was happy with it, realising that my exile was soon to end. I began my preparations without even an hour's delay, but the more I hurried the more trials I met. The most difficult concerned material things. Everybody knew that I and my family were poor. I would have hoped, therefore, that the parish priest, Father Joseph Nhã, would have taken charge of the material side of things, but he refused, saying in a caustic manner: 'If you enter religion it is for yourself, not for me, and you have the cheek to ask me to provide your trousseau?' What could I reply?

Faced with this refusal, I approached my adoptive mother. But this lady for reasons of her own did not want me to enter religion, but rather, she wanted me to be her heir. Because, as you already know, Father, this lady had only one daughter. She refused any responsibility, just like Father Nhã, saying to me: 'If you wish to enter religion, sort

(736)   things out with the parish priest. 'This is not my business.' She then added in a roundabout sort of way: 'Who does not know that I am a widow with an only daughter aged nine years, and who does not deserve any of your consideration. Go, therefore, where you will. We in this house, God will look after us.' I know that this lady was disenchanted from the day, one year earlier, when I had made known to her my intention to enter religion. She did not dare to say it openly for fear of being criticised. She satisfied herself with oblique words concerning her daughter's eventual engagement to me, on the ways of earning a living, on the difficulties one meets in administrative affairs etc. I understood all these things, although they were indirect, but I pretended not to understand them, and I continued straight ahead in the pursuit of my vocation.

Concerning myself and the young Sáu, we never had any thought of marrying later. We considered ourselves like brother and sister of the same family, living together happily as in the days of our childhood. Now that the hour of my departure had arrived, my adoptive mother was not afraid to tell me straight, that she and her daughter had need

(737)   of me after all that she had done for me. I made known to her the route by which God wanted to lead me and I added: 'So, it is God himself who will take care of you, to reward you in my place for what you have done for me. My first duty is to accomplish perfectly the will of God.' When I left she handed me a five piastre note, saying, in a voice broken with tears: 'Because I am unable to respond to your request, take at least this small amount for the journey.' Sáu, understanding nothing of her mother's words, looked at me, sobbing, and did not stop repeating: 'So now Van is lost to me! Van, my brother, pray for me, will you?'

Not being able to get anything from that source, I caught the train to go to my family on 27 June 1944, and I placed all my confidence in my mother's heart. On learning that the Fathers were accepting me in the community, my mother was, on the one hand, as happy as if a great favour had fallen on her from heaven; and, on the other, she could not hold back her tears on thinking of the moment of our goodbyes. Always ready to accept the sacrifice of my departure, she remained firm in her decision. But now that it was necessary to leave in such difficult circum- (738) stances she did not know what to do. The great difficulty was to provide the 'outfit' which the Fathers required. She often said to me with an unlimited generosity towards me: 'I will be willing to beg all my life and to sacrifice all I possess to prepare for your entry into religion.' But alas, my mother, just like me, had only two empty hands.

If I had known at that moment that the congregation did not insist on postulants bringing every article of clothing which figured on the prospectus I would not have been so anguished. But, unaware, I thought in my simplicity: 'The Fathers demand it; it is necessary to comply.' After a few days my mother had succeeded in obtaining a little money, in part, thanks to relatives who had clubbed together. This made me feel a little more relaxed, but once the problem of the money was resolved, the difficulty of finding cloth remained. Even if money was available, if there was no cloth how could clothes be made? During (739) more than a week my mother approached this one or that one to obtain tokens authorising her to buy a certain amount of cloth from the authorities, but it was necessary to forget this so-called favour since, by buying some metres of cloth from the authorities at a reduced price it was necessary to pay back-handers to a whole series of people stretch- ing from a subaltern to a sub-prefect. This came to a sum greater than the price of cloth bought on the black market. My mother had to seek the aid of some resourceful people who, secretly, searched for cloth merchants on the black market.

So my entry into the community was delayed. But what caused me most hurt was to see all the sacrifices my mother imposed on herself on my behalf. In spite of all this, my mother and I had been able to put up with everything until the time of our goodbyes. Yes, it was necessary for me to endure all these sad events, so that the words that Saint Thérèse had said to me more than a year before might come true. 'And, after having had your heart broken and trampled upon, your family will be for you once more a source of bitterness which will consummate your break with the world.'

A sorrowful separation: 15 July 1944

I intended to choose the feast of Our Lady of Mount Carmel for my entry into religion, since I would have loved the day of my admission into the monastery to coincide with a feast of the Blessed Virgin; but, because of circumstances and difficulties with transport, I had to bring my departure forward by one day. On the morning of the fifteenth my family, with the exception of my father, assisted at Mass with me, and although the Mass was not requested by my family, they had really wished to gather round the Lord to offer to him one of its members. The whole of the Mass and thanksgiving were spent by me in fervour and peace, but on returning to the house the sight of my family plunged in poverty and sadness threw me into such a state of anxiety that I could not hold back my tears. Casting my mind back ten years, I saw again my family but in different circumstances; although living in a

(741) modest house, it was, at least, resplendent with a bustling joy.

I had to go away at that time from the paternal home, but I left naturally and with joy, carrying in my memory all the souvenirs of my childhood and with the hope of returning one day to my sweet nest. Alas! Some time later my family was ruined! ... Today, although leaving without regret, my family's situation rekindled my sorrow. Everything I had seen previously was there still but changed entirely by circumstances. I knew that in leaving the world I was doing something which was nothing special, but at the thought of having to be separated from my mother ... O my God! My heart wanted to stop beating in my chest. The more my feelings were drawn to the past, the more I saw my mother's sufferings. Everywhere I looked I could see only the picture of my mother, covered in perspiration and drying her tears. As regards my father, my greatest suffering was to see him indifferent to my

(742) mother's labours and to see him add to her tears by his conduct. My family was now ruined, but if my mother had not been there it would have been the death of the family! ... My heart tightened, and I could only say to the good God: 'Dear God, I am going to leave soon and leave my mother in this lamentable situation! ... O my God, if you understand my heart, give me a little strength so that I can pass, courageously, through this final trial.'

Wiping my tears with my hand, I went through the door to enter the house. My mother was waiting there, and she had just sent my sister Lê to buy some extra food from the market for the farewell dinner. My little sister Tế had been excused school and, at that moment, my father had not yet risen. Having just stepped on to the veranda, I found my mother seated and drinking a cup of hot tea. She understood immediately when she saw my eyes red and misty with tears and, probably to contain her own emotion, she got up, her cup of tea in her hand and went into the kitchen and stayed there to avoid me. I understood my mother very well and, somehow or other, I had to see her to say some words of farewell. So a moment later, with a nonchalant air and trying very hard to hide my feelings, I went into the kitchen. On seeing me my (743) mother asked me, calmly:

'Have you already been to say goodbye to the parish priest?'

'Not yet, mammy.'

I stood there for a moment and then approached to speak to her. But, once again she spoke to ask me:

'Are you still short of anything?'

'I have all I need, mammy, except a pair of shoes, which has not been bought yet.'

'A pair of shoes? What sort of shoes?'

'Leather shoes.'

'Heavens! I haven't a sou left!'

Seeing the tears gather in my mother's eyes I hurried to say to her:

'There's no problem, Mamma. I remember that yesterday my cousin Khê* gave me five piastres, and my uncle Nhượng and my aunts have also given me something for the journey. I think I'll take this amount to buy the shoes. As for the journey, if it is necessary I can go on foot to the monastery.'

'Where have you put this money?'

'I gave it to Nhất.'†

'Nhất has already given it to me and I have spent it all to have your clothes made.'

And she began to cry.

At that moment, instead of comforting my mother, I began to cry (744) also. Then, leaning our heads one against the other, we shed many tears. Shortly afterwards, not having the strength to stand up straight, I went to my bedroom and threw myself on my bed and cried. As for my mother, sitting on the edge of the veranda and still crying, she listed all the difficulties which stemmed from the family's poverty, and which made it impossible for her to look after me as she would have wished. Nhất arrived at this juncture and, seeing us both crying, could not understand. He came to my room to find out what it was all about. I replied to him, sobbing: 'I have no money left to buy shoes, and mammy is crying.' Nhất went straight away to the kitchen to comfort my mother and she soon regained her composure. As for me, I continued to cry until my father became angry and threatened to beat me. I

---

* Khê. It was in fact cousin Ngăm whose first child was Khê.
† Nhất was an adopted brother.

was then able to hold back my tears. Then **Nhất** came back to my bedroom and quietly reproached me: 'Your mother has enough on her plate already. You must not sadden her any more. If you were short of something, why didn't you tell me?' This provoked further tears, and I explained to **Nhất** what had happened. He comforted me and gave me twenty piastres, which was enough to buy a pair of leather sandals. After that he told me to go to the presbytery to take leave of the parish priest, and to stay there long enough for my mother to regain her composure.

(745)

I went to the parish priest's house and stayed there until eleven o'clock. My little sister **Tế** then came to look for me for dinner. The parish priest, Father Joseph **Cầm**, gave me money for the journey. The catechist also had pity on my family's poverty, especially after having heard of the moving scene which had just taken place between my mother and me. Everyone helped me, more or less, in giving me something for my minor expenses. I would like, here, to express my gratitude to Father **Cầm** the parish priest and his assistants who, not content to help me, had always kept a watchful eye out for my family.

On my return to the house I saw my mother disentangling some silk on the veranda. I noticed that her blouse was damp from tears, and that they continued to flow on her chest each time that she blinked her eyes. Knowing that I had returned, my mother did not raise her eyes as she would normally do.

(746)

Nhất had gone to sell remedies at the market while my sister **Lê** was in the kitchen preparing the meal. On my return to the house I went immediately to check my luggage to make sure nothing was missing, and I stayed there until dinner. I went on tiptoe two or three times to see if my mother was still crying, since I had to say some words of farewell to this incomparable mother. But I would only have the courage to do so when my mother had recovered. Each time that I went close, I saw that she was still crying, and that from time to time she took out her crucifix to kiss it while murmuring some words. Overwhelmed with pain, I dared not cry any more for fear of causing her even more sorrow. So I returned to my room to say the rosary. I had the feeling that my prayer was meaningless. I could only think of both of our sorrows, my mother and me. I was agitated, incapable of standing or of sitting peacefully. I was behaving like a man who had lost his mind. When I wanted to sit I had hardly done so when I must stand up again

(747)

to walk, not being able to do anything else than to walk up and down in this dark room ... It is necessary to have lived the experience, it is necessary to have shed tears as the time of farewell approaches, to understand the grief of a soul at the time of departure.

Eleven o'clock: the farewell meal

The family meal was ready. I don't know why, but when my mother came to the table her face had changed completely. Her countenance was beaming, and showed an extraordinary joy. She made me sit beside her. During the meal she talked of the acts of self-denial prevalent in the religious life. She did not know exactly the Redemptorist rule concerning abstinence but she made some conjectures. 'Perhaps this is the last meal when you will eat meat. Who knows if from now onwards you can still eat it? Whatever, from now on you must make this commitment: "I accept cheerfully without complaint or demand the abstinence which will be imposed on me, later, by the rule of the congregation."'   (748) My mother allowed me to take a drop of alcohol on that day, as my father had already poured me a glass. Thanks to the watchful eye of my mother, I was never in the habit of taking alcohol. I left mine, therefore, to my father. Everyone was happy during the meal, and not a word was said to sadden the proceedings. Each one took it upon himself to distract the others from any sombre thoughts. My father, above all, did not stop telling amusing stories about the time of my childhood for the entertainment of all the family.

I got ready for the journey once the meal was over. My mother took it upon herself to accompany me to the jetty. I was very pleased with this privilege, and I was counting on this walk of seven kilometres to find an opportunity to open my heart to her and to express my gratitude. At the time of the farewells when I bowed my head to take leave of my father and brothers and sisters, I was very anxious and uneasy. I said goodbye in a choking voice and then I left, shedding many tears. My mother, carrying my luggage, left first and waited for me at the door; probably because she did not wish to witness my words which were stifled by emotion. When I left, seeing me sobbing, she said to me   (749) immediately: 'There, there! offer it all to the good God. Goodbyes are never without deep regrets ...' Then we took the road in silence, my mother ahead and me behind.

My mother, having nothing to say, began to say the rosary when we cleared the village gate. She took a short cut in the hope of avoiding questions from passers-by, and we could pray in a more relaxed manner. Once the five decades were finished silence reigned again. We walked by the side of the paddy fields. My mother continued to walk in front, and seemed to be praying quietly. We were able to walk side by side when we entered the village of Thị-Mão as the path was wider. It was then that my mother gave me her final words of advice in a trembling voice which betrayed her deep emotion. She counselled me above all to remain strong in my vocation right to the end, despite all the difficulties and trials I might encounter. I do not know when my mother has learnt these things, but this is what she said to me: 'A vocation is a very precious grace which the good God gives only once. If we refuse it, try as we might, we will never regain it. It is like a king who would ask for the hand of a poor girl from the country. If this girl realises that this is a very special favour coming to her from the king's bounty, could she not accept it? But if she refused it, later, come what may, she could not regain it; it would no longer be possible. The king, having suffered one refusal, would have chosen someone else for his queen. It is the same with the religious life. When one has refused to accept the Lord's call he gives this precious favour to another soul so he who has lost it will no longer be able to buy it back at any price.'

Little by little, my mother went on to the observance of the rule and gave me this advice: 'Never act against the will of God. This reveals itself in the rule, the customs of the community and in the superiors. Consequently, you must resign yourself to suppressing your own will in order to follow the will of God. Nothing would dishonour me more than to see you return to the world one day for not having known how to obey your superiors. When you were at **Quảng-Uyên** I heard that you were guilty of such a fault. But when you returned home I did not believe that you had acted in such a manner. I hope that you have really decided that for all your life you will never follow your own will, but only God's will. Remember, God only gives peace to those who search for his will and conform to it. This has been my experience many times. Everyone in the village knows that I have had to put up with great difficulties, but no one can understand how I can remain so joyful and manage to live in peace. Always remember my advice; never distance yourself from the path that the holy will of God has designed for you. If you wish finally to have peace and happiness, follow this path where the Lord is, always, and you will enjoy his protection.'

Having cleared the village of Thị-Mão and climbed the side of the dyke, we had walked a good distance when my mother stopped, gave me my luggage, and then, putting her hand on my shoulder, she looked at me with her eyes full of tears and, her voice shaking more than usual, she said to me: 'My child here we are close to the jetty. I'll stop here and wish you a pleasant journey. Remember the advice I've just given you . . . Pray a lot for me.' My mother began to sob with these words. I lowered my head silently, allowing my tears to flow freely. Then my mother added: 'How much more suffering will the family have to put up with because of your father? . . . Nevertheless . . . I accept everything cheerfully as it is a gift from God . . . I am relying a lot on your prayers. Ask the good God to give me more courage. Ask him, above all, for your father's conversion . . . I am letting you go in the hope that you will be an invigorating force

(750)

(751)

(752)

for the family and for me in particular. My child, being separated from you is causing me much suffering. From now onwards I no longer count on seeing you again! . . . But since God wishes it, it is with a cheerful heart that I am letting you go in peace! . . .'

I wiped my eyes and then, going close to my mother I said to her: 'Mammy, I beg your forgiveness for all my shortcomings and for all the pain I have caused you since my childhood until now . . .' Then, after sobbing a moment, I wished to continue but she prevented me, saying   (753) in a firm voice: 'I understand. That's enough! Go my child, I understand you . . .'

I put my travel bag on my back, saluted my mother by doffing my cap sadly and set off. After covering a dozen metres I looked round to see if my mother had already set off, but I saw her sitting beside the dyke, her face in both hands. Guessing that she was about to cry, I felt as if my legs were broken and unable to move . . . I walked a further few dozen metres and then, turning round again, I saw my mother sitting there in the same place but this time her eyes were following me. I again doffed my cap in acknowledgement, then, still looking at her, I began walking backwards. Seeing this my mother shouted to me to hurry up so as not to miss the bus, but she could not help giggling as, in walking backwards, I had almost fallen. Once I'd gone a fair distance I saw a group of buffalo-herdsmen running from the paddy field to bar my route and threaten me: I turned round, looking for my mother to ask her help, but she was already on her return path. Seeing that, I called for the people of the village to help me; from a distance, my mother,   (754) seeing that something unpleasant was happening, retraced her steps. The group of buffalo-minders surrounded me. One of them threw himself on me and grabbed my bag. Another, armed with a stick, held it at my mouth, saying: 'Be quiet or you're dead!'

Then they quickly questioned me:

'Where are you from?'

'From Ngăm-Giáo.'

'Who are your parents?'

'Mr and Mrs Liệt.'

Some young girls who were there intervened with these boys, saying:

'Come on, let him go. He's Mrs Liệt's child. She's a very good person who would never allow her son to intimidate you.'

Another young man made this threat:

'He is one of those lads from Ngăm, one of those Catholics who threaten everyone they meet. He can pay for the others!'

'I know nothing of what you're talking,' I said to him. 'Besides, have you ever seen me take part in rough games of that sort? The lads who   (755) threatened you are rogues without any education.'

'That's true,' said a young girl. 'Mrs Liệt's son has never behaved in such a bad way. Come on, let him go. Formerly my father often worked for this lady and he has never complained of being badly treated by her. That's enough, friends, let him go.'

Another young girl, coming back from the fields and being familiar with my story, made a detour to approach. On seeing me she cried out: 'Oh, it's Van, Mrs Liệt's son, who wants to become a Catholic priest. Why are you threatening him? Let him go for fear that heaven takes revenge, to our misfortune.' I heard my mother's voice behind me who cried out to the band of buffalo-minders: 'I am going to call the mayor to ask him to send a patrol to grab hold of this band, just as they deserve.' The boys all sneaked away on hearing this. As for the young girls, they begged my mother not to go to the village to call the mayor. They then added: 'But who would dare to threaten Van? It would be pure madness, since heaven would avenge it.'

(756)　　Once the group had dispersed I continued slowly on my way. I turned round after a certain distance and saw that my mother was still talking to the young girls of a short while ago. She wore an eloquent expression as if she were giving them a lesson of some kind. I doffed by cap to say farewell and she waved her hand telling me to walk quickly in order not to miss the bus. I turned once again a short distance further on, to see if she had gone back. The young girls walking beside me had escorted me up to the road which leads to the jetty. Before retracing their steps they said to me as a kind of farewell: 'We haven't done you any harm. You won't ask heaven to punish us, will you?' Then they cursed the buffalo-minders: 'Gang of good-for-nothings who have the audacity to bully the child of such a good person!'

As for me, I thanked the good God, because as I arrived at the landing stage a small boat was crossing the river, and the bus was actually waiting for the latest crossing before leaving. I went through Bắc-Ninh and arrived at Cẩm-Đường, the village where Father Nhã was born. After a night spent at the presbytery I caught the train for Hanoi very early the next morning, so as to present myself at the monastery.

(757)　　## Disappointment

16 July 1944. That morning I assisted at Mass and received communion fervently to celebrate the feast of Our Lady of Mount Carmel. I asked the Blessed Virgin to introduce me into a stable religious life and to help me to live there intimately with Jesus her Son, in conformity with the advice which my mother had given me the preceding day. I went to ring the doorbell at the 'blessed prison'* at about nine o'clock in the

---

* The Redemptorist monastery at Hanoi.

morning. Father Maurice Létourneau came and greeted me in a kind manner, but he could not hide his disappointment on seeing me still so small. In spite of this he questioned me in a cheery manner:

'Are you the one from Hữu-Bằng with whom I had arranged a meeting?'

'Yes, Father; I'm the one.'

'How old are you?'

'I'm sixteen.'

Father shook his head several times, smiled, and said to me jokingly:

'You are exaggerating a bit, if I'm not mistaken.'

'Father, I wouldn't dream of deceiving you.'

Father Létourneau, opening the parlour door, asked me: 'Did (758) anyone come with you?'

'No, Father, nobody was able to come with me, as we live a long way away, and my family is poor so I had to come alone.'

Without questioning me further, Father Létourneau opened the parlour door and then opened the interior door and led me into the monastery. When this door closed behind me it felt as if my boat had reached its port. Who would have guessed! Father Létourneau took me upstairs to meet the Father Rector who at the time was Father Pamphile Couture. Not finding him in his room he went into the office of the magazine *Our Lady of Perpetual Succour* where he was chatting with several fathers, and there I was interrogated for a second time.

On seeing me, Father Rector and all the fathers present were astonished at my small stature and could only exclaim: 'He is far too small.' Then Father Rector asked me:

'How old are you?'

'I'm sixteen, Father.'

Shaking his head he said:

'You were probably baptised four years before you were born.' (759)

The fathers burst out laughing. Myself, I had to hold back my laughter, but I was more ashamed than amused. Father Rector continued:

'Have you done any studying yet, and passed any exams?'

'I have studied since my childhood, Father, and I got my certificate of primary studies four years ago.'

'Do you know any French?'

'I have studied it a bit, Father, but I am not very proficient in that language.'

'If you wish, I shall register you in the Juniorate at Huê where you can continue your studies and later, God willing, you will become a priest.'

At this point I remembered the words of my sister Saint Thérèse who had told me one day that I would not be a priest. Faced with the gener-

ous proposal of Father Rector leaving me to choose, I said to myself:
'No matter what, I have to choose between two alternatives. If I tell him
that I accept his proposal I am deceiving him, since I know that I will
never become a priest. If, on the contrary, I don't accept, Father Rector
will send me back home and I will have to wait until I am big enough
to be admitted.' At that moment my mind was like a skein of tangled
silk. I did not know which solution to choose. Suddenly, on raising my
eyes, I saw the crucifix hanging on the wall of the room. My eyes filled
with tears but I had the courage to reply to Father Rector:

'Father, God does not want me to become a priest.'

'Why dare you say that?'

'Father, I was pursuing that path, but along the way the good God
made known to me that I must follow another way and he indicated this
monastery to me.'

'It's very good that you were able to know God's will so clearly as you
say. I can truly put you among the souls who live very close to God. But
I regret very much not being able to admit you immediately as an aspirant lay brother. You would probably not be able to put up with this life.
Accept having to return to the world for some time yet so as to become
stronger and grow a bit because, at the moment, you are too small.'

'Yes Father, but the atmosphere of the world cannot make me grow
a single millimetre. I can say with certainty that it cannot but make me
even weaker, and it is possible that I may die before the day of my
admission into the community. I beg you to have pity on me and receive
me now. Don't be afraid to give me any kind of work no matter how
painful. With God's grace I will be able to handle it.'

Father Rector remained thoughtful after I had finished speaking. A
father who was sitting in a corner reading a paper let slip these words:

'Let's face it, your voice hasn't broken yet. A boy like you would not
be able to carry a pick-axe handle ... So what good would you be?'

'That is true, Father, but I did say "with God's grace".'

It was only later that I learned that the priest was Father Sirois.
Father Létourneau interrupted me and gave me a sign to follow him.
He led me to his room and questioned me on the route I had to follow
to get to my village. He then gave me five piastres and said to me: 'Have
the patience to obey the superiors and let the good God sort things out.
Go home, work for a living and I will let you know immediately when
Father Rector agrees to admit you.' I could no longer hold back my
tears on hearing these words. Taking my bag I followed Father
Létourneau to the parlour while still crying like a child. Father, still in
a good mood, wished me a pleasant journey in a friendly manner. I had
hardly left the parlour when it began to pour with rain as if the sky
wanted to share my sadness.

Three months of waiting

I returned home with a broken heart and without being able to stem my tears. If this situation must last, all I could do was to hope to live until the day when I would have the happiness of entering religion. I should not have cried since I recognised that it was the will of God. The more I realised this the more my tears flowed. I was really sad! ... However, once back home and after a difficult time, I regained my optimism and my courage thanks to my mother's encouragement. It was precisely at this time that Thérèse came to comfort me and encourage me to follow (763) my vocation right to the end.

On hearing that I had to return home and that I still had a long time to wait, my father did not appear unhappy, and he suggested sending me to Father Nhã to ask him to allow me to pursue my studies as before. My mother was in favour of this solution at first, but later on thinking it over, and especially on seeing that it was very painful to me, she asked my father to forget it. She then busied herself with my return to the Fathers, because she was afraid that in keeping me at home my father might decide to change his mind which would have been even more painful.

This problem was hardly solved when another one arose. The devil made use of this time of weariness to come and disturb me. He suggested a reason to make me believe that my request to join the Redemptorists was pure illusion and based partly, on egotism. This crisis arose because some months previously I had been with a friend on pilgrimage to the chapel of Our Lady of Thái-Hà. Availing ourselves of the opportunity, we went to the parlour to visit a brother we knew. (764) As I wished to enter the Redemptorist Congregation I did not waste the opportunity to question this brother on the religious life and, in particular, on the Redemptorist model. Here is a brief summary of his reply: 'There is nothing difficult at the Redemptorists. The life is simple and comfortable. The cuisine is French and the work is compatible with one's strength,' ... etc. When he learned that I wished to enter the Redemptorists he was not greatly enthralled, and to put me off said to me: 'You won't be up to it ...' I was ashamed of this brother on that day who, although being a religious, spoke only of food. To eat French cuisine! This idea impressed people ordinarily because a lot of butter and meat was involved ... etc. That is why on hearing the brother talk of the French diet I felt a little ashamed that religious ate 'French style'.

On our return to Hữu-Bằng my companion repeated this story to everyone: 'The Redemptorist life consists only in eating in the style of the French.' So the catechists and young lads made fun of me, saying: 'You will soon be joining a community where French is spoken, where

(765) food is eaten as the French eat it, where you will give yourself the discipline as the French do, and where absolutely everything is French! So from now on you must try to act like a Frenchman.' I must admit that this teasing made me feel ashamed. This story of eating 'French style' finally reached my father's ears, so my determination to enter the Redemptorists and no other congregation prompted him to scold me: 'Do you want to enter the Redemptorists so that you can eat like the French?' However, the reasons that I subsequently gave were able to quash these false notions.

One night, however, when weariness was preventing me from sleeping, the devil made use of this to tempt me once more. He brought back to my mind this idea of eating like the French in order to make fun of me. But he did it skilfully, so as to let me believe that it was not a temptation against my vocation. Consequently I could not stop mulling over the idea of entering religion to eat in the manner of the French. Then I began to feel ashamed and to question my motives. Finally I was going to give up on my plan to enter the Redemptorists for fear of getting the reputation of someone who enters religion for the pleasure of eating *à* (766) *la française*. Unfortunately, during this night of silence I dared to risk taking such a decision without consulting Thérèse, my beloved sister, who was always at my side. Fortunately, at this moment of madness, Thérèse spoke up, revealing clearly the trick that the devil was plotting against me, her unhappy little brother, and she ordered me to reject these thoughts. She spoke to me in a firm voice, thus: 'Little brother, I am not reproaching your lack of faith, but I am not hesitating to tell you that you are very foolish; instead of occupying yourself with what deserved your attention, you go over in your mind things which have no foundation and which can only disturb you. Listen to me carefully. Reject these unreasonable thoughts. Don't be so naïve as to base your judgement of a religious community on the testimony of a brother who has not a hint of the religious spirit. If this brother is happy to enter religion because one eats like the French, too bad for him. A religious who looks only for the pleasure of eating is an idle religious, a religious in name or, worse still, a religious corpse. The happiness of the reli- (767) gious life does not consist in eating *à la française* as you will be able to judge easily once you have entered. You will find by experience if the French meals in the monastery are as tasty as those you are used to. You can compare them when you have entered. The important thing is, never to ask for French or Vietnamese dishes. Accept whatever is the food of the monastery, whether it is French or Vietnamese. That is the business of the one who prepares the meals. Don't listen to the devils who scorn you in your imagination and do not be at all ashamed. In fact the devils already know to what extent the French food in the community is salty, bland or succulent. What they want is, simply, to get you agitated, and make you lose your peace, so as to lead you to act against God's will. So, don't be afraid. Listen to me; reject this thought and then you will gain a complete victory.

'Don't be surprised, either, to see a religious whose only preoccupation is the table, and who only speaks of mounds of food. His is an isolated case, but later you will see many others who, if they are not as well fed as they would wish, can never accept things without complaining. Once again, don't let it surprise you. Simply put these religious in (768) the ranks of the idle, a sort who are religious only in their habit ... etc. And if the good God still tolerates these religious in his house, it is because he wishes to try the patience of the holy religious. God always wishes, of course, to see them become his worthy children, but the greater number of religious who have this fault find it difficult to correct themselves, even if they are the subjects of miraculous intervention. At most one can still forgive them if they have a small amount of good faith, if they acted unintentionally. But how much merit they lose! So, my dear little brother, rest in peace. I am giving you a kiss, and I want you to face the future with courage. Don't forget, tomorrow; tell your parents frankly that you are still resolved to join the Redemptorists and nobody else.'

The next morning, I followed my holy sister's advice to the letter, never suspecting that things would be resolved so quickly. Some days earlier my mother was still undecided, but later, seeing the firmness of my resolution, she immediately agreed with me and said to me: 'That's good ... Go there. Since God wishes you to make this decision it is also my wish. I will accept his holy will completely, whatever it might be.' (769) She sent me once again to Hanoi two weeks later to present myself to the monastery with a letter which made me entirely the responsibility of the community. This time neither my mother nor I shed a single tear at my departure. Nevertheless my mother was worried, fearing that once again the Fathers might refuse to accept me. This would have placed us in a still more critical situation, but we both had a firm confidence in the protection of our Mother Mary.

I presented myself to the monastery on 1 August 1944, and I gave the letter to Father Létourneau. The latter, after having taken note of it, told me to find lodging in the caretaker's house at the entrance to the courtyard. The next morning, 2 August, ignorant of the fact that it was the feast of the founder of the Redemptorists, and not knowing, either, that it was that morning the ceremony of profession of some members of the choir, I heard morning Mass and I then went straight to the Carmel chapel of Hanoi to cry and sigh near Saint Thérèse, the only sister of my soul. When I came back to the caretaker's house it was

(770) already past midday, and I had not a mouthful of rice to satisfy my hunger. Furthermore, I hadn't a sou to buy a snack. Towards three o'clock the brother in charge of the gardens, (Philippe Cơ) on the instructions of Father Létourneau, invited me to work in the garden. I felt very tired because I had eaten nothing since morning, and the previous evening having only ten sous, I had eaten only a small amount. So I had to admit frankly: 'Father, I'm a little tired ...'

I did not know how to distinguish at that time between priest and brother. That first time that I met Brother Gardener I was really surprised to see a priest become angry so easily. Hardly had he heard me say that I was tired than he rolled his eyes and said to me: 'Hm! You ask to enter religion but when you are told to work you complain of being tired. In that case I'll show you the door and there'll be no more question of religion.' On hearing these words I began to tremble and tears came to my eyes and I even allowed some to escape. I then felt a little ashamed because I heard laughing behind me. Seeing that, Brother Philippe glared at me again with his frightening eyes. Then he told me to hurry to the garden: 'Get a move on! Why, are you rooted to the spot? ...' I answered, 'Yes.' Then, taking my bag, I followed him

(771) to the garden. I had to steel myself to hold back my tears, all the more so because at that moment I was like a lost child haunted by the memory of his mother. The Brother led me across the community garden and took me into a building which served as a granary for the rice. After having climbed a ladder, I found myself on a floor where there was some free space. Then he told me:

'This is your lodging. Do you understand?'

'Yes, Father.'

I will never get over seeing Father with such a frightening appearance. He then gave me the following instructions:

'An old servant also lodges here. He is working at the moment. This evening you can prepare together a place where you can sleep. As for you, I will leave you to rest this afternoon.'

'Thank you, Father.'

And the brother turned round to climb down. Happily, as he was about to descend, he turned towards me and asked: 'By the way, have you eaten yet?'

'Not yet, Father.'

'You've had nothing since morning?'

'Nothing.'

'I don't believe it. You're already a great saint! ... Good. Sit down

(772) here, and I'll go to the kitchen and get you a little rice to eat.'

I turned round once the brother had left, and I looked in vain for a place to sit. The loft above my head was full of spiders' webs. The floor was covered with dirty straw scattered with mouse droppings and cock-roaches, and gave off an odour of rat holes. There was also a confused pile of broken objects which had been stuffed into a dark corner. As for any openings, I noticed that there were two windows: one in front with two shutters, and a smaller one at the back with only one shutter. As soon as I was brought into this attic, the brother, pointing at the big window, made this prohibition: 'It is forbidden, absolutely, to no matter whom, to open this window. Do you understand? If you want some air you may only open the window at the back.' Then, turning the lock, he opened the little window. The slats of the shutters were covered with a layer of dust so thick that it was impossible to recognise the colour of the paint. All that could be said was that the shutter was dust-coloured!

Although a little hesitant I decided to place my bag on the floor and then, pulling out a handkerchief, I brushed away the thickest dust (773) which was sticking to the window frame, and I sat there waiting for the rice. I glanced round the room once again, searching for a means to arrange things so that it was nice and clean, at least to accommodate two beds and to unpack my luggage. I was still reflecting on this when Brother Philippe climbed the stairs and handed me a dish of rice. I say a dish of rice to give it a bit of dignity, but in reality it was a mess-tin full of rice mixed with all sorts of food that one could call a 'mixture of varied dishes'. Handing me this plate, Brother said to me: 'Here, eat!' He was about to leave but, reaching the steps, he turned round to say to me: 'When you've eaten you can go into the garden and call the old fellow, Ẩu the servant, so that he can come and prepare the place with you. Do you understand?'

I had not yet got over my astonishment on seeing that a priest had such manners in speaking like that which, according to my upbringing seemed impolite if not downright rude. I did not yet understand how a (774) priest could speak in that fashion, so hard on the ears. Nevertheless, I made an effort to put up with everything, realising that at this time I was taking the most difficult step. The trial from the world was already over … I had victoriously overcome all the major difficulties, such as the farewells to my family, to reach this difficult passage, this suffering which tortured me internally without showing itself on the outside. I made the sign of the cross and said my grace and then, taking the dish of rice, I began to eat. I had to make an effort to hold back my tears whilst eating, but at the same time I had to smile on recalling that meeting with the brother who had told me that in the monastery only French cuisine was eaten! I was now tasting for the first time in the community, meals in the French style, and my impression was that it would be necessary to have an extraordinary spirit of mortification to enjoy meals *à la française* served in the Redemptorist community.

From this day until my admission as a postulant I ate in this manner, French style. The only difficulty was that, in the weeks that followed, I had to eat, together with the old servant, a mixture of all kinds of food served up in a soup tureen. Each of us, provided with a 'French spoon' took from the dish and brought the food to the mouth. It sometimes happened that there was only one spoon between us. We then ate alternately. After the meal we drank, in turn, mouthfuls of water contained in an earthenware carafe. This was our only dessert! Today, when thinking of these meals *à la française* I want to laugh and cry. It often came to my mind to write to my mother to tell her of my 'French style' meals, but I did not breathe a word for fear of making her sadder.

(775)

Once I'd finished my first French meal, I went to the garden in obedience to Brother Gardener to search for the old servant to prepare the lodgings. The garden stretched in all directions, but I had only been to where I had been led, that is, around the granary. Now I managed to get myself further acquainted. There was a coal cellar under my lodgings and at the side there was a hen house. At the side of the courtyard there were two banana tress that I had not noticed before. I then made a tour behind my lodgings where there was a long ditch* full of muddy water, which exuded a penetrating odour painful to put up with, because of the filth which came from the stable. On the other side of this little canal was a huge paddy field with, in the distance, an isolated village which had nothing of the romantic about it. I stood there for a moment, and I looked at the surroundings of my lodgings; I felt invaded suddenly by a sadness and a painful nostalgia for my family, and my sole desire was to return to them.

(776)

While I was in such a weary and indecisive state I heard Brother Philippe calling me from the granary.

'Van, Van, where are you?'

'Here I am.'

I ran to him and I saw that Brother had already called Ău the old servant. When I climbed up, Brother, both hands on his hips, gave us our work.

'Now then, start and make this room clean immediately, so that you can both sleep here this evening.'

Then he showed us how to put such a thing in such a place ... etc. In the end we prepared absolutely nothing since Brother decided that the old servant would lie on the bamboo rack covering the 'paddy'†, and he ordered me to place a piece of a door over an old bath tub, and then, pointing, he said:

(777)

---

* This narrow ditch was usually dry but became full temporarily after a shower.

† Paddy, i.e. rice not yet husked.

'That's your bed, all right?'

As for my luggage and clothes, Brother threw them into the rice storeroom so that the mice would not nibble at them! So, after Brother had ordered us to prepare the loft it remained just as it was before, without even a single spider's web being disturbed!

The old servant, peering at me from the corner of his eye, crossed his arms and said to the brother:

'Then, Brother, is it necessary to arrange anything?'

'Oh! . . . If it's not necessary leave things as they are.'

Then, apathetic, he withdrew, as if unaware of his indifferent attitude towards us. Until then I thought I was dealing with a Father but on hearing the old servant say 'Brother' I understood that he was a brother. And I had not yet recovered from my astonishment when the brother, hearing me call him 'Brother' was much harsher towards me than when, by mistake, I gave him the title of 'Father'. If I called him 'Father' he was very happy, and I got all I asked for. I then recalled the (778) words of Saint Thérèse that I heard one night: 'You will meet many brothers whose behaviour is totally bizarre, and totally at odds with the religious spirit.'

So, even before my entry into religion, I had already met two different specimens. The first found life easy in the congregation because of the French cuisine, and the second, with the airs of a great mandarin, loved to be called, respectfully, 'Father'. When one spoke to him it was necessary to use formal language, and to maintain a modest demeanour as if one were dealing with an important personage. These were two precious experiences, because if the good God had not allowed me to eat French cuisine in the manner and circumstances I described earlier, and if he had not allowed it that I receive orders in arrogant and harsh terms as I have just related, I do not know if I would ever have tasted such experiences. These were two precious experiences that God gave me and it is his precious heart which so arranged to grant them to me.

That night, obeying Brother Philippe, I lay on the piece of rough door, despite old Âu's suggestion not to sleep in the loft, where there (779) were many mice who would not neglect to tease me all night and prevent me from sleeping. The old servant carried his mat to the foot of the staircase to the section where the rice was shelled. I did not want to follow old Âu's advice, because I wanted to obey Brother completely. But the old servant's predictions came true to the letter. The mice prevented me from sleeping all night long. Not a single one was to be seen during the day, but as soon as the sun had disappeared behind the row of bamboos, mesdames the mice came out for the dance. They ran around and entertained themselves noisily all night. Those who were not dancing went in search of food. That night the entire village of mice was greatly astonished and they asked themselves where this man-sized prey came from that they noticed in their kingdom. They competed with each other to taste him. Alas, what a pity for their unfortunate prey! Hardly had he tensed up his legs which were bitten by a mouse, than he had to lift up his head because another was clawing his ears. He then felt a rat crossing across his stomach, and another, clinging to the shirt on his back, climb on to his head and swish his face with its tail

(780)   before sneaking away somewhere! ... O my God! it was really horrible! So much so that I had to have recourse to the names of Jesus and Mary and ask for the intervention of my guardian angel to recover a little calm. Without doubt it was a sleepless night!

I spoke about it the following day to Brother 'Site Manager' Philippe, and I asked him to show me some other place where I could sleep, but because inadvertently, I had simply called him 'Brother' he just stared at me and said:

'If you don't want to sleep there, sleep wherever you want.'

'Yes, Brother, with your permission I'll attend to it.'

He looked at me without saying a word, and went out grumbling. Therefore for the second night I had to follow Mr Ấu and go to sleep beside the rice-husking basin; but even there sleep was not easy because the scourge of mice was followed by that of mosquitoes. I could only defend myself when I was awake, or during periods of insomnia.

(781)   Nevertheless, when I was exhausted, even though the mosquitoes tried hard, I slept well in spite of their efforts. And if their stings upset me it was only the next day that I felt any pain. Because of these stings the skin on my face became rough like that of a leper, but it was a strange thing: I was still alive, I had no fever, and I remained as joyful as usual.

Now and again, when I appeared to be ignored or when I was criticised too harshly I felt sad and thought of my family. But at these moments my sister Thérèse came again to comfort me, and I found again peace and joy. As I have just said, the thought of having no value made me nostalgic for my family, and promoted the wish to return, since, in spite of its great poverty, I always found there a mother's warm affection. Here, in the space of two-and-a-half months, although living close to the Fathers and Brothers of the community, I have not heard a gentle word, nor met any evidence of an affectionate attitude which would have proved that an authentic and shining charity reigned in the

(782)   monastery. For me this happened only two or three times a week when I met the smile of Father Létourneau who came to get my news. That apart, everything added to my interior suffering and increased my tears.

When I first stepped into the rice loft I was startled, believing that I would find it very difficult to live there. Undecided at certain times,

I asked myself if I could tolerate such a situation for very long, but I was soon able to get over all these material difficulties fairly easily. After a week I was no longer put off by the sickening smell, nor the dampness, nor the uncleanliness which existed inside and around the loft. I had got used to it. Not all, not even many, but some of the brothers knew only how to pick on me and threaten me each time they met me, and to make me sense their deep antipathy towards me, so that fear and anxiety were added to the already painful sadness of my situation; so I ended up by thinking: 'I shall definitely not enter the Redemptorists. If the good God has pity on me I will ask to go to another community.'

Thérèse had to speak up and encourage me strongly in these critical (783) times, and it is thanks to her that I have been able to remain faithful to my vocation up till now. In spite of this, not a day passed that I did not shed tears. I was afraid of sharing my problems with anyone, so I was forced to hide them. This is why I did not make clear to Father Rector or Father Létourneau the state of my soul. I was resigned to putting up with it alone. Then on Sundays, when I could go to the Carmel, I opened my heart to Thérèse who, in fact, was the only person to whom I could confide my feelings.

A miracle: my boat reaches port

During this long period of two-and-a-half months trials did not cease to flow like so many waves pushing my little boat far from port. After having struggled for so long against the storm, it was as if my heart was submerged in an ocean of tears. They were the flavour of my life day and night. I lived among tears and I even only tasted joy in tears. My (784) pitiful state led the good God to take pity on me, and to shorten the time of waiting which had been imposed on me. An exceptional favour was necessary to facilitate my admission into the community. I obtained this extraordinary favour, and to me it's a miracle.

When Father Rector had sent me back to the world some months ago, he had said to me: 'You must wait two years before I can admit you.' However, only a little over three months had passed from the day when Father Rector had imposed this condition until the day when in fact I had been admitted as a postulant. Three months is not all that long; but in fact I was admitted after that time. If that is not an exceptional favour or, better still, a miracle, how was it that the Father Rector could change his mind so easily? My Father, so that you can see things clearly, let me relate this miracle to you.

In the month of October 1944 I heard it said that preparations were under way to celebrate the feast of Saint Gerard,* the patron saint of the lay brothers of the congregation. I felt a force inside me which propelled me to prepare fervently for the celebration of this feast. All I knew of Saint Gerard was gleaned from certain extracts of his life in the review *Our Lady of Perpetual Succour.* I did not pay much attention to them, neither had I ever asked a favour of him. Since I had got to know Saint Thérèse, this dear saint apart, I did not know how to communicate with any other saint. If I had some favour to ask, if I found myself in need of something, I knew only to have recourse to Thérèse, and it was with her that I accomplished anything. But it was Thérèse's wish that I enter into relations with other saints, no matter who. She wanted me to have confidence in each one, and to ask their help with the same intimacy that I adopted with her. However, I felt a certain fear in putting this into practice, and I did not know how to attach myself to anyone; consequently, I counted on her for everything.

(785)

Thérèse said to me one day during this painful time: 'Little brother, you know that according to the conditions imposed by Father Rector you still have to wait twenty months before being admitted as a postulant into the community. Now, if you wish this period of time to be shortened soon, there is no better means than to turn to your big brother Saint Gerard. I am therefore advising you to ask him to intervene, so that Father Rector will change his mind and admit you soon into the community. Saint Gerard's feast is coming. Prepare yourself to celebrate it with fervour and ask him, straight away, to grant you the favour I have just suggested. Do not be afraid. If you ask you will certainly obtain. Normally saints are very easily moved; consequently, they never refuse the graces which are asked of them, above all, when it is a question of a saint who will soon be your big brother, your patron and whose little brother you will be. If he finds someone to pray for in you there is no doubt he will not delay in admitting you to the community. Go each day to tell him how you are suffering in your heart, tell him what you hope from him and ask him to come to your aid. Act sincerely as you do with me. Don't believe that among the saints in heaven there is only your Thérèse who knows how to ask for favours. How many saints, powerful over God's heart, regret that my little Van has not had recourse to their intercession.'

(786)

It was 16 October shortly after this and I was lacking any enthusiasm. I had hoped that that very day would see Saint Gerard's miracle, but ... absolutely nothing happened. What a disappointment! The fathers, the students and especially the brothers celebrated this feast with great rejoicing. I ardently long for this joy but I waited in vain all day without

(787)

* Saint Gerard Majella, a Redemptorist brother whose feast day is 16 October.

a sign of the Father Rector coming down to admit me to the community as I had asked of Saint Gerard. Therefore tears of sadness, not tears of joy, were shed. My midday banquet with Mr Âu lost a little of its charm. Even Thérèse herself had no wish to speak to me. It was a failure. A total failure! The whole thing had misfired. Could I have committed some fault? I had acted in all sincerity, whatever it might be. What more could I do?

I dwelt on these inconclusive thoughts while chewing over my sadness when, just as I was going to the church for Benediction, Thérèse broke her silence. She joked cheerfully with me: 'Ah, Van, my little brother! What, are you annoyed with me? This morning I had (788) intended to let you have the good news, but, being busy wishing my brother Saint Gerard a happy feast day it was impossible for me to do so. It seems that you want to lose heart already. Come now, why are you so easily discouraged? There's still the octave of the feast. Anyway, your brother Gerard being very busy this morning he could not effect immediately the miracle for you. But now he can. Therefore, during Benediction don't forget to remind him of the favour you have already asked for, all right? Tell him what you desire and if you don't forget, that will be sufficient.'

I followed to the letter this advice of my holy sister but I spoke to Saint Gerard in a threatening rather than a prayerful mood. I said to him: 'If you don't bring my boat to port very quickly, if you don't obtain the miracle that I am expecting from you very quickly, I may, perhaps, lose my vocation, and then I will put the blame on you.' Gerard was probably not afraid of this simplistic threat. Nevertheless, he had pity on me because he granted my request. October 17th passed without any (789) sign, just like the day before, and yet, just as I was preparing to go to church for Benediction, my sister Saint Thérèse said to me: 'Don't forget to go to the parlour today and, without being afraid, wish Father Rector a happy feast day and ask him to admit you into the community. You know, doubtless, that tomorrow is his birthday.'

'Yes, but ... to have to ask him again to admit me to the community really frightens me! Allow me to do nothing. I went to make this request last week and I was well and truly rebuffed ... If I now go again to make the same request ... I'll be in trouble!'

'Come on, little brother, why are you so frightened? There's no reason to be.'

'So, my sister, you speak for me.'

'If you want a miracle you must speak for yourself ... The miracle is there. Your brother Saint Gerard has already done it. All you have to do is go and say a few words to Father Rector and it's yours.'

'But, my sister, what should I say to him?'

(790)   'What should you say to him? Begin first of all by wishing him a happy feast day; then speak to him about your request to be admitted into the community. You can say to him, for example: "Reverend Father, tomorrow the fathers and brothers are going to celebrate with you. I regret not having the happiness, like them, of being in the house to wish you a happy feast as I would like to. At least allow me to offer you from the simplicity of my heart my feelings of affection, of gratitude and of filial piety. I know that, strictly speaking, I cannot yet be called a child of your community. Nevertheless that is what I wish with all my heart and I wait only for the opportunity to arrive, and I beg you to grant me this precious favour. For a week I have prayed a lot for this intention, that is to say, I have asked God that I may be admitted to the community on your feast day, and yesterday I also asked Saint Gerard to intercede for me and to obtain this favour for me. That is why, today, I dare make this request known to you! I think that the good God has already heard my request. But I am waiting for nothing more than a 'yes' on your part, and my wishes will be fulfilled."'

(791)   I understood completely the significance of this very moving congratulation. I then went to the parlour with a heart beating like someone who was about to appear before a tribunal. When I was in the Rector's presence I had not yet had the time to sort out all I intended to say when my eyes were already brimming two streams of burning tears. Seeing this, Father Rector was very affectionate towards me, and then, gently stroking my hair, he said to me benevolently: 'Enough! Don't cry any more. You have been thoughtful enough to wish me a happy birthday, and I thank you with all my heart. Furthermore, in view of your great desire for me to admit you to the community, I have been moved and I can no longer refuse you this favour. So it is with joy that I am welcoming you into the community this very evening.'

On hearing these words I uttered a cry of delirious joy. I wiped my tears quickly, and warmly thanked Father Rector. My childlike behaviour made him burst out laughing. He then tapped me on the cheek, saying:

'Ah, you've stopped crying; now your heart must be overflowing with happiness.'

'Yes, Father.'

(792)   'Good! So tomorrow you must remember to pray much for me.'

'Yes, Father.'

'Now, go and get things ready, and I must go and warn Father Létourneau to come to the parlour to welcome you.'

'Yes! Thank you, Father.'

Hardly had Father Rector gone into the community than, overcome with happiness, I ran towards my loft, crying, jumping and singing while clapping my hands. I said proudly to all the fathers and brothers I met: 'Father Rector has admitted me to the community! It's true, he's admitted me!' The last person I met was Brother Tuyên*, a student, who was standing before the granary. Seeing my state of ecstatic happiness he said to me: 'You are really like little Thérèse when she heard the news of her admission to the Carmel, and you are certainly as innocent as she.' This was strange, because I had never dared let anyone know of the friendly relations between Thérèse and me, and yet each time that he met me Brother Tuyên jokingly called me the little brother of Thérèse of the Child Jesus. Is it Thérèse who has made this secret known to him, or the good God who has allowed him to penetrate the depths of my heart? I don't know and I have never dared to question (793) him on the matter. All I know is that these conjectures concerning my intimacy with Thérèse were true.

From the moment when I learned of my admission, my happiness made me forget everything. I had even forgotten to thank Saint Gerard. It was only the following day that I thought of expressing gratitude for the miracle of the day before. It was only from this moment that my relations with Saint Gerard became as close as those with Thérèse. At six o'clock that evening Father Létourneau came to the parlour to welcome me. He was happy as I was but with this difference; he did not jump up and down, nor did he show, as I had done, any childish reaction. He took me through the same door I had passed through on the first occasion. Then, having led me into the 'blessed prison' he gave me a warm, brotherly embrace. A few minutes later the other confrères came to greet me affectionately so that I had the immediate feeling of having found solid support in them. I understood that without knowing them these men were not strangers to me, that there existed amongst them a genuine charity and that willingly united in this (794) house they were all brothers. I understood it especially on hearing Father Létourneau's words of welcome, when he said to me in his customarily cheery manner: 'From now on, my brother, you will no longer be a stranger; you will no longer be the little lad lodging in a corner of the community, you are now the child of this house and our confrère. Therefore, in future, we will have this charity and this sincere affection for you which will replace all the affection you enjoyed in the world. Our only wish is to see you persevere in the congregation.'

At that moment I could only reply to these moving words with a simple: 'Thank you, Father', accompanied by tears of emotion. I was taken to my room and everyone dispersed, leaving me alone with my new impressions. I had hardly entered my room when a feeling came

---

* Brother Tuyên later became a priest.

(795) to trouble my heart which was invaded by a vague melancholy ... I collapsed on my bed and my eyes wandered around the four walls of the room. It was thanks to this glance that I was able to find a comforter. There were there, hanging on the wall, a crucifix and four prints. Jesus on the cross had a desolate appearance; his head was leaning forward and showed his eyes full of tenderness which he was trying to keep half-open. This look expressed an ardent love. But at what cost! The saints represented on the four prints all had their eyes on me. Our Lady of Perpetual Succour especially looked at me lovingly as if she were following my slightest movement in the room. I felt a power in her glance which drew me and would also protect me against danger and sadness.

(796) The room became for me a fervent place after these thoughtful glances around its walls. I felt comforted straight away and I felt: 'I am not alone in this room, a whole family lives here in intimacy and charity looking on me with the most tender affection.' Cries of joy escaped again, my heart began to beat stronger and tears, drop by drop, flowed gently from my eyes. I cried because I felt loved. This thought again came to my mind: 'I shall certainly have to fight a lot, later, against suffering but in this room I shall find invisible hands and loving glances to console me and dry my tears.' Oh, what happiness! What overwhelming joy! From now onwards Love will be my life's only treasure. I believe no longer that to live in religion is to lead a life of painful restraint, an unhappy life deprived of freedom and of all which pleases us. No, it is not like this! On the contrary I have found in the religious life a source of happiness; I have obtained the highest level of freedom, and I have never suffered any refusal on the part of Love. My joy is to love and be loved, and I possess this joy perfectly at this moment, O my God, how precious is the joy of living in your house!' When night came I saw on my pillow a wooden cross without a Christ. I understood that

(797) the cross was the personal portion of each religious, and that night, gripping the cross joyfully against my heart, the cross which was my heritage, I slept the deep sleep of the blessed which only happened to me when I was immersed in Love.

I had not forgotten that 18 October, the rector's birthday, was also my feast day. When I went to greet him, Father Rector said to me in a joyful manner: 'Everybody considers today to be your feast day rather than mine, and I also feel the same. Do not forget, also, that the fathers and brothers feel a very kind regard for you.' There were even some brothers who maintained: 'It took a miracle to get Father Rector to change his opinion.'

This was quite true. My brother Saint Gerard had performed a miracle the previous evening for his little brother. If it was not a miracle, how can you explain in human terms that a week previously, when I had employed every means, even my tears, to beg Father Rector to admit me, he had stubbornly refused, telling me to wait, while yesterday evening, after having made known my request to him, he admitted me so joyfully? No, without a miracle I would never have been admit- (798) ted to the community. I heard one Father who, in praising my tenacity, affirmed: 'Even though it was said he would not be admitted, he has succeeded, nevertheless, in getting himself accepted.'

I heard many other compliments which succeeded only in bringing me closer to God. I understood in fact that if this praise had continued indefinitely it could not surpass the level of endurance that I had to show from the day when I recognised with certainty that I had a vocation to the Redemptorists. I even think it was right to be prouder still for having succeeded in overcoming so many obstacles. Today my boat has reached its port. The huge waves have been repulsed far away. I have reached the shore of happiness where I receive displays of affection, acclamation and congratulations, so it is truthfully not without reason that I feel a holy pride.

The religious life: the first crosses (799)

My Father, as you have seen I was admitted to the community at a time when no one expected it; so much so, that my confrères paid more attention to me than to others. It was probably because I was still young and of small stature that they were sorry for me. Perhaps also, seeing me naturally unaffected and sincere in my manners and words, they were inclined to interest themselves in me and to help me with their advice. Yes, it is probably because the brothers still found in me childish attitudes that they paid special attention to me in order to correct me. That is why I was very happy in the midst of my brothers, and it is thanks to this that a solid and durable family spirit was formed in me.

But was it only for this reason that I loved to live in the community, or at least was it to find an easier life there? Not at all. In truth God has permitted that I was treated with tenderness during a certain time so as to bandage the wounds of my heart after the long trial I had just (800) endured, and even more, to strengthen me for the trials to come, since, in this world, there are no heroes without heavy trials. God in his wisdom has so arranged it. All in all, my life as a postulant contained nothing special. Externally my life was calm like that of my confrères, or, if there were any differences, they consisted in my still retaining some childish imperfections. Once or twice I would sniffle in the presence of my brothers. It was really ridiculous but it seemed that God

wished it to be so to give me practice in humility. Even today, when I recall my behaviour as a postulant, I can't help laughing. In my soul, however, God has introduced me to a new life, to a life very different from the one I led in the world. He has also made known to me the way of perfection and the conditions for reaching holiness. I understood these things skimpily when I was in the world. But once in the commu-
(801)   nity, God has made me see clearly each step on the way and the storms I would be subjected to. He has neither spared nothing, so that I can clearly feel the depth of his love. Truly, I led a life which could only be described as a life of the Redeemer.

In no time at all, after having kissed each day the cross placed on my bed, I have understood the profound meaning of the life of a religious Redemptorist. I understood that the Redemptorist must live and die like the Divine Redeemer. Also, from this time I knew only to look at the life of Jesus the Redeemer to live my own. I realised, in reading the gospel, that the whole of the life of the Redeemer is summarised in a single thought: conformity to the will of his Father. 'My food is to do the will of him who sent me.'* 'I came down from heaven not to do my own will but the will of him who sent me.'† It springs from this that all the Redeemer's life is summarised in obedience to his Father. Now who would dare to assert that all Jesus' life has been unhappy? And who
(802)   would dare to say that it has been perfectly happy? No! No one would dare to make such a suggestion. According to the gospel Jesus' life was a mixture of joy and sadness, but he was not the one who had chosen, spontaneously, to be partly happy and partly sad. He has only accepted what came to him from the will of his divine Father. His whole life has been an act of humble submission to the will of the Father which encompasses all his work of redemption.

However, to submit perfectly to the will of his Father, what sufferings and insults has Jesus had to endure. 'He was obedient unto death, even to the death of the cross.'‡ It is with this simple sentence that Saint Paul summarises all the Redeemer's life, but this sentence contains all the meaning of his life. Being placed in the school of the Redeemer, my only wish was to lead a life like his. I knew also that reciprocal love was not content to live for the beloved, to live one for the other, but it wished also to conform its life to that of the one it loves. Only this
(803)   resemblance can satisfy love and create unity. Thus, day and night, I fixed my regard on the cross and I was happy each time that the good God sent me crosses in abundance. Truthfully, in my efforts to model

---

*   John 4. 34.
†   John 6. 38.
‡   Philippians 2. 8.

my life on that of my divine master, God has spared me nothing and I have been fulfilled beyond my desires.

You see by that, Father, to what extent I have been spoilt by God! After the dazzling smiles and the consolations which have delighted the days following my entry, I have seen, little by little, these sweetnesses change into tears. The difficulties I encountered did not last for only one day, but they continued until the day of my profession. As the day of my entry was characterised by a gentle friendliness so it then changed into bitterness. I realised in a short time that there was a disagreement among the confrères in my regard. One said: 'He is so small he does not deserve the name of Brother.' Another reproached me: 'How can you become a religious when you cry at the drop of a hat?' I heard, again, someone target me indirectly: 'There's no rule which allows children into the community.' I noticed, moreover, that there was only one among the postulants who was favoured with such exceptional treatment. People were not afraid to speak of me as of someone who has not yet reached the age of reason, and who was incapable of doing anything. Regarding the other postulants, no one dared to speak to them in this manner, but with me it was normal. How I have to thank the Lord! Thanks to this, I learned to know myself a little better, and consequently I have been able to keep my heart pure and sincere, showing that I submitted not through human respect but because God wanted me to submit, that I did it because it was his will.

I must recognise, however, that if the way I was treated made me cry, it was partly my fault, since, as I have already admitted, I still had some childish habits and, above all, I was not accustomed to manual work. There was certain work in the community that, formerly, I believed I could manage but which I must now keep clear of. I had hardly entered (805) the congregation the evening before, when, during the following day Father Létourneau assigned me to helping in the kitchen. This consisted in scrubbing the cooking pans, taking the ashes from the fireplace, and cleaning the floor. I thought that this was not hard work but, once I had started, I realised that it required a lot of effort. The work in itself was not difficult but, in spite of all my good will to do it well, it was never considered as being well done. People thought that I disliked work and I heard observations of this nature: 'He may well be small, but here we don't distinguish between big and small ...' 'If he wants to stay with us he will have to work like us ...' Or again, on seeing me very tired because of the effort I was expending, it was thought, incorrectly, that I was lazy. Perhaps! But in fact only God knows the effort I had to put into it. Here is an example which will help you to understand more easily all the application I had to bring to the work because I wished to be faithful to my duty.

(806) During three long months my only resolution after each meditation was this: 'Today I am going to try to clean the pans well, to make the floor shine and to clean the fireplace with great care, all for the love of Jesus.' Also, each time that I began work I asked Jesus and Mary to come to my assistance so that I could do my work with even more care. After three months, this work to which I brought all my attention, instead of being difficult, became very easy. Once used to the fatigue, once used to acting 'for the love of Jesus', my will had become submitted entirely to love. Each time that I found myself in front of a dirty pan, I did not have to deliberate any more, or find a means of carrying it without dirtying my hands, which required more time than just grabbing it immediately and washing it. Therefore, when I had work to do, I did it straight away, no matter how difficult, and after each victory of this kind I would say, sincerely and proudly to Jesus: 'Look, Jesus! isn't your Marcel* clever?' Neither did I forget at the same time to seek his help for the next occasion. I still felt happiness in my successes even

(807) though I had acquired the habit of work, although I could never be considered as someone who enjoys work. From time to time I heard such words as: 'What's the point in a lad like him becoming a religious? He's as lazy as a donkey and yet he presents himself to become a religious! . . .'

At the beginning such words hurt me a lot, but, later, Thérèse recommended this to me: 'Everyone is mistaken apart from the good God, so be patient, turn a deaf ear to these provocative words, and firmly believe that God knows profoundly the sincerity of your heart.' I also feared that Father Rector, giving credence to these remarks, would form a wrong opinion of me and send me back to the world. Then who would come to my defence? Thérèse reassured me: 'God himself who reigns in your heart is the first superior. This superior is never mistaken and supposing that the superior of the house is deceived, God possesses all the means necessary to correct his mistake.' In spite of this,

(808) there was a time when I was worried and afraid of Father Rector. But later I saw that he always had the same feelings for me as on the day of my admission into the community. He never betrayed the slightest evidence that he was looking for faults in me so that he could send me home, as was often said to frighten me. Consequently, instead of being afraid I had more confidence in him.

If I told you in detail, Father, all the struggles and vexations I had to face during my postulancy, you would certainly not have enough time to listen to me. I now remember having a difficulty that I have never told to anyone. There was one among the postulants who was endowed with a

---

* Van's name in religion, *Marcel de l'Enfant-Jésus.*

very bizarre personality, and who worked in the kitchen with me. In his relations with the brethren in the community he gave the impression of being a 'living saint', but with the postulants the opposite was the case, and if he saw someone he could intimidate, he showed this person no respect. Although he was admitted to the community barely two months before me, on seeing me enter he adopted an imposing posture and did all in his power to create problems for me; so well that, in my astonishment, I came to ask myself: 'How is it that in a community like the (809) Redemptorists such imposing self-importance can be allowed? It was like the "great mandarin" attitude that one meets in certain degenerate presbyteries.' In fact, the only time that this postulant had the nerve to 'lord it' over me was in a corner of the kitchen or in the coal cellar but, as soon as he found himself in the presence of some Brother he became as gentle as a lamb, without, for all that, ceasing to criticise me. It was he who cut me to the quick with such bitter words as: 'What a specimen! If I were the superior I would get rid of him immediately without a word of warning.' He was also skilful at spying on me so as to find me wanting and report me to the chief cook or another brother including, above all, Brother Bonaventure who was my 'guardian angel'. This latter was very strict in any matter concerning the observance of the rule. When anyone accused me of such or such a shortcoming, he corrected me immediately without a second's pause. I often shed tears of repentance because of this for faults of whose existence I was unaware.

I also knew that this postulant did not appreciate my premature entry into the community. It also appeared that he liked Saint Thérèse of the Child Jesus a lot but, when he saw that my thoughts were similar to hers, he could not stand me. It was his custom to speak quite naturally of his closeness to Saint Thérèse of the Child Jesus but when certain circumstances in the life of this saint bore some resemblance to mine and I would allow myself to say: 'Brother, it's the same for me ...' He would stop his account and give me this lesson: 'Saint Thérèse is far from resembling you. Don't delude yourself that it is sufficient to enter the community early or to be small to resemble Saint Thérèse ... If you are ever canonised you'll have a long wait, by which time I shall have already been so myself.'

At the beginning, as with all the other stories of this nature, I found it very disagreeable and to stop them I wanted to break all relations with this postulant. Sometimes, in a moment of vexation, I considered making up stories so that one of us would be obliged to leave, because I was finding it insupportable to have to listen every day to such harsh (811) words. But once this moment of vexation had passed I placed my head on my Mother Mary's heart and I asked her pardon, and begged her to come to my aid or to show me a means of living in peace with this confrère. Subsequently, when I found myself in such painful circumstances, following the example of Saint Thérèse, I offered everything to God. I tried to respond to the brother with a lot of friendship; I even looked, skilfully, for opportunities to do him some service, but shortly afterwards he began to reject all my favours. I went, one day, with my customarily friendly face to help him peel the potatoes so that he could finish early. But he, taking his basket of potatoes somewhere else, said to me: 'Am I a child so that you have to mollify me? I don't need your help. I know you, you are only a child but you think you are an adult. I know all about your virtue! You are really very like Thérèse. I also know that your smile is as charming and scented as ... "pigs excrement".' The brother burst out laughing at this on thinking of the new name for a flower he had just invented.

(812)   From this moment I decided to put up with him in silence and to pray for him in imitation of Saint Thérèse with one of her sisters. I don't think this brother wanted my prayers either, as he said himself. It was very sad. We were both admitted, later, to the novitiate. Naturally the brother was not happy to see me admitted at the same time as him but since the superior had so decided he had to accept it. Nevertheless, he allowed himself to make this prophecy: 'It's my bet that Marcel will not be able to stay; he has a very shady look and if he ever perseveres in religion the heavens will fall ...'

What a pity! After three or four months of novitiate this prophecy rebounded. He had to say goodbye to the one he had judged incapable of living in religion, take off his soutane and return to the world. What has happened, subsequently, in the life of this 'prophet'?

(813)   My Father, you know better than me ... As for me, although I am not impeded by these false prophecies, I have, however, learnt a lesson which deserves to be graven on my memory for life. I have observed, once again, the truth of the words of the Divine Master: 'You will be judged by the way you judge others'. What this brother wagered would happen to me, God has allowed to happen to him in such a way that he has been the victim of his own threats. In spite of all that, I have never neglected to put into practice these words of Jesus: 'Pray for those who persecute you.' For myself, every time someone suspects me of committing some fault or other, I think, in all honesty, that without divine protection I would have been, without doubt, a thousand times more guilty than people thought. That is why I asked God, sincerely, to pardon me and to preserve me from the faults attributed to me.

Good examples

The good God has not always left me on a diet of bread mixed with bitterness. Now and again a new and pleasant taste would be added. I am speaking of confrères of deep piety who, being friendly towards me, allowed themselves to be easily moved by my entreaties and responded to the sincerity of my very small actions with a real affection. In my dealings with these brothers I was indulged like a little brother; that is to say, indulged in accordance with the way of perfection. These confrères supported and guided me; they made me understand clearly wherein lies true holiness and where lies error, not only by their words but also by their actions. I know well that, for a Redemptorist, to seek perfection is to try to imitate the example of the Divine Master. Now, among the religious close to us, God has given us transparent models which reflect (815) the sanctity of this Divine Master in order to teach us and lead us to model our lives on them. One should not, therefore, be content to read the gospel exclusively to learn the secret of holiness. It is also necessary to read the living gospels that God has placed around us. These living gospels are our brothers themselves who know how to keep the word of God and remain faithful to the Rule.

Of course, apart from Jesus our Redeemer and his holy Mother, the saints, no matter their level of virtue, are still subject to imperfections. But these imperfections do not merit that one should worry about them. They are often like the hard and rough bark which hides a delicious almond; it is necessary to savour the almond and not chew the bark. I noticed, therefore, among these holy confrères one who practised extreme poverty but who was still imperfect in the practice of charity; another on the contrary who was very charitable but who was often found wanting in observing the rule or a third who had a fiery temperament but who was very generous, etc. They were all sincere and their conduct was a model that I was free to contemplate for instruction in the life of the Redeemer. I can even say that Jesus our (816) Redeemer hid himself in them to practise virtue so as to teach me to imitate it. He did not practise, perfectly, all the virtues in a single confrère but he shared these virtues out amongst many of them, practising in each one a different virtue. So I was able to learn the practice of charity from one brother, and from another the practice of self-denial. In thinking in this way I felt the need to live more closely with the confrères without ignoring any, since all are models which the good God wishes to make use of to decorate my soul. Or, to speak in a more suitable manner, they are the colours that God has prepared for me to embellish the image of the Divine Redeemer living in me.

I have noticed one thing. After having learned to contemplate Jesus

(817)

hidden in my brothers and living out his life in the activities of each one in particular, I no longer felt any repugnance in learning, close to my brothers, the practice of virtue. Rather, I was happy when I managed to behave like them. The good God, seeing that I was happy to beg in this manner, had pity on me again and often gave me much more than I desired. It was really the fulfilment of this beatitude: 'Blessed are the poor in spirit for theirs is the kingdom of God.'* This kingdom of God is Love itself. But while waiting to reign with God it will be necessary for me to experience still a series of difficult trials.

Marcel de l'Enfant-Jésus†

(818)

A short time after my entry into the community my name Van was changed to that of Marcel. On receiving this name I would have been happier if the Father Rector had attached to the name of Marcel the qualification 'of the Child Jesus' as they had done for Thérèse. I wished to be called Marcel of the Child Jesus. This was a really childish thing, and for this reason Father Rector was not favourable to the idea ... I remember the morning Father Rector came to the kitchen and called me, in the presence of the brethren, to say to me: 'From now on you will no longer be called Van but Marcel.' I had wished for a long time to have the name Thérèse of the Child Jesus or, at least, to have the words 'of the Child Jesus' attached to my name, since, not content with loving the Child Jesus I wished, also, to carry his name. I had even asked the Child Jesus to grant me this favour.

(819)

I do not understand why Jesus had not intervened in any way on that day, allowing Father Rector to called me simply 'Marcel'. I did not really know what to think, but I kept saying to myself: 'If I had the words "of the Child Jesus" added to my name, how beautiful it would be.' Therefore, without saying anything to Thérèse, I went spontaneously to ask Father Rector to add to my name the words 'of the Child Jesus' so that it would be more beautiful. But my real motive was my great love for the child Jesus. I failed in my childish request. After having heard my request, Father Couture nodded his head and congratulated me heartily, and finally answered me, smiling: 'You live like the Child Jesus, which is very beautiful, and I am very pleased with that. However, it is not necessary to carry his name really to love him.'

'I would also like very much to be like Saint Thérèse.'

'It's the same thing. If you would like to resemble her, practise her

---

*   St Matthew 5. 3.
†   It was written in French in the Vietnamese text.

virtues and learn to act a lot like her. It is not important to be like her in name.' I was disturbed to see my bright idea dismissed so summarily, but I shall consider the affair as a lesson worthy of attention. I asked Father Rector, seeing that he was not in favour of the idea, to at least keep it a secret. He, seeing my great anxiety, tapped me gently on the head and said: 'Don't worry'. Then he left. I believed the episode would remain secret but, can you believe it, Father Rector found it so innocent (820) that he told it to the brethren so that, at midday recreation, everyone called me Marcel of the Child Jesus. I blushed and if I had not been the object of attention there would have been no shortage of tears.

A dream

I remember, a short time after my admission into the community, the trials I came up against had prompted fear concerning my vocation. On the one hand, my only desire was to attach myself closely to Jesus and to follow him right to the end and, on the other hand, in spite of all my sincerity, many things made me afraid, especially the words of my brethren as I mentioned before. Moreover, at this period the voice coming from heaven was seldom heard, so that my life became more and more sombre and full of anxieties. I did not know what the future had in store for me. If by good fortune I could remain in the congregation, my cup would be overflowing, but if it was my misfortune to (821) have to return to the world – o my God, that would be the worst of calamities! I was therefore very anxious, to the extent of losing my appetite and my sleep. Worst of all, I did not know whom to confide in. God, seeing me in this state, has in his love had pity on me and has sent me a dream to teach me not to be stopped by the erroneous arguments which the devil has used to deceive me.

Here is this dream. One winter's day when it was very cold, recreation had scarcely finished when I went to my room and stretched out on my bed to rest. Once laid down, without knowing why, I felt uneasy. I was unable to close my eyes and was troubled by a thousand sad thoughts. I left my bedroom, therefore, to walk on the upper floor. I was alone there, to walk the hundred paces on the corridor of Christ the King, where I had just spent recreation with the brethren. I looked absent-mindedly in the direction of the Nam-Đồng road whilst I was walking, which, at this moment, presented a very sad aspect; not a soul was passing. From time to time a gust of wind lifted up towards the sky a cloud of dust, which cast a shadow over part of the street. The trees were bare of their leaves, gusts (822) of wind shook some dead branches and carried them with the cloud of dust. Tired of walking, I took a rest. Looking at the sky I became sadder still without knowing the source of my sadness.

Suddenly, as I walked to the end of the corridor beside the novitiate, I saw Saint Thérèse who, coming out of the small corridor, came towards me. On reaching me, she hurriedly asked me: 'Marcel, my little brother, why aren't you resting? I can see you look sad.'

'Yes, my sister, I am very sad. I cannot close my eyes to go to sleep.'

At that moment, I saw myself the size of a small child of five years, whilst Thérèse was very big. She wrapped me in the left border of her cloak and, while walking, she spoke with me all the time on the theme of the love of God. As for me, I did not waste the opportunity to tell her of my trials and to say to her, sadly: 'Thus, it is not certain that I can (823) stay a long time in the community.' Thérèse listened attentively to the catalogue of all my trials. Then, in a comforting and encouraging tone, she made known to me what God would desire of me, and in what conditions friends of the Divine Redeemer can be called co-redemptors with him: 'God sends suffering to those he loves.' As for the temptations which were tormenting me, my sister exhorted me to reject them and not to tire myself unnecessarily in thinking about them.

Meanwhile, my sister took me into the little passage which leads to the community chapel. I had hardly crossed the entrance to this corridor when I saw a band of four or five little devils who were seated behind the oratory and chattering among themselves near Saint Anne's chapel. I trembled all over and I gripped Saint Thérèse's hand tightly. Of the five little devils, four were seated and the other stood up straight with his arms crossed behind his back. On seeing me they began shouting, and talked together about catching me. I gripped my holy sister's hand even tighter as I was even more afraid. Thérèse maintained her customary calm before this spectacle. She looked peacefully at the little devils and then looked again at me without saying a word. Her (824) demeanour reassured me a little and I was certain there was no danger. After standing there a while I came to the conclusion that these cunning little devils were incapable of harming us, since they were all as skinny as starving ghosts with legs and arms like withered twigs. I thought that by blowing heavily on them I could scatter all of them. They were as black as coal and with hideous faces they looked really detestable. They differed however from devils represented on pictures in that they had neither horns nor tails, but they were no less fierce-looking. After having made a short comparison of their strength against mine, I intended to throw myself at them to chase them from the corridor, which I had to pass to get to the oratory. Full of enthusiasm, I rolled up my sleeves and then, addressing my sister Thérèse, I said to her: 'My sister, with your permission I will go to try and give some blows to this band of little devils to teach them how to live.' At my provocation they became more angry and threw this challenge at me: 'Come on then! Come and see! ...' But Thérèse held me gently and said: 'Too bad for (825) them! It is sufficient for us to know that they can't harm us. Therefore it is useless to make trouble with them.' She then dragged me to the corridor outside to continue our walk. She spoke to me while walking but she paid no attention to the little devils who wished to hurt me. After having made several turns, Thérèse led me once again to the entrance to the corridor. The little devils ignored our presence. Seated head to head, they were absorbed in what seemed to be a very important conversation. The devil who earlier was standing up straight still maintained the same position, with his hands crossed behind his back, but he was also very attentive to the conversation of his four colleagues.

Thérèse and I, we stopped without exchanging a single word. We were happy to communicate by look and gesture. After a moment's conversation Thérèse put her finger to her lips, gave me a discreet smile and then, leaning towards me, she said very quickly into my ear: 'Go quietly behind the devil who is standing and without warning give him a sharp blow on the neck ...' Obeying Thérèse, I walked forward (826) stealthily. On getting near, my hair stood on end because of the stink which emanated from their persons, an unimaginable stink! I had to hold my breath to regain my strength, then, lifting my hand, I dealt a hard blow to the neck of the devil who was standing. He immediately fell head first in the middle of his companions who were seated. Seized with panic, each one got up painfully and fled, bellowing fearsome cries which made me shake all over! ... They turned round to look at me while running. They wanted to go into the oratory, but the door was closed. They then tried to enter the small Saint Anne's chapel, but this door was closed also, so they plunged, jostling each other, into the toilets which were at the side. Some jumped through the window which overlooked the roof of the kitchen, the others slid along the gutter and fled into the garden. I then saw clearly that they all had tails, and two horns. Seeing them flee, I pursued them to the window to see where they were going to hide. After a short time I saw them disappear, all five of them, behind the stable, from where they did not cease to scream in (827) a terrifying manner. In my joy at having been able to overcome them I clapped my hands on returning to Thérèse. I do not know how but, panic-stricken, I was banging my head against a wall ...

I gave a jump and realised that I had just been dreaming! I opened my eyes and groping around me I had the impression of smelling once again the stink which came from the band of little devils. Although it was a simple dream, I think it contained a lesson in prudence for me. How many times has my sister Thérèse said to me: 'Little brother, don't dwell on things of such a nature so as to trouble the peace of your soul;

these are lies invented by the devil.' But how many times, also, through having forgotten this lesson have I found myself in such a darkness that it could have led me to discouragement. The dream which took place has put an end to all these falsehoods invented by the devil.

(828)   **Interior peace**

From the day that I had this dream I took up again the tactic of peace. I mean, that, in spite of provocations and threats, I remained in peace and I abandoned myself entirely into God's hands, following the example of little Thérèse who, considering herself very small and without any talent, knew only to hide herself in God and to say to him with a sincere heart: 'O my God, you know that I am very small and that my enemies are powerful and fearsome. Given their number and their great power they would be capable of crushing me in the wink of an eye. However, my God, Supreme Being and all-powerful, allow me to huddle in your divine arms. The strength of your arms will triumph over the enemies of my soul. I will sing eternally of your supreme power.'

(829)   I don't always use such long formulas when I speak to God. A simple glance of love, full of confidence, suffices to move his pity and to obtain for me victory over the enemy. How many times, when imaginary thoughts or discordant words arrive to trouble me on the subject of my vocation, after having humbly implored the help of God, in spite of my weakness I have gained the victory incredibly quickly!

In a short time I regained peace of soul which, little by little, led me to a deep interior peace. Yes, peace of soul has been like the path which has led me to the highest peak of Love. Nevertheless I was followed everywhere by the cross, just as man is accompanied by his shadow. But when a soul lives in the strength of Love, the cross becomes like a flower with a delicate scent which is intoxicating.

(830)   **On the heart of God**

It was also at this time that the good God called me to exchange with him the feelings of his heart. I remember that it was in the silence of the afternoon, at the time when Jesus expired on the cross. As I was busy preparing the flour for the cakes, whilst meditating in my heart on the love of the suffering Jesus, I suddenly felt a change taking place in my soul, a change of a kind to make me feel uneasy and to give me the sensation of being transported by a current of mysterious thoughts. I had the feeling that God was very close to me, that he loved me a lot and that, on my part, I could only remain in a swoon faced with this immense and limitless love.

At that moment I heard a voice which said to me quietly:

'Marcel, do you love me a lot?'

'Yes, my God, I love you a lot, and beside you I do not know who else I could love more and I love you a lot, a lot.'

It was with these words that our conversation began. Jesus began to show me his intimate feelings in making his voice heard clearly by me. (831) At the beginning when I heard him speak, I found it difficult to understand. Whilst knowing well that it was God who was speaking to me, I did not understand how or in what manner I heard him. However, I did hear him, but not with my ears, although noise was a great obstacle to this conversation. Just as with the words of my sister Saint Thérèse that I have heard for a long time and that I understood clearly, I never managed to grasp how he arranged it so that I heard, whereas others around me heard nothing.

One day, by chance, I had in my hand a book translated by Father Lucas and which summarises the communications made by Jesus to Sister Benigna Consolata.* It is there that I understood a little of the intimacy of Jesus with souls, and this was sufficient to set my mind at rest and help me to work more determinedly in this new stage where I received the Lord's visit. From this day, I enjoyed continual intimacy with Jesus who communicated his teachings to me as he did with the apostles, (832) behaving towards me as a father does with his child. He usually used very ordinary language, but marked with such tenderness that it inflamed my heart with many sparks, and sometimes threw me into a certain anxiety which penetrated my most intimate being. It was as if my soul was outside itself; I had the feeling of being immersed into the depths of love, or of disappearing consumed in this love of the heart of God. In spite of this, my hands and feet continued to move and my work was always done regularly; the only difference being that I found that time passed very quickly. Subsequently, not only did Jesus speak to me, but he demanded that I speak to him. In his infinite goodness and condescension he asked me to tell him, in the smallest detail, all the little facts of my life. He wished, for example, that I speak to him of my daily work, of my problems with the brethren, of things which caused me pain, etc. He even wanted me to relate amusing incidents to him. I also spoke honestly to him of my faults and I asked him to help me correct them.

---

* Benigna Consolata (1885–1916) a sister of the Visitation order of Coma (Italy). She loved to converse with Jesus who asked her to be his little secretary.

(833) After having listened to my detailed and verbose stories, Jesus let it be known that he was very happy to have been able to hear me tell them with such sincerity. He said to me: 'I am happy to see that a soul such as yours exists which loves me as sincerely as yours does. Understand well that the simple words and the detailed stories such as yours, that people find childish and boring, for my Love all becomes extremely precious and interesting. I love nothing so much as a sincere love. And when it is sincere, love is meticulous. It does not hide from its beloved any of its least movements. If you love me you will always be sincere with me; your sincerity will make me find pleasure in staying with you, in giving myself to you and in embracing you even more with the fire of my Love.

My times of meditation had become sweet conversation with Jesus, and he, in his always faithful love, was so indulgent as to explain to me a host of many interesting things on the subject of love. Yes, these things were both very numerous and really captivating. As for me, I could only offer him in return stories of the kind I have described earlier. I think that Jesus found them pleasing simply because of the (834) sincerity of my heart. In fact, in my innocence I could only tell him of what I had seen and heard, only speak to him of the sadness and sufferings of my daily life, as also of my weakness and imperfections. As to applying my mind to reflect on the sublimity of the things of heaven as the great saints do, in my weakness that was out of the question. God already knew me very well. If in creating me he had made me an angel, I would certainly have had profound and splendid thoughts like the angels to praise him and converse with him. But since he has created me as a mere man, I can only put to his use human thoughts and activities. I think that if I had spoken to God of sublime things of the beyond, I would certainly have been described as a show-off. Therefore, I spoke to him in all simplicity, of the river when I saw a river, of the mountain when I saw a mountain, of my sadness when I was sad or of my joy when I felt happy. If I liked flowers I told him so. If I loved God I told him also of my love. God never neglects to listen to what one says to him provided that what one says to him is said in love and with the intention of pleasing him. How good he is, the good God! How he deserves to be loved! How can one manage to express in words all the love contained in his heart? And if one never manages to, (835) one can only conclude with these words: only the heart of God is in a position to describe the ultimate feelings of the divinity, and, consequently all language should be silent in this world in the presence of the infinite Love ...

In spite of this, after I had placed at his disposition my humble human condition, God himself in his infinite power has really wished to make known to me something of his divinity. He has told me of the fire of his ardent love. He has taught me a thousand easy ways of expressing my love, and how to please him while waiting for the day when I will belong to him completely, and will be transformed in him. Then he himself will be also all in me, and together we will be no more than one in the indestructible Love. There you have the mysterious secret of Love, a secret that cannot be described by dreams or illusions, but in the truth which only Love is capable of producing.

An unusual sign

One day at the time of solemn Benediction of the Most Blessed (836) Sacrament, God gave me an extraordinary sign which remains engraved in my memory down to the last detail. Allow me to tell it with necessary reservations. I dare not state that this prophetic sign really happened but I leave it to the future to bear witness to its truth.

If I don't deceive myself, this unusual sign occurred one evening in the month of June 1945 during Benediction of the Blessed Sacrament, and lasted until the end of meditation. I remember being on my knees and looking attentively at the Most Holy Sacrament and conversing interiorly with Jesus as usual. Suddenly I felt a change in me, which made me jump, as I saw Jesus clearly coming from a distance, and walking towards me. He came forward, his face impassive but marked with an extreme sweetness. His hair fell to his shoulders, but the most striking thing was above all the kindness of his gaze; an expression which was really the reflection of his heart overflowing with an infinite love, and I thought that such an expression would be sufficient to send (837) all souls into ecstasy. The colour of his clothing differed in nothing from representations one sees in pictures. He was wearing a light pink robe which reached to his heels, a cincture, and a red cloak exactly like the one of Christ represented on the picture of Jesus the Redeemer. Jesus came beside me and I then saw myself changed into a little child of two or three years. Before I even had time to be astonished I saw Jesus, sitting on a stone platform, take me in his arms and hold me tightly against his breast. Then we continued to talk together.

A short time afterwards I suddenly heard a far-off noise. Jesus immediately fixed his gentle gaze towards the front and, making a gesture in that direction, said to me: 'My child, look at this angry crowd which is coming towards me.' I looked quickly and then, O my God! I caught sight of a huge crowd composed of people of all conditions: children, adults, men and women, who came forward in a threatening manner, each one wearing on his forehead the same sign. They let out frighten-

(838) ing yells while walking. Passing before Jesus, they insulted him, lifting their feet and hands against him in an arrogant manner, and blaspheming his holy name. Then, some held sticks, and others gathered stones and threw them violently against the divine body of Jesus. Most of them were aimed directly at his face, but, don't ask me why, when these stones reached Jesus, they reached only his arms and legs. What an appalling spectacle! As for me, in my powerlessness, I knew only to clasp him firmly, to press myself against his heart and to shed tears. At a certain point I saw a stone coming straight for me. Terrified, I quickly moved to one side. Seeing my fear, Jesus pressed me against his breast and the stone only reached his knee. After having tormented him for a long time, these people stood there shouting insulting words. From time to time a stone or a stick, thrown from a distance, fell near him. In the middle of these insults Jesus' face remained stamped with goodness,

(839) and he gazed on the crowd with love. Yes, with love, with a great love! Then, seeing them persist in their attitude of mad arrogance, he was sorry for them, and tears dropped on to his chest.

Seeing his tears, mine redoubled and I felt a sadness in my heart capable of killing me. However, in contemplating the tenderness on his face, I felt comforted and, supposing that at that moment I wished to avenge Jesus, I think it would have been very difficult for me, if not to say impossible, to have had such an idea. Little by little the noise subsided, to stop completely. I stayed alone with Jesus and I was still crying. Jesus had pity on me, he comforted me whilst caressing me gently. While the crowd was still there, Jesus, at a specific moment, after glancing at me, looked at me again and said to me: 'My child, pray a lot and practise much self-denial for these unfortunate people. They really deserve pity. Yes, deserve pity! Save them in union with me.' Alas, how sad was my heart when I saw numerous children, still innocent, but who also collected stones to throw at Jesus. Finally, Jesus kissed me and

(840) recommended that I remembered in all its details, what I had seen. He then gradually disappeared.

When I heard Father Rector intone the Salve Regina I returned to a normal state, and I saw on my prie-dieu the tears that I had spilled. The next day, again at the time of meditation, I saw Jesus appear to me once again, as on the previous day, but the vision did not last as long, and it seemed to me that Jesus appeared even sadder than on the previous day. So as not to forget anything, I wrote down that very evening all that I had seen; but afterwards, having gone to reveal the matter to a brother whom I knew as having enough experience to make a judgement on this matter, he gave me this reply: 'Simple souls, like Thérèse, never had such dreams. Furthermore, the devil, in order to trick men, could very well be the author of such dreams.'

These words troubled me greatly, so to regain peace of mind I went to tell everything to Father Joseph Hiệp who was then prefect of the brothers. In the final analysis he gave me the same reply as Brother Marc; he advised me to leave such obscure things to one side, and if they reappeared to chase them away as tricks of the devil. I immediately (841) obeyed the prefect of brothers, and I threw all I had written into the fire and forced myself to forget this vision. Today, my Father, in order to obey you, I must write these things down once again. However, I dare not declare myself for or against. When Father Hiệp told me to put these visions to one side I obeyed him without delay and happily. Today, you are asking me to write these things down once again. All I know is to obey promptly without complaining at having had to put them to one side or at having to write about them again. All I know is to obey and if, later, you order me to burn all I have written, I will burn them willingly. I have not even weighed the pros and cons of the things that I have seen. It is sufficient that I conform to God's will, that I pray and practise self-denial for sinners as he wished. That is something I always did even before Jesus showed me what I have just related.

Although this vision has been a powerful stimulant for me, even without it I would have prayed and made sacrifices for sinners. That is why if the evil spirit, in order to trouble me, came one day to tell me that the extraordinary signs are the fruit of an imagination searching for something novel, I would answer him directly: 'If they are only (842) dreams, they will go away quickly, as dreams do; but if they come from God, it is then the work of God, and God will oversee the perfect fulfilment of his will. Myself, I only know how to follow his will sincerely and with all my heart.' In my opinion, when a soul gives itself totally to God it has no reason to worry any more, since God never abandons those who place all their confidence in him. This thought has helped me to remain in peace, in spite of all which has been difficult to understand in my life.

Nevertheless, from the day when Jesus appeared to me (I speak always with a certain reservation), his sad condition has stimulated me still more to think unceasingly of sinners. And at that moment I would never, either, forget my dear father. Every day I looked to impose many small sacrifices on myself, which I offered each evening with my tears, to ask that my father would make a good confession and lead a fervent life worthy of a Christian.

It was also at this time that something happened which showed that (843) my prayers and little sacrifices were pleasing to God. When Father Hiệp had just died, Doctor Le Roy Desbarres, who had cared for him during his illness, also fell gravely ill. Everybody knew he was a freemason, and in spite of the zeal with which he helped religious communities, he had never agreed to live in conformity with Christian doctrine. On hearing of his serious condition, all the brethren worried about his eternal salvation, as he was a great benefactor of the community. We thought of him and prayed for him to receive the grace of a happy death.

Personally, when I heard of his serious illness, I felt a great compassion for him and my soul did not stop worrying like a mother about to lose a child. I went immediately before God and opened my heart to him in these terms: 'Lord my God, I am very small, but what I am asking you is very big. You know that Doctor Le Roy Desbarres, a great benefactor of our community, is actually very ill and he will recover

(844)   with difficulty. Consequently, what I am asking you above all and as something very urgent, is that you will give him the grace of conversion before his death and to confess or, at least, to give a sign of repentance before breathing his last. My God, I ask this through the merit of the very precious blood which Jesus has shed for the salvation of the human race. I ask this through the intercession of the Blessed Virgin and of the saints and in particular of my sister Saint Thérèse. I offer to you from now onwards all my sacrifices, all my efforts, in union with the merits of Jesus, your Son, to expiate the doctor's sins and obtain his soul's salvation.'

From the beginning of the doctor's illness, Father Louis Roy, the prefect of brothers in place of Father Joseph Hiep, went every day to visit the sick doctor to encourage and help him to return to God. Alas! Each time the patient replied that he was not ready, that he was too tired. At the time of his last visit, Father Roy, in spite of all his suppli-

(845)   cations, suffered a final refusal, so that he came back with tears in his eyes, feeling sorry for the fate of the soul who has shown friendship so many times towards Jesus' friends. If the doctor lost his soul we would no longer have the chance to express our gratitude. On his return, Father Roy told us what had happened and added: 'We have exhausted all means of helping him. All that now remains is to confide his salvation to the merciful heart of Jesus.' He then told us that he was not sure that the doctor would last the night.

This news plunged me into a deep sadness, but I could not resign myself to allow a soul to be lost for whose salvation Jesus, himself, had shed his divine blood. I went, therefore, to tell Jesus all I had just heard and I asked him, as a matter of urgency, to give to the doctor the grace of repentance, or at least to do something so that the doctor belonged to God at the last moments of his life. I then asked Father Hiệp and my sister Thérèse to come to the doctor's aid in his final agony. I understood that there was only one means left: to ask Father Hiệp to come to the doctor's side since, apart from God, nobody could prevent him

(846)   from going to the doctor's bedside. That night, as usual, I withdrew to

my room to rest but before going to bed I thought of offering Doctor Le Roy Desbarres to God once again. I then went to sleep.

Towards eleven o'clock I awoke with a start as if someone had come to waken me. I then had the presentiment that the Doctor was perhaps in his agony at that moment. I got up straight away, and said three Hail Marys to obtain the grace of a happy death for the doctor. I did not forget to call Thérèse and Father Joseph Hiệp to come to his help at that decisive time. Then I went back to bed, but I was hardly asleep when once again I awoke with a jump, and I felt as if I was suffering from a strange fever. My head and limbs were burning. I felt a warmth all over my body making me feel as if I were closed in a trench full of hot air. My nostrils were blocked so that I had to breathe harder, even through my mouth, and, nevertheless, I still felt suffocated and uneasy. I sat on my bed and then, grabbing my wooden cross, I made the sign of the cross. Troubled and almost unconscious, I no longer knew where (847) I was until the moment when I touched the supporting post of my mosquito net. I then got off my bed, and thought first of all of going out on to the veranda to get some air. So I went out and stood near the window with both hands gripping the bars of the windows. I was expecting the wind to put an end to my fever. But what was the point in waiting? Before the window where I was standing, the branches of the trees were being gently moved by the wind which was blowing steadily right up to me. But, and it was a strange thing, this wind, instead of refreshing me, only made my malaise increase, and I had the feeling that a hot current of air was being directed straight at me. In holding on to the window bars I had the sensation of touching an iron bar on fire, and from that moment everything I touched seemed to be on fire. I have never felt such a fever, neither have I ever been so troubled and terrified.

After having stood for a short while before my window, I went back to my bed and lifted the mosquito net with the intention of resting again but I had hardly stretched out on my bed when I had the sensation of (848) resting on a sheet of burning iron. I jumped down from my bed and dressed quickly, to get to the tap to get water to wash my face and refresh myself. I had scarcely put my hand in the water when I found it boiling. I thought hard about it but I did not understand why. I went back to my room and stood at the window as before. Then looking by chance towards the oratory, I saw there was a light on. I spoke some words to Jesus, and then went straight to the oratory to put out the light, presuming that someone had forgotten to do so. On opening the door I saw Father Sirois kneeling before the open tabernacle. I understood then that Father was praying for the soul of Doctor Le Roy Desbarres. I knelt down for a few moments to adore Jesus, but since I had not got special permission I had to return to my bedroom. There my mind was haunted continually by the doctor's memory. Perhaps it was then the decisive hour of his agony. Then I let out a cry of satisfaction because I had just understood why the good God had sent me this strange fever. After that I went once more to bed and, although still (849)   uncomfortable because of the heat, I put up with this suffering without complaining or getting worked up, and I murmured prayers for Doctor Le Roy Desbarres.

I had then to fight against thirst. I had abstained from drinking since dinner, offering this sacrifice for the doctor since Father Rector had given permission to those who were able, to practise some self-denial to seek God's mercy for the doctor's soul, but I could only deprive myself of drinking. I had then a terrible thirst. My throat was so dry and ticklish that I was unable to say a word. I continued to battle until one o'clock in the morning. It was at that moment that the heat and the thirst began to subside, little by little, and I slept, but I do not know at what moment. In the morning I got up refreshed as usual but I was hardly awake when I learned, mysteriously, that the doctor had died. That is why, after my morning prayers, I said an Our Father, a Hail Mary and a Glory Be for the repose of his soul.

At nine o'clock on the morning of that day the community learned (850)   that the doctor had expired around midnight. This news saddened the brethren and a certain pessimist turned to say: 'Then that's it. We will never meet Doctor Le Roy Desbarres again.' But me, I did not agree. With my prayers, although weak and arid, I was certain that God could not refuse what I had asked for with so much sincerity. Neither could I believe that the blood shed by Jesus for this soul could become so easily wasted. No! It was impossible! Although I do not know with certainty on what evidence I can base my assertion that the doctor had been saved, I do not believe, either, that he was damned. I can only think, at the bottom of my heart: 'Who knows if at that last moment, touched by divine grace, the doctor has not come back secretly to God; and that sincerely and perfectly? Who knows also if at that last moment God has not sent Father Hiêp to help him as I had asked?' Furthermore, the extraordinary fever which had tormented me on that night was also, for (851)   me, a reason for comfort and confidence. I left the others to discuss as they wished and I continued to pray for the soul of the deceased. I believed he was in purgatory and not in hell as certain of my confrères believed.

However, in order to be sure, I went to find Jesus and say to him in all sincerity: 'My Jesus, you know that it is over three years since my father last went to confession. I do not cease to pray for his conversion, but I have heard no news of him for a long time. So, for my peace of mind and to allow me to pray for the doctor's soul, I am asking this favour of you: that my father may have the grace to go to confession and receive communion during this year. When I learn that he has confessed and gone to communion, that will be the sign by which you will let me know that the doctor has been saved.'

In fact, Father, I was really astonished by an amazing thing. Three days had not passed when a person from my village (Chú Tuyên, a neighbour) came to visit me to tell me that my father had confessed and had been to communion during the Easter period and since then he was leading a very fervent life. After having heard this news I went (852) immediately to my room and threw myself on my knees before the crucifix and melted into tears. They were tears of emotion, of joy and of happiness, since I had just learned two pieces of good news; on learning that my father had been to confession, I received in effect at the same time, the answer to my question I had asked of Jesus. I cannot find the words to express the joy which overflowed in my soul. I could do nothing other than get close to Jesus, throw myself into his arms and there on his breast express my gratitude and love with fervent glances and limpid tears. Truthfully, God is Love. How could he reject me? My sole preoccupation in eternity, in my extreme smallness and total powerlessness, will be to sing his Love.

Novitiate

It was in the month of August 1945 that I was admitted to the novitiate. This happy news came to me when I was not expecting it. Really, I did not expect to be admitted as soon. I had agonised for some time on the subject of my vocation. It is not that it occurred to me to leave the (853) congregation, but rather I had the impression that certain confrères were not happy with me. It caused me much suffering to live under such conditions. I was very anxious, waiting all the time to know what was the superior's will and being ready to carry it out. If he had indicated a return to the world, I would have bowed my head and left immediately but without feeling, besides, the slightest relief. But there: the opposite happened. At the moment when my soul was deeply worried, I got the news of my admission to the novitiate.

You can see by that, Father, that God refuses me nothing. He has made known to me the love of his heart in his own way without speaking. He has let me know that he is always pleased with me and he has inspired in me a greater confidence in him. To further the blossoming of Love in my soul and to alleviate the sufferings of those days of trial that I have just passed through, Jesus, the very close friend of my soul, has, during the fortnight of the retreat preparatory to the taking of the habit, filled me with special graces, of which the most precious was to be intoxicated by him with a very deep love.

(854)   The fortnight passed with the speed of a delightful dream. I had the impression of not depending on time any more; forgetting almost everything else, I felt all the time that God was near me, I heard his voice resonate quietly in the bottom of my heart, and during this retreat, what exquisite senntiments I exchanged with him on the theme of Love! How sweet Jesus is! His word cures all sadness and is the food and strength of a pure soul. It is he, Jesus, who has taught me to love, and has given a greater intimacy to my love.

I then began my novitiate and from that day Jesus, like a travelling companion, did not cease to walk at my side until the end of this year of trials. What have been my feelings and the changes occurring in my soul during this time? Father, you know very well for you have heard me recount them already and I think there is no need for me to give you further explanations. Yes, truthfully, Jesus-Marcel and Marcel-Jesus, there you have two names that are only one and it is you, my Father, who has been the witness of this union from its beginning. You know it well. I even think you know it better than me.

(855)   ## The day of union

I did not think that the day of my taking of the vows would happen at a time when I was plunged in distaste and aridity. I did not expect to be admitted so early into my religious profession for many reasons. I remained confident in spite of all, and I held myself ready to greet the happy day. During this time it was you, Father, who kept my confidence up; it was you who helped me chase away deceptive thoughts and who helped me, above all, not to listen to the critical words which were prompted by the devil. As you noticed, the closer the day of my profession came, the more I felt overcome by dryness. Each time that you questioned me on this subject, each time I explained to you my thoughts clearly in these terms: 'As for me, I am always ready: all I am waiting for is the "other side" to give its consent'. But why would it not give it? since, although Jesus had become indifferent towards me, especially during this time which closely preceded our union, it remains that this apparent indifference, accompanied by silence, helped me to understand that 'on that side' preparations were also being made, to give the day of our union due solemnity. It was because he was absorbed in these preparations that Jesus was forced to contain his feelings regarding the one he

(856)   loved; one never loves as much as when one acts only with love in mind.

Some time before my profession I had again the chance to make a fortnight's retreat. It seems that this retreat fulfilled my wishes even more than the first one, as I had already experienced the happiness that one tastes in conversation with the divine friend. Nevertheless it happened, once or twice, that aridity had caused a certain negligence on my part in the accomplishment of his will. However, Jesus is never far from me; he has always helped me to make this day of our union a perfect one. Oh yes, it is precisely thanks to this intention to do things perfectly that my friend Jesus has not spared anything – so well that things which seemed hopeless have turned out as I wanted.

Father, you certainly knew the numerous reasons for my unease concerning my profession which might perhaps be delayed or which, quite simply, might be refused me. The first reason was my state of health. Perhaps a more serious reason was the numerous faults, more appropriate to a child, that one noticed in my regard. I am sure that you understood, even better than me, that these faults caused me even more suffering than the discipline and other acts of self-denial, and it seemed that, at the time of my meetings with you, you rarely saw me (857) with dry eyes. I see there something magical, since it is also thanks to my imperfections that Jesus, my friend, has skilfully nurtured in my soul a thousand reasons to have confidence which have extinguished the movements of pride that one can easily see in me. Finally, it is thanks again to my numerous failings that I have gained the victory for the love of Jesus, and although in this victory I was myself the adversary, I did not remain less an honourable offering on the altar of Love. O what is there more honourable for love than to have been able to gain a victory over the adversary, a victory which consists in changing him by love. That I have been chosen with all my imperfections is therefore an obvious proof that Love does not hesitate before the greatest difficulties. So, despite the defects inherent in my human nature, my friend Jesus redeemed me with joy. He came to unite himself to me on that day, 8 September 1946.

The eighth of September. What a happy day! I see written there a (858) double memory, which will attract my attention each year. It is first of all, the birthday of the Mother of God and at the same time the day when my sister Saint Thérèse celebrated her spiritual marriage with Jesus, her spouse of love. Since the day when I got to know the book *The Story of a Soul* I have always wished to resemble Saint Thérèse, and I said to myself: 'If the day of my profession could coincide with that of the profession of my sister, how happy I would be!' Today this wish has become a reality, and it is once again a favour that Jesus wished for his friend ... with the difficult character!

Yes, my Father, that is Love. When one loves there is no difficulty, no matter how big, that cannot be overcome; above all when one is dealing with a friend as powerful as is my friend Jesus … Indeed, in the presence of this infinitely magnificent Love and its immense kindness, it felt as if my soul was immersed in a state of extreme intoxication. I would have wished to express to Jesus the love of my heart, but seeing how small I was, almost next to nothing, it would have been impossible for me to survive this instant of intoxicated joy if I had not been supported by the strength of Love. In truth I would have preferred that it had been thus, and I expressed this wish: 'If it is God's will he could take my soul to heaven, in this very moment of unprecedented happiness, as he did Saint Imelda,* who died of love.'

(859)

But it was only for a short time that the good God gave me this wish to die of love, so that I might come alive again to realise the promises he had made to me for the future, since during the entire year of my novitiate, the will of God for me tallied well with the question that Jesus had formerly asked his apostles: 'Little brother, if you love me, will you have the strength to drink the chalice of bitterness with me?' and during all this time he urged me to suffer and to sacrifice myself cheerfully. Thus my task consisted only in climbing with Jesus to the summit of Calvary and there to suffer death in union with him. So it will not be given to me to die through a surge of happiness, but rather after having sweated, and after my heart will have used up the last drop of my blood …

When will this vision be realised for which I thirst like a man gasping for breath …? So, here I am, still alive. What happened to Saint Imelda will not be re-enacted in my case, to my great sadness. This sadness made me fall into a melancholic state, which lasted for years, and even now you know very well that not a day passes without my knowing at least a minute's suffering in seeing that heaven is still so far away. Nevertheless, love has prompted me to play my part completely, and the greater my sadness, the more tenacious also is my desire to love. No matter what my state of aridity I never cease to hear this call from on high ringing out: 'Little brother, always believe that I love you and I shall love you eternally.'

(860)

I wish to describe the intoxication of my soul on this day of my union with Jesus. The closer the day came, the more troubled my soul felt. I was like a virgin holding a lighted lamp for her spouse. When I heard his call from afar, I felt my soul being pulled by an extraordinary power, but a power full of gentleness as if my head was leaning on my

---

* Saint Imelda (1320–33). A Dominican from Valpidietra, not far from Bologna. Her great love for the Lord made her worthy to make her first communion in a miraculous manner on Ascension Day 1333 before all the community. It was the moment when Jesus chose to take her to heaven.

beloved's arm. That is why I prepared in advance a written formula
where I expressed my soul's intoxication at the moment of meeting with   (861)
the spouse, quite sure that in this elated state, the soul can only let slip
vague words, although very sincere and full of love. I was ready therefore to say things to Jesus as I had written them:

'Jesus, the most dear friend of my soul, the happy moment has
arrived, but my love for you troubles me. It is that a thousand
things that I would like to say to you at this moment of intimacy to
calm it down, swirl around in my head since I see that you, Love
infinitely great and beautiful, have really wished to sacrifice yourself for a very small creature such as me. Furthermore, you have
deigned to look on me with a glance full of ardent love, as if I were
the only person on earth to possess a love which merits that you
love me so passionately.

'Jesus, my brother! My soul trembles with happiness to the
extent of being disturbed faced with this great favour, since, being
nothing, it has the good fortune to become your spouse.

'O moment full of delight! From this moment Love gives me the
honour of calling you spouse, the divine lover of my soul, but   (862)
where can I really find suitable words for the great happiness
which fills my heart, to say to you at least one word of love? Yes, I
feel an overflowing joy in the depths of my heart, a limitless love
which casts my soul beside itself. The word "love" alone remains
but in this moment even this word can be expressed only in
rapture and the deepest silence.

'Jesus, my friend, my brother, how beautiful you are! This
incomparable beauty renders me silent, leaving only my warm
glances and the beating of my human, confused heart to express
my love. Jesus, my brother, how I love you! and it really seems to
me that my expressions of love to you have succeeded in delight-
ing you. In fact it is not without reason that at this moment you
are remaining completely silent towards me. Ah! I now know your
love has made you, like me, beside yourself, in such a way that we
both understand each other solely by love, without the necessity to   (863)
have recourse to the language of love of this world, language
which can only express created love adequately.

'Jesus my brother, you know very well that I can easily lose my
temper and me, I know that you can easily become jealous. It
might happen that we must be separated from each other; if each
time we love each other, let us then both keep silent. In fact, in this
moment we do not cease loving each other, and it is because we
love each other a lot that we do not know what terms to use to

express our love. Love has changed us both so much that we are now only one. Ah! Unity! It is that which explains that we no longer have need of words to understand each other, since unity is the outcome of love.

'O Jesus, my loving friend, I love you deeply. At this time I only know one thing, it is that I, Marcel, I am Jesus and you, Jesus, you are Marcel himself. From now on it is unity between us two and, may it please God, I can affirm that this unity is eternal. I am trying to affirm it, all the same, by placing total confidence in you. I dare not count on myself too much, but I can say to you, "If from this moment I forget to love you for a second, or do not adjust the beatings of my heart to your love, or if again it happens that by my fault I take away from you the love I have vowed to you, I beg of you to use your divine power instantly to destroy both of us at that very instant. I am well aware that this is an impossible thing, but supposing that it could happen, it would still be better to let me carry in my heart a wound of which I could never be cured. Thus, my divine lover, from now onwards we will both live only by love ...

'O Jesus, I will hold you close to me, and I will never let you go. This day of our nuptials is a real heavenly day, and I am certain that it will be given to me to relive it one day in the courts of heaven. While waiting for this happy moment, O Jesus my brother, never allow my love to distance itself from your love for any reason, nor let it cool in contact with this tormented life. This is my firm decision, but I have need of your help to follow you without stumbling, on this path sown with thorns which leads to eternity, and there, on our very holy Mother's heart, we will taste together the happiness of loving each other as we do today.'

Marcel, your little spouse.
8 September 1946

(865)   In addition to what I wrote above, I have also indicated some favours that I intended to ask of Jesus. I did not ask these graces for myself but, because that particular day was my day of joy, I wished to draw Jesus' attention to those whom I loved. I thought a lot, therefore, about little children. I offered to Jesus all those who are alive, and those who will exist later on this earth, because these are the souls which are particularly dear to me. Neither did I forget the souls in purgatory, nor sinners and non-Christians.

My Father, you also understood very well that, my thoughts being identical to those of little Thérèse, the feelings which rose in my heart towards Jesus hardly differed from hers. I knew that the graces I asked for, even if they were huge, were still nothing much for Jesus since Love is always without limit. Alas, the happy day passed with the speed of a cloud carried by the wind! The whole day was full of delirious happiness. When evening came I intended to write down some thoughts but, on looking at the stars twinkling in the clear sky, I had to put my pen to one side and leaning against the side of the veranda, while contemplating the stars, I thought of little Thérèse on the evening of 8 September. I felt then a certain unease, and my soul was overcome by (866) an ardent desire to fly away quickly towards the divine spouse in the country of eternal life. After this moment of fervent desire and with my soul still full of unbounded love, I shed some tears silently, and I entered into this night which perhaps would have no tomorrow ...

The path which leads to Calvary

O intoxicating night! O silent night! But I awoke to an extremely painful tomorrow. The spouse of Jesus must live and die like him. On September 9 the sky's appearance had changed completely. Rain fell, and it fell as the tears of a soul which cries alone. My friend Jesus, whom I had seen the previous day shining like the midday sun, or like the light of the moon on a beautiful autumn night, had now lost his brightness and seemed to have disappeared into nothingness. I do not know how to describe all the sadness in my heart at this moment, when my love seemed to be struck with a thousand wounds. I longed for my divine Love, and my only wish was to leave this earthly life, and to find (867) it again in the place of life without end.

Nevertheless Jesus, the friend of my heart, had not yet had the courage to go away definitely from me. He came now and again to enlighten me further by his teachings, which were completely marked with intimacy. He did not cease repeating this advice: 'My child, my dear little friend, collaborate with me for the love of souls in the work of their salvation. Your part is cheerfully to sacrifice the moments of sweet intimacy that you will taste close to me, so as to allow me to go in search of souls.' Jesus did not forget to speak to me of the trials and sufferings which awaited me: 'In the future, my little friend, you will have to suffer at the hands of your superiors and brethren, but these trials will be a sign that you are pleasing to my heart. I am asking you to suffer thus with the sole intention of joining you to me in the work of the sanctification of priests, so that, in conformity with their vocation, they will work fervently so that Love will reign in men's hearts ...'

(868)   After these words, Jesus left me alone in darkness. Then, my Father, as you yourself, have fully understood all that happened in my heart, you have been the witness that not a day has passed when I have not had to suffer. Since God has wished that I place everything in your hands without hiding anything from you, not even a single thought, there was therefore, as I have just said, not a single detail which was not known to you during this period of my life. Jesus himself has said to me: 'You are the one who suffers, but it is your Director* who knows why'. Consequently, all I knew was that I suffered. But you, Father, knew well from whom and from where those sufferings came. In truth Jesus, wishing to prevent me from falling into error or to discourage me without reason, taught me to place total confidence in you, my Father, whom he called, 'the comfort, the love that he left beside me'. Therefore, while sending me suffering, he mixed with it a potion of sweetness in consideration of the low level of endurance possessed by a little, fragile soul like mine.

(869)   After a while, as you know, Father, my soul had become like a flower buried in the solitude and aridity of the desert. It was as if I had lost entirely all sweetness and closeness in my relations with God. Added to that, there were some regrettable external events which seemed to want to bury me in an abyss of sadness, especially from the time when I had to busy myself officially with the tailor's workshop.† Before this an unexpected suffering came to me from my family, a suffering so painful that it caused me to shed torrents of tears. My dear Father, is it appropriate or not that I try to write these lines? Anyway, I must write them, since I understand that it is your intention that I do not leave to one side any of my tears. Alas! I allowed these tears to fall into your hands and you have succeeded in taking away a little of their bitterness. How I must thank the good God because, if I have had the strength, it is also thanks to him who has put me into the hands of a man like you. It is impossible at this moment to put into writing the depth of the feelings I have for you, but what I cannot express in words I will express eternally by love. Thank you, Father, because during the hours of battle and suffering I have always found you near me to support me.

(870)   As you know, my Father, two months after having taken my little sister Anne Marie Té to Hanoi for her studies there was disagreement

---

*   Director of conscience, that is his spiritual guide. Father Boucher acted in this role until Van's death.

†   The workshop at which the brethren's clothes were made or repaired, as well as the house's linen. The tailor is also responsible for the vestry and the linen room. He is answerable to the Father Minister.

in my family.* Instead of maintaining a neutral stance between my father and my mother in the affair, as I should have done, it happened, and I am not sure why, that I sided openly with my mother, which resulted later in estranging my father from the family. Unfortunately I acted in a way that I consider still, today, as being unusually ungrateful ... Nevertheless, it was thanks to this action that I had been able to gain a victory that was totally unexpected. Without the help of divine grace and the wise counsel of my superiors, my decision could have had truly desperate consequences. Personally, I have not yet finished crying because of my family's tribulations. My affection for my father made me shed again copious tears which only stopped on the day when I was able to see my family reunited. The good God is wise, good and powerful! He has wrapped me in a curtain of shame! Can there be a greater shame for a child who loves his father with all his heart, than to have dared to declare that this man was his father no longer and to have denied him? However, behind this screen of shame, God has discreetly changed these hideous events into sweetness and deep joy.

After having lived unhappily for some time in his isolation, my father (871) wished to return to the right path. He purified his soul in a retreat; then, of his own initiative, he took steps so that the family was once again reunited. He has remained faithful to his promises until this day and I remain hopeful that never again will he fall into his former aberrations. My Father, it is not necessary to tell you; you can well understand with what an abundance of joy I was overwhelmed on this occasion. If I compare this joy with the sadness which preceded it, I see that neither is greater than the other, since it is already an immense joy to have been freed from a sadness, no matter how bitter it was. I wish to say, therefore, that Love has enveloped me, and that in Love I have been able to taste a happiness without limit. At that moment recollections of my childhood came back spontaneously to my memory. I tasted a happiness without parallel in remembering those afternoons when my

---

* It was in July 1947 that Van's father, tired of having to meet his friends to gamble, wished to set them up in his own home with the rest of the family looking after them. The family was firmly opposed to this idea, but the father remained obstinate. So the mother, accompanied by Lê and Nhất (adopted son) sought the help of her brother Nhượng. Having taken a decision they submitted it to the parish priest, Father Dominic Dư, who gave it his approval. It was necessary to make Van's father understand the lamentable situation into which he had plunged the family because of his passion for gambling. So all the family moved to Hanoi, leaving Nhất (who agreed) with the father of the family so as to look after him. It was then that Brother Marcel was made aware of the affair, and he sided with his mother. With the agreement of his superior he took steps to find lodgings for the family at Thái-Hà-Ấp. [Tế.]

dear father took me for walks, put me on his shoulders and ran like a horse, just to please me.

What sweetness! What happiness! Today, however, I am enjoying an even greater happiness in seeing my father live according to the Gospel and conforming more perfectly each day to God's will.

(872)   Once this trial had passed, my soul did not remain less overwhelmed by sadness. My friend Jesus had not shown himself again, and my soul continued to live in its loneliness. At certain moments of nostalgia, I thought it would be necessary to die to find my beloved again. It was only after a lot of effort that I succeeded in finishing my spiritual exercises, since it is at these times precisely that my soul was strongly inclined to think of Jesus. I remember having sometimes a feeling of fainting, such was the sentiment of loneliness in my heart in the absence of my beloved. The Blessed Virgin, fearing that I might die of sadness before Jesus' return, led my superiors to give me the responsibility of tailor, knowing well that in the exercise of this duty I would be obliged to be more attentive to the duties of my calling. That's what Thérèse said to me when she told me that I was going to be made responsible for the tailor's workshop, because in truth I had little aptitude for the work. Everybody was aware of this.

During the time when I was in charge of the tailor's workshop, my only consolation consisted in this, that the Blessed Virgin has never allowed me to lack either suffering or fatigue. I accepted everything
(873)   and, very often, there was more. It was also in performing this duty that it had been given to me to understand a little better that, even among the fervent brethren, there were those who wanted such-and-such a responsibility, perhaps one a little more prestigious or offering a little more free time. Certain brethren could not hide their surprise on seeing me appointed tailor. As for me, I found nothing unusual in this, although I was sometimes afraid; I was still very young and quite small, and I was therefore quite tempted to back away from it. But each time that I mentioned this, Father Rector replied: 'What you can't do, God will be there to help you, provided that you obey your superior completely.' Yes, the superior's will was truly my motivation in impelling me to overcome many difficulties, and because I was sincere God has helped me to do my work well.

After more than a year as tailor I was appointed sacristan. This change was quite unexpected, but it did not worry me greatly since the Blessed Virgin has made herself responsible for the complete accom-
(874)   plishment of my last activities. I took pleasure, on moving from the tailor's workshop to the oratory, in hearing the comments and criticisms of the brethren which were not particularly favourable in my regard. My Father, you doubtless know that I did not allow myself to be

demoralised by these gloomy words, since anyway having applied myself diligently to the work I had just left, I can say that it was success- ful. Nevertheless, giving way to my sensitivity, I had not been able to fight against a certain sadness nor prevent a few tears ... Obviously, Father, it was not right that I should cry for having been successful, but apart from this success what was there to comfort me? Truthfully, only God can know the bitterness I was overwhelmed with during the period of over a year when I was tailor. Now, to reward me, God has sent me another cross in allowing the brothers to criticise my lack of skill, in telling me that I was not strong enough to improve, whilst in my work I obstinately followed the prescriptions of the rule. This being so did not mean that I was in the wrong, but it was simply to fulfil the precic- tion of Jesus: 'You will have to suffer a lot from your brethren ...'

After having discharged me from my duties as tailor, Father Rector (875) made known to me his intention to give me a little rest, because for some time it had been noticed that I was showing signs of fatigue. In truth, finding myself for a while in the grip of some big problems, I had to go to Father Rector to explain to him my wish that the job of tailor be given to an older brother with more experience and talent than me, but since Father Rector did not share my opinion, he did not cease from encouraging me to accept the duty joyfully. This does not mean that I was looking for misplaced glory, as some brethren accused me of, by flattering the superiors in order to get important duties. Everything came from God's will. I also heard someone say: 'It is thanks to the suggestion of the master of novices* that Father Rector has given him this job.' These were fairly widespread views, but ones which, according to your advice, were not worthy of attention. It is a fact that if we put up with it cheerfully, God can only add to our reward. Is this not the case, Father? Father did not change his decision. His reply was unequivocal. God wished that I should drink the chalice of bitterness in a corner of the tailor's shop. The brothers thought it was an honour to be the senior tailor, but if they had had to do the work, they would have (876) found difficulty in finding any honour there. People usually attach honour to important functions but, according to our Father Saint Alphonsus, honour, for the Redemptorist, consists in accepting scorn cheerfully for the love of Jesus our Redeemer. So let me repeat, Father, the only glory I have looked for is that of the cross.

Jesus has shown me since my early days the dazzling beauty of the cross, and he has helped me to make the necessary efforts continually to collect crosses. I speak of effort because nobody likes to be despised but, in spite of all the bitterness in my soul, I forced myself to fulfil my

---

* Father Antonio Boucher.

duty as well as possible. In speaking of bitterness, I feel a little embarrassed and you, perhaps, cannot stop smiling on seeing the insignificant things that cause me suffering. In truth, you will have noticed that things that great souls would consider ordinary and of little importance are, for me, a heavy burden, and without divine grace I would not have been able to carry them. I know well that it must have been so, because my very small and imperfect soul easily becomes anxious and is unable to contain its emotion even before the smallest obstacle. This is why I (877)   wish to say with little Thérèse: 'Because I am very small I have only very little sacrifices to offer to the good God.'

From the day of my appointment as sacristan everything seemed to go as I wished. However, I must admit quite frankly that I was still full of self-will and often pretentious. I often did things without the permission of Father Rector or without telling him my plans with sufficient clarity. For example, when I had cut two cloths for the side altars of Saint Joseph and Saint Thérèse, although my work was artistic and admired by many brethren in the scholasticate, it is a fact that I had asked Father Rector's advice in a fairly vague manner so that, when the work was finished, he and the master of ceremonies* were not happy. I thanked the Lord with all my heart that it turned out like that since, thanks to this affair, the brethren who had formerly maintained that the Father Rector favoured me, then got the opportunity to understand things a little better. I also noticed that, from that time, Father Rector appeared to be stricter towards me. Nevertheless, it was better for me to put up with this trial for the love of Jesus, and to keep my soul in peace, than to have to put up with the displeasure of the Superior. I was no less sincere, nor did I lose confidence in my dealings with the Father Rector, and I believe that if the circumstances had been even more (878)   painful, my affection for him would not have changed. When one loves someone, this love never ceases despite the circumstances. Of course I did not dare think that Father Rector had distanced himself from me and no longer had any affection for me. God is my witness that I did not stop believing that he loved me always, and took care of me as he did the other brethren of the community. If God has allowed me to suffer emotionally, he has done so to make my love become stronger and stronger, thanks to a more pure and determined will.

The Saigon community

Once this period had passed, God, seeing his little rose about to be exposed to the rainy season took it a long way away, in order that the

---

*   The father responsible for the correct application of the rubrics.

prediction he had made could come true: 'You will have to suffer at the hands of your Superior.'

I had to leave Hanoi for Saigon on 7 February 1950 on an Air France aeroplane. Before my departure Father Louis Roy, who had become Rector, said to me: 'The Superiors are sending you to Saigon because they wish you to take some rest since in the house in Saigon there is not much work.' Whatever, I felt sad and unable to hold back my tears at (879) the thought of leaving this sweet nest which contained such dear memories for me, and from which I could not reconcile myself to depart. Father Rector was surprised to see me cry like a child; had he been able to see things more clearly he would have been more astonished again to perceive that my sacrifice, although little in itself, was immense beyond all imagination.

It was my Superiors' intention that I go to Saigon to rest, and during the two years that I lived there I had accomplished totally God's plans for me although, in the course of this time of suffering, I was so weak that God's will seemed, sometimes, to have no meaning. God, however, well understood my weakness and he gave me a very firm hope. One day when I was anxious and immersed in sadness and distaste, I called Jesus to come to me, and this is what I said to him: 'Jesus, I have had the feeling for a long time that you are always absent and at this time there is no one to let me know my shortcomings so that I can correct them. My dear brother Jesus, deign to speak to me to give me peace.' My beloved Jesus answered me straight away from the bottom of my heart: 'Dear little brother, listen carefully to my words; once the spouse knows the will of the beloved and acts completely in accordance with this will what need is there any more of words? Stay in peace. Continue (880) to live as you are doing: in this way you will always please me.' I recovered peace of soul after these words of Jesus, and this peace has not left me to this day, although at certain times I have been deprived of light and plunged into a dark night.

O the sweetness of Love! which shines on all occasions and which surpasses millions of times the sufferings of this world, and throws the soul into such intoxication that it seems one has never known any trial. In spite of all suffering, when one possesses Love, one also possesses paradise in all its splendour. Today, my Father, although the wound in my heart is getting worse still and my earthly pilgrimage is not yet finished, whatever may be the circumstances, my soul feels happy and at peace. Today, although the time has not yet come to speak of it, since I do not yet know the time of my death, in my peaceful cell I am very close to you, and my soul is full of the memory of your paternal solicitude in my regard. I still remember the stages of the happy times of my first novitiate, and it all makes my heart beat in overflowing gratitude and love ... How can I thank the good God sufficiently who, many times in my life, has allowed me to feel clearly his Love in all its intimacy? A Love I have experienced under a thousand forms, and, among many forms of this Love, God has left you close to me, my Father, like a gentle hand supporting my little soul, and, after each struggle he has placed me within reach of this caressing hand, to make me understand that his Love never distances itself from me.

(881)

At this time, dear Father, I cannot put my pen down before leaving on the paper a word of sincere gratitude. But how can I express myself when my soul is agitated and unable to pronounce a word and my trembling fingers are powerless to form one? I feel choked when I wish to say a word of gratitude! ... However, Father, I hope you understand deep down the feelings of my heart, just like Jesus my divine friend, who wished to confide to you the secret key of my heart. Anyway, it is necessary that I tell you at least once; my Father, I thank you with all my heart and I will repeat this 'Thank you' every time I say; 'Jesus, I love you!' 'It is no more possible for me to distance myself from you on earth or when I shall be in heaven than it is for my friend Jesus who always lives in your heart.'

(882)

And now here is the last word that I am leaving to the souls of whom you are the representative, as the Blessed Virgin stands near her son Jesus in his agony: I leave to them my love; with this love, small as it is, I hope to satisfy the souls who wish to make themselves very small to come to Jesus. That is something I would wish to describe but, with my little talent, I do not have the words to do so ...

From the most loving and smallest of your children,

J. M. T. Marcel, CSSR

Epilogue

The last years of Brother Marcel

On 10 July 1959, at **Yên-Bình** in North Vietnam, a large group of men expressed the wish to accompany one of their own to the place of his final rest. Only four prisoners from a neighbouring camp were authorised to carry the body. They wrapped it in matting and carried it to the spot where they placed it in the ground. One hour earlier, at midday, this body, exhausted by months of illness, had breathed its last. Joachim **Nguyễn-tân-Văn** was thirty-one years and four months.

Brother Marcel has made a large part of his story known to us in his *Autobiography*. When he had finished writing it, at the beginning of 1950, he was nearly twenty-two years of age. His birthday was 15 March. This was a little more than three years after he had made his union with Jesus on becoming a Redemptorist Brother. To construct the story of the last years of Marcel, we had to resort to his correspondence and to the testimony of people who saw him frequently.

On 7 February 1950, in obedience to the authorities of his religious community, he went on his first, not painless, aeroplane flight[*] en route to Saigon,[†] 1730 kilometres away in South Vietnam. He left North Vietnam where he was born and grew up. On leaving the city of Hanoi, Brother Marcel no longer had the opportunity to meet his spiritual

---

[*] Cf the letter to Father Antonio Boucher, 12.02.50. Saigon.
[†] Since 1975 this conurbation is called Hô Chí Minh City.

guide, Father Antonio Boucher, a Canadian missionary* and the Master of Novices of the Redemptorists in North Vietnam. Brother Marcel found in regular correspondence with Father Boucher (the one who had asked him to write the story of his life) the means of continuing under his spiritual guidance and, feeling himself prompted by Jesus to return to Hanoi, he consulted Father Boucher[†] before presenting his wish to the Superior Vice-Provincial.

> 'My situation has not changed since my last letter; I continue to live through days of suffering and sadness. These days are very long but for my heart which loves they are very short. For a long time, at the latest until the end of this month, the cup of bitterness which was my stay in Saigon will be emptied. In the course of these two years I have built the ramparts of the Saigon community at the cost of innumerable sufferings, sacrifices and fatigues. I hope that this will be changed later, as I have asked for with much insistence. (. . .) Still, in some days we will meet.'[‡]

At the end of February 1952, Brother Marcel was sent to Đa-lạt, 300 kilometres north of Saigon where the missionary community had recently built a house of formation. The beauty of the site and the freshness of the air were pleasing to westerners who compared this mountain resort to Switzerland. Brother Marcel found Father Boucher there who would guide him during his second novitiate in anticipation of his perpetual vows on 8 September. In anticipation of a reply from the Superiors of the congregation authorising him to return to Hanoi, Brother Marcel refined his obedience to God's will. He informed Father Boucher of his progress:

> 'With my dear sister Thérèse I am addressing some words to you.
> 'My Father, I have just realised that I was wrong on the 24th June in the request I had made to you. This afternoon when I was sitting darning some socks my beloved Jesus intervened to draw my attention to the request I had made to you to do without the collation at 4.30. He has made things clear to me that this was capable of making me separate myself from him and lose him. He has again reproached me in secret and more severely for not

---

*   The first Redemptorists from the province of St Anne de Beaupré arrived in Vietnam on 30 November 1925. It was established as a province on 27 May 1964.
[†]   Letter to Father Boucher, 15 Feb. 1952. Saigon.
[‡]   Letter to Father Boucher, 12 Dec. 1950. Saigon.

having enough confidence in him, for having wished to escape from his hands which are the divine lift taking me to the heights. Of my own authority, I asked to distance myself from the way of childhood that my dear and holy sister has traced out for me and along which she guided me: the way of love and total abandon (…)

'I now repent and renew my resolution … not to go to heaven by my own will but to go there by following Divine Providence.'*

In July 1954 the Geneva Accords recognised the authority of President Hô Chí Minh and the democratic republic of North Vietnam up to the Seventeenth Parallel. Numerous Catholic families, including that of Brother Marcel,† and nearly all of the religious communities were evacuated to South Vietnam. Some Redemptorists continued their ministry in the capital of North Vietnam in the parish of Our Lady of Perpetual Succour to the faithful who had remained. On 4 September Brother Marcel wrote to his sister Anne Marie Tế who had recently emigrated to Canada:

'At last I have just received very happy news that I am writing to share with you. I have received the order to go to Hanoi and stay there …

'Little sister, how happy and moved I am! My soul is almost in a state of ecstasy … since the favour which I have ardently wished for a long time has been granted to me by Jesus today. How happy I am! At this moment all I can do is repeat, my soul is full of happiness.'‡

To anyone who asked him why he wished to live in the Communist zone, he replied: 'I am going so that there is someone who loves God in the middle of the Communists.' On 4 September, furnished with the requisite authorisation, Brother Marcel rejoined his confrères in Hanoi. Some months later, when going to collect a moped which had been left in a shop for repairs, he intervened in a conversation and showed his opposition to an opinion which he judged erroneous. Shortly afterwards he was taken to the police station where he was interrogated. Sticking to his opinion, Marcel was sentenced to forced labour.

At the end of the year Brother Marcel succeeded in getting a letter to his sister Anne Marie, a novice with the Redemptorist nuns in Sainte Anne de Beaupré in Canada.

*   Letter to Father Antonio Boucher, 27 June 1952. Đa-lạt.
†   Cf letter to his sister Anne Marie Tế, 23 August 1954. Đa-lạt.
‡   Letter to his sister Anne Marie Tế, 4 September 1954. Đa-lạt.

'In prison, as in the Love of Jesus, nothing can take away from me the weapon of love. No affliction is capable of wiping away the loving smile that I wear habitually on my wasted face and for whom is the kiss of my smile if not for Jesus the Beloved?'*

Father Bích and Brother Clement visited him from time to time; they brought provisions for him to strengthen him. He wrote to the superior of his community, Father Denis Paquette:

'Concerning myself, since the day of my arrival in this camp of Mo-Chèn I am very busy, just like the little priest of a parish might be. Outside the time for forced labour, I have to welcome continually people who come to me, one after the other, looking for comfort from me whom they regard as someone who never gets tired. However, they can see that I, also, am not very strong.

'I am happy because during these months of detention my spiritual life has not suffered any harm. God himself has made known to me that I am accomplishing his will here. I have asked him many times for the favour of dying in this camp but each time he has answered me: "I am quite ready to do as you wish, as you always do for me, but there are souls which still have need of you; without you it will be impossible for me to reach them. What do you think, then, my child?" Lord, it's up to you to think for me.'†

In August 1957 Brother Marcel was transferred to Camp No. 2 at Yen Binh, more than 150 kilometres north-east of Hanoi, where the Redemptorists were no longer allowed to visit him. They learned, at the end of February 1958, that Brother Marcel's health was failing. A year and a half later a fellow-detainee, recently released, told them of his death.

None of the brethren was surprised at the news of his death; his convictions had carried him to the end. Other witnesses have told that he tried to get the Eucharist from outside the camp for his fellow-prisoners, but his attempt failed and resulted in his being put into the dungeon for long months. What is most surprising is the increasing interest in him among a growing number of people throughout the world. Nevertheless, apparently, he has done nothing extraordinary, nothing which could distinguish him from others who had lived in similar circumstances. In his life his brethren had noticed nothing in particular about him. It is in reading his writings that the truth is

---

* Letter to his sister Anne Marie Te, 17 November 1955, Hanoi.
† Letter to Father Denis Paquette, 20 July 1956, Camp No. 1 of Mochen.

revealed to them. The life of Brother Marcel is the life of the parable of the hidden treasure.* It is necessary to spend time reading his *Autobiography*, his *Dialogues*, his *Correspondence* and his *Other Writings*‡ to gain access to what is hidden from the eyes of the flesh. In the search for treasure it is not necessary to be a specialist; even children would learn something there. That reminds me of how a certain Jesus of Nazareth conducted himself . . . You've heard of him?

Father Mario Doyle, CSSR†

---

* Matthew 13. 44.
† Of the Redemptorist province of Sainte Anne de Beaupré, Canada. This is the same province where Father Denis Paquette lives in retirement, and where Father Antonio Boucher lived until his death on 4 July 1991.
‡ These works are in preparation.

Some notes on Vietnamese names

A Vietnamese name is usually composed of three words in the following order: family name, middle name and first name.

In Vietnam there are only a few hundred family names of which the most common is Nguyen, the name of the last emperors of Vietnam.

The middle component can be composed of one or more names, according to the wishes of the parents.

The first name can be almost any name and is, therefore, almost unlimited. It is by this name that Vietnamese call themselves and are addressed.

Christians can put a Christian name in the front of their name.

Thus for Joachim Nguyen tan Van, Joachim is the baptismal name, Nguyen the family name, Tan the middle name and Van the first name.

Van received the name of Marcel in religion but this is not part of his civil name.

Marcel Van is the name by which we know him.

In the genealogy list only the first name is used.

In Vietnam it is the practice to indicate parents by the name of their first born, thus Van's father is called Mr Liet and Van's mother is Mrs Liet or Mrs Mau.

Thus Van's sister does not know the name of her grandparents whom she calls by the name of their first-born.

Genealogy of Van's family

NGUYỄN Family

Khưởng	Hiệt (f)	Hoạt (f)		Đỗ (f)	Chi
Ngan (f)	Thạch (f)	Cầu (f)	Nguyễn (f)	Vinh	Khánh
Bội	Khánh	Đào	(from the second marriage of Hoạt's husband)	Khang	Đào (f)
	Van, o.p. Chuông (f)			Bảo (f)	Loan
	Đức (f)			Ban (f)	Dư
	Ty (f)				
	Tuyển (f)				

Triết † 25/11/58

PHẠM Family

Mậu *tante Khánh* † 25/06/75 *oncle Nhương*

Bá	Ngành (f)	Sởi (f)	Đũi (f)
Nhượng	Khỏe	Đích (f)	Nhuận (f)
Qui (f)	Bạo	Đáng (f)	Bình
Ly (f)	Bận (f)	Đường	An
Bình		Đường	Cư
Tuất		Bảy (f)	
Hay (f)			

Children of Triết and Mậu

Liệt	Lê	Van	Tế	Tú	Ly (f)	Lục	Nhất*
(1921-1954)	(1925)	(1928-1959)	(1932)	(1935)	(1937)	(1939-1976)	
	married Nguyễn Xuân Cư with whom she had 8 childrens		Sister Anne-Marie	died aged 4 months due to an epidemic	died aged 8 months from smallpox		

* Nhất was adopted when he was already married and the father of a family. He practised the profession of an itinerant pharmacist. It was when he was stationed at Ngàm-Giáo that he made his entry into Van's family. He became a great friend and providential support of the family at the time when the family had to endure great poverty.

Printed in March 2021
by Rotomail Italia S.p.A., Vignate (MI) - Italy